Bomber Command

To 'Bomber Boy' Roland W. MacKenzie DFC and His Brothers-in-Arms in Bomber Command and The Mighty Eighth who Served so Valiantly in Extreme Danger in The Second World War

Front cover: An Avro Lancaster of 75 (RNZAF) Squadron at RAF Mepal, 3 Group, being prepared by groundcrew for a combat sortie to Krefeld, north-west of Dusseldorf, on 9 February 1945. It has no front armament because these guns were usually kept in the armoury. The armourers collected them before the flight, and they were usually mounted in position during the pre-op air test.

Bomber Command

Churchill's Greatest Triumph

RODDY MacKENZIE

BOMBER COMMAND
Churchill's Greatest Triumph

First published in Great Britain in 2022 by
Air World
An imprint of
Pen & Sword Books Ltd
Yorkshire – Philadelphia

Copyright © Roddy MacKenzie, 2022

ISBN 978 1 39901 772 5

The right of Roddy MacKenzie to be identified as Author of this work has been asserted by him in accordance with the Copyright, Designs and Patents Act 1988. A CIP catalogue entry for this book is available from the British Library.

All rights reserved. No part of this book may be reproduced or transmitted in any form or by any means, electronic or mechanical including photocopying, recording or by any information storage and retrieval system, without permission from the Publisher in writing.

Typeset by SJmagic DESIGN SERVICES, India.
Printed and bound in the UK by CPI Group (UK) Ltd.

Pen & Sword Books Ltd includes the Imprints of Atlas, Archaeology, Aviation, Discovery, Family History, Fiction, History, Maritime, Military, Military Classics, Politics, Select, Airworld, Frontline Publishing, Leo Cooper, Remember When, Seaforth Publishing, The Praetorian Press, Wharncliffe Local History, Wharncliffe Transport, Wharncliffe True Crime and White Owl.

For a complete list of Pen & Sword titles please contact
PEN & SWORD BOOKS LTD
47 Church Street, Barnsley, South Yorkshire, S70 2AS, England
E-mail: enquiries@pen-and-sword.co.uk
Website: www.pen-and-sword.co.uk

Or

PEN AND SWORD BOOKS
1950 Lawrence Rd, Havertown, PA 19083, USA
E-mail: Uspen-and-sword@casematepublishers.com
Website: www,penandswordbooks.com

Contents

Preface by Allen Packwood vii
Letter from Air Chief Marshal Sir Michael Graydon GCB, CBE, FRAeS viii
Letter from RCAF Deputy Commander Major General Colin Keiver x
Foreword by Air Vice-Marshal Paul Robinson, OBE, FRAeS xii
Maps xiv
Introduction xvii

Part I: MY AWAKENING

Chapter One	Boyhood	2
Chapter Two	Manhood	14
Chapter Three	My Dad	21
Chapter Four	Discovering Bomber Command	32
Chapter Five	Leaders	41
Chapter Six	Harris	62

PART II: BOMBER COMMAND BACKGROUND

Chapter Seven	Opinions	82
Chapter Eight	The Plan	88
Chapter Nine	Warplanes	99
Chapter Ten	People	107
Chapter Eleven	Training	127

Chapter Twelve	Dad at War	140
Chapter Thirteen	Weaknesses into Strengths	154

Part III: GERMANY'S PERSPECTIVE

Chapter Fourteen	Germany's Research Institute for Military History	174
Chapter Fifteen	German Leaders – Especially Speer	190
Chapter Sixteen	Joseph Goebbels	201
Chapter Seventeen	Luftwaffe Leaders	211

Part IV: BOMBER COMMAND ACCOMPLISHMENTS

Chapter Eighteen	Air War	218
Chapter Nineteen	Sea War	240
Chapter Twenty	Assisting Allied Armies	247
Chapter Twenty-One	Germany's War Machine	256

PART V: REMEMBRANCE AND CONCLUSIONS

Chapter Twenty-Two	Dad Postwar	264
Chapter Twenty-Three	Bomber Command Postwar	268
Chapter Twenty-Four	Conclusions	284

Appendix I	Royal Air Force Distinguished Flying Cross	288
Appendix II	Royal Bank of Canada *Quill & Ledger* Letter	290
Appendix III	Halifax 57 Rescue (Canada) to Rescue Halifaxes	293
Appendix IV	Military Life Diarized by 166 Squadron	295
Bibliography		300
Acknowledgements		310
Index		316

Preface

This book began with one man's journey into the past: Roddy's personal quest to make sense of his own troubled relationship with his father. Roland MacKenzie won the Distinguished Flying Cross for his role as a Canadian bomber pilot in the Second World War, flying highly dangerous combat sorties over Europe in 1944. Like many of his generation he did not talk about it and the experience clearly scarred him.

History has had its own troubled relationship with Bomber Command and Churchill has been accused of supporting the bombing offensive during the war but then seeking to distance himself from it thereafter. Yet, the British Prime Minister recognised, as early as August 1940, that "night after night, month after month, our bomber squadrons travel far into Germany, find their targets in the darkness by the highest navigational skill, aim their attacks, often under the heaviest fire, often with serious loss, with deliberate careful discrimination, and inflict shattering blows upon the whole of the technical and war-making structure of the Nazi power".

We follow Roddy to airfields, museums, archives as his search for his father becomes a wider exercise. What begins as a personal journey becomes a wider story about recognising the importance and the sacrifice of the air offensive. It is a story of courage and, as Churchill also wrote, "Courage is rightly esteemed the first of human qualities because, as has been said, it is the quality which guarantees all others".

Allen Packwood,
Director, Churchill Archives Centre,
Churchill College, Cambridge.

Letter from Air Chief Marshal Sir Michael Graydon GCB, CBE, FRAeS

Air Chief Marshal Sir Michael Graydon GCB CBE FRAeS

The Barn
Eagle Hall
Swinderby
Lincs LN6 9HZ

18th July 2022

David Freeman
International Churchill Society
California State University
Fullerton CA

Dear David,

When you offered me the chance to read the draft of 'Bomber Command' I wondered if it would tell me anything new. It did. It traces the journey of its author Roddy, son of Roland MacKenzie DFC a Canadian Bomber pilot, in discovering his father's war and how it had changed his life.

In so doing, it provides a wealth of widely researched evidence including crucial information from German research which largely dispels the peddled ignorance which has clouded understanding of the Bombing campaign and the impact it had on the Nazi war effort. It wisely highlights the views of great soldiers such as Eisenhower, Alanbrooke, Montgomery and Horrocks who knew how Bomber Command was paving the way for armies and thus saving countless allied lives. The strong and vital relationship during the campaign between Harris and Churchill is described.

The journey takes him to many countries and contacts around the world; it makes good reading to learn how fruitful his numerous visits to UK were and how helpful retired RAF personnel were together with the Cranwell Library and Cambridge University's Churchill College. Great efforts have been made in the last 20 years to recognise the contribution of Bomber Command to victory in World War 2 and compensate for the disgraceful treatment afforded its men and women at war end.

It is no surprise that he is led to praise the bravery of Bomber Command aircrew, and their achievements, and in that process to understand the impact that such prolonged stress can have on mental health. It is good, too, to be reminded of the magnificent contribution and commitment of Canada to the allied cause. Roddy MacKenzie's comprehensive book is a fine tribute to a remarkable generation, but it offers much more than a trawl of history. In revealing the mental scars that war brought to his father, it will I hope provide some closure to other families who have experienced its consequences.

I was both informed and moved by what I read,

Yours sincerely,
Michael Graydon

Air Chief Marshal Sir Michael Graydon GCB, CBE, FRAeS

Letter from RCAF Deputy Commander Major General Colin Keiver

Deputy Commander
Royal Canadian Air Force

Commandant adjoint
Aviation royale canadienne

National Defence
Headquarters
Ottawa, Ontario
K1A 0K2

Quartier général de
la Défense nationale
Ottawa (Ontario)
K1A 0K2

September 7, 2022

There are history books, filled with facts, and there are good stories. Rarely are the two combined and this book, Bomber Command, is one of those rarities. It refutes, through brilliant research, widely held beliefs that the strategic bombing campaign of the Second World War was ineffective and it tells the story of those involved in that heroic effort in a deeply personal way. It makes clear that they contributed significantly to victory over tyranny and oppression.

It is in the telling of those stories that we are able to weave a fabric between the past, present and future. For an institution like the RCAF those stories are a critical means of remembering those who have gone before while reminding us of why we serve. I am honoured to commend this book and sincerely thank Roddy for sharing his father and his accomplishments with us in such a meaningful and heartfelt way. His dad would be even prouder of him than I am.

Most importantly, this book sheds new light on the real cost of war which is too often simply measured in terms of blood and treasure. It reminds us that there is a real and tangible cost to this unique and unfortunate human endeavour. Even those who returned physically unharmed bore scars that remained with them for the rest of their days. Today's RCAF stands ever ready to defend the values and freedoms we often take for granted and it does so on the shoulders of giants like Rolly MacKenzie.

Lest we forget,

Colin Keiver
Major-General
Deputy Commander, Royal Canadian Air Force

National Defence Défense nationale

Canada

RCAF Deputy Commander Major General Colin Keiver

Foreword

RAF Air Vice-Marshal Paul Robinson
OBE FRAeS.

A myth popular in the United Kingdom is that, until the United States entered the Second World War, Britain Stood Alone. Woe betide anyone expressing such a view within earshot of my friend Roddy MacKenzie. He would, rightly, point out that vast numbers of men and women from the British Empire and Commonwealth, the Axis-occupied lands and across the Free World, flocked here to fight against tyranny. He'd mention that many of these, hailing from sixty-two nations, served in RAF Bomber Command; and that the largest donor, in both blood and treasure, was Canada. Roddy taught me much about Canada's magnificent contribution - and not least that of his own father – subsequent to our first chance meeting in September 2018 at a memorial service for 166 Squadron, and his decision to write this book.

Another myth debunked by Roddy: that Churchill's support of the Command was lukewarm. Not so: having witnessed the slaughter of trench warfare and the impact of German air raids on Britain during the Great War, Churchill believed aerial bombing could deter aggression and, if it failed, prove an effective means of prosecuting war whilst avoiding horrific army casualties. During the War he

FOREWORD

defended the Command against pressure to divert its resources to other campaigns and, a fellow aviator, his praise of the 'bomber boys' was fulsome and heartfelt.

The final, most important myth Roddy has demolished is that, despite their skill, courage and sacrifice, the Command's people achieved little militarily. Roddy, through his analysis of German documents, has shown the reverse to be true. It proves that Bomber Command and the USAAF's 8th Air Force systematically dismantled Germany's military-industrial capability and, by attacking its land, air and maritime combat formations, effectively destroyed its ability to wage war.

In Roddy MacKenzie, Bomber Command has a formidable advocate: passionate, tenacious and intellectually curious. His book repays our debt of honour to his father and the million other aircrew, ground personnel, scientists, factory workers and politicians who made Bomber Command Churchill's greatest triumph.

Air Vice-Marshal Paul Robinson, OBE, FRAeS,
Leadenham, 11 August 2022.

Maps

xiv

MAPS

YUKON
NORTHWEST TERRITORIES
DISTRICT of MACKENZIE
NUNAVUT
Hudson
Bay
BRITISH
COLUMBIA
ALBERTA
SASKATCHEWAN
MANITOBA
ONTARIO
VANCOUVER
ISLAND
Fort Chipewyan
Fort McMurray
Peace River (Town)
Fairview
Dawson Creek
RCAF Cold Lake
Jasper National Park
RCAF Edmonton
Wetaskiwin
Camrose
Red Deer
Stettler
Prince Albert
RCAF Saskatoon
Oyen
RCAF Comox
Cochrane
RCAF Calgary
Banff National Park
Kananaskis
Kamloops
Vancouver
RCAF Vulcan
RCAF Moose Jaw
Nanton
Webb
RCAF Regina
RCAF Claresholm
Medicine Hat
Rocanville
RCAF Fort MacLeod
Lethbridge
Moosomin
RCAF Carberry
Winnipeg
RCAF Brandon
Waterton Glacier
Int'l Peace Park

Jutland
COPENHAGEN
NETHERLANDS
UNITED KINGDOM
Westerbork
AMSTERDAM
The Hague
Arnhem
Mimoyecques/
Cap Gris Nez
Zeebrugge
Dunkirk
Calais
Dieppe
Foret-Du-Croc
Belleville-sur-Mer
Wizernes
Vimy
Arras
Douai
Amiens
Antwerp
BRUSSELS
Waterloo (Battlefield)
BELGIUM
GERMANY
(see map opposite)
Utah Beach
Cherbourg
Omaha Beach
St. Martin-de-Varreville
Gold Beach
Juno Beach
Sword Beach
Le Harvre
Oisemont
Aulnoye
Bastogne
Rouen
Villers Bocage
Fontenay Le Marmion
Revigny-Sur-Ormain
Mantenon
PARIS
Mailly
Troussey
Rennes St. Jacques
Chateau Bernapre
Villeneuve-St. George's
Orleans
BAY OF BISCAY
FRANCE
Zurich
La Pallice
Pauillac
St. Medard-en-Jalles
Geneva

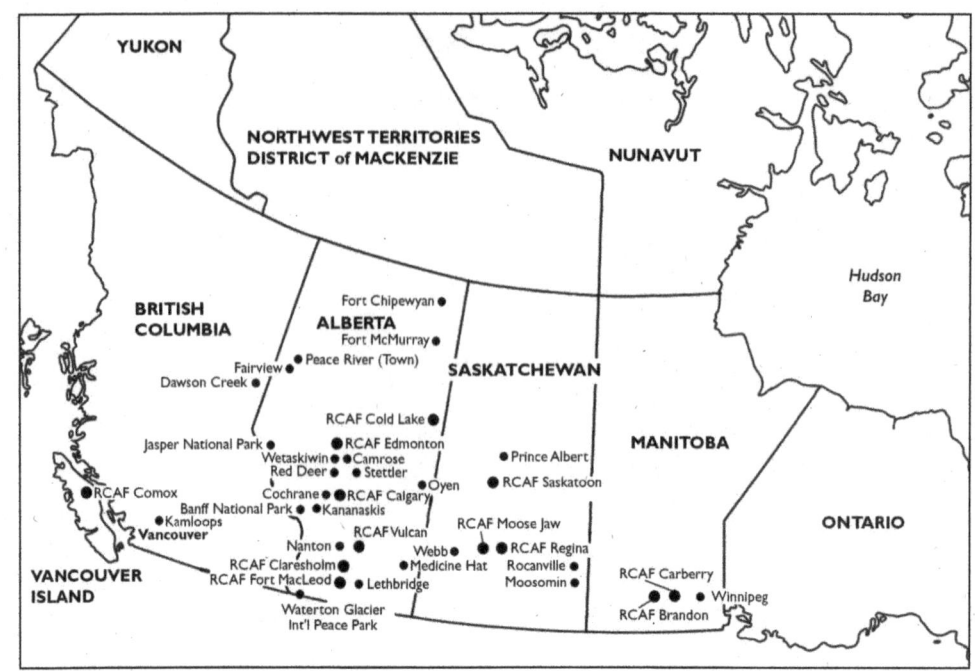

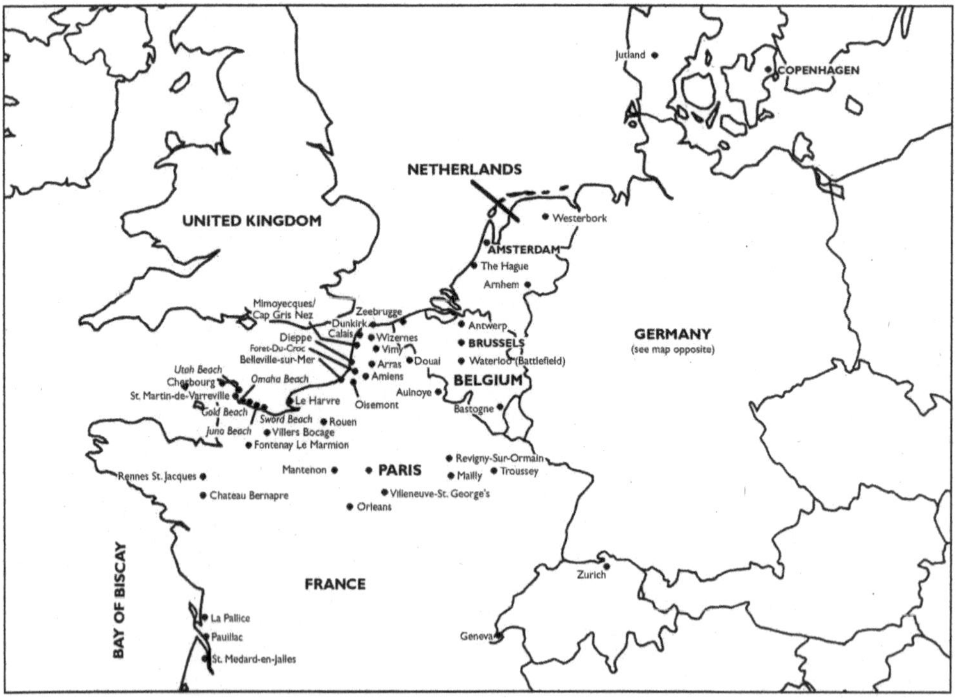

Introduction

Writing a book is an adventure. To begin with it is a toy and an amusement. Then it becomes a mistress, then it becomes a master, then it becomes a tyrant. The last phase is that, just as you are about to be reconciled to your servitude, you kill the monster and fling him to the public.

Sir Winston Churchill[1]

The maxim 'Nothing avails but perfection'
May be spelt shorter: 'Paralysis'

Sir Winston Churchill[2]

This is my first book. In it I weave together several stories. This book started as my quest as a Bomber Boy son to discover what my Dad did in the Second World War, and how it affected him. This evolved into my curiosity regarding Bomber Command – what it was, and what it accomplished. My research led me straight to Sir Winston Churchill. As I dug deeper, my awareness of Canada's contribution grew, and likewise that of 'The Mighty Eighth', America's bomber force in the UK. And, finally, all this led me to the Germans. They knew far better than we did what Bomber Command accomplished, both directly, and indirectly. It's quite the story.

Where did this begin for me? It began with my hero Sir Winston Churchill – his eloquence, both written and verbal, that ignited my lifelong interest in history, and especially the Second World War. Fortunately, our family library had a great collection of Churchill books, and as a boy I devoured all of them, largely because his writing style is captivating, and fun to read. As a teenager I occasionally went downtown to Calgary's Main Library to listen to recordings of Churchill speeches.

Perfection this book is not, but as honest an accounting as I can do it is. Also, I am not writing a textbook. My Bomber Command quest is to make meaningful what I have discovered. To accomplish this, I explore key characters as authentically as I can, and not as cardboard cut-out stereotypes. Hence my details, and detours.

---

1 Packwood, *How Churchill Waged War*
2 Note to General Ismay on 6 December 1942 on proposed improvements to landing-craft.

BOMBER COMMAND

So how did my story begin? It all started in Calgary three years after the Second World War when I was born a baby boomer boy. Calgary postwar was a young city filled with optimism, and set to explode into global greatness. I grew up in a brand-new Calgary suburban neighbourhood called St Andrew's Heights. There my friends and I were the first to occupy brand-new houses, almost all of which I think were of virtually identical size, albeit in a variety of designs, on identical 33 foot (10 metre) lots. As six-year-olds, we were the first class of brand-new Chief Crowfoot Elementary School. Six years later, we were the first class of brand-new Parkdale Junior High School. Six years after that, we were the first class of brand-new The University of Calgary. So much was new, a 'first'.

Increasing amounts of oil and gas were pumped up to fuel extraordinary prosperity. Alberta was fast evolving from having suffered severely in the Great Depression of the 1930s into its postwar emergence as an economic powerhouse. But, behind all this progress, all this newness, all this optimism, lay something gigantic that was seldom spoken of – the Second World War. This is the story of my evolving boyhood awareness of that war, and the role my Bomber Boy Dad played in contributing to our victory. This story is of greatness, of sacrifice, of honour, and of everyday people caught up in a worldwide conflagration in which they did what they could, did it well, and won. They were indeed what Tom Hanks and others call 'The Greatest Generation'.

And this is also the story of me as a Bomber Boy's son experiencing a paradigm shift in how I view my father. Through this quest, I have learnt that my Dad piloted a Lancaster for thirty-four combat sorties from April to August 1944 in Bomber Command's 166 Squadron of No. 1 Group RAF. Dad seldom spoke of the war. I did not learn much from him. But, commencing in 2017, especially through the Royal Air Force and Cambridge University, I have learnt a great deal.

Another way of saying all this is that I grew up in the 1950s and 1960s, riding the wave of Calgary's postwar boom of homogeneous optimism. But the society in which I was born and raised, and the schools which educated me, largely ignored Canada's trauma and magnificence in the Second World War. And this got worse. When in 1966 I entered the first class of brand-new University of Calgary, the Vietnam War was beginning to dominate the media. As well, hovering over everyone was the Cold War threat of nuclear bombs wiping us out. Both wars gave bombing a particularly bad name. And then, in 1968, Canada dealt two harsh blows to our military. First, it divorced the military from university students by cancelling popular military programmes on campus. That divorce between our military and university-educated Canadians still hurts. Second, Canada undermined the RCAF and RCN through unification with our Army. I am told even basic training for our aviators and sailors was discarded, with all recruits instead being forced to endure basic training for soldiers. This was followed by a succession of savage budget cuts in the ensuing 'decades of darkness' which further weakened our shakily unified military.

Long story short, for my 'Baby Boomer Generation' coming of age in the late 1960s Canada's military was receding into insignificance, the Cold War was

INTRODUCTION

terrifying, and the Vietnam War was escalating. My scant knowledge of Dad fighting the Second World War was contaminated by Vietnam carpet-bombing and our huge fear of nuclear wipe-out. Many my age became anti-war and anti-military. None of this was helpful for bridging the growing gulf between my Dad and me.

But, thanks to my great-uncle Leslie MacKenzie instilling in me pride in being a MacKenzie, as an adult I experienced the military in ways none of my friends did. My participation began in the mid-1980s when I became the first Commissioner for Western Canada, and thereafter the only Canadian President, of the Clan MacKenzie Society in the Americas. How did this involve me with Canada's military? In two ways. First, in 1987, the Seaforth Highlanders of Canada in Vancouver approached me to strengthen their connection with their heritage with our Clan. The Seaforths are a MacKenzie Regiment. Our MacKenzie Clan Chief, the Earl of Seaforth, raised the Regiment in 1778. Second, in 1991, our Navy approached me to strengthen the connection of Mackenzie-Class destroyer HMCS *Mackenzie* with our Clan. Starting with these chance invitations arising from my Clan MacKenzie leadership, I have remained active as a civilian volunteer in Canada's Army and Navy for over three decades. Surprisingly, given my Dad's service, I had no connection with our Air Force. That is, until 2015, when I was invited to join the Air Force Officers' Association of British Columbia. I was told that this invitation arose partly because of my interest in the RCAF, but mainly because of my Dad. In extending the invitation on behalf of the AFOA Board of Directors, the then AFOA President Wes Bowers said, 'Your Dad, Roddy, was RCAF royalty.'

Also surprisingly, it was not until 2017 that curiosity about Bomber Command arose in me, launching my quest which produced this book. On 18 June 2018, I began informally writing about Bomber Command at Westminster Abbey BC. On 01 September 2018, my sons and I represented Canada at a Church Service followed by a ceremony at what had been RAF Kirmington honouring my Dad's 166 Squadron. In April 2019 everything converged for me through the coming together of the RAF, RCAF, Churchill College at Cambridge University, and the International Churchill Society – aided by my mentors edging me into Bomber Command immersion. On 27 April 2019 in Lincolnshire I began writing this book. Fourteen drafts later, here it is. Researching and then writing it was far more challenging than I could have imagined.

Why did I do it? To find out and then make known what Bomber Command accomplished. To explain how this happened, I first share with you my growing awareness of Bomber Command, my MacKenzie heritage and my mentors. Without all these, for me this quest would not have happened.

In my journey of exploration, major figures emerge who are crucial to Bomber Command. These include the giants – Churchill and FDR, Eisenhower and Montgomery – and those who should be much better known, especially Canadian Prime Minister William Lyon Mackenzie King, Lord Trenchard and, in Canada, Lord Beaverbrook. And then there's Sir Arthur Harris, Air Officer Commanding-in-Chief of Bomber Command from 22 February 1942 until the end of war. Postwar, he was treated as shabbily as Bomber Command and Mackenzie King. And finally,

BOMBER COMMAND

I learnt how important individual relationships were, such as those of Mackenzie King with FDR and Churchill, and especially Harris with Churchill.

As mentioned, my quest has also led me to the Germans. My breakthrough happened on Saturday 18 May 2019 at RAF College Cranwell in Lincolnshire with my sons Guy Roland and Ruaridh MacKenzie and Royal Air Force Air Vice-Marshal Paul Robinson. That's the day and place Cranwell Assistant Librarian Tim Pierce introduced me to Germany's Research Institute for Military History. I learnt that the Allies could not be certain what Bomber Command accomplished because our intelligence inside Nazi Germany was poor, and postwar it was hard to discern much from rubble. But Germans knew. Their Institute, their military leaders, and especially Albert Speer and Joseph Goebbels, opened for me a flood of information about Bomber Command accomplishments. From all this, I learnt that much of my knowledge about Bomber Command, the Mighty Eighth, Mackenzie King and my Dad was wrong. This created a paradigm shift for me. I hope it will for you.

Churchill said, 'Never give up on something that you can't go a day without thinking about.'[3] That's me with Bomber Command. The result is this book.

---

[3] This is another of what many believe to be Churchill's famous quotes, cited repeatedly, but again I cannot locate where Churchill said it

Part I

MY AWAKENING

Chapter One

Boyhood

'Roddy! Come quick! Get in the car!'

Those words coming from my Dad, Roland W. MacKenzie, as he burst out the front door of our house and headed towards our car were unusual, indeed unprecedented. I was in our front yard working on our lawn, in which Dad took such pride, and for which he demanded perfection. Nothing normally trumped work on his lawns. What's more, Dad's words were enthusiastic. He usually wasn't.

So, as ordered, in a state of surprise, I dropped everything and dashed over to our gun-metal-grey 1952 Pontiac. I think Dad bought it brand-new, but I was too young in 1952 to know for sure. What I do know is Dad took remarkably good care of it, assisted of course by his son spending hours washing it. I longed for a new car, ours being so out of date in an era when cars seemed so important.

I scrambled into the front passenger seat at the very moment Dad entered the driver's side. He started the engine and off we went. It was Easter Sunday 1961. I was twelve years old, less than four months short of becoming a teenager.

As we drove, Dad explained, 'I just heard on the radio a Lancaster is flying towards Calgary. We're headed up to Nose Hill to get a good view of it.'

Nose Hill is a giant swath of original grassland which we called prairie wool. Fortunately, cattle love it, and eating it produces world-class beef. Nose Hill has a commanding view overlooking Calgary. It is also a major Canadian geographic phenomenon. From its eastern slope begins the famous Canadian Prairie stretching east a thousand miles (1,600 km) to about fifty miles (80 km) east of Winnipeg where forests take over. On Nose Hill's western side are Alberta's magnificent Foothills, stretching west from Calgary to the Canadian Rocky Mountains of Kananaskis and thereafter Banff National Park.

Many people have little concept of Alberta's gorgeous Foothills because the Trans-Canada Freeway connecting Calgary and Banff travels through what we called the Morley Flats or Plateau. It gives the optical illusion that one is still in the prairies.

Nose Hill is a geographic boundary between Prairie to the east, and the Foothills and Rockies to the west. It is also where my friends and I as boys wandered around and explored. It is pretty much the same as it was a thousand years ago. Today it is a 4.2 square-mile (11 square km) natural park created in

1980, surrounded on all sides by housing. In 1961 Nose Hill was open countryside at the edge of town.

Off to Nose Hill Dad and I dashed. This was one of few outings I remember of just Dad with me. We seldom did much together. But here we were, hurrying to Nose Hill. En route, I saw hundreds of others likewise racing towards good vantage points. I was surprised so many people wanted to see a Lancaster in the air. In addition, according to the *Calgary Herald* newspaper, about 15,000 people were waiting at the airport to watch this Lancaster land. Clearly something important was happening. But what was so important about a Lancaster?

Then that Lancaster came into view, leisurely approaching Calgary Airport. From 1938 until 1966, Calgary airport was called McCall Field to honour Calgarian Fred McCall, a First World War flying ace with thirty-five confirmed kills, an interwar aviation enthusiast, and Second World War RCAF squadron leader. The name was changed to Calgary International Airport when the City of Calgary sold the airport in 1966 for $2 million dollars, and several conditions, to Transport Canada.

While the Lancaster was airborne, Dad said nothing. But I remember how intently he watched that Lancaster fly. I wonder what memories it evoked. That was the first time, and one of the very few times, I had ever seen a Lancaster in the air. I knew about Lancasters, albeit not very much. I also knew Dad flew one in the Second World War, but I knew almost nothing about that. What I learnt on that fateful 1961 Easter Sunday is that Lancasters were important, so much so that thousands of Calgarians dropped everything at a moment's notice to see one flying into town. To distinguish it from the many other Lancasters in this book, I will refer to it as 'my Calgary Lancaster'. Every Lancaster has a unique serial number of two letters followed by three numbers. My Calgary Lancaster is FM136.

My Early Memories of Talking About the War

My earliest memory of talking about the war was when I was barely four years old. My Mom, Joyce Lenore Miller MacKenzie, had fallen ill with polio, and so was taken from our home in Calgary for a prolonged stay in the dreadful iron lung at the University Hospital in Edmonton about 200 miles (320 km) north of us. While she was there, and Dad was at work, my sister Susan and I were looked after by what at that time were called housekeepers. I remember asking one, an elderly woman whose name I do not know, 'What is Germany? Why are people afraid of it?' Her reply has remained with me all these years. It was my first inkling something scary had happened, from which my Dad helped save us. She said to me 'Germany is a big country far away. It was very powerful, and horrible. It did dreadful things. It tried to make slaves of us. But your Father and others like him crossed the ocean, fought the Germans, and beat them. That's why we are free.' As a boy so young, I developed a vivid imagination of Germans being terrifying monsters, fighting a David-and-Goliath-type battle, which my Dad helped us win.

BOMBER COMMAND

1959 Rocanville SK – Germany and Royalty

The summer of 1959 was for me unforgettable. Only ten years old, I flew with my sister Susan and my Mom in her wheelchair from ultra-modern, future-orientated, oil-boom-fuelled Calgary to my Mom's birthplace and childhood home – the village of Rocanville, Saskatchewan. Dad remained in Calgary. Mom and I flew aboard a Trans-Canada Airlines DC-3 propeller plane. TCA was created on 30 April 1937, and was not renamed Air Canada until 1 January 1965. We flew from Calgary to Lethbridge, then Lethbridge to Medicine Hat, then Medicine Hat to Swift Current, then Swift Current to Regina, then Regina to Yorkton where my Uncle Harold Miller lived. He was the eldest of Mom's four siblings. She was the youngest of the five. In only seven hours, we had flown all the way from Calgary to Yorkton. Amazing. Nowadays it's a nine-hour drive – 590 miles (950 km).

   We spent a few days in Yorkton before being driven to Rocanville. I have a photo with my maternal grandparents proving I had been to Rocanville as a baby, but I have no memory of that visit. This 1959 pilgrimage home was enormous for Mom -- her first time in Rocanville in a wheelchair, paralyzed by polio. I remember how she cried when we visited the graves of her parents. Polio had forced her to miss their funerals. What a shock Rocanville was for me. I went from Calgary's St. Andrew's Heights brand new state-of-the-art postwar suburban design including underground wiring to Rocanville's no electricity, no running water, wooden sidewalks and dirt roads. On their farm near Rocanville, likewise without modern amenities, I was the house guest of our Watson relatives, Great Uncle Roy and Great Aunt Jean. Some farm work was still done by people and horses. Life that summer seemed to me not much different than life hundreds of years ago. My good news is that, although I was only ten, I was allowed to drive the tractor. In Rocanville, we were house guests of my Mom's older brother Gordon, whom we called 'Gog'. He had inherited the farm implements business my Grandfather created in 1924. Uncle Gog liked teasing my super-city Mom with her most modern of everything. He drove a broken-down old pick-up truck, and wore the shabbiest of overalls and farm work clothes. He told me stories I would never hear in Calgary. He was unlike anyone I had ever met in Calgary, or anywhere for that matter. He was unique.

   A huge highlight for me was the excitement of the day we drove south 20 miles (32 km) from Rocanville to Moosomin, With my Mom in a wheelchair, we were put in the front row of a giant horseshoe of people from everywhere waiting for a special train. People gasped when it came into view. When it stopped, the most beautiful woman in the world emerged – our young Queen Elizabeth II. With her was her dashing husband Prince Philip whom my Mom thought was perfect. Everyone cheered. After the formalities, I remember the warmth of the Queen's smile as she approached us on her walkabout. People in my boyhood had commented on how much my Mom looked like the Queen. Now I saw these two together. I had left my camera back at the farm because one of my relatives said "You will never get close enough Roddy in that huge crowd to get a picture, and someone might steal your camera from you." So there I was with my Mom and The Queen but no camera. I've seldom made that mistake since.

My Grandpa Miller had died in 1953, so I never knew him. Grandpa was from Dashwood, Ontario. As early as fourteen, he left home, and worked all over Canada and America. Then, in 1905, he reached Rocanville as a grain agent. There he met and in 1906 married my Grandmother, Eleanor 'Nellie'. In Rocanville, Grandpa called himself John ('Jack') Miller. It wasn't until several years after my Mom's death in 1970 that I was astonished to discover that Grandpa was actually Jacob Mueller, and that his parents were German, not English. I'm told it was not uncommon for German Canadians to anglicize their names because Germans were not popular in Canada. And so, in 1959, I did not know my maternal Grandfather was German. But now I suspect my Uncle Gog did. In 1952, Gog's first wife Pearl Hanson died of cancer. In 1954, Gog married Wanda Klimke Rudiger. I liked her. But my goodness, Wanda was different. She was an old-fashioned European peasant-type country woman in dress and demeanour – perfect for Gog. Also, she was German. I now know she came to Canada postwar, having lost her first husband in the war. Like so many German soldiers, he was captured by the Soviets and never seen again.

Aunt Wanda had visitors while I was there in 1959. I thought they were her relatives. I remember they were a pair of incredibly handsome blond men. They were very respectful towards ten-year-old me. But I was astonished to learn both were Luftwaffe fighter pilots in the Second World War. In other words, my Aunt Wanda's visitors spent the war killing Allied airmen. While I was glad they did not kill my father, I did not know how one socialized with the enemy postwar. Was I betraying everyone they killed? It was a major turmoil for me. However, this gave me my first glimmerings that wars are wrong. I was seeing postwar the people fighting them becoming friends and even in-laws. Huge food for thought.

Memorable Moment at Chief Crowfoot Elementary School

The war was seldom mentioned in school. I do, however, remember when I was ten in Grade Five our teacher, Mrs Smith, somehow as an aside briefly referred to the war. She made specific mention of my Dad as having earned a tremendous medal for the extreme danger of flying a Lancaster to bomb Germany. That evening I asked Dad if he had won the Victoria Cross, it being the only 'tremendous medal' I knew of. All he said was no – his medal was a DFC, the Distinguished Flying Cross, whatever that meant. With that, Dad ended our conversation. Sixty years later, I learnt that the DFC was instituted on 3 June 1918 by King George V, grandfather of our Queen, just two months after the Royal Air Force was founded on 1 April 1918. In the Second World War it was the third-level – the Victoria Cross and Distinguished Service Order were above it. Until writing this book I had never heard of the Distinguished Service Order. All three are military decorations awarded to RAF, Commonwealth and Allied air force officers for 'an act or acts of valour, courage, or devotion to duty performed whilst flying in active operations against the enemy'. A citation describing the event or events for which the medal is presented accompanies each award.[1] I have attached my Dad's citation as Appendix I. Its contents are very interesting.

Miscellaneous Moments of Bomber Command Awareness

As a boy, I heard adults speak with admiration of my Dad's wartime service, and of his exceptional skill flying Lancasters. But these were all chance remarks, often overheard instead of in conversations with me. So I had little context, and even less knowledge. For me, Dad's role in the war was mysterious, a taboo topic. I do remember once as a teenager watching on our TV a wartime movie featuring Lancasters. I think it was the 1955 film 'The Dambusters'. There are two things I remember about that movie. First, my Dad telling me that something said about flying Lancasters wasn't right. Dad was sitting in his customary chair at the far end of our living room behind where I sat to watch TV. I'm not sure I realized he was there until he spoke. I remember no details regarding what he said, but I felt a trace of irritation that he would contradict what I was seeing on our TV screen. Who did he think he was? And, in typical teenage contradictory fashion where I was annoyed with my Dad one minute, and proud of him the next, the second thing I remember about that movie is a scene in which several pilots were at a reception in a very upscale location. In the hallway, one white-coated waiter with a silver tray said in awe to another 'Every pilot in that room is a DFC'. This reminded me my Dad was a DFC. That scene in the movie told me that being a DFC was impressive.

Sir Winston Churchill's Speeches – Content and Delivery

I won the Queen Elizabeth School Trophy in Social Studies, but graduated from that high school having learnt little about the Second World War. What I did know came largely from my love of reading books, especially those Churchill wrote. Sometimes I took trolley bus number 9 downtown to Calgary's Main Public Library. There I listened to Churchill's speeches. I also occasionally listened to speeches by FDR, and a couple of times even Hitler. I spoke no German, but I found fascinating and terrifying the way Hitler spoke – the changes of volume, the crescendos and diminuendos. Also terrifying was the roar of the frenzied crowds. I heard, however, none of that extraordinary energy in the recordings of Churchill's speeches. It was not until 27 April 2021 that I learnt why.

That April I watched a webinar hosted by my mentor Allen Packwood featuring author and politician Lord Michael Dobbs, who wrote both *House of Cards* and *Winston's War*. I met Lord Dobbs on 7 October 2021 at the RAF Club reception for the World Churchill Meeting in London. It turns out he and I are the same age.

---

1 Birrell, *Johnny – Canada's Greatest Bomber Pilot*, p. 68

BOYHOOD

The 27 April 2021 webinar included a clip of Lord Dobbs interviewing 'Darkest Hour' Churchill actor Gary Oldman who so brilliantly played Churchill in that movie. I was astonished when Oldman said recordings of Churchill's speeches were often made after, not at, the event he was speaking. That is why these recordings do not have the energy and gusto of Churchill's inspired delivery to audiences. That's why, as a boy in the Calgary Library, while I was hearing the content of his speeches, I was not hearing Churchill's brilliance as an orator.

The clip included the entirety of Churchill's famous 'Beaches – We Shall Never Surrender' speech as uttered by Oldman in parliament in the movie. Lord Dobbs said this was one of the greatest speeches in the English language. What a difference from the recordings I listened to in the Calgary Library. During that Beaches speech in parliament in 'Darkest Hour', I also vividly remember the momentary view of the establishment leaders sitting frozen in shocked silence while MPs whooped for joy during the speech. It made clear that Churchill's followers were the people of Britain, not the establishment.

When I was eighteen, I was aboard a passenger train from Edmonton to Saskatoon. A German teenager about my age sat beside me. Fortunately, he grew tired of the incredibly flat scenery, and wanted to practise his English. While we talked, I asked him what was so mesmerizing about Hitler's oratory. How did Hitler whip crowds into massive frenzies of adoration? He replied 'I have no idea. When I have heard recordings of his speeches, I hear them knowing they led to total catastrophe, so nothing about them appeals to me. Also, it was impossible to talk about the war at my house. My parents would sooner have told us about their sex lives than say anything about that war. And we Germans are really prudish about sex, especially when talking to our parents.'

My Tale of Four Lancasters

As mentioned, a recurring image of increasing importance in my boyhood was that most iconic of Second World War aircraft, the Lancaster. Essentially, my Alberta boyhood wartime awareness largely arose from four of them – my 'Tale of Four Lancasters'. The power of these planes to a young boy, especially a boy who knew his Dad flew them, is difficult to describe. I knew they were our biggest aircraft in the war, and they certainly looked big to me. But they were more than that. Much more. They were a visible statement of power, of winning, of doing something incredibly difficult, incredibly dangerous, and absolutely essential to our well-being. And, whatever that was, in some way my Dad was part of it.

My Calgary Lancaster

My Calgary Lancaster research was complicated partly because, as I have now discovered, there were actually two Lancasters in Calgary. When my Dad and

BOMBER COMMAND

I watched my Calgary Lancaster flying into Calgary from Fort MacLeod on 9 April 1961, the *Calgary Herald* headline was 'Winged War Relic Arrives in Calgary'. More to the point, the subheading declared 'Lancaster here'. It had been purchased about three days earlier by Lynn Garrison from the Crown for $975. On 11 April 1962, my Calgary Lancaster was lifted up onto a huge pedestal by three big cranes. On Saturday 14 April 1962, it was dedicated. The inscription says:

> Dedicated to all personnel who served and trained in the British Commonwealth Air Training Plan. The most important centre of this Plan was Calgary, and this area saw nearly 30,000 men and women trained from 1941-45. From here personnel went to all theatres of combat throughout the world. Dedicated by Chief of the Air Staff, Air Marshal Hugh Campbell, CBE, CD, April 14, 1962.

Even though I was born and raised in Calgary, I did not know until researching for this book that Calgary was 'the most important centre of The Plan'. That lack of knowledge arose in part over convoluted confusion in the 1960s involving my Calgary Lancaster and the Calgary Airshow Lancaster, the complexity of which is beyond this book, but led to reducing Calgary as an aviation centre and its memory of its role in the Plan in the Second World War. However, Calgary rebounds magnificently. For example, CTV News announced on 6 April 2022 that de Havilland Aircraft of Canada Limited is launching a new firefighting bomber known as the DHC-515 that will be manufactured in Calgary.[2]

My strongest memory of my Calgary Lancaster was its location. It was the first sight every person arriving by plane had of Calgary when emerging from Calgary's airport terminal, and the last sight of Calgary when leaving. It was the highest profile aviation real estate in Calgary. Even I as a teenager could figure out by its location that, for whatever reason, Lancasters had been very important. In 1977, that Terminal was replaced by the present one at the opposite end of the airport. My Calgary Lancaster was removed from its pedestal and kept outside on the ground beside McKnight Boulevard at the south end of the airport. Today it is housed there inside one of a pair of huge hangars with other vintage aircraft at The Hangar Flight Museum. It still thrills me to see it. My 6 July 2015 visit was memorable. My daughter Mary Anne MacKenzie and I were driving in from Calgary airport for the funeral that day of our beloved Aunt Sheila MacKenzie. Although our timing was tight, I made stopping to see my Calgary Lancaster a priority. Mary Anne and I were photographed with it. That's how powerful the pull of Lancasters continues to be. The Lancaster has an aura of greatness. My most recent visit was on 10 September 2020 when I was hosted by Director Don Ross and Executive Director Brian Desjardins. It still looks magnificent.

In addition, Calgary has an RCAF Bomber Command display in what was Calgary's Museum of the Regiments when it was formally opened on 30 June 1990

---

2 Fleming, 'New Jobs for Calgary's Aviation Industry,' CTV News 6 April 2022.

by the Queen. On 03 June 2006 by announcement of HRH Sophie, Countess of Wessex and spouse of HRH Prince Edward, it was renamed the Military Museums because it now includes the relocated Naval Museum of Alberta and the Air Force Wing I just mentioned. It is the second largest Military Museum in Canada. The largest, of course, is the Canadian War Museum in Ottawa whose Second World War Historian Jeff Noakes has helped me with this book.

Calgary Airshow Lancaster[3]

In April 1964, Lynn Garrison purchased Lancaster KB976 which, to avoid confusion, I will call the Calgary Airshow Lancaster. Garrison says Canada's then Minister of Defence, Paul Hellyer, authorized the Calgary Airshow Lancaster being flown in RCAF colours on 4 July 1964 at the Calgary International Airshow at which Hellyer was guest of honour.[4] Four years later, Hellyer became intensely disliked for his 1 February 1968 unification of Canada's armed forces into one service, ushering in 'decades of darkness'. This Calgary Airshow Lancaster flight was captained by Garrison, with his 403 Calgary Squadron RCAF colleague, Flight Lieutenant Ralph Langemann as co-pilot. I had an informative and enjoyable meeting with Ralph on 1 September 2020 in Calgary where I was astonished to learn that neither Lynn nor Ralph had flown a four-engine plane before that fateful Airshow. Decades later, after being bounced around North America and Europe, the Calgary Airshow Lancaster was purchased by Kermit Weeks, and awaits restoration in his 'Fantasy of Flight' in Orlando, Florida. It may fly again.

My Red Deer Lancaster

My Calgary Lancaster was not my first; my Red Deer Lancaster KB885 was. As mentioned, in about June 1952 my Mom contracted polio. She was taken to Edmonton and put in the iron lung. Dad would take me with him on what was then a six-hour drive north to Edmonton (and now is only three hours), but I was never allowed to see her. Instead, in Edmonton I stayed with my Uncle Bruce MacKenzie and his family while Dad alone visited Mom. More on that later.

Halfway between Calgary and Edmonton is Red Deer, today Alberta's third largest city. The 'Queen Elizabeth II Highway', a beautiful freeway, now connects all three cities. But then it was just Alberta Highway No. 2 – the oldest, longest and most used highway in Alberta. At one time it was called the Calgary Trail by Edmontonians and the Edmonton Trail by Calgarians. On my long drives as a little boy with my Dad to Edmonton, I always looked forward to our approaching Red

---

3 Garrison, 'KB976's last RCAF flight and The Air Museum of Canada Lancaster KB796', Section 3 Canadian Civilian Life www.timefadesaway.co.uk/strathallan/kb796/kb_976_3.html

4 Skaarup, *Canadian Warplanes* iUniverse Inc., New York, 2009, p. 25

Deer, partly because the stretch of road leading into town from Calgary was called 'Gasoline Alley', partly because I liked Red Deer, and partly because I particularly enjoyed seeing my Red Deer Lancaster parked on the east side of the highway. For me it was a thrill driving past my Red Deer Lancaster. I have now learnt Charlie Parker purchased it for $275 in 1947, and parked it next to his gas station, of course on Gasoline Alley. He called his gas station 'Bomber Service'. I'm told Mr Parker allowed people to tour inside my Red Deer Lancaster, but we never did. Sadly, for health reasons, in 1956 Mr Parker sold my Red Deer Lancaster. The new owners then sold it to Americans as a fire-fighting water bomber. It was going to carry 4,000 gallons of water to drop on forest fires. In January 1957 came the big day. After much work by mechanics, my Red Deer Lancaster was deemed airworthy again. Pilot-mechanic E. Robinson taxied it through the snow to its makeshift runway. Just before take-off, hydraulic problems developed, igniting a fire in the interior of the nose of the plane. The nose section fell off. My Red Deer Lancaster was sold for scrap. Even now, whenever I enter Red Deer, I longingly remember my Red Deer Lancaster.[5]

My Nanton Lancaster

The fourth of my boyhood Lancasters became by far my most important, but I had no way of knowing that as a boy. My Nanton Lancaster FM159 first appeared beside Alberta Highway No. 2 at the north end of Nanton in 1960. I later learnt its history from Dave Birrell's book *FM159 The Lucky Lancaster*. Built in Canada, it was in Britain only six weeks in 1945 before being designated for deployment to Okinawa as part of Tiger Force. Tiger Force ended after America's B-29 Superfortress 'Enola Gay' dropped an atomic bomb on Hiroshima. In the 1950s, my Nanton Lancaster saw service with the RCAF at 103 Search and Rescue Unit at RCAF Station Greenwood in Nova Scotia. Next it was flown by 407 Squadron at RCAF Station Comox in British Columbia. From Comox it flew ice-reconnaissance patrols in the northern annual Operation NANOOK. On 12 July 1955, my Nanton Lancaster flew a weather-reconnaissance flight from Resolute Bay to Isachsen on the northern part of Ellef Rignes Island (79 degrees north). Then my Nanton Lancaster flew its most memorable flight – twelve-hour 25-minute ice-reconnaissance flight from Resolute Bay followed by a diversion to Alert, the northernmost point in Canada (82.5 degrees north) on Ellesmere Island just 490 miles (790 km) from the North Pole. On 21 July 1955 my Nanton Lancaster arrived back in Comox, and two weeks later was flown to California to accompany HMCS *Ontario* to enable the ship's company to hone their anti-aircraft gunnery skills while my Nanton Lancaster escorted the ship back to BC. Other RCAF deployments included to Portugal, Londonderry, Northern Ireland, and Kodiak Island Alaska. My Nanton Lancaster's last RCAF operational flight was in October 1958.[6] Then, in 1960, it

---

5 *Bomber Command Museum of Canada*, Nanton Alberta www.bombercommandmuseum.ca

6 Birrell, *FM159 The Lucky Lancaster*, pp. 17-49.

appeared in Nanton, a town of about 2,000 people an hour's drive south of Calgary on Highway 2, now a freeway, but then MacLeod Trail. We would drive through Nanton en route to Lethbridge to visit my Mom's sister Dorothy and her family. I liked exploring Lethbridge's coulees of the Old Man River with my cousin Don. Guess what their surname is? Lancaster! Aunt Dorothy married Ken Lancaster of Ventnor, on the Isle of Wight.

We would also drive through Nanton to visit Waterton Glacier International Peace Park, 'Head Smashed In' Buffalo Jump, the marvellous beef restaurant several miles past Claresholm on what I now know was a former British Commonwealth Training Plan air base, or as part of a scenic circle drive from Calgary. On 9 August 2021, my wife Ka Hyun and I managed to find and photograph the Claresholm RCAF Second World War airbase at which I now know my Dad was a flying instructor in 1943. More on that later. I also now know locals purchased my Nanton Lancaster in 1960. It sat outdoors beside Highway No. 2 for thirty years until the Nanton Lancaster Society, which was formed in 1986, completed a hangar to house it in 1991. More, too, on that later.

The Ever-Increasing Power of Lancasters Over Me

The enduring power of my four boyhood Lancasters grew even stronger as I moved into manhood and encountered my fifth Lancaster in Toronto. More on that in the next chapter. Thereafter, other Lancasters enriched my expanding reality. As a boy, either alone or with my Dad, I built model Lancasters. I watched my Dad carve a model Lancaster from wood with a knife, and then paint it in wartime colours. My Dad also built models on the same scale of a Halifax, a Wellington, a Mosquito and a Tiger Moth. He had them on display on a wall in his bedroom. I thought these were all aircraft he flew, but the Mosquito does not appear in the back of Dad's logbook, so I now know I was wrong about that. Sometimes I would take my friends into Dad's room to see them. Through all of this, the iconic Lancaster became deeply embedded in my sense of my Dad, and my growing awareness of the war in the air over Nazi Germany.

My MacKenzie Heritage Aroused By My Great Uncle Leslie MacKenzie

My life has been greatly enriched by a series of awesome mentors, one of the first being my Great Uncle Leslie MacKenzie, Grandpa's older brother. Uncle Leslie's greatest gift to me was the awareness he gave me, and the pride he aroused in me, of my MacKenzie heritage. That brought marvellous people into my life, including the friendship of our MacKenzie Clan Chief, the Earl of Cromartie, who is also known as John Mackenzie, and to MacKenzies as 'Cabarfeidh'. John and his wife Eve reside in Castle Leod near Strathpeffer in the Scottish Highlands. Said to be the most authentic castle in Scotland, it is featured in the *Outlander* books and drama series. When you enter this castle, you will see a plaque declaring that *Outlander* author Judith Gabaldon and I are two of the 'Guardians of Castle Leod'.

My Great Uncle Leslie MacKenzie and his wife, my Great Aunt Anna MacKenzie, were pillars of Calgary society, and an enormous influence on my boyhood. They brought great joy into my life. Uncle Leslie was one of Dad's closest friends, and Aunt Anna was one of Mom's closest friends. Sadly, Uncle Leslie died of cancer on 28 February 1965, just a month after Churchill's death on 24 January. I was only sixteen years old. Aunt Anna died two years later on 29 January 1967 while I was in first year at the University of Calgary. I still miss them both. Their only child, Elizabeth, married Arthur Hutson. He, too, seriously expanded my outlook, and strengthened my values. In the Second World War Arthur had distinguished service in the US Army in China. On 16 November 1943, Arthur while a major was ordered to China to teach Chinese troops how to use American weapons, and to learn Mandarin as quickly as possible. In June 1944, Arthur was made liaison officer with the 30th Chinese Division, and on 19 January 1945 he was made commanding officer of the combat forces of the Chinese 89th Division. Postwar, returning to the reserves, Arthur taught military intelligence at Fort Ord on Monterey Bay near Salinas, California. He retired from the US Army as a full colonel in 1967. Arthur shared with me positive views of Mao Zedong and Zhou Enlai, and negative ones of Chiang Kai-shek as corrupt and ineffective. Arthur's words shocked me. They were contrary to the prevailing view of the late 1950s and early 1960s that all 'Commies' were the devil, and leaders like Chiang Kai-shek were wonderful. I mention all this because, through his wartime stories, Arthur opened my mind to critical thinking, and not believing something just because others did. Critical thinking enriched me as a lawyer, and in researching to discover the truth for this book.

Postwar, Arthur became a professor at the University of California, Berkeley, where he served as assistant to President Clark Kerr during the 1960s Mario Savio Student Movement which spread through campuses worldwide from Berkeley. The Hutsons asked me to live with them, and earn my BA in Political Science at Berkeley, but Dad wanted me in Calgary, saying my Mom needed me. Tragically, Elizabeth died, to my shocked sorrow, on 18 April 1972 of what I think was a heart ailment. That was just a couple of weeks before I graduated from law school. The plan had been for me to visit the Hutsons later that month. Another terrible shock – their only child, and Uncle Leslie's only grandchild, my second cousin Danny Hutson whom I liked, was killed in a traffic accident on 5 October 1992, age fifty-three. Years after Danny's death, his daughter Anna Elizabeth Hutson managed to find me on the Internet. We've been friends ever since. They would have loved her. I mention all this to show how important my Great Uncle Leslie was to me. He and his family gave me the strength, discernment, and awareness needed to write this book.

BOYHOOD

Entering Manhood in the Scottish Highlands

On 22 June 1969 I was a young solo backpacker looking pathetic while standing on the side of a primitive road in the rain. I had walked a mile from the Ratagan youth hostel to reach that road. There I was hitch-hiking near Loch Duich and Eilean Donan Castle in what in those days were the wild Scottish Highlands. A luxurious yellow Rover, which went well with the yellow Scottish broom in bloom that day on Highland hillsides, came to a halt, its occupants feeling compassion for my plight, and I was welcomed in. My hosts were Ted and Norah Cossey of Devon. Conversation turned to the war, I think because I am Canadian. The Cosseys' reaction was unforgettable when I said my Dad flew a Lancaster. They had enormous admiration for 'Bomber Boys' who they told me were among the greatest heroes of the war. In Newtonmore of Clan MacPherson, located at the exact geographical centre of Scotland, the Cosseys hosted for me one of the most elegant multi-course meals of my life up until then. After this mid-day feast, they took me to Blair Castle, ancestral home of the Chiefs of Clan Murray – the Dukes of Atholl.

I have visited Blair Castle twice since, first with my children Mary Anne and Guy Roland MacKenzie in 1992 as guests of the Duke in my capacity as President of the MacKenzies in the Americas. That visit was during my children's first day in Scotland – we were en route north to the MacKenzie Clan lands. The Duke was extraordinary – one of the wealthiest men in Britain, and having the UK's only legal private army. He showed us recent photos taken of US President Ronald Reagan and his Secretary of State George Schultz sitting in the same chairs we now occupied. My second visit to Blair Castle was in the summer of 1998 in my capacity as Scoutmaster of the 27th Vancouver Scout Troop. We were attending a jamboree in the grounds of Blair Castle of scout troops from about twenty European countries. Ours was the only troop given a full tour inside that beautiful castle.

After Blair Castle, the Cosseys drove me over Killiecrankie Pass where they made a point of showing me the Queen's View at Pitlochry. I now stop there each time I pass through because it was Queen Victoria's favourite, and because Pitlochry is the boyhood home of Canada's second prime minister, Alexander Mackenzie. The Cosseys did all of this, and more in subsequent years including in 1972 hosting my bride and me in their home for a week of our four-month honeymoon, because it enabled them to say Thanks! They told me they were thrilled to be entertaining the son of a Bomber Boy. They said the hope Bomber Boys instilled in the British, and those conquered by the Nazis in Europe, was one of their defining memories of the Second World War. They told me men like my Dad were at as great a risk of being killed as they were in the front line during the war. For me, this heartfelt food for thought aroused awareness that possibly what Dad did was important.

And that led me into my manhood.

Chapter Two

Manhood

'Which squadron Roddy did your Dad fly with in the war?'

These were the words of the City of New Westminster's very first city planner, my colleague Barry Chaster. Barry had been a Lancaster pilot in the Second World War. Whenever Barry asked, my answer was always: 'I don't know'. On 19 July 1976, the day after my twenty-eighth birthday, was my first day as the super-young, brand-new City Solicitor of British Columbia's first capital city – the Royal City of New Westminster. It was named by Queen Victoria, and it was there I saw Queen Elizabeth II. It was also there that Barry Chaster came into my life – and so did the most remarkable of men, New Westminster City Administrator Doug Manning, one of my greatest mentors. My non-answer to Barry's question of course gave rise to his unspoken suggestion that I ask my Dad. I never did, because Dad and I seldom talked about anything important, and least of all the war. And I was annoyed that Dad kept me in the dark.

From the outset, Doug Manning and I developed an extraordinary relationship that transcended our work environment and covered every aspect of our lives until Doug's death on 21 November 2013. On 30 November 2013 I delivered his eulogy to a packed hall of mourners. The turn-out was so huge that more were outside the hall than in. Doug's widow Betty Manning, when asking me to do this eulogy, said: 'You always speak from the heart Roddy. That's one of the things Doug liked so much about you.' That is what I am doing my best to do here in this book – speak my truth from my heart. Doug recognized early on my strained relations with my Dad. Every now and again, Doug would ask when Dad and I had last spoken. Doug would then order me to pick up the phone right there in the City Hall and call Dad in Calgary, which I always did. But our chats were superficial. No depth developed.

Doug and Barrie lived on New Westminster's two-block-long Courtney Crescent. Another pair of remarkable men who resided on Courtney with Doug and Barry were New Westminster City Clerk Peter Larkin and Chief Medical Health Officer Dr John Blatherwick. John and Betty are the only two of this great group still there, indeed still alive. Both are cherished friends of mine. Peter's face was disfigured. It for me was transformed from disfigured to heroic the day I learnt it happened when German Panzers blasted Peter out of a Royal Westminster Regiment Canadian tank in the 1944 Battle of Normandy. I had a view of the

MANHOOD

Westies Armoury across our shared parking lot from my beautiful City Hall office. Peter was hospitalized for many months after that battle. He later married his nurse Rose. They were a happy couple who produced a lovely family. And there's more. On 30 March 2022 my FitFellas classmate Jim Graham told me Peter's assistant city clerk, Isabelle Graham, whom I remember, was Jim's mom. What's more, Peter was Jim's scoutmaster. Small world of wonderful people.

As mentioned in my Acknowledgements, Dr John Blatherwick became New Westminster's Chief Medical Health Officer when I became City Solicitor in 1976. At the time of his retirement, John was Canada's longest serving medical health officer. He served postwar in the RCN, the RCAF and Canada's Army, and so has earned ranks in all three. John is the published author of several books. He helped me write this, his enthusiasm kept my nose to the grindstone and his friendship was a major motivator whenever the enormity of this task overwhelmed me.

RCAF Flight Lieutenant J. Barry Chaster

Barry's story, as I remember him telling me in bits and pieces over several years, was that the Lancaster he piloted was shot down and Barry evaded capture all the way across Nazi-occupied Europe from The Netherlands south to Spain. From there he was repatriated to Britain. Barry mentioned he had a major scare in a movie theatre in Belgium. Someone asked him a question, and Barry inadvertently answered in English. English in Nazi-occupied Belgium was a singularly dangerous language. Barry quietly departed the theatre before the movie concluded. Barry also told me his greatest regret was that his fateful flight took off from England moments before word arrived that he had been commissioned as an officer. As a result, the whole time Barry was evading the Germans in Europe, he mistakenly thought he was still an NCO. Barry told me, with a twinkle in his eye, this meant sleeping in ditches while officers slept in haystacks, and other indignities he would have been spared had he only known he was an officer. He may have slightly stretched this, given his wonderful dry sense of humour. Bomber Command aircrew were a band of brothers, and so unlikely to differentiate rank while being hunted by Germans. Speaking of rank, some heavy bomber aircrew, and especially pilots, not being officers was a continuing source of conflict between Canada and Britain. Canada maintained everyone aboard should be an officer while Britain, still steeped in its class system and with a sharp eye on costs, persisted in restricting the number of aircrew made officers. One resulting absurdity was pilots such as Barry were in charge of the aircraft while some of their aircrew were officers, but they were not. The seven aircrew aboard a Lancaster were a tightly-knit entity that should not have been separated into different messes and barracks.[1] All should have been officers.

---

1 Feesey, *The Fly By Nights – RAF Bomber Command Sorties 1944-45*, p. 70

BOMBER COMMAND

But what were the details of Barry's story? After he died on 24 April 2007, I feared I would never know. And then, on 4 July 2019, while the house guest of my friend Jim Bartlett, the widower of Ka Hyun's beloved Godmother, Deirdre Bartlett, in Kamloops, I struck gold. Jim's extensive library included the book *We Flew, We Fell, We Lived* by Philip Lagrandeur,[2] five pages of which to my delighted surprise are devoted to Barry. From that book I discovered Barry's story is far more powerful than I ever imagined – it turns out Barry's sortie was important, and his experience terrifying. Barry had the self-effacing modesty that was widespread among Bomber Command veterans, if they spoke at all. Barry gave me no hint of the importance, or the terror, of his final flight. For starters, I erroneously assumed Barry flew with an RCAF squadron when in fact he flew with RAF 207 Squadron of 5 Group. From 11 September 1939 to 22 November 1940, 5 Group had been commanded by AVM Arthur Harris. Starting 28 February 1943, almost two months after Barry was shot down, it was commanded by AVM Ralph Cochrane. Its most famous squadron was 617, the Dambusters, led by Guy Gibson to bomb the Mohne, Eder and Sorpe dams on 17 May 1943. That was just over five months after Barry was shot down. No. 5 Group was noted for navigational innovation and low-level target marking to the annoyance of Australian AVM Don Bennett, the air officer commanding No. 8 Group Pathfinders. I discovered Barry played an important role in this innovation and low-level marking.

Lagrandeur starts out saying Lancaster Pilot 'Flight Sergeant Chaster', not knowing he had just been promoted to flight lieutenant, departed England on 3 January 1943 on a sortie to Essen in Germany. RAF AVM Paul Robinson tells me this sortie was part of a trial to test night blind bombing with 10/10ths cloud cover. Nineteen Lancasters were guided by three Pathfinder Mosquitos using the new navigational device OBOE, our first airborne, precision-bomb-aiming radar system. It was so successful that Bomber Command immediately adopted it. Three Lancasters were lost that night. One was Barry's. What happened to Barry was a tragedy. Lagrandeur says that, while returning to England, Barry encountered Luftwaffe ace *Oberleutnant* Manfred Meurer, a German fighter pilot with sixty-nine kills. At 18,000 feet, Meurer shot down Barry's Lancaster. Four of Barry's crew were killed in the attack – Walter Harris, Ivan Lineker, Bill Moger and Ken Pugh. Barry's navigator, Gordon Marwood, and bomb aimer, John Banfield, survived, albeit seriously injured. As for Barry, Lagrandeur reports:

> A wall of flames had trapped Chaster in his cockpit. He smashed the jagged perspex from one window frame, tore his parachute pack open and shoved his canopy out. The slipstream filled the silk canopy like a sail and pulled him into the sky. Miraculously, he cleared the two spinning propellers and the tail plane.[3]

---

2 Lagrandeur, *We Flew, We Fell, We Lived – Stories from RCAF Prisoners of War and Evaders*, pp. 343-7.

3 Lagrandeur, pp. 343-4.

MANHOOD

Barry's evasion of Germans through The Netherlands, Belgium and France to Spain was fraught with danger. Lagrandeur writes that the Dutch had no escape network. This is confusing because Bob Porter says he owed a great debt to the Dutch Resistance escape network when his RCAF Lancaster was shot down over The Netherlands.[4] Whatever the truth of Dutch resistance, Barry was saved by brave Dutch citizens risking their lives to take him to the Belgian border, and helping get him across. The first Dutch family he met removed shards of perspex from his scalp, bandaged his head, and gave him an overcoat to cover his RCAF uniform. He had to leave their home almost immediately because Gestapo agents were billeted next door. Barry told me he impersonated a deaf mute when dealing with Germans while successful evading capture in Europe. Lagrandeur's book confirms this. In Belgium, Barry was saved by the 'Comet Escape Line' from there to Spain through which 120 Allied airmen had been successfully rescued from occupied Europe. However, at the very moment Barry was entering Belgium, collaborators who had infiltrated the Comet Escape Line were betraying it to the Gestapo. As a result, Barry was one of the last to use it, and at terrible cost. The Comet Escape Line collapsed just as Barry slipped through. At least four of his helpers were sent to concentration camps. Joseph Heenan survived two horrific years in Dachau. Three Belgian women who helped Barry also survived two years in German concentration camps. They were Mesdames E. Warnon, E. Leigois and Paulsen.

Barry chose the name 'Knut Rockney' for the Swedish passport the Belgians gave him. Knute Rockne was the famous Norwegian-American football player and coach at Notre Dame University adjacent to South Bend, Indiana. In Brussels, Barry was handed over to Albert Grindel, a revered Belgian nobleman whose brother Jean oversaw the operation of the Comet Escape Line. Albert Grindel escorted Barry from Brussels to Spain. His brother Jean died in Nazi custody. Over 100 of the 1,000 helpers in the Comet Escape Line were executed by the Nazis. But Lagrandeur points out that their heroic work both saved Allied airmen's lives, and gave all Allied air force aircrew hope when they were shot down. In addition, these resistance heroes buoyed the morale of people in countries occupied by Nazi Germany, and their resistance demoralized German military morale, tied down German manpower needed at the front, and gave Allied intelligence invaluable information about German operations. And, best of all, they saved the lives of heroic Allied aircrew evaders such as Barry. I liked Barry as a friend, I admired him as a pioneering city planner, and now I'm in awe of him as a Canadian who heroically helped us win the war. But my lack of knowledge and indifference to Bomber Command in the 1970s when Barry and I worked together in New Westminster City Hall deprived me of knowing him so much better, and deprived Barry of knowing anything about my Dad in the war. To not deprive others of knowing any of this is one of the reasons I am writing this book.

---

4 Porter, Bob (ex-RCAF PoW) *The Long Return – A True Story of a Young WWII Airman – One of Two Survivors of a Plane Which Was Blown Up Over Nazi-Occupied Holland* http://www.intergate.bc.ca/business/boport

My Toronto Lancaster

My fifth Lancaster was in, of all places, Toronto. The first time I flew into Toronto as a young man, and took the airporter downtown, I was pleasantly surprised to see it in Coronation Park on the south side of Lake Shore Boulevard across from the Canadian National Exhibition. My Toronto Lancaster FM104, like Calgary's, was perched on a pedestal, which they call a plinth. My Toronto Lancaster was assembled at Victory Aircraft at Malton, Ontario, where on 25 March 1958 Canada's iconic Avro Arrow fighter jet first took off. Postwar, the RCAF used my Toronto Lancaster in Newfoundland for anti-submarine patrols and search and rescue work. It was SOS (Struck off Strength) by the RCAF on 10 February 1964, exactly twenty years after rolling out of the Malton factory. My Toronto Lancaster was sold to the RCAF Association Toronto Region which put it on display at the 1964 CNE, and then donated to the City of Toronto. It was moved across Lake Shore Boulevard from the CNE to Coronation Park where I saw it perched on a plinth as a permanent war memorial.[5]

I always looked forward to seeing my Toronto Lancaster. Then it disappeared. Sadly, I now know it had been victimized by both weather and vandals. And then, in July 2018, my Toronto Lancaster re-appeared with a vengeance. It turns out it had been disassembled and placed into storage because no one knew what to do with it. The Canadian Warplane Museum at Hamilton wanted it, evidently promising they would work to get it airborne again one day, just as their Lancaster FM213 is now flying. But Toronto City Council rejected Hamilton. Some media speculated Toronto Council was suspicious the CWM would not get it airborne, but instead would cannibalize it to keep their own Lancaster in the air.

Then Toronto City Council did something that caused me to utter the three words born and bred western Canadians seldom say – 'Thank you Toronto!' On 24 July 2018, Toronto City Council voted to give my Toronto Lancaster to the British Columbia Aviation Museum[6] on Norseman Road beside Victoria International Airport. British Columbia was the centre of Lancaster activity in Canada post-war but, until Toronto did this, there was nary a Lancaster anywhere in Canada's third largest province. And now, thanks to Toronto, BC finally has a Lancaster. My Toronto Lancaster is in a ten-year, five-million-dollar, restoration project by a group of volunteers including my friend Russ Hudson to get it airborne. And so, I conclude by again saying: 'Thank You Toronto!'

My Nanton Lancaster Returns – And Packs a Major Punch!

But for me the power of this iconic aircraft arose most from my Nanton Lancaster.

In about 1987 something important happened. It began while my Dad and I were driving to Lethbridge. Just the two of us. This was unusual, given at that time

---

5 Filey, 'The Way We Were – Historic Avro Lancaster will one day take to the SKIES again,' *Toronto Sun* newspaper 30 May 2020

6 Liz Braun, 'Toronto Lancaster Headed West', *Toronto Sun*, 24 July 2018

MANHOOD

I was a married 37-year-old-lawyer raising a family in Vancouver. On that fateful day circa 1987, en route to Lethbridge, Dad and I entered Nanton. Dad was at the wheel, as usual. We were pretty quiet together, as usual. My Nanton Lancaster was still parked outside beside the highway, as usual, where it had been weathering the elements since its arrival back in 1960. But in 1987 our passing through Nanton was different. First, the Lancaster was set back from the road with a small white picket fence surrounding it, and parking beside it. Second, Dad and I stopped in the parking lot and got out to have a look. We had never done that together before. Third, a handful of others were milling around, also admiring the aircraft. As is my wont, I piped up, saying to everyone 'My Dad flew one of these in the war!' A couple of men looked at us with interest, their eyebrows slightly raised. One said to my Dad 'Really?' My Dad nodded. They quietly exchanged a few words with Dad. Then one said to us both 'I have the keys to this aircraft. The two of you are welcome to climb aboard, and spend as long inside her as you wish.' We did.

I have no idea how long Dad and I were alone aboard her – half an hour, perhaps an hour. I was aware we were sharing something extremely significant, although I wasn't sure what. What I also did not know until over three decades later was we were in one of the only Lancasters the interior of which is still authentically as it was in the Second World War. Most others are reconfigured internally for other uses postwar. While we were aboard, little was said. Dad gave brief explanations, mainly about where people sat and what they did, and especially what Dad did to fly the plane. But mostly we sat in silence. Time passed. It was serene. Then suddenly Dad snapped out of whatever trance he was in, and announced: 'Time to go!' We were quickly out of that aircraft, thank-yous and goodbyes said, and into our car and back on the highway heading south and then east to Lethbridge.

My Dad Tells Me How to Pilot a Lancaster in Combat

But as we departed Nanton for Lethbridge, something remarkable happened. Something I had never experienced before, and would never experience again. My usually taciturn father started talking, while I sat in complete silence listening. Speaking slowly and deliberately, with a quiet voice in a measured pace, choosing his words with care, two hands on the steering wheel, never taking his eyes off the road, Dad talked nonstop. I didn't interrupt, not even once. That, too, was unusual. I simply sat there, trying to absorb what Dad was saying. Afterwards, I have often wished I'd had a recorder, because what Dad was telling me was so important.

Dad explained in great detail exactly what was involved in (1) getting a Lancaster to a target exactly on time, especially when flying with hundreds of main force bombers, (2) hitting that target, and (3) getting out without getting killed. He explained *flak*, and told me about Germany's devastating dual anti-aircraft and anti-tank guns. He told me about the Lancaster's ability to corkscrew. He described German night-fighter aircraft, how they attacked, how they killed. Dad explained what pilots had to do to survive all this, and how remarkable a Lancaster was if the pilot knew enough about flying it. He explained that there was no margin for error. Any error, no matter how seemingly innocuous, could and too often did result in death. The depth of his knowledge was extraordinary. I got glimpses of just how intelligent he was, how brave, how determined. It also struck me that, if Dad had not been blessed with all those attributes, I would never have been born, because he would have been killed in hostile skies over Nazi-occupied Europe in the bloodbath known as Bomber Command. Dad also told me about navigational problems, weather problems, equipment problems, morale problems. He told me how freezing cold Lancasters were, except for the navigator who was in danger of being burned by the heater. But what he did not tell me was with which squadron he flew, which bomber group he was in, from which RAF station he flew combat sorties, how he got the DFC, or anything else that would enable me to learn more about his time overseas. As we approached Lethbridge, Dad stopped talking. He never mentioned the war to me again. Four years later, he died of emphysema.

Who Was My Dad?

So who was Roland W. MacKenzie DFC, the father I never really knew? And why was it so hard to connect with him emotionally on any meaningful level? Where did Dad come from, what sort of a man was he and, most of all, what happened to him in Europe in the Second World War? It has taken several years of researching and writing this book for me to find out.

Chapter Three

My Dad

An Unusual Volunteer

In September 1941 an unusual volunteer commenced training with the Royal Canadian Air Force. He was unusual because he was much older than most recruits, being 29, and he had for thirteen years been a banker with the Royal Bank of Canada. I'm told he was seen to have a bright future with the Royal Bank. Who was he? He's known in RCAF and RAF records as Roland W. MacKenzie DFC. Among his wartime RCAF and RAF colleagues, he may have been known as Grandpa.[1] Among MacKenzies, he was Roland. To his Royal Bank colleagues, and our Calgary friends, he was Rolly. To me, he was Dad. I am his only son. So who was my Dad? That is a great question. He was a decorated veteran, but the only time I ever saw his medals on display was beside his coffin at his funeral in August 1991. I never knew him to attend Remembrance Day services, or have contact with his wartime colleagues. It was difficult knowing my Dad, hard to connect with him emotionally. I now know I am one of many sons of Bomber Boys who were adversely affected by their fathers' horrific wartime experiences in Bomber Command. We were also adversely affected by the RAF's and modified RCAF's concepts of LMF – Lack of Moral Fibre. And we were adversely affected by the shabby way Bomber Boys were treated postwar. More on this later.

Outer Hebrides to North America

I am told Dad was the first member of the sixth generation of our MacKenzie family in Canada, and that the first generation of our MacKenzie ancestors to reach Canada made the perilous voyage across the stormy unforgiving Atlantic Ocean in 1779. They came to Pictou County from Stornoway on the MacKenzie Clan lands of the Isle of Lewis in Scotland's wild Outer Hebrides. I am told they were led by my namesake, '4xGreat' Grandfather Roderick MacKenzie.

Five years earlier in 1774, ten-year-old Alexander Mackenzie departed Stornoway with his Dad for New York City. Two years later, the American

---

1 Birrell, *Johnny – Canada's Greatest Bomber Pilot*, p. 26

Revolution began, so in 1778 young Alex was sent to Montreal for safety while his father and uncle joined the King's Royal Regiment of New York as lieutenants to fight the rebels. In Montreal, Alex apprenticed with Finlay, Gregory & Co., an influential fur-trading company which in 1787 merged with the North West Company. Then he discovered the Mackenzie River, on which he travelled north by canoe for sixteen days, reaching the Arctic Ocean on 14 July 1789. But for Alex it was the River of Disappointment, because his quest was to reach the Pacific Ocean, not the Arctic. His round-trip from Fort Chipewyan via the Mackenzie River to the Arctic Ocean was over 3,000 miles (4,800 km).[2] On 20 July 1793, at the age of 29, Alex achieved his goal, reaching the Pacific Ocean at Bella Coola in what is now British Columbia. He was the first European to cross North America by land north of Mexico. His accomplishment is one reason British Columbia became British instead of American from the south or Russian from the north.

Another notable to cross the Atlantic from her birthplace in Stornoway was Mary Anne MacLeod. She departed Scotland 2 May 1930, arriving in New York on 11 May, the day after her eighteenth birthday. On 11 January 1936 she married Fred Trump. On 20 January 2017, their son Donald became America's forty-fifth president. My sons Guy Roland and Ruaridh and I saw, with Ka Hyun, her Stornoway home in 2017.

The first Scots emigrating from Scotland to Nova Scotia arrived in Pictou on 15 September 1773, only six years before my family. They were aboard the *Hector* (Canada's *Mayflower*). That auspicious event gave Pictou the honour of being 'The Birthplace of New Scotland'. William MacKenzie, age eighteen in the summer of 1773, compiled the most complete passenger list that exists. It says 189 passengers were aboard.[3] Most spoke only Gaelic and most boarded the ship at Lochbroom, also in the MacKenzie Clan lands. School teacher William McKenzie was one of the few who also spoke English.[4] I'm told the first three generations of my family in Canada continued to speak only Gaelic, so my MacKenzie grandparents could barely speak with their grandparents, given my grandparents spoke only English.

Getting back to my Dad, on 21 April 1912, the same day that Queen Elizabeth II was born fourteen years later in 1926, he was born Roland Waldo MacKenzie in Westville, in Pictou County on the northern coast of Nova Scotia across Northumberland Strait from Prince Edward Island, to my grandparents Roderick MacKay MacKenzie and Mary Catherine Gunn MacKenzie, both of Pictou County. This makes Dad 'a-Son-of-a-Gun', an expression common when I was a boy, although I never really knew what it meant. It seemed to me an affectionate expression but, for whatever reason, Dad did not like it. The names of everyone who married into the first five generations of our MacKenzie family in Canada since 1779 suggest they were all Highland Scots. I asked Grandma how she chose Waldo. She replied she named Dad after Ralph Waldo Emerson whom she admired.

---

2 Tabitha Marshall and Keith Mercer, *The Canadian Encyclopedia, Sir Alexander Mackenzie (explorer)* Published Online 7 January 2008, Last Edited 4 March 2015

3 *Heritage Hector Quay* www.shiphector.ca

4 Wikipedia, Hector Ship

MY DAD

For me Emerson's most compelling observation was 'Fear defeats more people than any other one thing in the whole world'. I wonder whether Dad was aware of that Emerson quote. It might have helped him survive Bomber Command.

Westward Ho!

My Dad was the last in our family to be born in Pictou County. While Dad was still a baby in 1913, his parents moved west with him from Westville Nova Scotia to Medicine Hat Alberta. At that time, both of Grandpa's brothers lived in Medicine Hat. My Great Uncle Chester MacKenzie soon returned to Westville. His only offspring, Jean and Alice, spent their lives in Nova Scotia. My Great Uncle Leslie MacKenzie, Grandpa's older brother, of course moved to Calgary. Dad's boyhood consisted of moving from town to town in Alberta and Saskatchewan while Grandpa helped build them and their neighbouring towns. Grandpa was an accomplished carpenter, and ultimately a superintendent of what was then called Crown Lumber. It later became Crown Zellerbach, which sadly disappeared through a hostile takeover in 1985, the year Grandpa turned 100. However, houses Grandpa built did not disappear. They can still be seen in Westville and Stettler. All are still occupied today. The house Dad was born in 1912 in Westville and our MacKenzie family home in Stettler for forty years both still have exceptional street appeal. I visited Grandpa's Westville house with my children. The owners opened their home to us, and even took us into the room where Dad was born on 21 April 1912.

Of all the towns he grew up in, Dad told me he loved Webb, Saskatchewan the most. Sadly, Webb today is pretty much a ghost town, with just a handful of houses still occupied. That was the fate of so many of Canada's small towns which before the Second World War bustled with life. Postwar Canada urbanized. Many Canadians abandoned their farms and small towns to move into our rapidly growing cities. The expression during my boyhood was 'How can you keep them down on the farm after they've seen Paris?' Dad lived in Webb from 1918 until 1920. Turning six on 21 April 1918, Dad began school in grade one in Webb that fall. In those days Webb was a vibrant community he loved. It was ideal for a young boy to run free. It is also where my Uncle Jack MacKenzie was born.

In 1920, the year Dad turned eight, our family moved to Kindersley, Saskatchewan for five years, by the end of which Dad was a teenager. I have a photo of Dad wearing a boy scout uniform and holding a horn, perhaps a bugle. My Uncle Bruce MacKenzie was born in Kindersley. Then, in 1925, our MacKenzies departed Kindersley to return permanently to Alberta. Their first two years were in Big Valley. In 1927, when Dad was 15, they moved north twenty-one miles (34 km) to Stettler, the wonderful community in which my Grandparents resided for the next forty years. It's known as the 'Heart of Alberta'. I discovered while exploring the Stettler Museum that Dambusters' hero Guy Gibson visited Stettler in September 1943 as part of his victorious Cross-Canada tour selling Victory Bonds. Photos disclose that Gibson was exceptionally popular with Stettler's girls.

My MacKenzies Go to War

It is interesting Canadiana for me to note that, to the best of my knowledge, the first five generations of my MacKenzie family living in Canada had no military connections. Grandpa was considered too old to be slaughtered in the First World War, thank God. As well, he was married with two young children, the elder being my Dad. Our family's non-involvement with the military since our arrival in Nova Scotia in 1779 changed dramatically in the Second World War. Canada fought that war the way Canada fights all wars – with volunteers. Our family volunteered.

I must qualify this. My friend RCAF Colonel (Retd) Patrick Dennis, an editor of this book, a military historian and a published author, reveals the little known fact that Canada did towards the end of both world wars make limited use of some draftees for fighting overseas. Instead of draftees, Canada calls them conscripts[5] which sounds like convicts. Some distinguished themselves in battle to our great benefit.

Canada entered the Second World War with about 11 million people. Of these, about 1.2 million volunteers were accepted into the Canadian Armed Forces. These volunteers included my Dad, two of his younger brothers, my uncles Jack and Bruce MacKenzie, and two of their brothers-in-law, my uncles-in-law Glen Harrison and Dr Warren Irvine. My beloved MacKenzie grandmother told me when I was a boy staying with her in Stettler, as I did every summer, that she did not get a single night's decent sleep while three of her sons were fighting overseas. I as a boy was impressed by military brass bands, medals and flags. Grandma was not. She did not have a single good word to say for war, but she knew Nazi Germany had to be stopped, so we had no choice but to fight.

The Royal Bank of Canada

The definitive experiences of my Dad's professional life were three-fold – RBC, the RCAF and the RAF. Dad never knew the term RBC – during his lifetime the Royal Bank of Canada was known as the Royal Bank, or simply the 'Royal'. The name RBC came in 2001, ten years after Dad died. Royal Bank history states it began way back in 1869 as the 'upstart Merchants' Bank of Halifax'. The *Canadian Encyclopedia* says it was founded in 1864 by a small group of merchants as a private bank, and received its 'official federal charter' in 1869 as a public company. In 1887 it opened its first British Columbia branch in Vancouver. Vancouver was incorporated on 6 April 1886, so the Royal was here essentially from the start. In 1901 it renamed itself the Royal Bank of Canada, and in 1903 opened its first Toronto branch. I say all this because I was raised in a Royal Bank family, and the Royal took great care to include us kids so we too would feel part of the Royal. The Royal also took great care of its Second World War volunteers.

---

5 See Patrick Dennis *Reluctant Warriors – Canada's Conscripts and the Great War*

MY DAD

My Royal Bank research reveals Dad's forty-four years with the Royal included the duration of his 1941 to 1945 wartime service with the RCAF and the RAF. Forty-four years! Dad's forty-four wonderful years with the Royal. Years so good that, following his retirement in 1972, Dad and the woman he married that spring, Verna Tate MacKenzie, served for several years as Royal Bank historians. RBC even created in its Alberta Head Office in Calgary a beautiful space easily seen by the public and named in gold letters the 'MacKenzie Room'. It housed Dad's and Verna's historical bank work. I remember its beautiful rich reddish wood trim, and the many bank artefacts Dad and Verna had acquired. He and Verna created a history of pretty much every RBC branch in Alberta. It became apparent through their work that the history of the Royal in Alberta was an integral part of the history of Alberta. For example, Dad told me that, in 1884, the Union Bank opened in Lethbridge the first branch of any bank in Alberta. In 1925, the Union Bank became part of the Royal.

Dad's lifetime with the Royal began in Stettler in 1928. That June, at age sixteen, Dad graduated with Junior Matriculation in grade eleven from Stettler High School. He was the first of our family to earn a high-school diploma, just as a generation later I was first to earn university degrees. Immediately after graduating on Friday 29 June 1928, Dad chose to stop school and start work with the Royal in Stettler on the next workday, which was Tuesday 3 July 1928. Monday was a national holiday then called Dominion Day, and now called Canada Day. Dad's job at the Royal arose in part because Grandpa was friends with Stettler's Royal Bank manager. Perhaps Dad thought a year later that opportunity might not still exist. Whatever were Dad's reasons, his decision to accept work with the Royal in 1928 launched Dad into a remarkable lifetime of professional fulfilment, and his timing was amazing good luck. Good luck also helped him survive the Second World War, even though he volunteered to serve where the chance of death was greatest.

I say Dad's timing was unbelievable good luck because, the year after Dad joined the Royal, the stock market crashed. This contributed to Canada plunging into our 'Ten Lost Years'[6] of the Great Depression. During that dreadful decade, known today as the 'Dirty Thirties', being a Royal Banker would have been highly coveted employment. And the Royal was noted for its fine treatment of its staff. That was particularly so during the Second World War, much to Dad's benefit.

Dad's Paradise – Peace River Country

My understanding from casual family references is that Dad worked for the Royal in Stettler 'for a couple of years'. Then RBC transferred him way up north to a place called Fairview in Alberta's wild Peace River Country. Dad told me the happiest years of his life were with the Royal in Fairview. I had no idea why. Dad was one of a staff of two. They lived above the Royal Bank. In those days, the Peace River

---

6 Broadfoot, *Ten Lost Years*, Doubleday, 1973. An oral history of the Great Depression

Country was so isolated, so primitive, so far north, that to an urban postwar Calgary boy like me, Dad might as well have been transferred to the North Pole. For this book, I needed to know why Dad was so happy in that wilderness.

And so, in August 2021 my wife Ka Hyun and I visited Fairview. What we discovered was important. Settlement of Peace River Country was dependent on the railways because, without trains, the muskeg separating it from southern Alberta made access by settlers virtually impossible. Muskeg is a Cree word meaning low-lying marsh. The first railways from Edmonton reached the towns of Peace River and Grande Prairie, Alberta in 1916. They were built under contract from the Alberta government by John Duncan ('JD') McArthur, a railroader who got things done. It was not, however, until 1928 that a railroad reached Fairview. In 1929 the village was incorporated and in 1930 both the United Church and the Royal Bank arrived. Think about it. Dad joined the Royal Bank in Stettler at age sixteen in July 1928. Two years later he was up north as part of a staff of two opening the Royal's brand-new branch in Fairview. He didn't turn eighteen until 21 April. The Royal had sufficient confidence in him that they made him one of only two Royal bankers in Fairview. Given their extreme isolation, those two would have largely relied on themselves as to how to operate their branch, and deal with financing the explosion of settlers pouring in, many of whom were penniless. In Fairview he would have experienced every aspect of banking – in Fairview he thrived. To me, Dad succeeding in frontier Fairview with RBC mirrors a decade later his succeeding with the RCAF and RAF in Bomber Command. Both times, he was thrown into the deep end of the pool to sink or swim. Dad swam.

Something happened at Fairview's The Old Bistro that sticks in my mind. Ka Hyun and I were enjoying coffee in that picturesque historic house just a block from the Royal Bank on 20 August 2021. Inside and outside, The Old Bistro was delightful. While I was seated in a wingback chair by the bay window absorbing the ambiance, Ka Hyun was browsing. She found a coffee-table style book about pioneer families in the area called *Reminisce with Freidenstal* funded by the Friedenstal Historical Society and the Municipal District of Fairview. Friedenstal was a small community just three miles (4 km) miles south-east of Fairview. When Ka Hyun showed me that book, what caught my attention was a pair of photos. The first is of a penniless family newly arrived from Russia in rags about 1928. Included in that photo is their seven-year-old son. These people had nothing. Without the aid of their new neighbours, they would have starved or frozen to death. But they were helped, they worked hard, and they prospered. The second photo was also of their son, this one taken about 1940. Now he wore the uniform of the Royal Canadian Air Force. He had volunteered to serve Canada in the Second World War. The RCAF had commissioned him as an officer, and had presented him with his wings as a pilot. He was no longer a penniless refugee in rags from Russia. Now he was a Canadian hero fighting for our freedom.

These two photos caused me to realize what an extraordinary unifier Canada's Armed Forces became in the Second World War. Differences dissolved when people donned the uniforms of the RCAF, RCN or Canada's Army. Who they had been, or where they were from, no longer mattered. In our armed forces fighting a war we had to win, they were Canadians.

On 22 August 2021, I concluded my visit to Alberta's Peace River Country by attending the Sunday Service at St Paul's United Church in Fairview. I did that because Dad was a life-long United Church of Canada member since its creation by parliament on 10 June 1925. St Paul's United was built in 1930. At the 22 August 2021 Service, I was among about thirty socially-distanced worshippers, given the Covid-19 Pandemic. Early in the service, after noting no birthdays or anniversaries, the minister asked whether there was anything anyone was grateful for that week. At first, no one responded. Then, impulsively, from where I was sitting towards the back of the sanctuary I put up my hand. The minister looked at me with surprise, partly I think because I was a stranger, then asked me to speak. Everyone turned around to look at me as I stood up. I said, 'I'm here this morning to express the gratitude of my Dad. While still a teenager, he was transferred by the Royal Bank from Stettler to Fairview in 1930. He had worked since high school at age sixteen in 1928 with the Royal Bank in Stettler. Here in Fairview, he was one of only two Royal Bankers. They slept in quarters above the bank. It was such an important time for Fairview. The railway arrived in 1928, the village was incorporated in 1929, and both the United Church and the Royal Bank arrived in 1930.' Someone asked his name. I replied 'Roland MacKenzie, but in Fairview he was likely called Rolly'. I then concluded by saying 'My Dad told me the happiest years of his life were living here in Fairview in the 1930s. For that I thank you!' My words were warmly received.

Dad's Prewar Personality

In these past few years, I've increasingly focused on who my Dad was prewar by asking those who knew him then for their memories. My interest was aroused by my awakening knowledge of Bomber Command. I needed to know how Bomber Command changed Dad. Our family seldom discussed such things, so I was pretty much in the dark. I learnt much about my Dad from my Uncle Bruce MacKenzie with whom I met several times during the last couple of months of his life. Uncle Bruce died on 26 June 2017. From my inquiries, I learnt that:

My Mom and Dad met at RBC where they both worked in Calgary before Dad went overseas, not postwar at Knox United Church Young People's in Calgary as I had assumed. I'm told Mom was one of the Royal's first female tellers. I had not realized they knew one another before Dad went overseas to fight. Tragically, letters Dad and Mom exchanged while Dad was overseas were destroyed over thirty years ago. I didn't know they had existed until after they were destroyed.

It caught me by surprise to learn prewar my Dad was relaxed and easy-going, that he had a remarkable sense of humour, that he was really funny, and that he often told funny stories. I have almost no memory of him doing any of that. What I do remember is Dad telling me once when I was a student at the

University of Calgary, and we were standing by the open door of our garage, that Dad's 'greatest regret' while I was growing up was that 'there had been almost no laughter in our house'. I did not associate Dad with laughter. I mention the garage because such conversations were so unusual I can remember exactly where we were standing.

Another surprise for me was hearing that, in the middle of the Great Depression, Dad and a couple of his friends in an old beat-up car drove all the way from Alberta to Illinois to attend Chicago's 1933 World's Fair. Roads in those days were terrible, so that road trip was an extraordinary feat. My Dad never mentioned that, or any other of his adventures, to me. My image of him was that of a serious senior banker, a straight-laced perfectionist expert at drawing my attention to my many imperfections, not a daredevil happy young man bent on seeing the world.

Also during the Great Depression, residents of Stettler were starting to acquire radios. Grandpa said the MacKenzies didn't need one, because reading newspapers gave the necessary news. But then, to our family's pleased surprise, Dad while visiting from the Peace River Country, presented his parents with a beautiful full-sized console radio. It was given a place of honour in the MacKenzie living room. Grandpa every evening carefully listened to all the news on Dad's radio, especially while he had three sons including Dad overseas fighting in the Second World War. I'm told this wonderful, expensive gift was seen as so thoughtful given Dad was such a young man just starting out in life in such tough economic times.

Dad Goes to War

RCAF records, which it took me a long time to extract from unhelpful officials in Ottawa, disclose that on 3 July 1941 Dad appeared at a Calgary recruiting centre to volunteer for aircrew with the RCAF. That was exactly thirteen years after he had commenced work with RBC in 1928. In an undated RCAF Interview Report, presumably that day, the interviewing officer wrote that his opinion as to Dad's character and suitability for the RCAF was: 'Good type, intelligent, clear eye, not nervous, very willing to serve in any capacity in Air Crew. Should be excellent material for Observer [Navigator] – good in Mathematics'. The report also disclosed that Dad was: '29 years old, 5 foot ten, 145 lbs, confident, easy, upright, neat, conservative, clean, slender, of clear speech, quick, deliberate, alert, sincere and reserved'. However, the report pointed out that Dad had only three years of high school, that he had no military training, that his flying experience was 'Nil', and that he was 'average'. How could anyone think my Dad was 'average'? That's presumably why the report concluded by stating Dad was not suitable for commissioned rank, although he was accepted for pilot or observer training. Noting in the report that Dad was 'very willing to serve in any capacity in Air Crew', the RCAF of course gave him the lowest possible aircrew rank of AC2 (Aircraftsman 2nd Class), for which the pay was a glorious $1.30 per day ($474.50 per annum). Compare that to the $1,550 per annum the Royal had been paying him. Fortunately, the Royal counted time its staff served in the military in the Second World War as if they were still working for RBC. And so, commencing 12 October 1941, the Royal supplemented Dad's RCAF $474.50 annual pay by adding a Royal Bank allowance of $558.83. Royal Bank records reveal that RBC released Dad to the RCAF on 20 September 1941. That day the RCAF transferred Dad from Calgary to RCAF No. 2 MD (Manning Depot) in Brandon Manitoba. There on 21 September 1941 Dad's RCAF training in the British Commonwealth Air Training Plan (the 'Plan') commenced.

A year later, on 11 September 1942 in Saskatoon, the RCAF:

- presented Dad with his Wings
- commissioned him as a pilot officer AND
- raised his pay from what had become $1.50 per day plus $.75 (yes, 75 cents) flying pay all the way up to $6.25 per day, which was $2,281.25 per year.

That's because in a single day Dad had risen from the lowest of RCAF aircrew ranks all the way up to a commissioned officer and pilot.

RBC Goes to War Too!

The Royal Bank's commitment to the war effort was impressive. The *Royal Bank Magazine* Christmas 1942 front cover features in uniform with huge smiles walking arm-in-arm towards the camera four Royal Bankers in the uniforms of the Royal Canadian Navy, Canada's Army, the Canadian Women's Army Corps and the Royal Canadian Air Force. The majority of Royal Bankers appear to have volunteered to serve in the RCAF. Inside this magazine was inserted a special 'Greetings' card which appears to be the actual original fountain-pen signature of the Royal's general manager [today his title would be president] Dobson. His card said, in part 'To the 1,830 of our men in the armed forces I send special greetings. At sea, on land, and in the sky, you are writing one of the proudest chapters in the history of the bank.'

Page 11 is devoted to Royal Bank airmen who earned their wings or commissions

Pages 12 & 13 name Royal Bankers on active service in Canada's Armed Forces

Page 14 is devoted to former Royal Banker Lieutenant Colonel Cecil Merritt receiving the Victoria Cross, and two Royal Bankers receiving DFCs. Postwar, in Vancouver law firm Bull Housser & Tupper (now Norton Rose), Cec Merritt became Royal Bank Counsel in British Columbia, and one of Canada's most distinguished barristers. As an awesome gesture to a new young lawyer, he gratuitously helped me structure one of my earliest municipal law litigation cases for the Courtroom with insightful strategy advice I have followed throughout my legal career.

Page 19 is special for me. At the top is a photograph of Dad in his RCAF uniform under the heading 'Class Leaders'. It proudly advises that Dad 'headed the graduating class at No. 4 Service Flying School, passing with special distinction. He received his pilot's wings and with them his commission as Pilot Officer'. It also mentions that Dad joined the Bank in 1928, and took leave of the Bank on 20 September 1941 to join the RCAF. Page 19 also includes news that a Royal Banker at Vancouver's Davie Street Branch graduated first in his class in Quebec, and likewise received his commission. And there's a photograph of an RCAF Royal Banker with his bride on their wedding day.

Page 20 is devoted to Royal Bank head office women sending Christmas cheer to Head Office staff serving Canada in our armed forces overseas, and advises of another Royal Banker who was commissioned as a pilot officer.

Page 21 has yet another RCAF Royal Banker graduating at the head of his class. It refers to the article he published entitled 'What a Bomber I'll Make!'. That page also features the heroics of Royal Bankers in the Royal Canadian Navy.

Page 22 is devoted to Canada's Army at Wolsley Barracks, No. 1 District Depot in London, Ontario where all eleven soldiers pictured in the Army Pay Office were Royal Bankers.

Pages 24 and 25 report another DFC and list in their Roll of Honour with photos those Royal Bankers killed in action, missing in action, or prisoners of war.

To conclude concerning the pride the Royal took in Dad's wartime involvement, I found the 14 September 1942 letter the Royal Bank's manager in Saskatoon wrote to the Royal Bank's supervisor in Calgary regarding Dad graduating first in his class at Saskatoon's RCAF Service Flying Training School. It says 'I enclose clipping from Saturday evening's issue of the *Saskatoon Star-Phoenix*, reporting up the last Graduating Class at the local Service Flying Training School. I understand that the number one student, LAC RW MacKenzie, was a member of the Bank's staff in Alberta prior to his enlistment and you will no doubt be interested to learn that his marks were the *highest that have been recorded* at No. 4 School since its inception.' (Emphasis Mine)

My Dad the Pilot

While Dad was immersed in training within the Plan as an RCAF LAC2, the lowest of the low, and later an LAC1, something amazing happened. Dad became an exceptional pilot. He was so good that:

MY DAD

- In Edmonton on 22 May 1942, he achieved the highest general standing in his class for which he was presented with a sterling silver engraved cigarette case from Edmonton Flying and Training School which I have; and
- In Saskatoon on 14 September 1942, he was not only first in his class but achieved the highest marks in the history of Saskatoon Service Flying Training School.

Remembering the adage that no good deed goes unpunished, the RCAF kept Dad in Canada training others to fly. I say 'unpunished' because Dad told me instructing students to fly was more dangerous than anything he experienced over Germany. Dad's admiration for wartime flying instructors was enormous.

Chapter Four

Discovering Bomber Command

Bomber Command had the finest aircrew of any Air Force anywhere in the world ever! Your father flew with the best of the best!

United States Air Force Officers
The Pentagon 26 February 2018

Bomber Command

Nowadays controversial words. In the Second World War, what was Bomber Command? I knew as a boy my Dad piloted a Lancaster bomber, but I'm not sure I'd even heard the words Bomber Command, much less knew what they meant. But in my manhood after Dad's death, two major Canadian events focused my attention on Bomber Command. The first shocked me. The second upset me. Both defamed Bomber Command. Both were inaccurate, yet effective. Both were rebutted, but scarcely anyone remembers, or like me even heard, the reasoned rebuttals. Meanwhile many who heard the scandalous assertions still think they are true. That is how fake news takes hold. Here are the two events.

The first happened on 19 January 1992 when CBC broadcast across Canada the National Film Board documentary *Death by Moonlight – Bomber Command* episode of *The Valour and the Horror*. It was an earthquake. It was so awful I actually felt grateful my Dad died the previous August, and so was spared this. Brian and Terrance McKenna's documentary essentially said Bomber Command went out night after night to bomb cities of no military value just to kill innocent Germans, and that its contribution to winning the war was minimal, if any. Canadian veterans' groups and prominent historians, including Jack Granatstein, the author of *Who Killed Canadian History*, attacked that show as 'highly inaccurate and offensive'. David Taras wrote that this was 'among the most controversial programmes ever broadcast on television'.[1] He noted it was watched by an estimated six million viewers. Veterans formed the Bomber Harris Trust, suing the CBC and the

---

[1] Taras 'The Struggle Over The Valour and the Horror: Media Power and the Portrayal of War,'. *Canadian Journal of Political Science* Flight 28, No. 4 December 1995 pp. 725-48

DISCOVERING BOMBER COMMAND

filmmakers for defamation.[2] The $500 million class action suit was dismissed – the Ontario Court of Appeal ruled the veterans did not have standing for a class-action suit, although that same Court of Appeal in 2019 ruled Uber drivers do have standing for class-action suits. The Supreme Court of Canada dismissed the veterans' appeal without comment, as it always does with dismissals.

The Senate of Canada conducted an Inquiry. Its sub-committee reviewing the veterans' claims concluded 'that the criticisms levelled at *The Valour and the Horror* are, for the most part, legitimate. Simply put, although the filmmakers have a right to their point of view, **they have failed to present that point of view with any degree of accuracy or fairness**.' (my emphasis). I was unaware that the Senate had done this until my research for my first Bomber Command talk in the summer of 2018. The CBC/NFB documentary was broadcast across Canada, but the Senate's conclusions were so poorly reported I was unaware of them until this book. Too many remember the erroneous assertions, not the reasoned rebuttals. As Canada's national magazine *Maclean's* said,[3] 'the biggest controversy stoked by *The Valour and the Horror* was over its depiction of the aerial bombing of German cities late in the war as morally depraved and strategically unnecessary'. By the time the McKennas were making their film, Tim Cook[4] astutely observes, Cold War anxieties about nuclear bombs falling were ingrained. 'This modern fear of mass death reshaped how some viewed the bombing campaign of the Second World War,' he writes, 'while others questioned it in light of the new international law about the treatment of civilians in a war zone.'

The second of these two events upset me. It occurred in June 2007 while I was visiting my son Guy Roland MacKenzie in Ottawa where he had won an awesome internship in Bank of Canada. My memory is the headline in the *Ottawa Citizen* newspaper which declared Canadian Bomber Command aircrew to be war criminals. The moment the new Canadian War Museum opened the following morning, I was there and rushed in to see for myself. Sure enough, the Bomber Command exhibit called Canadian Bomber Command aircrew war criminals. I was furious. I knew in the core of my being that this was wrong. My confrontation with Museum officials caught the attention of a CBC TV crew there for another purpose. CBC asked whether I was willing to express my views on television. I definitely was. They turned on their camera, and I talked! What they did with that footage I do not know, but my memory is I was told it was broadcast across Canada. I hope it was. Fortunately, other Canadians shared my concern. The reaction was enormous. I was later told the Museum replaced the offensive Bomber Command text with a more accurate commentary. I also heard

---

[2] A *Battle for Truth: Canadian aircrews sue the CBC over Death by Moonlight: Bomber Command* Toronto Public Library 1994

[3] Geddes 'Lest We Forget Again – For decades, Canada largely ignored World War II. What prompted our national change-of-heart?' *Maclean's*, Canada's National Magazine June 2020 p. 73

[4] Cook *The Fight for History: 75 Years of Forgetting, Remembering, and Remaking Canada's Second World War*, Penguin Canada, 7 April 2020

33

people were fired for creating the offensive text. I hope that is true. But again, it was the erroneous assertions, not the reasoned rebuttals, that people remember.

RAF Kirmington

It turns out RAF Kirmington was my Dad's Second World War RAF combat sortie airbase. Paul Robinson tells me my Dad flew 'on B Flight, 166 Squadron at Royal Air Force Station Kirmington. RAF Kirmington was part of 13 Base (HQ at RAF Elsham Wolds), 1 Group (HQ at RAF Bawtry), Bomber Command (HQ at RAF High Wycombe). Simple!'[5] From RAF Station Kirmington, Dad piloted a Lancaster with 166 Squadron RAF for all thirty-four of his operational sorties. I learnt too that Dad was also a deputy flight commander, but I knew not what that was. RAF Kirmington's call sign was 'Risky' and its aircraft code letters were HS. My 'Road to RAF Kirmington' was a rocky one, filled with unexpected twists and turns. But at last I learnt it was at a village in North Lincolnshire. During the war, North Lincolnshire was part of Lincolnshire. Ka Hyun and I headed to Kirmington. I wondered what I would discover. Our trip had become a pilgrimage. At Kirmington on 24 July 2017, Ka Hyun and I stopped first at the Marrowbone & Cleaver Pub. I learnt it was where 166 Squadron personnel spent some happy wartime hours. They called it 'The Chopper'. Ka Hyun and I ate the food they ate, and drank the beer they drank. The Chopper is a lovely living memorial to 166 Squadron. This pub dates back to 1871. Happily for us, it was purchased in 2017, just months before our arrival, by Guy Martin,[6] a local who attended Kirmington Church of England Primary School and later became a celebrity motorcycle racer turned television presenter. And guess what? Guy Martin was named after Dambuster legend Guy Gibson.[7] Also, Guy Martin's lovely sister Sally Martin does a brilliant job of running the pub.[8] Every time I visit, her meals are fine pub fare, and she even has a special beer from Bateman's Brewery. Best of all, The Chopper displays 166 Squadron Second World War memorabilia, including framed wartime photos of 166 Squadron aircrew and an impressive mural of Lancasters.

At The Chopper, I struck gold. Its preservation of 166 Squadron memories includes the *166 Squadron Book of Remembrance* and 166 Squadron's *Visitors' Book*. I signed the 166 *Visitors' Book*, and then photographed pages where signatories included their e-mail addresses. That evening I e-mailed those people. I was rewarded with valuable replies, especially from Martyn Wright, the son of 166 Squadron's Jim Wright who I discovered wrote the wonderful book *On Wings of War*. Jim joined 166 Squadron in the fall of 1944, about a month after Dad left,

---

5 e-mail from AVM Paul Robinson to the author 25 May 2020

6 Abby Ruston 'Speed star Guy Martin 'breathes life back into' village where he grew up by buying the local pub' *The Mirror* 24 December 2016 www.mirror.co.uk

7 Wikipedia Guy Martin England

8 Lisa Porter 'Guy Martin buys village pub in Kirmington' *Lincolnshire Live* 2 January 2017, updated 6 June 2017 www.lincolnshirelive.co.uk

so I doubt they met. Martyn and I, however, have become friends. On 15 May 2018, while I was in Liverpool visiting him and his partner Ann-Marie, in a gesture of extraordinary generosity, Martyn gave me a signed copy of his Dad's marvellous masterpiece book. It helps me hugely, being invaluable for my understanding of 166 Squadron. Best of all, it gives me details for all of Dad's sorties. It's been called one of the most beautifully written books about Bomber Command. Sadly, it is out of print and its plates were lost in a fire.

At Kirmington good news welcomed me. First, while the RAF disbanded 166 Squadron on 18 August 1945, and RAF Kirmington like so many others fell into disuse, in 1970 the runway from which Dad flew was chosen to become Humberside International Airport. Second, when Ka Hyun and I arrived on 24 July 2017, we happily discovered a Hampton by Hilton Hotel had opened alongside that runway just six days before our arrival. Out of respect for my Dad, Hilton staff placed Ka Hyun and me in a room on the Hilton's top floor with a perfect view of the runway. We were the first guests to occupy that room. Contrast a brand-new Hilton in 2017 to Dad's wartime Kirmington accommodation.

RAF Wing Commander Tony Lark came into my life with a bang when e-mailing me on 16 December 2017 in response to my voice-mail inquiry whether there would be a 166 Squadron reunion in 2018. Tony's e-mail was incredible. He replied YES, there would be a 166 Squadron Memorial Service and Wreath Laying at Kirmington Village on Saturday 1 September 2018 beginning with a Service at the village church. He went on to say he could arrange for me to attend the RAF Elsham Wolds Reunion Dinner that Saturday evening, and he could have RAF Scampton opened for me on the Sunday. Pulling out all the stops, Tony concluded with his fateful words 'It is the hundredth anniversary of the formation of the RAF next year, so it should prove a special one for everyone concerned with those who flew or served with the RAF.' There in his welcoming speech to everyone, with a huge smile Henk mentioned me twice and Bomber Command three times!

That sold me. I decided to come. My sons Ruaridh and Guy Roland MacKenzie of London came too. And the icing on the cake – Kirmington and Croxton Parish Council Chairman Councillor Terry Marsden chose my sons and me to represent Canada at these Ceremonies. Our experiences from 31 August to 2 September 2018 in and around Kirmington were decisive in launching my quest to understand Bomber Command. And those ceremonies brought into my life RAF Air Vice-Marshal Paul Robinson, his wife, Deputy Lieutenant of Lincolnshire Sarah Robinson, RAF Air Marshal Sir Christopher Coville and Lady Coville.

PENTAGON Perspective

And then there's 26 February 2018 at the Pentagon. Superlatives abound for the Pentagon's gigantic building -- the world's biggest, and America's extraordinary armed forces – the world's best. I was astonished when USAF officers there told me Bomber Command aircrew such as my Dad were 'the best of the best in any air force anywhere ever'. Once they knew who my Dad was, Ka Hyun and I were treated like royalty. With us were fifteen United States Air Force elite air cadets, each being the best from that cadet's region of America. They were brilliant and gifted. All had at least a 3.8 grade average (out of 4.0). They were also very interested in my Dad, so much so that a decision was made to waive the prohibition of photography so that a photograph could be taken of them with me. Afterwards, the Cadets thanked me for that photo. Second World War Bomber Command is held in the highest esteem by the Pentagon and its elite air cadets.

Prince Harry's Wedding and the RAF

One of Canada's national television networks, CTV, asked me to provide commentary for its Canada-wide coverage of Prince Harry's 19 May 2018 wedding. My friends Fiona MacKenzie Try and her husband, Geoff, residing only a block from the castle made my attendance possible. My assignment was to explain to Canadians that CTV was not televising a wedding of celebrities, but rather that the Monarchy is core to Canada's governance and legal system.

During my half month in Britain, however, I found myself increasingly hijacked by Royal Air Force and 166 Squadron RAF families, and especially Martyn Wright and Wing Commander Tony Lark who summoned me to Lincolnshire on 14 May. While waiting to board my train from London to Lincolnshire, I asked a seventeen-year-old passer-by whether he could fix my smartphone. He did, in less than two minutes. But then he asked why I was there. That launched our Bomber Command conversation. We spoke for an hour. He told me he could not comprehend how British teenagers were so dedicated in the Second World War that they actually volunteered to serve in Bomber Command with its horrendous fatality rate. He said he does not see that level of commitment or unity of purpose about anything among those he knows nowadays. He also told me he had known nothing about Bomber Command until he met me. When it was time for me to board my train, while saying goodbye I asked which train was his. He replied he was not catching a train. Instead, he had been hurrying through the station as a shortcut. He said he's glad he did because knowing about Bomber Command is important. Having not then decided that I must write this book, it never occurred to me to obtain his contact details so I could name him herein.

Kirmington Ceremonies

On 31 August 2018 my sons Ruaridh and Guy Roland and I arrived in Lincoln. At the time, Ruaridh was 27, and Guy Roland 34. My first stop with my sons when our train arrived from London was to buy clothes for the 1 September 166 Squadron ceremonies because my luggage had been lost on my Budapest to London Luton flight the previous day. Our second stop was the Lincolnshire Aviation Heritage Centre in East Kirkby. There we saw Lancaster NX611, 'Just Jane'. It and my Nanton Lancaster are the only two in which all four engines work but neither aircraft is yet airworthy. We met Andrew Panton, who kindly kept the centre open to accommodate us and with whom I have kept in contact ever since. Andrew is a nephew of farmers Fred and Harold Panton who rescued that Lancaster. These brothers started the Museum in 1988 in memory of their elder brother Christopher Whitton Panton who, as a flight engineer with 433 RCAF Squadron aboard Halifax HX272, was killed on Bomber Command's 'Black Friday' raid on Nuremberg the night of 30/31 March 1944 in which 108 aircraft were lost, 665 aircrew were killed and 159 aircrew were taken prisoner. After East Kirkby, my sons and I reached Kirmington and visited The Chopper. We spent the next two nights at the Hilton in rooms overlooking Dad's wartime runway.

Then came 1 September. Guy Roland, Ruaridh and I represented Canada at the Kirmington Village Church Service and thereafter the RAF ceremonies at the nearby 166 Squadron RAF Memorial Garden. There we laid the Canada Wreath. Representing the RAF were Air Marshal Sir Christopher Coville and Air Vice-Marshal Paul Robinson. Paul soon became my mentor who helps me hugely.

At the 1 September Elsham Wolds Reunion Dinner that evening, RAF Wing Commander Tony Lark with his elbow jabbing my ribs ordered me to stand up and make an impromptu speech. I gave a real barn-burner. It was so well received by the surprised attendees that it further solidified my intention to speak and write about Bomber Command. As promised, Tony arranged for RAF Scampton to be opened for the three of us the following morning, a Sunday on which the base was closed. Flight Lieutenant Mark Wood gave us a marvellous tour. RAF Scampton was the home of the Dambusters and the Red Arrows, so I was photographed seated at Guy Gibson's desk and my sons were photographed in Red Arrow cockpits and with Tall Boy and Grand Slam Lancaster bombs. Harris called Gibson 'as great a warrior as these Islands ever bred.'[9] Next we drove to Lincoln to behold with awe the great Spire with the names of those killed. Dave Gilbert is the inspired volunteer who works with such dedication tracking down every name, and learning something about each airman. We also toured the International Bomber Command Centre which opened in April 2018. I hope it will rework its software to articulate what Bomber Command accomplished, and why it was vital to victory.

All of this contributed to a paradigm shift of my understanding of my Dad, and my admiration of him and his fellow Bomber Boys. These men were extraordinary.

Dutch Support

The country in which Canada is so beautifully remembered in the Second World War is The Netherlands. Commanding Officer Blair McGregor made me the 'meet and greet' person for the Seaforth Highlanders of Canada in The Netherlands in 2005 to celebrate the sixtieth anniversary of the end of the war. My Dutch counterpart, General Ben Bouman, and I became friends for the rest of his life.

---

9 Gibson VC, *Enemy Coast Ahead*, p. vii

BOMBER COMMAND

A highlight was General Bouman's ten-minute introduction of my friend Eric de Ridder and me to Princess Margriet, then a sister of Queen Beatrix and now an aunt of King Willem-Alexander. Princess Margriet spoke to us about the incredible importance of Bomber Command to the Dutch, and of Operation MANNA in which Bomber Command squadrons including Dad's refitted their Lancasters from dropping bombs to dropping food to the starving Dutch in areas of The Netherlands still occupied by the Nazis. She told us that, without our food, over a million Dutch could have starved to death in the *Hongerwinter* of 1944-45, instead of the 20,000 who did die. Princess Margriet told us there are four reasons why the Dutch love Canada. They are (1) the Dutch Royal Family was given refuge in Ottawa during the war, and on 19 January 1943, Princess Margriet was born there – Canada declared the Maternity Ward in Ottawa Civic Hospital to be temporarily Dutch for her, and FDR and Queen Mary became her godparents; (2) Canada was key to liberating The Netherlands; (3) we remained as an Army of Occupation for a year to help the Dutch – never had they been ground down so low; and (4) no country welcomes Dutch immigrants more warmly than Canada. These include Dutch war brides marrying into the Canadian military. Of Canada's Second World War brides, 80 per cent married Canadian soldiers and 18 per cent married RCAF airmen.[10]

On 25 October 2018, for the first time a Dutch prime minister addressed the Canadian Parliament. PM Mark Rutte used that event to thank Canada for liberating The Netherlands. He waxed eloquent about Canadian soldiers, but nary a mention of Canadian airmen. Dutch Consul General Henk Snoeken, while hosting lunch for me on 20 November 2019, assured me no offence was intended. He pointed out that in Dutch the word 'soldier' includes sailors and airmen. However, Canada's role in Bomber Command was so enormous that it should have been praised, but almost never is by politicians. Ever gracious, after our two-year Covid-19 pandemic lockdown since our lunch, Henk invited Ka Hyun and me to his beautiful home, the mansion in which the Dutch house their Consuls General in Vancouver, on 27 April 2022 for The Netherlands' King's Day Celebration.

The person who summed up Dutch feelings about Bomber Command best for me was my longtime friend Joost Blom QC. Joost came with his family from The Netherlands to Canada as a boy after the war. His Dad was here to help us with dykes after the dreadful Fraser River floods in the Lower Mainland of BC in 1948. The Bloms liked it here, so stayed. Joost in due course became the much-loved Dean of my alma mater UBC Law School. Joost e-mailed me:

====== Original Message --------

From: **Joost Blom**
Date: Sun, 28 Oct 2018 at 16:30
Subject: Dutch PM Deeply Disappointing
To: Roddy MacKenzie

---

10 Rebecca Priegert Coulter *War Brides* The Canadian Encyclopedia published online 21 February 2006, updated by Tabitha Marshall 9 August 2019

DISCOVERING BOMBER COMMAND

Hi, Roddy.

Thanks very for letting me know about Mr Rutte's visit and about your correspondence concerning Mr Rutte's speech to Parliament.

My impression is that Dutch people generally are vividly aware of the bomber crews' contribution, especially because of those planes that still, now and then, emerge from the water in the IJsselmeer. Anybody (like my parents) who lived through the war remembers the emotion of seeing the allied fleets of bombers overhead on their way to their targets or, as you mention, dropping food packages for the starving people in the western Dutch cities.

Hope all is well with you and the family. Cheers,

Joost

In a similar vein to Joost's message, a Dutchman wrote to Harris on 26 January 1946 saying 'We shall never forget the nights when your squadrons passed us in the dark on the way to Germany. The mighty noise was like music for us and it told us about happier days to come. Your passing planes kept us believing in coming victory, no matter what we had to endure.'[11]

Writing This Book

Although informally I began writing my book at Westminster Abbey BC on 18 June 2018, and I had been writing papers complete with footnotes for my Bomber Command presentations since 14 August 2018 at Vancouver, Round Table, the big day I formally started writing this book was Saturday, 27 April 2019. I was in room 144 of the Premier Inn on Canwick Hill above Lincoln, and across the street from the inspiring Bomber Command Memorial Spire. I remember powerful winds swirling around my hotel as I wrote that day. I wondered how Dad and his colleagues could get their planes airborne in a place that was being whipped by such power of the wind. I had no inkling then of the enormity of the task I commenced. During my three weeks in Lincolnshire, wonderful people in various ways enlightened me about Bomber Command, encouraged me, hosted me, and assisted me in my quest. I had, however, in my first week a major wake-up call that Lincolnshire has those who did not want me praising Bomber Command because they feared Bomber Command critics. People I erroneously thought would help me did not want any controversies. Rather, they wanted a heart-warming story about me with my Dad which they could quietly file with many others while hopefully I would return to Canada, never to be heard from again. That was depressing. What could I do to keep going in those fragile early days of writing my book in the face of such opposition?

---

11 Probert, *Bomber Harris*, p. 363

BOMBER COMMAND

Then on 3 May 2019 it came to me. I awoke thinking CAMBRIDGE. I realized I must upgrade my Lincolnshire research with work in the supportive environment of the archives at Churchill College in Cambridge University. I needed a powerful jolt of stimulation to counter Lincolnshire discouragement, and I needed quality information not available in Lincolnshire to sustain my motivation. So I began my day by telephoning Churchill College Archives Director Allen Packwood. Allen was delighted to hear from me. This was thanks to our mutual friend David Freeman in California perceiving the need we each had to know the other. David had brought us together digitally on 11 March 2019, thus enabling Allen to follow my progress thereafter. Allen told me how much he was enjoying following my adventures through my emails. I told him about my troubles in Lincolnshire. Allen sprang into action, arranging for me to be an accredited Churchill reader and obtaining for me a 'Churchill College Fellows Guest Room' accommodation. Allen is an awesome mentor and fine friend. But first I had important work to complete in Lincolnshire, including with RAF Air Vice-Marshal Paul Robinson and RAF College Cranwell. Both proved crucial to this book.

In the fall of 2019 there were two wonderful events. First, editor David Freeman published my paper 'Churchill's Greatest Triumph: Bomber Command'[12] in Issue 185 of *Finest Hour*, the sleek, intellectual, and deeply-respected magazine that goes to every member of every Churchill Society worldwide, and to many others as well. The whole of issue 185 is devoted to Churchill's relationship with the Royal Air Force. David gave me the honour of writing about Churchill's relationship with Bomber Command. Churchill and the RAF caught fire – I'm told this was the most successful issue of *Finest Hour* since its founding in 1968.

Second, in Montreal at the urging of Frank Borowicz QC, I spoke on 2 November 2019 in English and French to a packed audience of 2,500 about Bomber Command. The occasion was the 'Violins of Hope Concert' of L'Orchestre Metropolitain in the Maison Symphonic at Place des Artes for the world premiere of Jaap Nico Hamburger's 'Children War Diaries Symphony'. Moments before I stepped onto the stage, Frank urged me to give it all I've got. That ignited in me an intense need to make my points as powerfully as possible. I doubt Montreal had ever heard anything quite as emotionally charged about Bomber Command. The explosion of applause when I concluded drowned out the Pipes and Drums about to march in. Afterwards, veterans with tears in their eyes warmly shook my hand while thanking me for speaking the truth about Bomber Command, truth sadly suppressed for so long postwar. And in Montreal Ka Hyun and I stayed at the Fairmont Queen Elizabeth where my Dad stayed when at the RBC HQ at Place Ville Marie across that street. I'd been amazed he went from the train to the hotel to the bank without ever going outside. In my boyhood Montreal was awesome.

These happy events conclude my introduction to Bomber Command.

---

12 Roddy MacKenzie 'Churchill's Greatest Triumph: Bomber Command,' *Finest Hour* No. 185, Third Quarter 2019, pp. 24-8.

Chapter Five

Leaders

Bomber Command was about people. My deepening research into Bomber Command shed light on several singular leaders. These for me include Lord Beaverbrook, Mackenzie King and FDR, and culminate with Bomber Command's greatest champion, Sir Winston Churchill. My growing awareness of these men, their relationships with one another, and the cast of characters supporting or challenging them, tells the story of where Bomber Command came from and what it did. The Bomber Command leader of greatest importance is, of course, Sir Arthur Harris, so much so that I have devoted a separate chapter to him.

Beaverbrook

In my first two drafts of this book, I made no mention of Lord Beaverbrook. However, after Allen Packwood spent three days reviewing in its entirety my second draft during Thanksgiving 2019, he fully briefed Paul Robinson and me of his impressions and suggestions. He expressed surprise I made no mention of Beaverbrook. Allen and Paul then insisted I include Beaverbrook. But who was he? Although a Canadian, he is not well known in Canada. I knew little more than that he was a powerful newspaper baron in Britain, and that he was formerly Max Aiken of New Brunswick. Former Canadian Prime Minister John Turner, with whom I was acquainted, says Beaverbrook was a great friend of Churchill, and a giant who did an outstanding job as Minister of Aircraft Production, and later Minister of Supply during the Second World War.[1] That aroused my interest. But again, who was Max Aiken, and why was he so successful, and so important?

My research reveals he was smart, hardworking, and superb at making friends with awesome mentors. This Beaverbrook skill is shown early on by his being mentored by a pair of future prime ministers, one British, the other Canadian, both from New Brunswick. In Britain, it was Andrew Bonar Law, the only British prime minister born in Canada, and the only one born anywhere outside Britain until prime minister Boris Johnson who was born in New York City. In Canada, it was R.B. Bennett, later Viscount Bennett, Canada's prime minister from my hometown

---

1 John Turner's Foreword for Terry Reardon *Churchill & Mackenzie King*, p. 11.

BOMBER COMMAND

Calgary. He is well known to me partly because Calgary's Queen Elizabeth High School, which I attended, and Calgary's Viscount Bennett High School had two of Alberta's best high-school bands, conducted with great rivalry by the Dow brothers. I played trombone. We won the championship. My other Bennett connection is that I was a member of the Calgary law firm Bennett founded. More on that in a moment.

The Beaverbrook/Bennett story starts with the birth of Richard Bedford Bennett in Hopewell Hill, New Brunswick on 3 July 1870, the eldest of six children. Nine years later, his protégé, Max Aiken, was born in Maple, Ontario on 25 May 1879, one of ten children. A year later, the Aiken family moved to Newcastle, New Brunswick. Bennett became Max's mentor while Max was Bennett's office boy and articling student in Chatham NB. Max persuaded Bennett to run for Alderman on Chatham's first town council. Max ran the campaign and Bennett won. Afterwards, Bennett was furious when he heard the promises Max made on his behalf. Max Aiken's ability to infuriate was legendary. In 1897, Bennett left New Brunswick for my hometown, Calgary, to become a law partner with James Lougheed, Calgary's richest resident and the grandfather of Alberta icon Premier Peter Lougheed. Bennett worked with Max to create the Alberta Grain Company, Canada Cement and Calgary Power for which I did so much work in his law firm in the early 1970s. Bennett and Max had many successful ventures including stock purchases, land speculation and buying and merging small companies.[2] Then Bennett and Lougheed had an acrimonious split after which Bennett founded in 1922 his law firm which I joined fifty years later in 1972. In politics, Bennett rose to lead the Conservative Party and defeat Mackenzie King's Liberals in 1930. His reward? Bennett as prime minister was blamed for the Great Depression. In 1972, we had a spectacular Fiftieth Anniversary Dinner. Today his firm, known now as Bennett Jones, is one of the finest in Canada, with over 400 lawyers plus 500 staff – that being somewhat larger than in Bennett's day.

The Beaverbrook/Bonar Law story starts with the birth of Andrew Bonar Law in Kingston, New Brunswick on 16 September 1858. Kingston is now called Rexton. Bonar Law Memorial High School is there. Bonar Law's mother died in 1861, so her sister Janet came from Scotland to help raise Bonar Law and his siblings. On 1 July 1867, New Brunswick became one of the four original provinces that created Canada. This made eight-year-old Bonar Law a Canadian. Three years later in 1870, Bonar Law's father remarried, and allowed Bonar Law, aged eleven, to accompany his Aunt Janet to Scotland. At age sixteen in Scotland, Bonar Law left school to work in the iron industry. By age 30, he was wealthy. In 1900 he and Churchill were elected for the first time as Conservative members of parliament.

Bonar Law is important to this narrative because of his role mentoring Max Aiken. Max had become wealthy with various ventures, many with Bennett, but his ambitions exceeded Canadian opportunities, so in 1910 Max arrived in Britain from Canada a millionaire at age 30. There he quickly made friends with fellow New Brunswicker Bonar Law – both were sons of clergy, and of Scottish Canadian ancestry. Max

---

2 Wikipedia, R.B. Bennett

LEADERS

persuaded Bonar Law to support Max's 1910 election as an MP which Max won by 196 votes on 3 December 1910. Not bad for an immigrant to Britain to win election as an MP the year of his arrival. At the start of his campaign, it is said Max told a reporter 'Go easy on me. I've only been in politics a week!'[3] Another first-time winner in that election was George Lansbury, later the Labour leader of His Majesty's Loyal Opposition, and grandfather of actress Angela Lansbury, whom I admire.

Even for Max, 1911 was amazing. Compliments of his unique personality and extraordinary abilities, much happened. King George V invested him as a knight. Max bought Cherkley Court, a Victorian mansion and 370-acre estate, his home for the rest of his life, at which Churchill first visited him circa 1915. And then, on 13 November 1911, Bonar Law became leader of His Majesty's Loyal Opposition. Bonar Law's ascendancy greatly aided Sir Max, and Sir Max likewise aided Bonar Law. At the outbreak of the First World War, Sir Max helped create Canadian War Records in London, and caused newspapers in both Britain and Canada to publish articles about Canada fighting the war. Sir Max's welcome visits to the Front as an Honorary Canadian colonel, his books, and his newspapers all served the cause. He was especially effective in promoting the sales of war bonds to the general public.[4] In December 1916, Bonar Law turned down the offer of King George V to become prime minister and instead recommended Lloyd George. The King appointed Lloyd George the next day. Bonar Law served in the newly-formed coalition government as Leader of the House of Commons, a member of the War Cabinet, and Chancellor of the Exchequer.[5]

In 1917 Sir Max hit the big time. That January, King George V elevated him to the peerage as 1st Baron Beaverbrook. Sir Max chose Beaverbrook because it sounds Canadian, and is the name of a place near his New Brunswick boyhood home. Lord Beaverbrook immediately entered the House of Lords as a Lord Temporal, and served there for forty-seven years until his death on 9 February 1964. The following year, on 10 February 1918, Prime Minister Lloyd George ushered Beaverbrook into the Cabinet and Privy Council by making him Chancellor of the Duchy of Lancaster and Britain's first Minister of Information. There he managed propaganda in Allied and neutral countries. On 4 November 1918, a week before the First World War ended, Beaverbrook resigned due to ill-health – a tooth infected with actinomycosis that almost killed him. English doctors could not help him, but a Portuguese medic saved his life.

On 23 October 1922, King George V made Bonar Law prime minister. Bonar Law called a general election on 15 November 1922 in which he won a majority but Churchill, who had an operation for appendicitis that October, lost his seat. This caused Winston to famously remark that he found himself 'without an office,

---

3 Adams, Richards, *Extraordinary Canadians – Lord Beaverbrook*, Chapter 9, 'Knighthood' Penguin Random House www.penguinrandohouse.ca/series/B9X/extradordinary-canadians

4 Taylor, *Beaverbrook: A Biography*, Hamish Hamilton, London, 1972

5 Editors of *Encyclopedia Britannica,* Bonar Law Prime Minister

without a seat, without a party and without an appendix'.[6] Churchill did not like Bonar Law. When Bonar Law died of throat cancer on 30 October 1923 Churchill, while making the customary complimentary remarks about the deceased to the media, reportedly interrupted himself in mid-sentence to ask 'Are you sure he's dead?' That made the mundane memorable, as Churchill so often did. Churchill's question was the first I had heard of Bonar Law. It aroused my curiosity. Imagine my amazement when I discovered this virtually unknown prime minister was from Canada. Prophetically, Prime Minister H.H. Asquith remarked at Bonar Law's funeral at Westminster Abbey that they were 'burying the Unknown Prime Minister next to the Unknown Soldier'.[7]

Between the wars, Lord Beaverbrook built up the circulation of his flagship *Daily Express* from under 40,000 a day in 1919 up to 2,329,000 a day by 1937. He also expanded his media empire and his wealth. After the Second World War, Beaverbrook's *Daily Express* became the largest-selling newspaper in the world.

Only four days after King George VI made Churchill prime minister on 10 May 1940, Churchill appointed his friend since the First World War Lord Beaverbrook Minister of Aircraft Production. Beaverbrook worked wonders, overhauling all aspects of wartime aircraft production. He also took control of aircraft repairs, having bombers and fighters repaired with blinding speed. He replaced the management of underperforming plants, and seized supplies destined for other departments.[8] Many feathers were ruffled. Beaverbrook had a talent for ruffling feathers. Beaverbrook's fame spread, so much so that, at the height of the Battle of Britain, America's *Time Magazine* cover story declared: 'Even if Britain goes down this fall, it will not be Lord Beaverbrook's fault. If she holds out, it will be his triumph. This war is a war of machines. It will be won on the assembly line.'[9] Air Chief Marshal Hugh Dowding, Air Officer Commanding-in-Chief of Fighter Command in the Battle of Britain, praised Beaverbrook hugely, saying 'Lord Beaverbrook gave us those machines, and I do not believe I exaggerate when I say that no other man in England could have done so.'[10] Churchill, when praising Beaverbrook's increased bomber and fighter aircraft production, said that 'his personal force and genius made this Aiken's finest hour.'[11] And I should mention Beaverbrook's son, Wing Commander Max Aiken Jr, served as an RAF fighter pilot credited with sixteen kills.

Beaverbrook's personal relationship with Churchill was an important behind the scenes feature of Churchill's wartime leadership. Not many know, for example,

---

6 Tolppanen, *Great Contemporaries:Max Aiken, Lord Beaverbrook*, The Churchill Project Hillsdale College, 17 June 2016 from Richard Langworth *Churchill in His Own Words*

7 The Right Honourable The Lord Blake (Robert Blake) *The Unknown Prime Minister. The Life and Times of Andrew Bonar Law*, 1858-1923, Eyre & Spottiswoode, London, 1955

8 Wikipedia *Max Aiken, 1st Lord Beaverbrook*

9 'Great Britain: Shirts On', *Time Magazine,* 16 September 1940.

10 'Battle of Britain in the Words of Air Chief Marshal Hugh Dowding', Spitfiresite.com 20 August 1941

11 Wikipedia *Max Aiken, 1st Lord Beaverbrook*

that in August 1941, Beaverbrook accompanied Churchill aboard the battleship HMS *Prince of Wales* to meet FDR in Placentia Bay in Newfoundland, the first of Churchill's eleven meetings with FDR in the Second World War. In September 1941 Lord Beaverbrook led Britain's first delegation to Soviet Russia since Hitler had invaded the Soviet Union that June. Averell Harriman was his American counterpart for their three days of talks with Stalin in Moscow. Beaverbrook went on to serve as Britain's Minister of Supply, and briefly as Minister of War Production. He was also Lord Privy Seal from 24 September 1943 until Churchill's election defeat in July 1945. But what mattered most throughout the war was that Beaverbrook remained a close confidant of Churchill. They were often together until 'the wee small hours'.[12] Suffice to say they enjoyed one another's company, and each aided the other in successfully fighting the Second World War, as Sir Max and Bonar Law aided one another in the First World War.

To conclude where I began with former Canadian Prime Minister John Turner – Beaverbrook was a giant. And this is how he came to be in my book.

Mackenzie King

William Lyon Mackenzie King was Canada's longest-serving prime minister. First elected PM in December 1921, he led Canada out of limited self-government and into sovereign autonomy, out of the Great Depression and into victory in the Second World War, followed by postwar prosperity. He resigned as PM for health reasons on 15 November 1948 and died on 22 July 1950. Yet remarkably, he is among the lesser known, and is without question the most misunderstood, of Canada's prime ministers. He was neither charismatic nor loveable, but he was a brilliant political strategist, a shrewd judge of character, and deeply devoted to Canada. He was mysterious, and virtually invisible even in plain sight. As I plunged deeper into my Bomber Command research, I came to realize he was also one of the great heroes of our victory in the air. But, sadly, now he is either forgotten or defamed, largely because of his Diaries, and sensationalist biographies arising from them.[13] His unfair postwar fate largely mirrors that of Bomber Command and Harris. *Canadian Encyclopedia* says Mackenzie King's Diaries are among the most valuable documents Canada has regarding our governance in the first half of the twentieth century. That's ironic, given how they hurt him.

Mackenzie King was a man of many names. FDR called him Mackenzie. His most intimate friends called him Rex (Latin for King). His mother called him Willie. Virtually everyone else called him Mackenzie King. Growing up in Calgary, I never heard him referred to as Prime Minister King. He was always referred to as Prime Minister Mackenzie King, or simply Mackenzie King. I remember, however, a newspaper headline 'King Meets Queen in Winnipeg'. No, King George VI was

---

12 Wikipedia *Max Aiken 1st Lord Beaverbrook*
13 Stacey *A Very Double Life*

not meeting his spouse Queen Elizabeth there. The headline was referring to John Queen, the labour activist who served a year in prison for leading the Winnipeg General Strike of 1919, and afterwards was elected Mayor of Winnipeg, meeting with Prime Minister Mackenzie King.

It was by chance that I saw for myself the power of Mackenzie King. This happened in Westminster Abbey, the Benedictine Roman Catholic Monastery in Mission BC. My friendship with the monks began in 1970 via my friend Eric Stathers, and is unusual given I am Protestant, born and raised in the United Church of Canada. For over half a century now, the Benedictine monks continue to welcome me into their sacred world of Christian immersion of fifteen hundred years for which I am profoundly grateful. Much of this book was written in their monastery, where Brother Luke had me teach their fourteen-year-old students about Bomber Command, and on another occasion about leadership, in which Mackenzie King was included. Through these students I learnt that young Canadians, though unaware of Bomber Command or Mackenzie King, have the capacity for enormous interest in both. By chance I had $50 bills in my wallet. They have Mackenzie King's portrait, so I gave one bill to each row of students for them to examine and then pass along. They were impressed to see him on Canadian currency. Afterwards I told Brother Luke how happy I was to have had those bills to show the students. Brother Luke dryly responded how happy he was that I emerged with the same number of bills after class as I had before class.

To understand Mackenzie King, one must understand his heritage. He grew up in modest circumstances in Ontario, but with a strong sense of being a Mackenzie instilled in him by his mother Isabel Grace Mackenzie whom he adored. It is interesting that Mackenzie King, FDR and Churchill all shared strong feelings of affection for their mothers, as do I for mine. Mackenzie King, like me, was named after his MacKenzie grandfather, in his case William Lyon Mackenzie, the first Mayor of Toronto and the Leader of the Mackenzie-Papineau Rebellion of 1837. I remember reading when I was a boy that Mackenzie King when he was a boy told his teacher he intended to become prime minister 'to restore the great name of Mackenzie'. His teacher, William Diefenbaker, was the father of future Canadian Prime Minister John Diefenbaker, an honorary member of Bomber Command.

Fellow Clansman Alexander Mackenzie served as Canada's second prime minister from 1873 to 1878. He was a simple stonemason about whom Governor General Lord Dufferin, after meeting him, said 'However narrow and inexperienced Mackenzie may be, I imagine he is a thoroughly upright, well-principled and well-meaning man.'[14] Mackenzie gave Canada secret ballots, and both the Supreme Court of Canada and our auditor general. As a stonemason, he was very involved in building Canada's stone Parliament Buildings and other great stone structures. He brought honesty, effective governance and fiscal prudence to Ottawa. So did Mackenzie King. Alexander played a major role in helping build the Canadian

---

14   Wikipedia Alexander Mackenzie (politician)

Pacific Railway from Montreal to Vancouver, thus making Canada the second largest country in the world. Mackenzie King played a major role in leading Canada from limited self-government to sovereignty, and in Canada helping win the Second World War. Neither Prime Minister is much known today.

Money -- the UK and the US

It takes money to win wars, mountains of money. As mentioned, Canada's 11 million people raised $14 billion in Victory Bonds. That's right – $14 billion. Canadians trusted Mackenzie King's government to make the best possible use of their money, and he was determined that this precious money be well spent looking after our armed forces and helping our Mother Country. In 1942, Canada gave Britain a 'Billion Dollar Gift' coupled with a $700 million non-interest loan. In 1943, Canada gave Britain a second grant of aid through our 'War Appropriation Act 1943'. And, to top it all off, at war's end Canada gave Britain an additional $3 billion dollars, and forgave $425 million of flying training debts owed by Britain to Canada. Canada also gave Britain immediately after the war a $1.3 billion loan which was not fully repaid until 2006. Britain's position in 1940 and 1941 was one of extreme danger. It was Canada, more than any other nation, who came to the rescue. Britain's danger was so extreme that British professor Richard Holmes wrote[15] 'in 1940-41, Britain would not have survived as an independent nation had it not been for the agricultural, industrial and financial aid received from Canada.'[16] Canada also had the RCAF in Britain, Canadian aircrew in the RAF, and the Royal Canadian Navy fighting U-boats and protecting convoys of supplies to the UK in the Battle of the Atlantic. The RCN grew to become the world's third largest navy. And then there's Canada's Army. At Dunkirk, British soldiers were miraculously rescued but massive amounts of British military equipment had to be abandoned. This meant after Dunkirk the best equipped and functioning force in the United Kingdom was the First Canadian Army. A controversial person, but politically astute student of our history, Conrad Black, observes that 'under Mackenzie King, Canada became the most important ally of the Anglo-Americans, except for the Soviet Union (an unreliable ally, to say the least)'.[17]

And then there are the Americans. As part of his policy of keeping Canadians and our Allies well aware of what Canada was doing to help win the war, Mackenzie King spoke in New York on 2 December 1942. His speech was broadcast throughout America and Canada, and to other countries. He focused on Canada's increasing industrial capacity. He pointed out that Canada provided 95

---

15 Reardon, *Churchill & Mackenzie King*, p. 135
16 Holmes, *In the Footsteps of Churchill – A Study in Character*, Basic Book,s 2009, First Published 2005
17 Black, 'Canada must return to being a grown-up nation, now and post-COVID-19', *National Post*, 3 April 2020

per cent of the nickel and 40 per cent of the aluminium used by the Allies. In addition, Canada had North America's largest small-arms factory, built 300,000 military vehicles, and had increased aircraft production from forty a year to 400 a month. He said Canada had supplied Russia with $100 million in tanks and other military supplies. He announced that Canada's overall war production in 1942 was $2.5 billion. All this from 11 million people! Mackenzie King concluded his speech with the astonishing statistic that 'we are supplying about two hundred pounds of food per annum for every man, woman and child in the United Kingdom'. Then he departed New York for Washington DC to accept FDR's invitation to spend the weekend at the White House.[18]

Propaganda and Postwar Prosperity

Until the end of 1942, the Second World War was going badly, so badly that Mackenzie King had become 'anxious to clear up the war information business'. He felt that government and country were suffering from 'not having proper publicity.'[19] He looked to Dr Norman Archibald Macrae, 'Larry', MacKenzie to chair Canada's Wartime Information Board, a position Dr MacKenzie could occupy while simultaneously continuing as President of the University of New Brunswick. As board chair, Dr MacKenzie reported directly to Mackenzie King. On 18 September 1943, expressing gratitude for Mackenzie King's scrupulous avoidance of any political interference in the board's work, he wrote to Mackenzie King, 'I think it is a tribute to you and your colleagues ... for it would be a very easy and in some respects a natural thing to use the Board for political or personal purposes.'[20] This tribute to the non-interference of Mackenzie King in War Information Board work reminds me of Sir Arthur Harris praising Churchill regarding Bomber Command when Harris wrote 'But I want to make it quite clear that I was never pressed by Mr Churchill to do anything at his dictation, or anything with which I was not personally satisfied.'[21] Dr MacKenzie became University of BC President in 1944 and served until 1962, raising UBC from being a glorified agricultural college to becoming one of Canada's greatest universities. In fact, UBC was ranked the second best university in Canada in the 2022 edition of *Times Higher Education* (THE) World University Rankings. I met Dr MacKenzie in 1969 while I was in first-year law at UBC. We discovered our families lived near each other in Pictou County – his on Green Hill and mine on Rogers Hill, just a few miles apart. He even knew some of my MacKenzie relatives. He inspired me!

---

18 Reardon p. 230

19 Waite, *Lord of Point Grey – Larry MacKenzie of UBC*, The University of British Columbia Press, Vancouver, p. 99

20 Waite, p. 100.

21 Harris, *Bomber Offensive*, pp. 106-7

LEADERS

In 1944 Mackenzie King created the Department of Veterans' Affairs and made Vancouver MP Ian Mackenzie Canada's first Minister of Veterans' Affairs. Postwar support was provided for veterans in many ways, including housing and education.[22] This helped launch Canada's postwar prosperity. But Mackenzie King's greatest contribution was avoiding the terrible French-English spilt on conscription (drafting men into the military) that so deeply divided us in the First World War. His policy on that topic became his most famous: 'Conscription if necessary, but not necessarily conscription.' Mackenzie King's commitment to Canadian unity was so clear that Quebec forgave him for the Conscription Crisis of 1944, and helped re-elect him on 11 June 1945, albeit as a minority government.

Something I admire in Churchill, FDR and Mackenzie King is that they attracted the best talent available, people far more knowledgeable in specific areas than they were. Many leaders are frightened of having more brilliant colleagues, but those three were not. Mackenzie King brought to Ottawa his 'Dollar-a-Year Men' – brilliant business executives to work in government, largely in the Department of Munitions and Supply, and on the Wartime Prices and Trade Board.[23] C.D. Howe, Canada's wartime 'Minister of Everything' created a re-armament programme using 'dollar-a-year men' such as E.P. Taylor, ultimately one of Canada's richest people. And Mackenzie King brought, and helped keep, Churchill and FDR together.

Mackenzie King died 22 July 1950. The crowd on Parliament Hill in Ottawa, followed by a half-million in Toronto, watched in silence his coffin pass on a gun carriage. He is buried in Toronto's Mount Pleasant Cemetery. Canadians never loved him, but they respected him, and they glimpsed his greatness.[24] In his will, Mackenzie King used the $100,000 gift John D. Rockefeller gave him for his seventy-fourth birthday to create the Mackenzie King Scholarships – travelling scholarships and open scholarships for graduates of Canadian Universities plus one student each year graduating from his alma mater, Harvard University chosen by Harvard's President to pursue postgraduate studies at a Canadian University. My friend Joost Blom QC chairs the board of trustees for these scholarships, and the selection committee which chooses the recipients each year. Mackenzie King attached huge importance to education, and was our best-educated prime mininster.

Roosevelt

Just as Mackenzie King knew America well, Franklin Delano Roosevelt, whom I refer to as FDR, knew Canada well. This mutual knowledge aided the Allies enormously in winning the Second World War. FDR was the first American president to visit

---

22 Waite, p. 116

23 *Canadian Encyclopedia* 'Dollar-a-Year Man'

24 Hutchinson *The Incredible Canadian – A Candid Portrait of Mackenzie King*, Oxford University Press, 2011, as quoted by Reardon 'History has been kind to Mackenzie King', *Waterloo Regional Record*, 22 July 2013

Canada while president, having spent his first thirty-nine summers on Canada's Campobello Island in New Brunswick, commencing when he was a one-year-old boy in 1883. Ka Hyun and I visited FDR's thirty-four-room 'cottage' on Campobello Island on our honeymoon in 2010. I think it should be one of the most important homes for tourists in Canada. Tragically, it was at Campobello Island in August 1921 that FDR, age 39, was stricken with polio, just as my mother Joyce Lenore Miller MacKenzie, who was born in 1921, was stricken with polio in Calgary thirty-two years later in 1952. It is said that polio and the atomic bomb were America's two greatest fears.[25] Polio was terrifying. It left my Mom and FDR paralyzed from the waist down. I should note, while FDR was told he had polio, some say he may in fact have had GBS – Guillan-Barre Syndrome.[26] On 03 October 1924 FDR first visited Warm Springs in Georgia. Swimming there, FDR immediately felt better. In 1926 he bought the resort and 1,200 acres at Warm Springs and, in 1927, organized the non-profit Warm Springs Foundation to which he gave his property. In 1938 it became the National Foundation for Infantile Paralysis[27] in which FDR remained active for the rest of his life. He spent time healing at Warm Springs every year except 1942. It was at his beloved Warm Springs that FDR died on 12 April 1945. In 1992, I took my daughter Mary Anne, aged nine, and my son Guy Roland, aged eight, to Warm Springs because I wanted them to better understand both Roosevelt as president, and polio which had also inflicted their grandmother. It was moving being in FDR's modest two-bedroom cottage.

I was surprised to discover, and not many know, that both of America's Roosevelt presidents used Mackenzie King as their 'channel of communication' with Britain. When, in 1908, Theodore Roosevelt asked Mackenzie King to come to Washington for lunch at the White House, Mackenzie King and Prime Minister Sir Wilfried Laurier were astonished, especially given Mackenzie King was not an elected official, but instead Canada's first Deputy Minister of Labour. Over lunch at the White House, TR asked Mackenzie King to be his channel of communication with the British. Laurier concurred, so off to London Mackenzie King went.[28]

As an aside, TR did not react well to Churchill. They met in Albany in December 1900 while TR was Governor of New York. As David Freeman, editor of *Finest Hour*, says 'unlike his distant relative Franklin, Teddy Roosevelt never took a liking to Churchill – and no wonder. Their personalities were too similar. There could never be enough oxygen in one room to sustain two such egotists.'[29]

In May 1940, President Franklin Roosevelt, an admirer and fifth cousin of Theodore Roosevelt, and husband of TR's niece Eleanor Roosevelt, did the same as TR in 1908 – FDR also asked MacKenzie King to be his channel of communication

---

25 PBS Documentary 'American Experience: The Polio Crusade' *Los Angeles Times* TV Review 2 February 2009

26 United States Senate Congressional Record 17 August 1967 page 23043

27 Thompson p 111

28 Reardon pp 31-2

29 David Freeman *Prelude to Power – Churchill and the American Presidency* p 10

LEADERS

with the British.[30] Mackenzie King had won the trust and confidence of both Republican President Theodore Roosevelt of Oyster Bay, New York, and Democrat President Franklin Roosevelt of Hyde Park, New York. This aided Canada, America, and Britain.

No American president officially visited Canada until FDR on 31 July 1936. He met with Mackenzie King in Quebec City. It became his chosen location in the Fairmont Chateau Frontenac for two of his most important Conferences of the Second World War, on 17-24 August 1943 and 12-16 September 1944. On 18 August 1938, Canadian-American relations fundamentally changed from mutual unfriendly indifference to what became later known as the 'Special Relationship'. Accompanied by Mackenzie King, on 18 August FDR as mentioned came to Kingston to accept an honorary doctorate from Queen's University. Eight decades later, our son Kai MacKenzie earned his Masters in Economics at Queen's in 2019. Some say FDR's speech at Queen's was one of the most important speeches in Canadian history. At Queen's FDR announced to the world that America would come to Canada's aid if Canada were ever threatened by a hostile power – making himself crystal clear, he said an attack on Canada would be regarded by America as an attack on the United States. This was a dramatic change in American foreign policy. It created quite a stir. It reminds me of President James Monroe's Doctrine of 2 December 1823. FDR later remarked he was surprised his announcement created so much controversy because, as FDR said, 'any idiot looking at a map could see the untenable position America would be in if a hostile power conquered Canada.' FDR was, of course, referring to our 5,500-mile (8,900 km) US-Canada border. FDR's speech meant Germany attacking Canada would find itself at war with America. Two days later, Mackenzie King stated that Canada would never allow enemy forces to cross Canadian territory 'by land, sea or air' to threaten America.[31] Americans were impressed, and pleased.

Regarding America, Mackenzie King was a realist. He knew Canada needed far better relations with Americans than had been the case from Confederation in 1867 until FDR's speech at Queen's University on 18 August 1938. And so, Mackenzie King negotiated with FDR two extremely important bilateral agreements. The first was their 17 August 1940 'Ogdensburg Agreement' for mutual defence of both nations. It created the Permanent Joint Board of Defence to oversee the defence of America and Canada that still operates today. Some saw it as abandoning Britain. Churchill was angry. But Mackenzie King persuaded Canadians it was necessary for security, it improved relations with America, and it moved America closer to war. As well, Canadians were pleased Canada resolutely refused to give America control of Canada's armed forces. Postwar, this led to NATO, NORAD [North American Aerospace Defence Command which was known until March 1981 as the North American Air Defence Command] and 'Two Eyes', the latter two being exclusively bilateral between Canada and America.

---

30 Reardon pp 108-9
31 Thomson p 78

The second Agreement happened on Sunday, 20 April 1941. Mackenzie King as an economist came to realize that Lend-Lease, while benefiting Britain, had the potential for bankrupting Canada. He rushed to Springwood, FDR's Hyde Park home, with a proposal in hand that we now call the 'Hyde Park Declaration'. Mackenzie King alone pleaded his case, and FDR, also alone, and his Hyde Park neighbour, US Secretary of the Treasury Henry Morgenthau, concurred. This enabled Canada to charge to Lend-Lease components it bought for military equipment Canada made for Britain and increased American purchases from Canada, thereby eliminating Canada's trade deficit and enabling Canada to accumulate an enormous trade surplus. This was all through Mackenzie King on a Sunday negotiating alone at FDR's New York home with FDR one of the most important trade agreements in Canadian history. Mackenzie King's solution to the threat posed by Lend-Lease was marvellous, and possible only because FDR respected him, trusted him, liked him, and so agreed with him. It was helpful, too, that Mackenzie King had thoughtfully visited Morgenthau in Washington days earlier to wish him a happy twenty-fifth wedding anniversary and, 'by the way' to mention this proposal. Properly informed in advance, at home at Hyde Park that Sunday, Morgenthau concurred with FDR to approve Mackenzie King's proposal. Then FDR wrote on the document 'done by Mackenzie and FDR at Hyde Park on a grand Sunday'. These two agreements also brought Canada and America closer together to the benefit of both nations in winning the Second World War and prospering post-war without lessening Canada's respect for Britain and the Commonwealth, the admirable worldwide association of fifty-four nations in which Canada remains so prominent.

But what was the relationship FDR had with his friend 'Mackenzie'?[32] For starters, they both had Harvard degrees, and they met twenty times. Mackenzie King was a house guest nine times in the White House. These included long conversations into the night, and morning meetings in FDR's bedroom while he was still dressed informally. He was also FDR's house guest a couple of times at Hyde Park, and he was possibly the only foreign leader FDR had as a house guest at Warm Springs. FDR's daughter Anna, who had accompanied FDR to Yalta, told Mackenzie King FDR told her when referring to Mackenzie King that there was 'a great friend of his coming to the White House, one of whom he was very fond'.[33] When FDR died on 12 April 1945, the only foreign leaders America's Secretary of State immediately cabled were Churchill, Stalin and Mackenzie King. At the private funeral conducted by invitation only at Hyde Park, Mackenzie King was the only member of a foreign government present. He was placed in the front row, between Treasury Secretary Henry Morgenthau and Secretary of State Edward Stettinius, at the latter's insistence. Eleanor Roosevelt told Mackenzie King how happy she was that he had come to the funeral, and that she knew Franklin would be very happy too that Mackenzie King was there.[34]

---

[32] Thompson, pp. 52, 47, 59, 66, 67, 77, 81-7, 90-6, 111-14, 134-37, 155-60, 187-8, 194-203, 224-6, 229-33, 242-9, 254-67, 348-58, 385-99

[33] Thompson, pp. 391-2

[34] Thompson, p. 398

LEADERS

Churchill

We meet to honour a man whose honour requires no meeting—for he is the most honoured and honourable man to walk the stage of human history in the time in which we live. By adding his name to our rolls, we mean to honour him—but his acceptance honours us far more. For no statement or proclamation can enrich his name—the name Sir Winston Churchill.

President John F. Kennedy 9 April 1963
Making Churchill an Honorary American

JKF was right – Churchill needs no introduction. All I am sharing here is my perception of him as it grew from my boyhood living at home in Calgary. I remember then reading *Reader's Digest* declare Sir Winston Churchill was the 'Greatest Person of the 20th Century'. I wondered how they could be so certain, given that the twentieth century was barely half over. By the end of the twentieth century, I felt they were right. Then the BBC in 2002 declared him the 'Greatest Briton'.

As a boy, I found Churchill particularly fascinating because he was so easy and enjoyable to read. For me, reading many historians was like the heavy weight of wading through wet cement. My parents had a great Churchill library in which I read everything. I naively took all I read by Churchill at face value, but Churchill was human and, while fascinating and appealing, he was not perfect. An example is his failure to champion Bomber Command in the spring of 1945. A second example is wartime Churchill seldom uttering the words Canada, Australia or New Zealand. Instead, he felt all was encompassed by 'British' or 'Anglo'. Likewise, he preferred 'Empire' to 'Commonwealth'.

My problem with this is it seriously discounted my understanding of Canada's contribution to winning the war. Churchill's words gave me the impression that Canadians, including my Dad, were marginal players. My research reveals the exact opposite is true. It is not widely known that Churchill on one important occasion did focus attention on Canada's wartime contribution. That happened on 19 May 1944, shortly before D Day. Both Churchill and FDR invited Mackenzie King to Washington DC. There he was seated beside the Duke of Windsor (formerly King Edward VIII) in the Executive Box to hear Churchill speak to Congress. Churchill said to Congress 'It is my special duty to promote and preserve this intimacy and concert between all parts of the British Commonwealth and Empire, and especially with the great self-governing Dominions, like Canada, whose Prime Minister is with us at the moment, and whose contribution is so massive and invaluable.' Back at the White House that afternoon, FDR told Mackenzie King and Churchill that he had listened on the radio to Churchill's speech to Congress, with which he was pleased, and he 'noted the hearty applause Congress gave Mackenzie King'.[35]

---

35 Reardon, p. 238

Words are important, but even for events as big as the 1943 landings in Sicily, and D Day in 1944, Churchill stuck to 'Anglo-American'[36] in spite of Mackenzie King wanting Canada specifically mentioned. FDR and Eisenhower, however, happily complied with Mackenzie King's request, so America used the phrases 'Anglo-American-Canadian forces' and 'British, American and Canadian troops'.[37]

Another of Churchill's famous words is the 'Few'. Most people I know are aware that one of Churchill's most famous speeches was in 1940 about the 'Few'. Like too many others, I erroneously thought he was referring to a small number of fighter pilots. I was astonished in 2018 to discover that his immortal words praising the 'Few' were praise for all RAF aircrew, not just fighter pilots. What's more, his emphasis in that speech was on Bomber Command, not Fighter Command. Here in full are Churchill's words in parliament on 20 August 1940:

> The gratitude of every home in our Island, in our *Empire*, and indeed throughout the world, except in the abodes of the guilty, goes out to the *British* airmen who, undaunted by odds, unwearied in their constant challenge and mortal danger, are turning the tide of world war by their prowess and by their devotion. *Never in the field of human conflict has so much been owed by so many to so few.* All hearts go out to the fighter pilots whose brilliant actions we see with our own eyes day after day, but we must never forget that all the time, night after night, month after month, our bomber squadrons travel far into Germany, find their targets in the darkness by the highest navigational skill, aim their attacks, often under the heaviest fire, often with serious loss, with deliberate careful discrimination, and inflict shattering blows upon the whole of the technical and war-making structure of the Nazi power.' (emphasis is mine)

Churchill, Trenchard and the RAF

Key to my growing awareness of Churchill was his relationship with the Royal Air Force, especially Bomber Command. My curiosity was aroused by Churchill's famous memo to Cabinet in September 1940 saying 'The Navy can lose us the war but only the Air Force can win it. Therefore, our supreme effort must be to gain overwhelming mastery in the air. The fighters are our salvation, but the bombers alone provide the means of victory.'[38] My research reveals that Churchill's RAF relationship far preceded 1940. In fact, I learnt from Boris Johnson that Churchill's passion for the air force began much earlier than the RAF's formation as the world's first independent air force on 1 April 1918. My Finnish friend Pekka

---

36 Reardon, pp. 280-1,

37 Reardon, p. 242

38 Birrell, *Johnny – Canada's Greatest Bomber Pilot*, pp. 29-30

LEADERS

Moisio points out to me that Finland's air force was formed on 6 March 1918, almost a month before the RAF. However, unlike the independent RCAF in the war, but like the RCAF today, it was not independent. Instead, it was a branch of the Finnish Defence Forces just as today the RCAF is a branch of the Canadian Armed Forces. Johnson says the idea of an independent air force in Britain started at the beginning of 1913 when Churchill, then First Lord of the Admiralty, visited the naval air station at Eastchurch on the Isle of Shepppey. Johnson says Churchill instantly saw the potential. He wanted a proper division, with its own identity and esprit de corps: and so began what became the Royal Air Force.[39]

I also discovered that Churchill was not alone. That discovery happened by chance while my sons Guy Roland and Ruaridh and I were being shown RAF Scampton in Lincolnshire on September 2018 by RAF Flight Lieutenant Mark Wood that Sunday morning. There I noticed a large portrait of a distinguished-looking gentleman, so I asked Mark who he was. Mark replied that he was Hugh Trenchard, a name I would probably have immediately forgotten if Mark had not added 'the Father of the RAF'. That moment at RAF Scampton, Mark had introduced me to Marshal of the Royal Air Force, Hugh Montague Trenchard, 1st Viscount Trenchard GCB OM GCVO DSO. Lord Trenchard is known as the 'Father of the RAF' partly because, for eighteen of its first nineteen years of existence, he was its Commander-in-Chief. In addition, Churchill wrote to RAF Air Marshal Sir Bertine Sutton saying: I consider that Marshal of the Royal Air Force Lord Trenchard is the founder of the Royal Air Force.'[40] Lord Trenchard declined formal appointments in the Second World War, saying younger men were needed. However, his influence and friendship with Churchill continued. For example, on Churchill's 66th birthday, 30 November 1940, they had lunch together at Chequers. And Lord Trenchard remained a major morale booster for the RAF and a strong supporter of Sir Arthur Harris throughout the war.

And I learned through my research that Lord Trenchard was also revered in America where he is known as the 'Patron Saint of Air Power'.[41] The Mighty Eight's commanding general, Ira Eaker, writes that

> All American leaders recognized Lord Trenchard, as did the RAF, as the author of the concept of strategic bombing in World War I .... General Spaatz and I had contacted Lord Trenchard soon after arrival in England as observers in the Battle of Britain. He was always kindly and courteous in a fatherly fashion. The visits of this world-famous patriarch to our combat groups, during the early operations, proved a valuable morale factor.[42]

---

39 Johnson, *The Churchill Factor*, p. 56
40 Courtenay, 'Churchill as Honorary Air Commodore', *Finest Hour* No. 185 Third Quarter 2019 p. 50
41 Boyle, *Trenchard Man of Vision*, Collins, London, 1962, p. 732
42 Murray, *A Thousand Shall Fall*, p. ix

BOMBER COMMAND

Postwar, Lord Trenchard was consulted by America's highest ranking air force General, Hap Arnold, and wartime commander of America's strategic air forces in Europe, Carl Spaatz, regarding the formation in 1947 of the United States Air Force.

That raises the question of how did the UK, Australia and Canada acquire independent air forces a quarter of a century before America? I discovered that the short answer to this interesting question is the combination of Winston Churchill and Hugh Trenchard. There was movement in Washington DC at the end of the First World War to create a separate air force, but America had no equivalent to Churchill-Trenchard, so America's Army and Navy managed to quash the idea. In postwar Britain the Army and Royal Navy likewise wanted to terminate the Air Force as a separate service, but they were out-manoeuvred by Churchill and Trenchard. This Churchillian out-manoeuvring began on 17 July 1917 when British Prime Minister Lloyd George reclaimed Churchill from the political wilderness he had been thrown into following the disaster at Gallipoli. On that day, Lloyd George brought Churchill back into the Cabinet as Minister of Munitions. There Churchill was exceptionally effective, just as was in the Second World War Albert Speer for Germany and Lord Beaverbrook for Britain as British Minister of Aircraft Production, Minister of Supply and Minister of War Production. As well, Churchill as Munitions Minister ensured that Britain's brand-new Royal Air Force was well equipped and supplied.

On 13 June 1918 the six-week-old RAF formed its first bomber squadron[43] and guess what? It was 166 Squadron with which my Dad flew twenty-six years later. As a direct order from the British Cabinet, in retaliation for the Luftwaffe bombing London, 166 Squadron was to bomb Berlin. It was the first RAF squadron to be equipped with the Handley Page V/1500 heavy bomber, designed for long-range bombing. When all was finally ready for this incredibly difficult operation, and days of bad weather had passed, just before take-off word was received to cancel the sortie – an armistice had been signed at 11am. It was 11 November 1918. As a result, Berlin was not bombed. That meant the First World War was never fought inside Germany. This enabled post First World War Germans to develop the myth that they been 'stabbed in the back'. Allied failure to bring the First World War to Germany was not repeated in the Second World War.

Post the First World War, on 10 January 1919, Churchill was made Minister of War and Minister of Air. In this latter capacity, Churchill 'concocted' with 'Father of the RAF' General Sir Hugh Trenchard 'methods of using bombers to control large areas of sparsely populated territory' through 'force substitution'.[44] This was important. Churchill and Trenchard saw the air force as an offensive (no pun intended) weapon, rather than just defensive. Churchill's enthusiasm made the RAF for many years the largest air force in the world. Also, Churchill's support of British air construction helped save Britain in the Second World War. On 20 June 1941, US Army Air Corps units were designated as the United States Army Air Forces, but it was not until postwar on 18 September 1947 that America created the United States Air Force.

---

43 Wright, *On Wings of War*, p. 6
44 *Air Force Blue*, p. 35.

LEADERS

In the early 1920s, after attempts to disband the RAF failed, there was enormous political pressure to reduce its size. Rather than destroying the extra aircraft, I am told Churchill and Trenchard shipped them to Canada, Australia and New Zealand. Canada formed the Canadian Air Force on 17 May 1920. King George V granted Royal consent, transforming it into the Royal Canadian Air Force, into which it was officially formed on 1 April 1924.[45] Australia preceded Canada by three years with the Royal Australian Air Force being formed on 31 March 1921. The RAAF had been preceded by the Australian Flying Corps which had been formed on 22 October 1912. New Zealand came after with the Royal New Zealand Air Force being formed 1 April 1937. The RAAF, RCAF and RNZAF are the three Commonwealth air forces that joined the RAF's Bomber Command which had been formed in 1936.

From the outset, Churchill saw with singular clarity the importance of Bomber Command to winning the Second World War, so throughout the conflict he insisted on continuing its dangerous heavy bomber operations regardless of the staggering cost in aircrew killed and aircraft destroyed. He saw Bomber Command as our only way of attacking and weakening Hitler's Fortress Europe before D Day, and essential to winning the war all the way into 1945. In addition, he invariably cited Bomber Command whenever Stalin pressured him for a second front.

Without Churchill, Bomber Command would likely have been side-lined early in the Second World War because of the horrific cost in aircrew killed and aircraft lost for marginal benefit. Looking at the broader picture, with anyone but Churchill as prime minister in May 1940, Britain would likely have negotiated peace with Hitler – peace Hitler would have violated as soon as convenient for him. One point: before Churchill became prime minister Britain and France had done little in the Second World War. This was the so-called 'Phony War'. It ended with Germany's *Blitzkrieg* in the spring of 1940. As for Bomber Command, I discovered that in April 1940 Prime Minister Chamberlain's 'failure to embark on any sustained bombing raids against Germany since September 1939' was a key criticism of the Watching Committee of Peers and Members of Parliament that played a major role in the demand for his resignation.[46] Even in Churchill's wartime coalition government, his Deputy Prime Minister and Secretary of State for the Dominions, Clement Attlee, was no fan of Bomber Command.[47] But, for Churchill, Bomber Command was vital to victory.

Sadly, the spring of 1945 was not Churchill's finest hour, and that included Bomber Command. His March 1945 message to General Hastings ('Pug') Ismay, followed by his failure to mention Bomber Command in his Victory Speech praising the armed forces,[48] caused Bomber Command aircrew considerable grief postwar, and helped fuel Bomber Command controversies. More on that later in this book.

---

45 Royal Canadian Air Force Wikipedia
46 Gilbert, 'Churchill and Bombing Policy', *Finest Hour* 137, Winter 2007-08
47 Churchill & Attlee – The Unlikely Allies Who Won the War
48 Geddes, 'Lest We Forget Again – For decades, Canada largely ignored World War II. What prompted our national change-of-heart?' *Maclean's*, Canada's National Magazine, June 2020, p. 73

Churchill's Women and the 'Special Relationship'

Churchill and Mackenzie King were of one mind regarding the importance of what came to be known as the 'Special Relationship' Britain and Canada developed with America through their leaders' friendships with FDR. Since the Second World War there has been much talk about this 'Special Relationship' without much clarity. The diversion on topic I find interesting is that of the contribution of Churchill's women to this Special Relationship. After Pearl Harbor and Hitler's foolish declaration of war on America on 11 December 1941, high-ranking Americans poured into London. Two of Churchill's married women formed their own special relationships. His married daughter, Sarah, had an affair with John Winant, America's wartime Ambassador to Britain from 1 March 1941 until 10 April 1946, after which Winant tragically committed suicide. Churchill's married daughter-in-law Pamela Churchill had an affair with Averill Harriman, US Ambassador to the Soviet Union from 23 October 1943 until 24 January 1946 and US Ambassador to the UK from 30 April 1946 until 1 October 1946. Their affair, as Erik Larson tells it, began at the Dorchester.

On 16 April 1941 Harriman attended a dinner to honour Fred Astaire at London's Dorchester Hotel where he was seated beside Pamela Churchill, who had married Sir Winston's son Randolph on 4 October 1939 aged 19. She gave birth to their son Winston Spencer Churchill on 10 October 1940, five months to the day after his grandfather became prime minister. In February 1941, Randolph was transferred to Cairo and spent the remainder of the war in Eastern Europe and the Middle East. After dinner, Harriman invited Pamela back to his apartment. It was the day after her twenty-first birthday. Then a major Luftwaffe raid began. As Erik Larson succinctly reports: 'Bombs fell; clothes were shed ... a big bombing raid is a very good way to get into bed with somebody.'[49] On 27 September 1971 Harriman married Pamela. He was 79. He died fifteen years later on 26 July 1986. Seven years after that, on 30 June 1993, Pamela became America's Ambassador to France. While still the Ambassador, she died on 5 February 1997, aged 76, and is buried with Harriman in Arden NY. During the war, young Pamela developed more of her 'special relationships' with Americans, including affairs with US Army Air Forces General Fred Anderson who, in 1943, became commanding general of VIII Bomber Command Europe[50] under General Ira Eaker, and with Edward R. Murrow and William S. Paley of wartime CBS media in London.[51]

Kay Halle, the author of several Churchill books and lifelong friend of the Churchill family, had an affair with Randolph Churchill but refused his proposal of marriage, and had an affair with Averell Harriman but likewise refused his proposal of marriage. She was instrumental in Churchill becoming an Honorary American.

---

49 Larson, *The Splendor and the Vile*, pp. 429-30

50 US Air Force Biographies Major General Frederick Lewis Anderson Jr. www.af.mil/About-Us/Biographies

51 Costigliola, 'Pamela Churchill, Wartime London, and the Making of the Special Relationship,' *Diplomatic History* Vol. 36, No. 4, September 2012, p. 753

Meanwhile, Averell Harriman's daughter Kathy had an affair in 1942 with FDR Jr, who was married to Ethel Du Pont of the chemical family.

Quite the collection of wartime special relationships.

Churchill The Pilot

A fun fact I discovered about Churchill is that, while First Lord of the Admiralty, in 1912 he took flying lessons. Unfortunately, 'although he had many hours' instruction, he was not allowed to fly solo, so he never qualified as a pilot.'[52] This was because Churchill's enthusiasm for flying was not matched by aptitude. His friends and relatives were opposed. His cousin Edith, Lady Londonderry, said his interest in flying was 'evil'. Edith's maternal grandmother, the Duchess of Sutherland, was Anne Hay-Mackenzie, an important ancestor of our current MacKenzie Clan Chief, John Mackenzie, the Earl of Cromartie. That is because, on 21 October 1861, the Earldom of Cromartie was restored, and Anne became in her own right Countess of Cromartie. The Cromartie title had been forfeited after the loss of the 16 April 1746 Battle of Culloden which crushed the Highlanders.

Churchill's cousin Sunny, the Duke of Marlborough, also opposed Churchill flying. He wrote to Winston:

> I do not suppose I shall get the chance of writing you many more letters if you continue your journeys in the Air. I consider you owe it to your wife, family and friends to desist from a practice or pastime – whichever you call it – which is fraught with so much danger to life. It is really wrong of you.[53]

Nor was Churchill's enthusiasm for flying shared by his wife Clementine, presumably because his flying lessons included near-death experiences. An example is his last flight over the Channel when his aircraft engine lost power. Churchill described this brush with death to British press magnate Sir George Riddell, who recorded in his diary that Churchill said

> I saw that things looked serious. I knew that if the engine just ceased to cough we should fall into the sea. We were too low down to have an opportunity to rectify matters. I wondered if I could unstrap myself and unstrap the pilot, and how long the machine would float and how long I could swim after that.

---

52 Courtenay, 'Churchill as Honorary Air Commodore,' *Finest* Hour, No. 185 Third Quarter 2019, p. 49

53 Johnson, *The Churchill Factor*, p. 57

Fortunately for the free world, his aircraft engine restarted, and Churchill avoided death yet again. Although an air enthusiast for the remainder of his life, Churchill gave up on becoming a pilot, and wisely left the flying to others.[54] On the RAF's twenty-fifth anniversary on 1 April 1943, Churchill was awarded by the Air Council with the approval of King George VI 'honorary wings' – the flying badge of the RAF.

Canada The Linchpin

One of Churchill's most famous speeches about Canada was at the 4 September 1941 Luncheon at the Mansion House, the official residence of the Lord Mayor of London, to honour Mackenzie King. Churchill said

> Canada is the linchpin of the English-speaking world. Canada, with those relations of friendly, affectionate intimacy with the United States of America on the one hand and with her unswerving loyalty to the British Commonwealth and the Motherland on the other, is the link which joins together these great branches of the human family, a link which, spanning the oceans, brings the continents into their true relation and will prevent in future generations any growth of division between the proud and the happy nations of Europe and the great countries which have come into existence in the New World.

Canada being in Churchill's view the linchpin is something I heard often. It is one of my earliest understandings of Canada in the world, as seen by the 'Greatest Person of the 20th Century'.

This leads me into a unique combination that enormously aided winning the war and Bomber Command – the combination of Churchill and Mackenzie King.

Churchill Mackenzie King Combo

> **Churchill:** 'We met in Canada… I think I made a frightful ass of myself on that trip, didn't I?'
>
> **Mackenzie King:** 'Well Mr. Churchill, there were many Canadians who thought so. I was one of them.'
>
> Their Second Meeting, London September 1906[55]

---

54 John Maurer *Churchill, Air Power, and Arming for Armageddon* Finest Hour No 185 Third Quarter 2019 p 12

55 Reardon, *Winston Churchill & Mackenzie King – So Similar, So Different*, Dundurn, Toronto, 2014, p. 30

LEADERS

While Churchill's first meeting with Mackenzie King in November 1900 was not a success,[56] their relationship soon improved, and lasted a half century until Mackenzie King's death in July 1950. When Churchill became Britain's prime minister in May 1940, Mackenzie King had already served as Canada's prime minister for fourteen years and they had known each other for forty years. This is important – the leaders of the second and third most powerful western Allies having known one another for four decades, and Churchill and Mackenzie King certainly knew one another. They had many similarities, starting with being born only eighteen days apart in 1874, and some significant differences. Churchill was a man of action while Mackenzie King said 'It is what we prevent, rather than what we do, that counts most in Government.'[57] Their biggest difference was that Churchill saw the Dominions as part of the Empire, while Mackenzie King saw them as independent sovereign nations who were voluntarily helping, but not serving, Britain at war. This divergence of views directly affected the RAF with the RCAF in the Second World War.

Another difference concerns Hitler. Churchill tried to arrange a meeting with him in 1932, but Hitler declined. Hitler did, however, meet with Mackenzie King in 1937. The night before meeting with Hitler, Mackenzie King made a point of sleeping under his Mackenzie tartan blanket, saying rather romantically in his diary that he felt 'the whole Mackenzie Clan were communicating in my diplomatic mission.'[58] Mackenzie King also met with Göring, reflecting his interest in controlling the air.

A major, indeed monumental, similarity is:

- In a survey of scholars by Canada's national news magazine *Maclean's* in 1997, Mackenzie King was ranked first among Canadian prime ministers.
- In a television poll conducted by the BBC in 2002, Churchill was ranked the 'Greatest Briton'.

The Churchill-Mackenzie King combo served the Allies well – these men entered the war knowing each other for four decades, sharing the same commitment to controlling the air, and balancing one another with their divergent personalities.

---

56 Reardon, 'Winston Churchill and Mackenzie King,' *Finest Hour*, 130, Spring 2006
57 Canada, Library and Archives Canada, *William Lyon Mackenzie King*, 26 August 1936
58 Hopper, 'The Day Mackenzie King Met The Führer,' *National Post*, 15 May 2017

Chapter Six

Harris

It is right that we should not forget those dark days of war when we were in grave danger and Bomber Command gave us hope and the means of salvation. Sir Arthur Harris was an inspiring leader who carried a heavy burden of responsibility for more than three years ... .

The Queen Mother while unveiling the statue of
Sir Arthur Harris on The Strand,
31 May 1992

I doubt whether any single man did more in winning the war than he did. I doubt whether that is generally realized.

Field Marshal The Viscount Montgomery
Speaker at Chamber of Shipping
Annual Dinner, Grosvenor House,
6 July 1950[1]

Sir Arthur Harris is now bearing the brunt of the charge of unnecessary 'civilian brutality' by RAF Bomber Command. No one knows better than I that such charges and claims are entirely false and wholly unfair.

Lieutenant General Ira Eaker,
America's Counterpart to Harris[2]

One of the most controversial, and misunderstood, Allied military leaders of the Second World War was euphemistically known as 'Bomber' Harris. My Bomber Command quest has taken me to him, where I discover almost everything I thought I knew about Harris is wrong. Who was he?

---

1 Probert, *Bomber Harris*, p. 370
2 Peden, *A Thousand Shall Fall*, p. x

HARRIS

Harris Served in the RAF for Three Decades

Harris gave the RAF three decades of service spanning two world wars, starting on 6 November 1915 when he joined the Royal Flying Corps as a second lieutenant. Having learned to fly in late 1915, he was promoted to lieutenant on 29 January 1916. In France in 1917, he became Commanding Officer of 45 Squadron. When the RAF was created on 1 April 1918, Harris became one of its original officers. The rank of flying officer was created when the RAF was formed. Prince Albert, who on 11 December 1936 became King George VI, was also one of the RAF's original officers. Harris continued with the RAF until the end of the Second World War. On 1 July 1937, he was promoted to air commodore and in 1938 became Air Officer Commanding-in-Chief (AOCinC) of No. 4 Group Bomber Command. Then he was posted to Palestine and Trans-Jordan as RAF commander. Throughout this period, he pressured his superiors for large strategic bombers capable of taking the war from Britain to Germany. On 1 July 1939, just two months before the UK entered the Second World War, Harris was promoted to air vice-marshal. When war broke out, he took command of No. 5 Group Bomber Command. In November 1940, he was made Deputy Chief of the Air Staff, a position he found frustrating. Harris was a man of action.

Air Marshal Sir Arthur Harris, was RAF Air Officer Commanding-in-Chief (AOCinC) of Bomber Command from 22 February 1942 until the end of the war. He was sometimes called 'Butch' by aircrew, 'Bert' by friends, 'Buddy' by colleagues such as Ira Eaker,[3] and even today 'Bomber' by the media.[4] I will refer to him as 'Harris'. My limited knowledge of him was negative. I envisioned him being a cold-blooded mass murderer. What surprises I unearthed while researching the reality. For example, what Harris accomplished was, to quote Supreme Allied Commander in Europe General Dwight Eisenhower, 'miraculous'.

Some accuse Harris of mindless carpet bombing of innocent civilians, while contributing little, if anything, to winning the war. CBC's January 1992 *The Valour & The Horror* is an example. In reality, to again quote Eisenhower, Harris was one of the most effective and innovative parts of Eisenhower's whole organization. The Queen Mother called Harris an 'inspiring leader'. Harris indeed inspired his aircrew for over three long years of constant danger to carry out work vital to our victory in spite of horrific casualties. I remember when Harris was under heavy attack in the media in the early 1990s, the Queen Mother speaking out loud and clear in his defence. My deep respect for her awakened my curiosity and sowed the seed that my negative impression of him was wrong.

---

3 Probert, *Bomber Harris*, p. 178.
4 *Reap the Whirlwind*, p. 75

BOMBER COMMAND

Churchill Saves Bomber Command

As the war entered 1942, pretty much everything was going badly for the Allies, and Bomber Command was in need of rescue. It was in danger of being side-lined, indeed perhaps even shut down. Its numbers of aircrew killed and aircraft lost were astronomical, and its results were pitiful. It was under political attack at home. Abroad it was enduring loss of supplies from America and devastating attacks by the Luftwaffe. Morale was plummeting. It was Churchill who saved Bomber Command by summoning Harris home from America and, on 22 February 1942, appointing him Bomber Command's Air Officer Commanding-in-Chief.

My research reveals Harris picked up the pieces and built Bomber Command into one of the most war-winning weapons the world has ever seen, while restoring the morale of the magnificent young men who fought and, in too many cases, died in this most horrific form of warfare. Martyn Chorlton says 'Harris's arrival and the fresh ideas he brought to Bomber Command was the equivalent of turning a wild horse into a thoroughbred.'[5] Dave Birrell says 'Harris was introducing new tactics, taking advantage of increasing numbers of the new, four-engine bombers, and implementing new, electronic navigation aids. The most significant of these was GEE.'[6] Rebecca Grant says 'Perhaps no airman had ever been given a more difficult job'. In *Air Force Magazine* under the heading of Harris 'In a New Light' she wrote:

> Harris' record is worth a reconsideration, however. For one thing, he faced major challenges building up the kind of Bomber Command that could produce such impressive operational results – including surprisingly effective support for land force operations in the last year of the war. Perhaps no airman had ever been given a more difficult job: to create from scarce resources a bomber force that would be the one sure means of taking the war directly to Nazi Germany. That was Harris' task from 1942 to 1945.[7]

What was it about Harris that inspired such high praise? What did he do? What was his form of leadership? How could anyone lead a group sustaining such horrific casualties? My curiosity about Harris grew. And then it struck me – even though one quarter of all Canadians in uniform killed in the Second World War died in Bomber Command, Canada sustained more casualties in five days on Vimy Ridge in the First World War than fatalities in five years in Bomber Command in the Second World War. In addition, Bomber Command, unlike Vimy, was vital to victory. The most comprehensive statement about Harris as a

---

5 Chorlton, *The Thousand Bomber Raids*, p. 165

6 Birrell, *Johnny – Canada's Greatest Bomber Pilot* p. 50

7 Grant *Air Force Magazine* the Official Publication of the Air Force Association, 17 May 2008

leader I have seen is from Air Chief Marshal Sir Edgar Rainey Ludlow-Hewitt, Bomber Command C-in-C until 1940 and Inspector General of the Royal Air Force until November 1945. Sir Edgar, who Harris says 'was the most brilliant officer I have ever met in any of the three services' wrote to Chief of Air Staff Sir Charles 'Peter' Portal:[8]

> I have had considerable experience of Air Vice-Marshal Harris's work and I am very impressed with the rare qualities of personality which arise from an exceptionally active and stimulating mentality. He has an exceptionally alert, creative and enterprising mind balanced by long practical experience together with energy and force of character to give his ideas practical shape and realization. He has rendered great service in respect of improvements in the technical equipment of the aircraft in his command, and also in the creation and organization of novel methods of dealing with the extremely difficult problems of crew training. His particular talents lie mainly along practical lines, but his ideas are inspired by an unusually well-developed imagination, and it is this combination which makes him a very valuable officer in any task where creative ideas and the energy to put them into effect are required. As a commander his exceptional air experience gives him a sympathetic insight into the attitude of mind of the crews, which is well understood and appreciated by them.

My research tells me Sir Edgar was right, and the vicious attacks tossed at Harris postwar were wrong. Of all the military leaders who led us through the Second World War, Harris suffered the greatest amount of unjust abuse postwar.

Harris and Churchill

Above all, Harris had the support of Churchill. Churchill recognized Harris as a man of steel when many other commanders bent and snapped under the heavy responsibilities with which he entrusted them.[9] An indication of just how highly Churchill valued Harris was that the Churchill family asked Harris to serve as a pallbearer at Churchill's funeral. During the war, Harris lived near Chequers so he and Churchill sometimes dined together.

---

8 Probert, p. 95

9 Hastings, *Finest Years – Churchill as Warlord 1940-45*, HarperPress Paperback, 2010, First published HarperPress London, 2009, p. 249

Harris and Eisenhower

Harris says Eisenhower, was 'a wise and immensely understanding man'.[10] Eisenhower says Harris was 'one of the most respected and co-operative members of this team' and that Harris 'achieved the impossible'.[11] Harris elaborates:

> The comparatively brief period[12] when the strategic bomber forces both of the RAF and of the USAAF were placed under the control of Eisenhower for all operations related to the invasion of Europe and the defeat of the German air force was absolutely the only time during the whole of my command when I was able to proceed with a campaign without being harassed by confused and conflicting directives. It was in many ways a great relief after two years of working under other directions.[13]

Eisenhower, when re-assuring US General George Marshall that return of control of Bomber Command to the RAF in September 1944 would work well wrote:

> You might be interested to know that ACM [Air Chief Marshal] Harris not only willingly supports the ground operation, but he actually proved to be one of the most respected and cooperative members of this team ... . I have no real fears for the future when the great battle comes to the real entry into Germany, he will be on the job.[14]

What's more, Eisenhower told Marshall that he regarded 'British Bomber Command as one of the most effective parts of our entire organization, always seeking and finding and using new ways for their particular type of aircraft to be of assistance in forwarding the progress of the Armies on the ground'.

When releasing Harris from direct Supreme Command control, Eisenhower reinforced his respect by saying to Harris 'If at any time you believe that we are neglecting opportunities for striking the German in his own country, do not hesitate to tell me about it.'[15] Harris first visited postwar America in 1946. On 6 April 1946, Eisenhower presented him with America's Distinguished Service Medal.

---

10 Harris, *Bomber Offensive*, p. 215
11 *Bomber Harris – Straight from the Horse's Mouth Video*
12 March to September 1944 – which covers the entire time my Dad flew his thirty-four combat sorties
13 Harris, *Bomber Offensive*, p. 214
14 Brookes (RAF Wing Commander) 'An Interview With "Bomber" Harris, 8 September 1975', *Royal Air Force Historical Society Journal* 74, 2020, p. 63
15 Nichol and Rennell, *Tail-End Charlies*, p. 214 & Probert, *Bomber Harris*

Harris in America

In May 1941, Harris was sent to America as the head of an RAF delegation to expedite delivery to Britain of needed war materials. What Harris really wanted was a field command. But at least America depressed him less than being in the Air Ministry.[16] Ten days after his arrival, Harris was summoned to the White House for talks with FDR about the 22 June 1941 German invasion of Soviet Russia. Harris also became friendly with General George Marshall and Admiral John Towers, the first US admiral to rise through Navy ranks as naval aviator. These added to the friendships Harris made with Generals Henry 'Hap' Arnold and Ira Eaker in the 1930s.[17] In 1938 Harris was in the US for six weeks buying aircraft.

It was fortuitous that Harris was in America in 1941 because much happened that year in the evolution of American airpower. The US Army Air Forces, renamed from the US Army Air Corps, were created on 20 June 1941, two days before Germany attacked Russia. General Hap Arnold became Commanding General of the Air Forces, and acting Deputy Chief of Staff for Air. General Ira Eaker, second-in-command of the US Army Eighth Air Force, would be sent in 1942 to England to form VIII Bomber Command, America's counterpart to RAF Bomber Command. To avoid confusion, I will refer to the USAAF's VIII Bomber Command as the 'Mighty Eighth' and the entirety of America's bomber force as 'America's Bombers'. On 1 December 1942, Eaker became Commander of the Mighty Eighth. He advocated at the January 1943 Casablanca Conference round-the-clock bombing by the Mighty Eighth during the day and Bomber Command at night.

Harris in America also met famous pioneer American aviator Jacqueline Cochran. She spoke of female pilots for ferrying. Arnold suggested she take qualified female pilots to Britain to study the ATA use of female pilots. This led in September 1942 to America's WAFS – Women's Auxiliary Ferrying Squadron. Cochran became wartime head of America's WASP – Women Airforce Service Pilots. It employed about a thousand female pilots to ferry planes. Postwar, on 18 May 1953, Cochran was the first woman to break the sound barrier.

Harris was still in America when the Japanese bombed Pearl Harbor. Harris says:

> The first effect of the entry of America into the war was rather to nullify the efforts which the RAF delegation had been making in Washington. The United States at once put a total embargo on the export of munitions to the allies, being driven to do so by the very serious position their own forces found themselves. For the time being, the effect on the RAF was serious, and especially on the

---

16 Harris, p. 59

17 Grant. 'Bomber Harris,' *Air Force Magazine the Official Publication of the Air Force Association*, 1 January 2005

bomber forces, which it had hoped to expand very soon by sending aircraft from America.[18]

However, Churchill soon decided Harris was needed at home.

Harris and Americans

The first of a steady stream of American guests Harris entertained at Springfields was US General Ira Eaker, his counterpart as CinC of the Mighty Eighth. Eaker came to dinner, and stayed several weeks. Harris insisted Eaker be their house guest until his own home was ready, so Eaker lived with Harris until July 1942. On his departure, Eaker wrote Jill 'the warmest of thank-you letters', recalling the comfort and charm of Springfield, and their grand dinners. He said he would never be able to repay 'Jillie' and 'Buddy' for their many kindnesses. Theirs was a lifetime friendship between the two families – the two men even shared the same birthday, for Harris 13 April 1892 and Eaker 13 April 1896.[19] Eaker also accepted Harris's invitation to locate the US HQ with Harris at RAF High Wycombe in Walters Ash, until Eaker found and made operable the Mighty Eighth's HQ. Eaker selected Pinetree at High Wycombe, chosen to ensure close co-operation. It had been an exclusive girls' school, Wycombe Abbey.

On 12 April 1942 General George Marshall visited Harris at Springfields to learn as much as he could about the strategic bomber offensive in which his American airmen would soon participate. Visits followed from other distinguished American airmen, including Generals Carl 'Tooey' Spaatz and then Hap Arnold himself. US Ambassadors William Bullitt, John Winant and Averill Harriman also paid visits, as did Soviet Ambassador to the UK, Ivan Maisky, on 19 July 1942. Other groups of Russians followed, and one of Chinese. Everyone came to enjoy Springfields' hospitality, learn about Bomber Command and meet Sir Arthur Harris.

Harris sums up his relations with the Mighty Eighth in three ways:[20] First: 'If I were asked what were the relations between Bomber Command and the American bomber force, I would say that we had no relations. The word is inapplicable to what actually happened; we and they were one force.' Harris goes on to say both sides did everything possible to help one another. Second, regarding American bomber leadership 'We could have had no better brothers-in-arms than Ira Eaker, Fred Anderson and Jimmy Doolittle, and the Americans could have had no better commanders than these three. I was, and am, privileged to count all three of them as the closest of friends.' Third, regarding American bomber aircrew: 'As for the American bomber crews, they were the bravest of the brave, and I know I am speaking for my own bomber crews when I pay this tribute.'

---

18   Harris, p. 66.
19   Probert, p. 178
20   Harris, *Bomber Offensive*, p. 246

Harris and Germans

Germany's Research Institute for Military History (the 'Institute') says Harris pulled Bomber Command together, and turned it into the lethal force it became.[21] Concerning the character of Harris, the Institute says 'For Harris, the Air Force was the most important service. He did not share the inferiority complex suffered by many RAF officers owing to the lack of tradition in the Air Force as compared with officers of the other two services.'[22] Concerning the relationship of Churchill and Harris, the Institute says:

> In the course of 1942, his ... relationship with Churchill became more and more confident. Churchill's country home, Chequers, was only three minutes [sic] from Harris's house, and Churchill often invited him over, particularly on weekends. He defended Harris, if necessary, against the Air Staff and the aviation minister, and although he never put him under pressure or ordered him to do anything against his convictions, he brought him under his spell. As Harris wrote: 'I never failed to return from those visits invigorated and full of renewed hope and enthusiasm.'[23]

In short, with Harris in charge, Germany's Defence of the Reich Campaign and our strategic bombing offensive had become, to borrow an American expression, a brand-new ballgame.

Another charge laid against Harris is that he thought he could win by smashing German morale. I explore this further later in this book. Suffice to say here it served the Allies well that Hitler believed that smashing German morale was what Harris was trying to do. Harris says 'The idea that the main object of bombing German industrial cities was to break the enemy's morale proved to be wholly unsound ... the Gestapo saw to it that they were docile ... "morale" bombing was comparatively ineffective against so well organized a police state as Germany.'[24]

Harris at Home at Springfields

The house Harris, his wife Jill and their young daughter Jackie (Jacqueline Jill Harris, born 1939) lived in while he was CinC of Bomber Command was called Springfields (sometimes Springfield). It is a spacious mid-eighteenth-century home at Cryers Hill set on four acres of grounds, with formal and kitchen

---

21 Institute, Vol. VI, p. 562
22 Institute, Vol. VI, p. 562
23 Institute, Vol. VI, p. 563
24 Harris, pp. 78-9

gardens, a paddock and an orchard.[25] It is near the village of Great Kingshill in Buckinghamshire, and about five miles (8 km) from Bomber Command HQ at RAF High Wycombe in the village of Walters Ash. It had a bomb-proof en-suite bedroom, doors reinforced with steel, and a shower of the toughest bullet-proof glass. It is described as 'impenetrable, providing a haven from any type of attack.'[26] Best of all, it was a ten-minute drive to Churchill at Chequers.

Although some dismiss Harris as an anti-social recluse, I discovered thanks to Henry Probert[27] that Harris and his wife Jill entertained family, friends and those important to Bomber Command a great deal at Springsfields. His first guests included Lord Trenchard, Father of the RAF, and Sir Richard Stafford Cripps, Lord Privy Seal and Leader of the House of Commons. Others soon followed, including Herbert Morrison, Home Secretary; Anthony Eden, Foreign Secretary; Clement Atlee, Deputy Prime Minister; Ernest Bevan, Minister of Labour; Archibald Sinclair, Secretary of State for Air; Brendan Bracken, Minister of Information and Churchill confidant; and nine Canadian and American production chiefs in October 1943. His naval guests included RN Vice Admiral John Henry Godfrey, Head of Naval Intelligence; and US Admiral Harold Stark, Commander of US Naval Forces in Europe. Prime ministers Jan Smuts of South Africa and Godfrey Huggins of Southern Rhodesia visited Harris, as did Canadian High Commissioner Vincent Massey. On 10 January 1944 Harris had as his overnight house guest General Sir Bernard Montgomery. Monty had just returned to England to take command of 21 Army Group. During that visit, Monty and Harris laid the groundwork for Bomber Command's participation in the D Day operation less than five months hence.

Harris and Royalty

From the Royal Family, first came the king's younger brother Prince George, the Duke of Kent, an RAF officer, on 31 March 1942. Next came the king's sister-in-law, the Duchess of Gloucester, Princess Alice. She was head of the WAAF (Women's Auxiliary Air Force) from 1939 until 1945. She became viceregal consort of Australia when her husband Prince Henry, Duke of Gloucester, also a brother of the king, served as Governor General. She continued to rise in the RAF. By the time of her death on 29 October 2004 at age 102, she was not only the world's longest lived Royal, but also an RAF air chief marshal.

Then, on 7 February 1944, Harris received a Royal Visit from King George VI and his consort, Queen Elizabeth. Her Majesty as Queen Mother postwar served as Patron of the British Bomber Command Association. She was a major champion

---

25 'Top security house on sale for £1.75 million,' BBC News, 17 August 2001

26 Claridge 'Bomber Harris's VERY elegant bunker: 18th Century house which was home to RAF Marshal Harris could be yours for £3.75 million,' *The Mail on Sunday*, 24 June 2017.

27 Probert, *Bomber Harris*, pp. 160 & 177-81.

of Sir Arthur and his heroic Bomber Boys. Extra Air Equerry RAF Group Captain James Pelly-Fry described how absorbed His Majesty was in all he saw on their 7 February visit, and how the Queen demonstrated her immense charm and special style of communicating with people. Their visit was a Harris highlight.[28]

Harris, Churchill and Portal

I mention all this to demonstrate that Harris was no recluse. He worked hard, not only leading Bomber Command, but also proclaiming its accomplishments to a wide range of wartime leaders and opinion-makers. You may, however, note no mention of Churchill or of Harris's immediate superior RAF Chief of Air Staff Sir Charles 'Peter' Portal. That is because Harris dined with Churchill at Chequers and met with Portal regularly in London.

A quick aside regarding Chequers. Chartwell was regarded as too risky because of its location in Kent, and its visibility. When 'the moon was too high' Chequers also was regarded as too visible and so vulnerable to air attack. Churchill instead spent those weekends at Ditchley Park. It was virtually invisible from the air.

Harris and Hostile Media

Harris also entertained leaders of the media, knowing he and his Bomber Boys were subject to continuous public scrutiny, praise and criticism. Denis Richards, the author of the Introduction to the 1990 edition of Harris's book *Bomber Offensive* (first edition 1947), said Harris was easy to misquote and misrepresent because

> Harris was fond of bold generalizations, which in conversation he would deliver with an air of mischievous humour, but which do not also impress in print … . He was not a man to weigh every word as is the habit of some senior officers and politicians, nor was he a man who would spend more time analyzing something he had written than he had spent writing it.'[29]

Not all media trashed Harris. One newspaper, noting in 1992 criticism of the Harris statue in The Strand, remarked that 'Had it not been for the Boys of Bomber Command and thousands more British servicemen like them, Europe would not exist, and the only statue in the Strand would be of Adolf Hitler.'[30]

---

28 Probert, p. 179
29 Hampton, *Selected for Aircrew*, p. 338
30 Cooper, *Target – Dresden*, p. 241

Harris and Canada

Harris initially resisted Mackenzie King's demand that the RCAF operate a separate RCAF group within Bomber Command. Mackenzie King prevailed, and No. 6 Group RCAF was formed on 25 October 1942, and first flew combat sorties in January 1943. No. 6 Group had a shaky start – in 1943 it was the least effective Bomber Command group, although No. 3 Group, still operating with Stirlings, wasn't great either. Also, in spite of Canada's demand for Lancasters, No. 6 Group was given inferior Halifaxes and Wellingtons. But times change. In autumn 1943, No. 6 Group was the first to receive the more powerful Halifax Mk III with comparable performance and bombload to Lancasters, although the Halifax bomb bay could not carry Tallboy or Grand Slam bombs.

For the RCAF, 28 February 1944 was pivotal – that day a new leader took command of No. 6 Group. He was RCAF Air Vice-Marshal Clifford ('Black Mike') McEwan. Under Black Mike's leadership, No. 6 Group RCAF rose to become what some say was the most effective of the bomber groups. It achieved both the highest survival rate and the best accuracy rate of all bomber groups.[31] Statistics? No. 6 Group RCAF flew 40,822 sorties, lost 814 aircraft and 4,255 aircrew, and earned over 8,000 decorations for bravery.[32]

At war's end, Harris acknowledged that No. 6 Group RCAF and Canadian airmen were second to none. Harris joined Black Mike on 31 May 1945 at RCAF Middleton St George in Yorkshire to bid farewell to the first RCAF contingent returning home to Canada. Harris told his Canadian airmen: 'You leave this country, after all you have done, with a reputation that is equal to any and surpassed by none. We in Bomber Command have always regarded the Canadian Group and Canadian crews outside the Group as among the very best.'[33]

Postwar – Rhodesia

Godfrey Huggins, the prime minister of Southern Rhodesia (now Zimbabwe), asked the British government to appoint Harris Governor of Southern Rhodesia. Huggins wanted a 'Rhodesian' for this position, so saw Harris as ideal. Harris, who self-identified as 'Rhodesian' his whole adult life, agreed that being governor would be perfect for him. The problem was timing. He would have to start in January 1945. Some say bombing had worn out its usefulness by 1945, indeed after D Day, but Churchill knew otherwise, so he opposed Harris departing in January. Churchill called it 'that critical point in the war'.[34] In fact, nor would Harris have willingly departed Bomber Command then. He and Churchill both knew Bomber

---

31 Wikipedia 'Clifford McEwen'

32 Bomber Command Museum of Canada, Nanton Alberta, www.bombercommandmuseum.ca

33 *Reap the Whirlwind*, p. 362

34 Probert, p. 358

Command remained vital to victory in the final months of the war, and Harris was essential. As it happens, on 11 December 1979, Churchill's son-in-law, Lord Soames, became the last Governor of Southern Rhodesia. His wife was Churchill's daughter Mary. His successor in Southern Rhodesia on 18 April 1980 was Canaan Banana as President of Zimbabwe.

The reason Harris self-identified as Rhodesian is that, at the tender age of 17 in 1910, to the disappointment of his family, he emigrated to Southern Rhodesia. They wanted him to stay in England to continue his education, or commence a career. In Southern Rhodesia, young Harris earned his living as a miner, coach driver and ultimately farmer. Then the First World War broke out. Harris volunteered in the 1st Rhodesian Regiment. When the South-West African Campaign ended in July 1915, his regiment was disbanded and Harris discharged on 31 July. He returned to farming but the War continued, so in October 1915 Harris arrived in England among a party of 300 Southern Rhodesian volunteers. He was rejected by the Royal Artillery, but then accepted by the Royal Flying Corps.[35] He remained in what in 1918 became the RAF until November 1945 – thirty years.

Victory Honours List Omission

Something which still stings today was the omission of Harris, and by implication Bomber Command, from the Victory Honours List in 1945. The one man my research reveals to be most responsible was John Strachey. Originally a disciple of the British Fascist Oswald Mosley, Strachey was elected an MP in 1929, broke with Mosley in 1931, lost his seat that year, and was a communist sympathizer in the 1930s. He broke with the Communist Party in 1940 and joined the RAF. There, astonishingly, he served in planning and public relations roles including in the Air Ministry's Directorate of Bombing Operations. Strachey made official broadcasts about Bomber Command. Harris complained, and was threatened by a senior officer he would be sued for libel if he did not 'shut up'. Strachey was elected a Labour MP in 1945, and Clement Attlee became Labour prime minister. Attlee immediately appointed Strachey Under Secretary of State for Air. Harris says of Strachey, 'It was partly due to this individual trying to get at me that Bomber Command did not get the credit it deserved, and to some extent he succeeded.'[36]

---

35 Wikipedia *Sir Arthur Harris 1st Baronet*
36 Brookes, 'An Interview with "Bomber" Harris 8 September 1975', *Royal Air Force Historical Society Journal* 74, 2020, pp. 56-7

Postwar Air Ministry Battles[37]

The Germans had scarcely ceased firing at the end of the Second World War when Harris found himself in a prolonged war of attrition with his own Air Ministry superiors. Harris said, 'However, for some extraordinary reason, the Air Ministry propagandists – call them what you will – have never played up the bomber offensive properly'. At the heart of this was the Harris *Despatch*. Detailed summaries of Second World War activities from senior officers of every major army, naval and air force command were published as *Despatches* in the *London Gazette*. The Harris *Despatch* was conspicuous by its absence, given how important Bomber Command was. Why was no *Despatch* published from Harris? Bomber Command silence was particularly noticeable, given prompt publication of Lord Downing's Fighter Command *Despatch* on the Battle of Britain.

Under a covering letter of 18 December 1945, Harris submitted his *Despatch on the War Operations undertaken by Bomber Command from the 23rd February, 1942, when I assumed command, to the 8th of May, 1945 when warlike operations were concluded*. Harris noted his submission was in conformity with 'King's Regulations and Air Council Instructions', paragraph 47b. His *Despatch* was about 150,000 words. One hundred copies were made and circulated. The Harris *Despatch* caused quite a stir. Bomber Command was no longer popular with politicians – they were seeking reconciliation with our former enemies in Europe. Harris reminded them of Second World War directives they now preferred to forget. Worst of all, from the bureaucrats' perspective, Harris seriously criticized other areas of government affecting Bomber Command.

Criticisms by Harris of the wartime British Government included:

- There was insufficient provision of airfields
- The Works Department suffered 'from lack of experience and supervisory personnel'
- Bomber Command aircraft were 'constantly diverted from their main job of destroying the enemy's will and capacity to resist in favour of targets of secondary importance which are causing annoyance to one or other Government Department'
- Armament design for his aircraft 'showed throughout a standard of incompetence which had the most serious repercussions on the efficiency and effectiveness of the Bomber Offensive'
- Harris recommends the most drastic overhaul of the design personnel concerned and the organization responsible
- Loose talk about planned flying could have undermined Bomber Command effectiveness and resulted in 'a considerable reduction in bombs dropped, thereby leading to a prolongation of the War'

---

37 Grehan & Mace, *Bomber Harris – Sir Arthur Harris' Despatch on War Operations 1942-1945*, pp. 1-7

- Some numbers Harris used did not tally with official records, particularly regarding success in controversial areas such as area bombing

The public's demand to see this *Despatch*, and its growing public unhappiness over lack of recognition of Bomber Command's contribution to winning the war, further complicated Air Ministry thinking on how to handle (or should I say bury) the Harris *Despatch*. Worse, from the Air Ministry's perspective, some RAF leaders defended Harris. For example, Air Vice-Marshal Baker, wartime Commander of No. 12 Group and now RAF Director General of Personnel, wrote on 10 September 1946 'The Marshal [Harris] was never one to mince matters, and I am sure his *Despatch* would lose much of its historical value and interest if we watered down too far the forthright language he has used throughout.' Air Vice-Marshal Sir Ralph Cochrane, wartime Commander of No. 5 Group and now Commander of Transport Command, was highly supportive of Harris and said his *Despatch* 'provides a very fair summing up of the situation'. The most detailed analysis of the Harris *Despatch* was by Air Vice-Marshal Sydney Osborne Bufton. In wartime, he was a Director of Bomber Operations under Harris. Bufton's 28 December 1946 report stated that the Harris *Despatch* is 'well presented, comprehensive, and supported by a wealth of statistics and technical information'. Bufton also observed the reality that the Harris *Despatch* was written from a Bomber Command perspective, and therefore in Bufton's words 'tended to find virtue at home, and all waywardness elsewhere'.

The Harris *Despatch* generated a tremendous flurry of internal Air Ministry counter-attacks. It is amazing how ingenious bureaucrats were then, and still are today, in protecting themselves, shifting blame, and attacking Harris. Soon the issue became whether this *Despatch* should be published. The situation escalated to the point where a decision had to be made by the Chief of Air Staff, Sir Arthur Tedder. He dithered. He said reasons for not publishing the *Despatch* were: it is argued it has errors; the Soviets might find it useful; and it has 'strongly expressed criticism of the Air Ministry'. On the other hand, he understood public demand for the *Despatch*, and that the Press is saying 'Bomber Command's contribution to victory has been insufficiently recognized by H.M.G.' Then Tedder decided. His decision? On 5 October 1947, Tedder made his 'final conclusion and recommendation that the *despatch* by Sir Arthur Harris should *not* be published.' (my emphasis). On 20 February 1960, British prime minister Harold Macmillan shafted Harris in much the same way, for much the same reason. Some things never change. More on Macmillan momentarily.

Harris Postwar – Safmarine[38]

Postwar, Harris was particularly easy to defame because he disappeared. He returned to the land he loved, southern Africa. His RAF pension was woefully inadequate.

---

38 Probert, *Bomber Harris– His Life and Times*, pp. 365-9

Harris had a young family. He needed a job. Thwarted from becoming postwar governor of his beloved Southern Rhodesia, Harris looked elsewhere for work and found it in South Africa. In November 1945, Harris accepted the position of Managing Director Safmarine – the South African Marine Corporation – to create direct shipping between America and South Africa. In February 1946, he moved his family from Britain to America to finalize details for this new venture. Then off he and his family went to South Africa. Arriving in Cape Town on 18 May 1945, Harris immediately set up Safmarine and invited his Bomber Command aide Peter Tomlinson to join him. During the war on photo-reconnaissance duties, Tomlinson crash-landed through engine failure in 1941 and so spent the remainder of the war as a PoW. His captors never discovered his connection to Harris.[39] Tomlinson was the godfather of Harris's daughter Jackie.[40] Delighted to be invited, Tomlinson resigned his RAF commission and arrived in Cape Town on 25 June 1946. Harris inspired great loyalty in his staff. They established their offices in Old Cape Town adjacent to the Parliament Buildings which I visited in September 2019 and were seriously burnt by arson on 2 and 3 January 2022. In both South Africa and America, Harris's tremendous work ethic and organizational skills proved invaluable, as did his reputation and contacts. An example is Averell Harriman, wartime US Ambassador to the Soviet Union and postwar to the United Kingdom. Harriman had, on 7 October 1946, become President Truman's Secretary of Commerce. His personal support was essential to the success Harris had in persuading the US Marine Commission to release victory ships to Safmarine. Safmarine and Harris himself soon gained 'an increasingly favourable press for the standards of its ships, the facilities for its passengers, and the quality and treatment of its crews.'

Postwar Praise[41]

Since leaving Britain, Harris maintained few formal RAF connections, but in July 1946 did accept being President of the new Cape Town Branch of the Royal Air Force Association. On 22 September 1946, while Harris was in South Africa, Fighter Command C-in-C for the Battle of Britain Lord Dowding declared in the Albert Hall in London at the Royal Air Force Association Festival of Reunion 'how Sir Arthur Harris hated the work he had to do, with what inflexible determination did he carry it to its conclusion, and how magnificently was he supported by his bomber boys. Truly, if Fighter Command's Calvary was measured in months, theirs was reckoned in years.' In April 1947, while on Safmarine business in Canada, Harris spoke in Montreal at the first No. 6 Group RCAF Bomber Command Reunion. In 1950, Harris on Safmarine business, made his first postwar trip back to Britain. He was entertained at dinner on 19 June at the Dorchester by the Pathfinder

---

39 Probert, pp. 159-60

40 Probert, p. 87

41 Probert, p. 370

Association. Father of the RAF Lord Trenchard attended. Six years later, Harris served as a pall-bearer at Lord Trenchard's funeral. Of all Harris supporters, Lord Trenchard gave him the most unqualified backing, including by introducing him to key people.[42] While still in London, on 6 July 1950 Harris attended the annual dinner of the Chamber of Shipping where feature speaker Field Marshal Viscount Montgomery, as I have previously mentioned, declared about Harris 'I doubt whether any single man did more in winning the war than he did. I doubt whether that is generally realized.'

Back in South Africa, on 11 September 1950 Afrikaner Boer general in the Boer War and then long-time South African Prime Minister and close Churchill confidant Field Marshal Jan Smuts died. Postwar Harris had maintained friendly personal relations with Churchill, including sending 'goodies' Churchill loved every Christmas. Churchill asked Harris to represent him at Smuts' funeral. Afterwards, Churchill wrote to Harris 'Dear Bert, I am proud and honoured to have acted, through you, as one of the Pall Bearers at this farewell to a great friend and comrade.'[43] Three years later, with weakening health, his wife Jill longing to return home, and his daughter Jackie turning 14, thereby raising questions regarding her education, Harris in autumn 1953 resigned from Safmarine and returned to Britain. He remained, however, on Safmarine's board for part-time duties in Britain and America until 1960. One of his final Safmarine acts in 1953 was to engage wartime No. 8 Group Pathfinders Commander Don Bennett to draft plans for an airline flying Comets to connect South Africa to America.[44]

Back in Britain

On 4 May 1953, Harris and Jill arrived at Southampton aboard the RMS *Queen Mary*. His arrival received national media coverage. Four days later, he attended his first Bomber Reunion – the annual dinner of the Pathfinders' Association. And of course 2 June 1953 was the Big Day – the Queen's Coronation. Probert observes, regarding Harris riding to the Coronation in the RAF's first carriage, 'As he rode in the RAF's first carriage with three fellow Marshals, Douglas, Slessor and Tedder, Harris was for the first time in his proper place, a position reinforced on 15 July when at Odiham he attended the Queen's Review of the Royal Air Force. The *Daily Express* wrote simply of this day, 'Bomber Harris seems to have made his peace with the RAF.' In October 1953, Harris attended the opening of the RAF Runnymede Memorial which I visited with my sons Ruaridh and Guy Roland MacKenzie on 1 June 2019. In May 1954 Harris attended the unveiling at Lincoln Cathedral of the Memorial Window to the 55,000 killed in Bomber Command which I visited with Lancaster Memorial Spire Lead Volunteer Dave

---

42 Probert, p. 160
43 Probert, *Bomber Harris*, p. 370
44 Probert, *Bomber Harris*, p. 372

Gilbert on 12 May 2019. In November 1955, Harris attended the York Minister Thanksgiving Memorial.

As mentioned, Harris served as a Pall Bearer at Lord Trenchard's funeral in Westminster Abbey in February 1956. Then Harris spoke at the Cambridge American Military Cemetery in July 1956, attended the unveiling of the Smuts statue in Parliament Square in November 1956, and was invited to occupy one of the stalls allotted to the Knights of the Bath that month in the presence of the Queen at the Henry VII Chapel in Westminster Abbey.[45] In 1957 Harris attended the reception for Commonwealth Prime Ministers, in 1958 the Royal Air Force fortieth Anniversary Dinner, and in 1959 the dinner President Eisenhower hosted at the American Embassy to honour Churchill and other top Allied leaders of the Second World War. Harris also attended at RAF Scampton in 1959 when the Queen Mother presented its Standard to 617 Squadron. But other than these events, Harris largely declined RAF invitations in the 1950s.[46]

Two Prime Ministers Fail Harris

Harris sustained blows by a pair of British prime ministers in 1960 which helped fuel Bomber Command misconceptions still current among too many today.

Prime Minister Clement Attlee: In November 1960 the *Sunday Times* published an article about Attlee's forthcoming memoirs. Attlee was reported in the *Sunday Times* as thinking that Harris was 'never frightfully good', and that Harris 'should have concentrated more on military targets, particularly oil, instead of attacking cities'. Attlee apologized when Harris challenged him, and purportedly made changes to his memoirs, citing 'the dangers of failing memory' for errors, but refused to publish an apology.

Prime Minister Harold Macmillan: On 20 February 1960 Macmillan followed in the 5 October 1946 footsteps of Sir Arthur Tedder in sacrificing Harris, Bomber Command, and the truth to protect instead the government's image. For Tedder, it was the 18 December 1945 Harris *Despatch*. For Macmillan, it was the four-volume Official History of the Royal Air Force *Strategic Air Offensive Against Germany* in the Second World War as part of the *History of the Second World War* series.

The Official History was written by Sir Charles Webster and Dr Noble Frankland. Harris in South Africa had been informally contacted by Webster, but not invited to officially consult with the historians, and so had no involvement in its creation. Had Harris been officially invited, he could have intervened on matters he disputed.

---

45 Probert, p. 375-6
46 Probert, p. 378

When in 1959 the draft was being reviewed by RAF and civilian experts, and the Cabinet advisory panel, Harris was not included.

On 10 October 1959, Harris entered the fray, strongly disputing the Webster and Frankland *Official History* findings. Harris later said his objections included:[47]

- The authors 'didn't even take the trouble to look at the Bomber Command records to see what we did and where we went'.
- One of the authors, Dr Nobel Frankland, was a junior officer in Bomber Command who flew a single tour as a navigator, whose views were already known in his thesis for his doctorate, and who 'dammed with faint praise everything Bomber Command did'
- The authors made too much of the 'bloody nose' Bomber Command got at Nuremberg on 30 March 1944 and were wrong about what happened after
- The authors relied too heavily on American postwar reports on the effectiveness of the strategic bombing offensive

This controversy rapidly escalated up from the Air Ministry to Macmillan as prime minister. On 20 February 1960 Macmillan decided the risk to his government of publishing this flawed *Official History* as it now stood was not as great as the risk of being accused that the government 'gagged the authors', so he authorized its publication. It was published on 2 October 1961. The *Times* welcomed its publication with the newspaper headline 'Row Breaks Over Last War Bombing – Sir Arthur Harris's Retort to Charge of Costly Failure'. Harris himself said every smear-monger belittling the efforts of the bombers written since was based on this *Official History*. And so, to his shame, Macmillan's 1961 handling of this *Official History*, in which Macmillan cared more about politics than the truth, led to Bomber Command being branded a 'costly failure'. Speaking of shame, Macmillan's 1962 Vassall affair in which Admiralty clerk John Vassall was passing secrets to the Russians, followed by Macmillan's 1963 Profumo affair, the sex scandal involving Macmillan's Secretary of State for War John Profumo and Christine Keeler, led to the collapse of his government and a year later Labour Party leader Harold Wilson being elected prime minister.

Not a Politician, But a Leader

Harris was ill-suited for public political battles where rhetoric prevails over truth. This meant Harris was unable to override Churchill's flawed March 1945 signal to General Ismay, Churchill's failure to mention Bomber Command in his praise of the armed forces, and endless defamation thereafter. Harris was not equipped to fight politicians and the media. The resulting trashing of Bomber Command

---

[47] Andrew Brookes RAF Wing Commander *An Interview with 'Bomber' Harris 08 September 1975* Royal Air Force Historical Society Journal 74, 2020

brought great grief to the final years of the Bomber Boys. Some even believed these terrible falsehoods. Tragically, they died thinking they had failed. In reality, their selfless service in extreme danger had been vital to victory.

However, the revered Father of the RAF, Lord Trenchard, on 29 April 1945 wrote to Harris

> Words are of little use but I would like to try. Your great task is over and by your relentless efforts you have succeeded. I know no man that could have been more determined to carry out what you did. I know no one who could have combined such determination with technical and operational knowledge. I give all credit to your staff and your wonderful aircrews and maintenance crews and all. But it was your leadership and knowledge that made Bomber Command the magnificent force it was. The world should thank you. Words I cannot find to say what I feel about the part the Royal Air Force has played in this war. Forgive this inadequate letter.[48]

David Bashaw cites Henry Probert's opinion that Lord Trenchard's letter probably touched Harris more than the host of accolades Harris would later receive.

I think the best way to sum up Sir Arthur Harris is by quoting Eisenhower. After serving two terms as America's president, Eisenhower wrote to Harris 'as one of my close associates in OVERLORD, a special word of thanks should go to you for your skill and selfless dedication to the cause in which we all served. No historian could possibly be aware of the depths of my obligation to you.'[49]

---

48 Bashaw, p. 437

49 Brookes, 'An Interview with "Bomber" Harris 8 September 1975,' *Royal Air Force Historical Society Journal* 74, 2020, pp. 63-4

Part II

BOMBER COMMAND BACKGROUND

Chapter Seven

Opinions

Allied Leaders

Churchill said 'The Fighters are our salvation ... but the Bombers alone provide the means of victory.'

FDR said 'Hitler built a fortress around Europe, but he forgot to put a roof on it.'

Stalin said 'I welcome the bombing of Essen, Berlin and other industrial centres of Germany. Every blow delivered by your Air Force to the vital German centres evokes a most lively echo in the hearts of many millions throughout the length and breadth of our country.'[1]

Eisenhower said 'I have come to regard British Bomber Command as one of the most effective parts of my entire organization, always seeking and finding and using new ways for their particular type of aircraft to be of assistance in forwarding the progress of the Armies on the ground.'[2]

Montgomery said 'First of all you must win the battle of the air. This must come before you can start a single sea or land engagement. If you examine the course of my campaign you will find that we never fought a land battle until the air battle had been won.'[3]

Harris elaborates – 'Victory, speedy and complete, awaits the side which first employs air power as it should be employed. Germany, entangled in the meshes of vast land campaigns, cannot now disengage her air power for a strategically proper application. She missed victory through air power by a hair's breadth in 1940'[4]

---

1 Cooper, *Target-Dresden*, p. 230

2 Cooper, op. cit.

3 Cooper, p. 238

4 Inspiring Quotes www.inspiringquotes.us/author/2176-sir-arthur-harris-1st-baronet

OPINIONS

Field Marshal Lord Alanbrooke, Chief of the Imperial General Staff, wrote in his private diaries (that were published postwar) of the 'brilliant skills of Bomber Aircrew' and the 'outstanding assistance they gave to Allied Armies during the Invasion'.

General Sir Brian Horrocks, a Corps commander in North-West Europe post D Day, says 'In my view the continuous Allied strategic air offensive was the most important operation of the war. Apart from the devastation it caused, its effect on allied morale was great. The air power at our command made it almost impossible for German reinforcements to move into Normandy by day, I am firmly convinced that the airmen did more to defeat the German armies than any action that was fought on the ground.'[5]

Montgomery sums it up best, saying 'the British bombers are the greatest of all in the destruction of the German Armies as a whole.'[6]

Dominions

Australia[7] Under the heading 'Australians in Bomber Command' Australia says

'Australians contributed to, and suffered greatly in, the British Royal Air Force (RAF) Bomber Command. Of the 55,000 aircrew who 'failed to return' or were 'missing in operations' during the Second World War, 3,486 were Australians of Bomber Command. These men represented 20 per cent of all Australian service personnel 'killed in action' in all theatres of the war. (Royal Australian Air Force) No. 460 Squadron dropped the greatest tonnage of bombs and flew the most Lancaster sorties during the war. The Roll of Honour lists the names of 589 Australians who died serving that squadron.' In other words, while Bomber Command had only 2 per cent of the Australians fighting in the Second World War, 20 per cent of Australians killed in combat died in Bomber Command.

As mentioned, I am a member of the Bomber Command in Australia Association, Inc. I'm told that, until a few years ago, Australian failure of remembrance of Bomber Command was just as shameful as it remains today here in Canada. However, their Bomber Command Association grows stronger each year thanks to the children, grandchildren and great-grandchildren of Australian Bomber Command aircrew unhappy with Australia's postwar failure of remembrance. These next three generations, now known as the 'Bomber Command Family in Australia', number a *quarter of a million* Australians.[8] Imagine how many Canadians are members of the yet to be formed Bomber Command Family in Canada. And keep in mind the many Bomber

---

5 Hampton, *Selected for Aircrew*, pp. 214-15

6 Cooper, p 238

7 www.anzacportal.dva.gov.au

8 Bomber Command Association in Australia Inc. *Newsletter* No. 69, Autumn 2019, p. 4.

Boys who have no descendants because they were killed. Their nieces and nephews and their descendants should also be counted in each nation's Bomber Command family.

Canada[9] Under the heading *Canadians In Bomber Command* Canada says

> The efforts of the approximately 50,000 Canadians who served with the Royal Canadian Air Force (RCAF) and Royal Air Force (RAF) in Bomber Command operations over occupied Europe was one of our country's most significant contributions during the Second World War …. By the end of the war, we had the fourth largest air force of the Allied powers. Approximately 250,000 brave men and women served in the RCAF, many of them with Bomber Command …. The men who served in Bomber Command faced some of the most difficult odds of anyone fighting in the war. For much of the conflict, the regular duration for a tour of duty was 30 combat sorties. The risks were so high, however, that almost half of all aircrew never made it to the end of their tour. Despite the heavy losses, Bomber Command was able to maintain a steady stream of aircraft flying over U-boat bases, docks, railways and industrial cities in Germany, as well as enemy targets in occupied Europe from Norway to France.

In addition, Canada's *National Bomber Command Memorial* says:[10]

> The bomber offensive mounted by the Commonwealth countries during the Second World War has been described as the most gruelling and continuous operation of war ever waged. It lasted for some 2,000 days, and for four long years, while the world waited for the tide slowly to turn, Bomber Command offered the only weapon capable of waging war against Hitler's European fortress. Bomber Command's successes were purchased at a terrible cost. Of the volunteers who flew, over 55,000 were killed. 10,000 of these were Canadians.

New Zealand. Under the heading *New Zealanders in the Royal Air Force* New Zealand says:[11]

> By 1944 more than 6,000 New Zealanders were based in the United Kingdom, serving in the Royal Air Force (RAF). From the formation of the Royal New Zealand Air Force (RNZAF) in 1937, young men had been trained as officers at Wigram and posted for short stints to the

---

9 Government of Canada Website www.veterans.gc.ca
10 Canada's Bomber Command Memorial and Museum, Nanton Alberta www.bombercommandmuseum.ca
11 www.nzhistory.govt.nz/war/d-day/nzers-in-the-raf

RAF. As the Second World war loomed, the New Zealand government offered more airmen to the RAF. When war was declared the RNZAF was mobilized and volunteers were called for to serve in either the RNZAF or the RAF for as long as the war lasted .... From April 1940, 7,000 more New Zealanders sailed for Canada as part of the Empire Air Training Scheme .... New Zealanders trained in Canada as pilots, navigators, wireless operators, air gunners and bomb aimers. Once in England, the New Zealanders were posted to Operational Training Units before being assigned to squadrons. The average age of the men when they began their operational careers was 21 years. They were expected to fly a 'tour' of 30 sorties, or combat flights, before being given time out. There were seven squadrons with a New Zealand identity in the RAF, manned largely by New Zealanders. Two of these were in Bomber Command (75 and 487) .... The majority of New Zealand airmen in the RAF were not in New Zealand squadrons but flew alongside men from Canada, Australia, South Africa and the United Kingdom. New Zealand was represented, at some stage, in almost all RAF squadrons.

These percentages are gigantic. Paul tells me that 45 per cent is the overall loss figure across all 125,000 airmen from sixty-two nations. With such enormous casualties suffered by all four Bomber Command nations, why is not Bomber Command better known and better understood? Inaccurate books, articles and documentaries, some sensationalist, and too many defamatory, obscure official Allied commentary.

Royalty

Australia, Britain, Canada and New Zealand share the same Head of State. During the war, our shared Head of State was King George VI. Today it is his daughter, Queen Elizabeth II. Our mutual Sovereign is a major unifying force for good. And the Royal Family remain staunch supporters of Bomber Command and Harris. Royal Family support has shown itself in many ways. Highlights include:

First World War: Prince Albert, the future King George VI, was the Officer in Charge of Boys in the Royal Naval Service training at Cranwell when the RAF was created 1 April 1918. Prince Albert transferred with Cranwell from the RN to the RAF. He was the first member of the Royal Family to be a pilot. Towards the end of the First World War, Prince Albert served in Trenchard's staff at RAF HQ in France.

26 April 1923: Prince Albert married Lady Elizabeth Bowes-Lyon, the future Queen Mother, in his RAF uniform. His great grandson Prince William was likewise married to Catherine wearing his RAF blue sash with his wings over his red Guards uniform on 29 April 2011.

BOMBER COMMAND

Second World War: King George VI and his Queen visited multiple Bomber Bases during the war. 'Visits to the [Bomber Command] operating stations by Royalty were always of huge significance.'[12] Here is my sampling of these visits.

1 February 1942: The Duke of Kent visited 405 (Vancouver) Squadron RCAF[13] at Pocklington. No. 405 was an Article XV Squadron formed on 23 April 1941 as Canada's first bomber squadron. The duke was King George VI's youngest brother. He was commissioned an RAF group captain in 1937. On 23 July 1941, he was made air commodore on the Welfare Section of the RAF Inspector General's Staff, in which capacity he paid official visits to RAF stations to help boost morale.

30 April 1942: Princess Alice visited 405 (Vancouver) Squadron RCAF.[14] She was the last surviving grandchild of Queen Victoria, and the wife of the Earl of Athlone, wartime Governor-General of Canada from 1940 until 1946. The Earl was the brother of Queen Mary. Queen Mary was the mother of King George VI and the grandmother of Queen Elizabeth II. Princess Alice was the Honorary Air Commandant of the Royal Canadian Air Force Women's Division.

25 August 1942: The Duke of Kent was killed in a plane crash. This was the first time in 500 years that a member of the Royal Family was killed on active service.[15]

25 May 1943: The King and Queen paid an official visit to No. 8 Bomber Group Pathfinders Headquarters at RAF Wyton.[16]

7 February 1944: The King and Queen paid an official visit to Air Marshal Arthur Harris at Bomber Command Headquarters at High Wycombe.

11 August 1944: The King and Queen and Princess Elizabeth visited No. 6 Group RCAF Station Linton-on-Ouse, a 62 'Beaver' RCAF Operational Base, where the King presented Commanding Officer RCAF Group Captain John Fauquier of Ottawa a Bar to his Distinguished Service Order. Johnny Fauquier is known to some as the 'King of the Pathfinders'[17] and 'Canada's Greatest Bomber Pilot'.

8 June 1945: King George VI and Harris were among those at Cranwell for the RAF College's Silver Jubilee.

---

12 Birrell, *Johnny - Canada's Greatest Bomber Pilot*, p,.47
13 Birrell, p. 47
14 Birrell, p. 59
15 *Newbattle at War* Newbattle Parish in WWI and WWII www.newbattleatwar.com
16 Birrell, p. 99
17 Birrell, p 147

OPINIONS

13 June 1945: King George VI presented Harris with his GCB (Order of the Bath) Knighthood

2 June 1953: Harris rode in the RAF's First Carriage with fellow Air Marshals Douglas, Slessor and Tedder for the Queen's Coronation

November 1956: Harris was installed [given his own stall] in the Henry VII Chapel as a Knight of the Order of the Bath in the presence of The Queen.

July 1964: Harris was invited to Buckingham Palace to attend The Queen's presentation of a new Colour for the Royal Air Force

November 1969: At the funeral of RAF Air Marshal Lord Sholto Douglas, Harris represented The Queen and so was transported to Westminster Abbey in The Queen's Rolls Royce complete with Crown.

October 1972: Harris was asked to perform what he regarded as the most exalted ceremonial task in this life – in the presence of The Queen and her guest, President Gustav Heinemann of West Germany, Harris installed Five Knights of the Garter.

12 April 1983: The Queen Mother opened the Bomber Command Museum which had been supported strongly by the Duke of Edinburgh. Her Majesty remarked how 'particularly pleased' she was that Harris was present because he 'would always be identified with the wonderful achievements of his Command'.

31 May 1992: The Queen Mother personally unveiled the statue of Harris on The Strand in London amid great controversy that she with elegance chose to ignore.

1998: Harris's son-in-law, the Honourable Nicholas Assheton, served as Treasurer to the Queen Mother from 1998 until her death in 2002. Assheton's wife Jackie [Jacqueline Jill Harris] was Harris's youngest daughter. She was born in 1939.

29 April 2011: Prince William married Catherine wearing his blue RAF sash and wings over his Guards' uniform

28 June 2012: The Queen brought with her twenty-three members of the Royal Family[18] when Her Majesty unveiled London's magnificent Bomber Command Memorial in Green Park. How's that for Royal Family support? I'm told not a single politician showed up, and no government money was contributed

---

18 Hazel Dobbie *NZ Bomber Command Veterans Remember Those Who Died* Royal New Zealand Air Force HQ New Zealand Defence Force 28 June 2012 ywww.airforce.mil.nz/about-us/news/media-releases

Chapter Eight

The Plan

> The Germans never had the sense to organize
> a proper scheme of training air-crew in time,
> and now had to pay for this lack of foresight.
>
> Sir Arthur Harris[1]

The British Commonwealth Air Training Plan (the 'Plan'), is sometimes called the British Empire Air Training Plan. It was a four-nation Commonwealth undertaking which produced magnificent results – the world's finest aircrew. Speaking about these dual names for the Plan, Australian author and Bomber Boy Don Charlwood observed that 'Canada, more independent of Britain than the rest of us, eschewed mention of Empire; besides she had her French population to placate. But if the official line was more independent of Britain, we found most English-speaking Canadians as loyal to the Crown as we were ourselves, perhaps even more loyal.'[2] The awesome effects of the Plan were soon felt, so much so that, on 21 February 1941, Churchill reported to Mackenzie King that the Plan had become 'one of the major factors, perhaps the decisive factor, in winning the war'.[3] But Churchill remained fixated on the Empire, of which he saw Canada being part, and so concluded his message by saying 'What a pleasure it is to see the whole Empire pulling as one man, and believe me my friend, I understand the reasons for your success in marshalling the great war effort of Canada.'[4]

The British Commonwealth of Nations came into being on 11 December 1931 with six founding nations – Australia, Britain, Canada, Ireland (more correctly Saorstát Éireann; the state didn't become Ireland until December 1937), New Zealand and South Africa. On 26 April 1949 the 'London Declaration' dropped the word 'British' from the Commonwealth's name. This was part of a constitutional change to enable India to remain a full member even though India, since 15 August 1947 a Dominion, advised it would become a Republic, which it did on 26 January 1950.

---

1 *Bomber Offensive*, p. 194a
2 Charlwood, *Journeys Into Night*, p. 21
3 Reardon, *Churchill and Mackenzie King*, p. 137
4 Churchill, *The Grand Alliance: Second World War*, Vol. 3, Cassell & Co., London, 1950, pp. 739-40

THE PLAN

Today the Commonwealth thrives, with an impressive membership of fifty-four nations worldwide having a combined population of 2.4 billion people. The leaders of its member nations meet each second year. The Head of the Commonwealth is Queen Elizabeth II. In addition, she reigns as Queen of Australia, Queen of Canada, Queen of New Zealand, Queen of the United Kingdom and Queen of her other Realms and Territories worldwide. The Queen is by far the greatest reason for the endurance, relevance and impressive roster of successes of the Commonwealth. The first Head of the postwar Commonwealth of Nations as formally constituted by the London Declaration on 26 April 1949 was her father King George VI. On his death on 6 February 1952, Queen Elizabeth II became and remains the second Head of the Commonwealth. On 19 April 2018, by the unanimous agreement of the heads of government of all fifty-four member-nations at the Commonwealth's 25th Heads of Government meeting in London, Prince Charles was designated to become the third Head of the Commonwealth following The Queen.

In the Second World War, of the British Commonwealth's six members, Ireland was neutral while South Africa was pre-occupied with the air war in Africa and Italy. Accordingly, South Africa operated with the RAF a parallel programme to train 33,347 aircrew at thirty-eight South African air training schools.[5] In Ottawa on 17 December 1939, Mackenzie King's birthday, the other four of the six British Commonwealth members signed an agreement creating the Plan. They were Australia, Britain, Canada and New Zealand. That agreement was set to expire in March 1943. On 5 June 1942, a new agreement was signed to extend the Plan until 31 March 1945, give Canada increased control over training, and allow for changes necessitated by the evolution of aerial warfare since 1939. The Plan enabled Canada to transform over a hundred thousand men such as my Dad from civilians with no flying experience into the world's finest aircrew. The Commonwealth played a major role in Bomber Command. According to Britain's Imperial War Museums:

> The bomber war was fought largely by young civilian volunteers from Britain and the Commonwealth, commanded by men who joined up before the Second World War. The vast majority of aircrew were in their late teens or early twenties. Only 25% were officers. An increasing flow of Canadians, Australians and New Zealanders meant that one in four aircrew came from the Dominions.[6]

To finance the Plan in Canada, Australia contributed $65 million, Britain $54 million (plus $162 million in used equipment), and New Zealand $48 million. Canada contributed $1.6 billion. That's right: $1.6 billion. But Canadians did far more than that. Canadians in the Second World War bought about $14 billion

---

5 Wikipedia, *British Commonwealth Air Training Plan*

6 Mason, *Life and Death in Bomber Command* Imperial War Museums 25 June 2018 www.iwm.org.uk/ history/life-and-death-in-bomber-command

in Victory Bonds; that's over $250 billion today. Canada and America were the only Allies to pay their way throughout the war. Both helped others postwar. If you would like to know the exact numbers for the total cost of the Plan, here they are:

- Canada spent $1,617,955,108.79
- Britain contributed $54,206,318.22 in cash, plus equipment valued at $162,260,787.89
- Australia contributed $65,181,068
- New Zealand contributed $48,025,393
- America's contribution through Lend-Lease[7] was evaluated at $283,500,362
- The total cost was *$2,231,129,039.26.*[8]

For this, Mackenzie King demanded that Britain agree air training would take precedence over other aspects of the Canadian war effort, and that distinct Royal Canadian Air Force squadrons would be formed.[9]

USAF General Robert Dixon offers an interesting comparison of American and Canadian aircrew training before America entered the Second World War. Dixon was a wartime contemporary of Murray Peden in the RCAF, and ultimately a USAF general who, for his final five years of service, commanded America's Tactical Air Command. In his Foreword to Murray Peden's excellent book *A Thousand Shall Fall*, Dixon says that in summer 1941 he was in basic training at age 21 at the US Army Air Corps' Randolph Field in Texas. However, he was 'washed out – declared unsuitable, by lack of inclination to discipline, to become a military pilot'. Within a year, Dixon was in Canada commissioned as an RCAF pilot officer graduate of the Plan. He says it was 'not a wholly joyous day' when he left the RCAF to transfer back to the USAAF once America was at war. Dixon says the fundamental difference between Canadian and American aircrew training was that America was focused on ground discipline in the cadet atmosphere where his 'youthful refusal to consider cadet "hazing" as a practical military discipline' resulted in his being 'washed out'.

In Canada, in Dixon's words 'The same youthful attitude, moulded by a training system dedicated to the needs of a free commonwealth of nations at war, produced a trained and usable pilot – in my case and others.' Dixon makes another point about the Plan that is easily overlooked, but goes to the heart of morale – and aircrew morale in Bomber Command was nothing short of astonishing. The additional point Dixon makes is 'My close association with Commonwealth aircrews – the British,

---

[7] *An Act to Promote the Defence of the United States*, enacted 11 March 1941

[8] Hatch *Aerodrome of Democracy: Canada and the British Commonwealth Air Training Plan 1939-1945*, Canadian Government Publishing Centre, Ottawa: PDF Version Modified 2018-03-08, Epilogue, p. 195. My addition of those numbers reveals a total of $2,231,129,037.90, creating a discrepancy of $1.36.

[9] Website, *Bomber Command Museum of Canada*, Nanton, Alberta

THE PLAN

Canadians and Australians I went through training with – gave me a window on a wider world of airmanship, fellowship and esprit ... All of these experiences were of fundamental continuing value.'

The Plan was such a marvellous undertaking that FDR, who referred to America as the 'Arsenal of Democracy',[10] called Canada the 'Aerodrome of Democracy'. That memorable phrase was coined for FDR by future Canadian prime minister Lester ('Mike') Pearson stationed in the Canadian Embassy in Washington at the time.[11] On 19 April 1943, Canada's 4th Victory Loan Campaign was launched in Toronto. Speaking to the nation in support of it, Mackenzie King praised the Plan, and proudly quoted FDR's 'Aerodrome of Democracy' designation for Canada.[12]

The statistics are staggering. The RCAF administered the Plan through 107 flying schools and 184 auxiliary units operating at 231 locations across Canada. To do so, the RCAF employed 104,113 staff and used 10,906 aircraft.[13] What's more, I discovered that most training schools had three runways, each 100-feet (30 metres) wide and 2,500-feet (760 metres) long. The runways were made extra wide to make it easier for students to find them and land on them without killing themselves and their flying instructors. These airstrips required so much cement that Canada could have instead built a highway 20 feet (6 metres) wide from Ottawa to Vancouver.[14] By air, the distance from Ottawa to Vancouver is farther than London to Istanbul; it is approximately London to Baku in Central Asia.

Training and Graduating

Regarding training, Canada says[15] 'Training in the BCATP was challenging and rigorous. Pilots, wireless operators, air gunners, air observers, and flight engineers went through months of training at specialized schools.

The pilot training was the longest and most difficult. From Initial Training School, they went to Elementary Flying Training School, where they got their first chance to fly, followed by Service Flying Training Schools where they were separated into fighter and bomber pilots. From there they went into Advanced Flying and Operational Training Units before going overseas.

---

10 FDR, *Fireside Chat*, 29 December 1940

11 Pearson, *Mike, The Memoirs of the Right Honorable Lester B. Pearson*, University of Toronto Press 1, 1972, p. 208.

12 Reardon, p. 236

13 Canadian Encyclopedia www.thecanadianencyclopedia.ca

14 Veterans Affairs Canada https://www.veterans.gc.ca/eng/remembrance/history/historical-sheets/britcom

15 Veterans Affairs Canada https://www.veterans.gc.ca/eng/remembrance/history/historical-sheets/britcom

BOMBER COMMAND

Of the Canadians trained in the BCATP, 25,747 would become pilots: 12,855 navigators; 6,659 air bombers; 12,744 wireless operators; 12,917 air gunners, and 1,913 flight engineers.'

Noting the small number of flight engineers, I am reminded that when RAF Air Vice-Marshal Paul Robinson was hosting my sons Guy Roland and Ruaridh and me in Lincolnshire on 17 October 2021, he mentioned that almost every heavy bomber flight crew had a British flight engineer aboard. On 18 January 2022 Paul elaborated, saying flight engineers were not necessary until the dominance of the Lancaster, and so were late coming to training in the Plan. Halifaxes and Stirlings initially used co-pilots, but these were expensive and lacked the needed specialist engineering knowledge. Then RAF engine and airframe fitters and mechanics were given a flying course and turned into 'flight engineers'. They were older than the rest of the crew because of their previous service, and they did not join bomber crews until the Heavy Conversion Unit stage of training. Initially, only the RAF trained these flight engineers so they were also posted into Canadian and Australian aircrews. However, early in 1944 the RCAF sent its own students to these RAF flight engineering courses, and then started its own courses within the Plan in Canada. The first Canadian flight engineers were posted to No. 6 Group RCAF.

As New Zealand's *Bomber Command Association Newsletter* proclaims, the Plan trained and graduated 131,553 pilots, flight engineers, navigators, air gunners, bomb aimers (air bombers) and wireless operators for the four Commonwealth air forces. The breakdown of graduates per Commonwealth Air Force is:[16]

42,110	Royal Air Force
9,606	Royal Australian Air Force
72,835	Royal Canadian Air Force
7,002	Royal New Zealand Air Force
131,553	Total
	and in addition
5,296	Royal Navy Fleet Air Arm

And there's more. Through the Plan, the RCAF also trained aircrew from Argentina, Belgium, Ceylon (Sri Lanka), Czechoslovakia (Czechia and Slovakia), Fiji, Finland, France, Greece, The Netherlands, Norway, Poland, Rhodesia (Zimbabwe), South Africa and, most important of all, the United States of America.[17] That won FDR's admiration, and American financial assistance.

---

16 Veterans Affairs Canada https://www.veterans.gc.ca/eng/remembrance/history/historical-sheets/britcom

17 Canadian Encyclopedia www.thecanadianencyclopedia.ca/en/article/british-commonwealth-air-training-plan

THE PLAN

America and the Plan

When America declared war on Japan on 8 December 1941, the day after the Japanese attacked Pearl Harbor, and Germany and Italy declared war on America three days later on 11 December, 6,129 American volunteers were in the RCAF. Of these, 3,883 were still in training. With America now at war, in due course 3,797 of these American volunteers transferred home to the United States Army Air Forces. Others continued to serve in the RCAF. One of the most famous and revered Americans in the RCAF was Pilot Officer John Gillespie Magee Jr. He composed the immortal poem 'High Flight' which, as mentioned, my Dad had in his cockpit. Magee was killed on 11 December 1941 flying his Spitfire, just four days after Pearl Harbor. The original manuscript of 'High Flight' is in the Library of Congress in Washington DC.

While America was officially neutral prior to Pearl Harbor, with the explosion into hugeness of the Plan, Canada found itself short of pilots. This led to looking for Americans via the 'Clayton Knight Committee' created by Clayton Knight and the RCAF's Director of Recruiting, Air Marshal Billy Bishop VC, one of Canada's greatest aviation heroes. The committee opened its first office in New York's Waldorf Astoria Hotel in the spring of 1940, and then established bureaux in Atlanta, Cleveland, Dallas, Kansas City, Los Angeles, Memphis, San Antonio, San Francisco and Spokane. Although the official goal of the Clayton Knight Committee was to attract trained pilots for non-combat duties, increasingly it was attracting American raw recruits eager to join our fight against the Nazis. These raw American recruits constituted 85 per cent of the Americans who joined the RCAF.[18]

Today, these American RCAF Second World War recruits are back in the news. Congressman Tim Ryan of US Congress 13th District Ohio is sponsoring bi-partisan legislation, the 'American Patriots of WWII Through Service With the Canadian and British Armed Forces Gold Medal Act of 2019' to award them a Congressional Gold Medal. This proposed Bill 1709 in the 2021-2022 Congress has, I am told as of November 2021, five additional Congress members sponsoring it. The Bomber Command Museum of Canada, of which I am a life member, enthusiastically endorses Bill 1709. So do America's National Association of County Veteran Service Offices, AMVETS, American Legion, National World War II Museum, Air Force Association, American Fighter Aces Association, Ernie Hall Aviation Museum, VFW Post 2662 and American War Memorials Overseas. This Bill is also endorsed by the No. 1 British Flying Training School Museum, Aircrew Remembered, the Canadian Harvard Aerobatic Team, *20th Century Aviation Magazine*, the Hickory Aviation Museum and the Florida Aviation Historical Society.[19]

---

18 Halliday, 'Canada's Yanks: Air Force, Part 16', *LEGION* Canada's Military History Magazine, 1 July 2006

19 Please Support the Award of the Congressional Gold Medal to UN Nationals Who Volunteered to Serve in WWII in the Canadian or British Armed Forces in Recognition of Their Dedicated Service. https://honoring-american-ww2-volunteers.com/

Faint Evidence Remains of the Plan

From my earliest years as a small boy, I and my friends were aware of the Plan, albeit dimly. How could we not be aware, you might ask, given Alberta was the site of so many airfields for the Plan just fifteen years earlier? Sadly, by the late 1950s, most evidence of this massive undertaking had virtually disappeared. I remember one small roadside stone cairn west of Cochrane on the old Highway 1A from Calgary to Banff. This cairn had affixed to its stones a brass plaque. Stopping to have a look, I discovered this small monument proclaimed the importance of the Plan, and stressed that it was a Commonwealth undertaking. This Commonwealth fact gets lost in so many of the official histories. One of the most important moments in my life was when the local Alberta Driver Licensing Bureau doors opened on 18 July 1964, my sixteenth birthday. I was standing there, waiting to be let in. I passed the test, and was awarded my all-important driver's licence. My friends did likewise, so soon we were enjoying driving around Calgary and the surrounding countryside. Once we had graduated from university and were earning enough money, a special trip we particularly enjoyed was the drive south from Calgary to Claresholm to dine on some of the best beef in Alberta in a house we vaguely knew was a holdover from an airstrip that had taught aircrew through the Plan. I did not know Dad taught there.

I also did not know this then, but my research now reveals the Claresholm airstrip students first arrived on 9 June 1941, and No. 15 Service Flying Training School opened officially on 16 August 1941 to train pilots. It was closed on 30 March 1945, and then re-opened in 1951 as No. 3 Flying Training School to train pilots for the Korean War. It was also used to train NATO pilots. It was closed and abandoned in 1958. That summer I had my tenth birthday. To me as a Calgary boy, the war seemed remote, and so did the traces of visual evidence throughout the prairies of the Plan. One speaks of ghost towns. The Canadian prairies postwar had scores of ghost airstrips, most almost invisible. With Bomber Command Memorial and Museum Curator Karl Kjarsgaard as host and guide, on 3 September 2020 I was permitted through normally-locked gates into something wonderful. It was the RCAF Vulcan Flying Instructor School at which Dad was taught in the fall of 1942 to become a flying instructor, and which Calvin Pocock and I had seen from a distance on 28 August 2020. It still exists. Hidden miles from anywhere, it still has a half-dozen or more of its gigantic hangars intact. Best of all, the runways were never ripped up. Instead, they were covered up by blowing dirt, and so blended in with the fields surrounding them. Now the dirt is being removed, and those runways can be seen and walked on. It was an exciting event to see them with Karl, and to stand on those runways knowing they were used by my Dad. It amazed me how wide they are. Karl said that gave fledgling pilots as much room as possible, especially in bad weather. The property is owned by John Sands who restored one of the hangars and is uncovering the runways. As mentioned, it is wonderful.

THE PLAN

Flying Instructors MacKenzie, Middleton and Miles

My curiosity about flying instructors was aroused in July 2011 during Prince William and Catherine's visit to Calgary, because they paid particular attention to the memory of Catherine's grandfather, a wartime flying instructor stationed at Calgary Airport. He was RAF pilot Peter Francis Middleton (1920-2010), whom Prince William reportedly knew well. Middleton served from May 1942 for a couple of years as a flying instructor at No. 37 Service Flying Training School at the southern end of what is now Calgary International Airport. His location was just off McKnight Boulevard, where my Calgary Lancaster and other aircraft are today on display in the Hangar Flight Museum. About 800 pilots received their wings at Calgary's No. 37 SFTS.[20] My Dad meanwhile was a flying instructor at RCAF Claresholm, nowadays only 88 miles (143 km) south of Calgary's McCall Field by freeway, so he and Middleton may have known one another. My wife Ka Hyun and I visited the Claresholm site of the Plan for the first time on 9 August 2021. Back in Britain in August 1944, the month my Dad concluded his thirty-four combat sorties, Middleton commenced flying combat sorties in a Mosquito fighter-bomber. Sadly, Middleton died age 90 in 2010, just a few days before William and Catherine announced their engagement. Prince William was with him on his 90th birthday, and a few months later attended his funeral. As it happens, in 1962 Catherine's grandfather toured South America with Prince William's grandfather. RAF Captain Peter Middleton, who was then a British European Airways pilot, served as Prince Philip's co-pilot for forty-nine flights Philip piloted on his 1962 Royal flying tour of South America.[21] For this, Middleton received Philip's letter of appreciation and gold cuff-links. Little did they know during their time together in 1962 that their grandchildren would marry.

I was vaguely aware my Dad was also a flying instructor in Canada before his transfer to Britain sometime in 1943, but I did not know when Dad instructed, or where, or who. As mentioned, Prince William's 2011 visit to Calgary caused me to further wonder what my Dad actually did in the war. And that begins with training. Wartime flying instructor Jack Miles, who died aged 103 on 11 December 2021, was very involved with me in writing this book. It started when Jack passionately urged me to write this book while thanking me at the conclusion of my Bomber Command speech at the Air Force Officers' Association formal dinner to celebrate the RCAF's 95th Anniversary on 30 March 2019. And Jack helped me hugely right up until his death through constant telephone conversations and e-mail exchanges. Jack made real for me what my Dad, Peter Middleton and he were doing. Jack was six years younger than my Dad. Like Dad he was a banker before volunteering for the RAF, but Jack was a British banker in Buenos Aires with the Bank of London and South America (now Lloyds). Jack

---
20 Bomber Command Museum of Canada www.bombercommandmuseum.ca
21 *Daily Mail*, mailonline, 15 Nov 2019

tells me that the Royal Bank of Canada also had a prewar branch in Buenos Aires. Jack volunteered for the RAF in Buenos Aires in 1939, two years before Dad, and chose Canada for the place of his demobilization in 1946. Unlike Dad, Jack did not return postwar to banking, but instead returned to Buenos Aires to work as a civilian pilot, and ultimately became Vice-President of Canada's Pacific Western Airlines. His grandson, John Miles, is Director of Corporate Finance at YVR (Vancouver International Airport). Jack like Dad began his wartime training at the Manning Depot in Brandon, Manitoba.

Jack tells me Dad sealed his fate as a flying instructor by coming first in his class in both Edmonton and Saskatoon flying schools. Jack says whoever came first in each class was automatically diverted into being a flying instructor. That was how important the RCAF and RAF knew flying instructors were. Jack told me where in Dad's logbook was the list of planes Dad flew, and explained to me the aircraft Dad used to teach future pilots. Jack brought to life for me the whole experience. In addition Jack, like Mike Mathews and Paul Robinson, taught me how to 'read between the lines' in what my Dad was writing in his logbook.

The Plan Museum and RCAF Memorial

Although I did not know then that Dad began his RCAF training at the Manning Depot in Brandon, my knowledge of the Plan took a giant jump in Brandon on 29 June 2016. My wife Ka Hyun and I were returning home, driving west along the 4,860-mile (7,821 km) Trans-Canada Highway through Manitoba, from visiting our friends Fred and Marion Wright on McKenzie Portage Road on Lake of the Woods in Ontario. Fred's stepfather was a mid-upper gunner in Bomber Command. As Ka Hyun and I approached Brandon, Manitoba's second largest city, I saw signs on the Trans-Canada Highway for the British Commonwealth Air Training Plan Museum and the RCAF World War Two Memorial at Brandon Municipal Airport. On impulse, we took the airport exit and drove in to have a look. I am so glad we did. We ended up spending several meaningful hours there, viewing the exhibits, absorbing the solemn importance of what we were learning, reading aircrew letters to family and friends, watching videos, seeing those powerful black-and-white photos, and wondering which of these earnest young men were killed fighting for our freedom. The Plan's Museum and RCAF Memorial are memorable, indeed profoundly moving. Individual stories there are heart-warming, and all too often heart-breaking. Visiting this Museum and Memorial became yet another major milestone in my growing awareness that Bomber Command was important, and that I knew too little about it. But in 2016 my knowledge of my Dad's service was still virtually non-existent. Until that was remedied through the Royal Air Force in 2017, I remained essentially paralyzed. According to the Museum's brochure:

THE PLAN

> The Commonwealth Air Training Plan Museum is Canada's only museum dedicated solely to the story of the RCAF personnel who trained and served the Commonwealth during WWII (1939-1945). Travel to the 1940s as you wander through a vintage hangar (a National Historic Site) and see aircraft, vehicles and hundreds of artefacts from that era. The RCAF WWII Memorial is a 300-foot granite wall etched with the names and ages of over 19,000 fallen. It is Canada's only permanent public memorial which serves as lasting recognition of all the members of the Royal Canadian Air Force and all Canadians serving in any Commonwealth air force, who lost their lives during World War II.

It speaks poorly of Canada that the Plan's only Museum for the Second World War is in Brandon, Manitoba, and Bomber Command's only Memorial is in Nanton, Alberta. Both should also have places of honour in Ottawa.

New Zealand to the Rescue

Fortunately for me, thanks to New Zealand, more answers about the Plan's aircrew training came to me in 2019. My New Zealand connection arose through my Bomber Command work in Canada leading to my admission to memberships Down Under in the Bomber Command Associations of both Australia and New Zealand. An important benefit of my New Zealand membership is New Zealand's excellent *NZ Bomber Command Association News*. Its Editor, Peter Wheeler QSM, is also the Executive Officer of New Zealand's Association. Fortuitously, with my membership, Peter kindly mailed me back issues of his *Newsletter*. In his October 2018 issue, Peter wrote a tribute to Canada's role in the Plan. Peter's headline is 'The Canadian Effort'. His article commences by saying 'Except to the many Veterans who were trained in Canada, this country's effort is often overlooked'. How true that is.

Peter goes on to tell about Canadians spending more than a billion dollars operating the Plan in over 100 schools during the five war years, and graduating a total of 131,553 airmen in the air forces of the four Commonwealth nations. All of this has been almost forgotten postwar because Canada so often ignores the declaration in the Gospel of St Matthew that 'Thou shall not hide thy light under a bushel'. We too often hide ours and, in my research since 2017, I have learnt that is especially true for Bomber Command. Peter's New Zealand *Newsletter* certainly aroused my attention! The story is astounding! And, best of all for me, Peter lists all these Canadian schools with important details on each, including their locations and their coding. At last, I had my first significant key to understanding the Plan. Just seeing the long list printed in his New Zealand *Newsletter* is overwhelming.

Churchill's Perspective on the Plan

And as usual I refer to Churchill. In December 1942 Churchill wrote to Mackenzie King:[22]

> When I look back on the remorseless growth of the Air Forces of the United Nations and survey the shattering punishment we have already begun to inflict upon the enemy, I realize how much of our success is due to the great scheme which has been so energetically developed in Canada. Canadians in their thousands have answered the call of the air.

Churchill concludes by saying 'Our thanks are due to the Government and people of Canada, and especially to the officers and men of the Royal Canadian Air Force, who by their wholehearted endeavours have established the plan on a sure foundation, and from it are now forging a potent instrument of victory.'

On 30 March 1945, Churchill wrote to Mackenzie King regarding Canada's dismantling of the Plan.[23] Sending his 'warmest regards' to the RCAF and Canadian Government, Churchill summed up the Plan:

> This master plan has done much to speed us along the road to victory. In Canada alone, trained air crews, of which more than half were Canadian, have been turned out at an average rate of 25,000 a year over the last five years. Moreover, the quality of the training has been outstanding, and has shown itself triumphantly in the superiority which we have gained over the enemy in every type of air combat.[24]

In other words, Churchill is telling us the Plan was a success.

---

22 Reardon, pp. 231-2
23 Reardon, p. 313
24 Churchill, *'Victory': The War Speeches of Winston* Churchill, Vol. 6, p. 121

Chapter Nine

Warplanes

Bomber Command flew an array of aircraft in the Second World War, some of which were failures, some just mediocre, and some superb. To me the 'Big Four' are the Lancaster, Halifax, Mosquito and Wellington. Here is what my Bomber Command research reveals to me about each of them.

1. LANCASTER

Where the Spitfire was a dashing rapier
The Lancaster was a mighty broadsword
The Spitfire's central role was to provide protection
The Lancaster's to inflict destruction

Leo McKinstrey[1]

I believe that the Lancaster was the greatest single factor in winning the war.

Sir Arthur Harris[2]

Roy Chadwick Designed the Lancaster

Roy Chadwick is the genius who designed the Lancaster from his failed Manchester. The Lancaster went from drawing board to combat sorties in only two years. It is a wonderful example of the famous expression 'thinking outside the box'. Not every British bomber had proven to be highly successful. What was wrong? Chadwick thought about wingspans. He wondered what would happen if he lengthened the wings. To find out, Chadwick added twelve feet to what was the Lancaster's failed

---

[1] Leo McKinstry *They took a lot of flak: the lives of the Lancaster bombers – But their courage, and the dark missions they flew, eventually won the war* The Spectator Magazine 06 June 2020 reviewing John Nichol's book *Lancaster, the Forging of a Very British Legend* Simon & Shuster 28 May 2020
[2] Harris to Sir Roy Dobson of A.V. Roe, 6 December 1945

predecessor, the Manchester, thereby making the wingspan 102 feet (30.5 metres). In addition, Chadwick replaced the Manchester's two problematic 24-cylinder Vulture engines with four less powerful but more reliable Rolls Royce Merlin V-12s.[3] I once owned a 12-cylinder Jaguar. On those rare occasions in which all twelve cylinders functioned in sync, it was pure magic.

Through extended wingspans and four more reliable engines replacing two problematic ones was born the Lancaster, the most successful bomber of the Second World War. The Lancaster's first test flight was on 9 January 1941 and its first combat sortie was on 3 March 1942 when four Lancasters of No. 44 (Rhodesia) Squadron laid mines in the Heligoland Bight. Its first major operational bombing mission was on 17 April 1942 when twelve Lancasters flew a thousand miles across France and Germany in broad daylight to bomb the U-boat diesel-engine factory at Augsburg in Bavaria.[4] Tragically, seven of those twelve Lancasters and eighty-five aircrew were lost. The Lancaster unprotected by fighters was not suited to daylight combat sorties.

Roy Chadwick was killed on 23 August 1947 on a Tudor test flight because of a servicing error of inadvertently crossed aileron cables, so he never saw to fruition another of his designs, the Vulcan. He was 54. His bust is on display at the RAF Club London, and at the Chadwick Centre at the IBCC.

At War, and Today

I've now learnt that 7,377 Lancasters were built for the Second World War. They carried out 156,192 combat sorties in which 3,431 Lancasters were lost in action and 246 crashed en route.[5] Approximately another 400 crashed in testing or in training. This raises an important question. It's seventy-five years since the Lancaster bomber first roared aloft. So why do our leaders still refuse to celebrate the giant – and its awesomely brave crews – that smashed the Nazi war machine?[6] This question is part of what led to my writing this book. All Lancasters were built in Britain, except for 430 constructed in Canada. Canada constructing Lancasters was an accomplishment given it was primarily an agrarian nation. A half-million manufacturing operations were needed to build a Lancaster; Lancasters had 55,000 parts, with engines and turrets regarded as one part each, and not including small items such as rivets, nuts and bolts. On 21 October 2020 Russ Hudson showed Dr John Blatherwick and me an enormous number of pieces that still have to be assembled to rebuild the Toronto Lancaster for display in British Columbia at the BC Aviation Museum adjacent to Victoria's Airport.

On 12 September 1941 Canada decided to build Lancasters, and created a Crown Corporation called Victory Aircraft to do it. Victory Aircraft ultimately

---

3   Bomber Command Museum of Canada www.bombercommandmuseum.ca

4   Edwards *The Iconic Lancaster, Still Capturing the Public's Imagination* www.google.com/amp/s/richardedwards.info/2015/03/27/the-iconic-avro-lancaster

5   Middlebrook & Everett Bomber Command War Diaries

6   Robert Hardman *Daily Mail* Newspaper 23 January 2016

employed about 10,000 people making a Lancaster a day. On 1 August 1943, the first Canadian Lancaster, KB700, nicknamed the 'Ruhr Express', rolled off the assembly line. It flew two sorties with 405 (Vancouver) Squadron RCAF in No. 6 Group, Canada's first bomber squadron. This was followed by forty-seven combat sorties with 419 (Moose) Squadron RCAF, also of No. 6 Group. The highest number of combat sorties flown by a Canadian Lancaster was by KB732, designated as VR X-Terminator which completed eighty-four missions, also in 419 (Moose) Squadron RCAF of No. 6 Group.[7]

Of the two that still fly, one is in the RAF's Battle of Britain Memorial Flight (BBMF) based at RAF Coningsby in Lincolnshire. On 13 May 2019, Richard Tillotson-Sills gave RAF Wing Commander Tony Lark and me a thorough personal tour of it. Tony had been Richard's superior in the RAF. It is ironic that this Lancaster is in the Battle of Britain Memorial Flight, given that the Battle was in the summer of 1940, and the first Lancaster prototype did not have its first test flight until 9 January 1941.[8] As mentioned, my son Guy Roland and I saw it fly at Prince William's Wedding 29 April 2011. The other Lancaster still flying is based at Canada's Hamilton Airport at Port Hope in Ontario. It was acquired by the Canadian Warplane Heritage Museum (CWHM) in 1977 from the Goderich Ontario Branch of the Royal Canadian Legion. Prince Charles is the CWHM Patron and officially opened the CWHM's new facility on 26 April 1996. As mentioned, my son Ruaridh and I saw it fly in May 2011.

And there's more. In summer 2014, the Canadian Lancaster crossed the Atlantic to fly together with its British counterpart in airshows throughout the UK. Hundreds of thousands saw this pair of Lancasters airborne, and millions more saw them on television. This was the first time a pair of Lancasters had flown together in the fifty years since a pair last flew over Ottawa in 1964.

As mentioned, an additional two Lancasters have all four engines working. One is at the Lincolnshire Aviation Heritage Centre at East Kirkby in England. The other is my Nanton Lancaster in Alberta. The East Kirkby Lancaster gives taxi rides on the runway as part of its full-day 'Lancaster Experience'. My Nanton Lancaster attracts crowds when it is pulled outside and all four engines are fired up. My Canadian Lancasters in Calgary, Nanton and Toronto all sat outside through decades of rough Canadian winters. That these three Lancasters sat outside with no protection for so many years told me that Lancasters were tough aircraft. How tough I would later learn from my research. Their toughness was one reason the Lancaster became an iconic aircraft of the Second World War.

Navigator John Curnow of 103 Squadron at Elsham Wolds was succinct in his letter home of 1 November 1942, saying 'The squadron is now converting to a new kite, ten times better than the Halifax. It is the Lancaster, and are we pleased! The best way that I can compare the two is, I think, by saying the comparison is

---

7 Birrell, *FM159 The Lucky Lancaster,* pp. 10-15.

8 Military Factory www.militaryfactory.com

like that of a racehorse to a carthorse, the 'Lanc' being the racehorse.'[9] John was shot down 10 March 1943, his twenty-fourth combat sortie, after bombing Munich. Time and again thereafter he escaped his captors and was recaptured until 16 April 1945 when the British Army liberated him and his fellow PoWs.

The Lancaster was versatile in what it could carry. It could carry up to 10 tonnes of bombs,[10] far more than other bombers in the European theatre. Its long, unobstructed bomb bay enabled it to carry multiple bomb-load combinations.[11] Barnes Wallis provided Bouncing Bombs for Dambusters, followed by his Tallboy (6 tonnes) and Grand Slam (10 tonnes) deep-penetration earthquake bombs. They could destroy previously impregnable German fortifications.[12] The Lancaster was the only aircraft that could lift those bombs. Lancasters dropped over 600,000 tons of bombs in 156,000 combat sorties.

The Lancaster had a maximum speed of 275 mph (443 km/h), a cruising speed of 210 mph (322 km/h), a service ceiling of 25,700 feet (7,833 metres) and a range of 2,520 miles (4,056 km). The Lancaster was intentionally constructed to maximize structural strength per weight, enabling it to withstand significant damage, as was proven in my Dad's 11 August 1944 flight for which he received the DFC. A strong, seasoned pilot assisted by a strong flight engineer could accomplish miracles in Lancaster manoeuvrability under attack. Having said that, as mentioned, 3,249 Lancasters were lost in action.

Nothing sums up Lancasters better than Harris himself. On 6 December 1945, Harris said to Sir Roy Dobson, the wartime Managing Director of Avro (A.V. Roe & Company) and postwar Founder of Avro Canada, 'I would say this to those who placed that shining sword in our hands – without your genius and efforts we could not have prevailed, for I believe that the Lancaster was the greatest single factor in winning the war.'

2. HALIFAX

The Halifax was: a virtual failure.... utterly unsatisfactory....
The Halifax's shortcomings: Its performance was too low,
It had vicious handling habits, its exhaust flame damping was
unsatisfactory, and the attempts to make it carry the necessary
defensive armament rendered it practically useless for operations.

RAF Air Marshal Sir Arthur Harris[13]

---

9 Curnow, *Shot Down*, p. 56
10 https://www.historyextra.com>period
11 BAE Systems www.baesystems.com/en/heritage/avro-683-lancaster
12 Canadian Warplane Heritage Museum www.warplane.com/aircraft/collection/details.aspx?aircraftId=4
13 Probert, *Bomber Harris: His Life and Times* pp 219-20

WARPLANES

*The Halifax was the greatest airplane
in all 110 years of flight in Canada*

Karl Kjarsgaard
Founder Halifax 57 Rescue (Canada) &
Curator, Bomber Command Museum of Canada

The other great Commonwealth four-engine heavy bomber of the Second World War was, of course, the Halifax. Harris initially intensely disliked it, partly because of deficiencies in the aircraft and partly because he personally disliked Sir Frederick Handley Page, founder of the company that produced Halifaxes. That evidently is why Harris gave Halifaxes instead of Lancasters to No. 6 Group RCAF, which he also disliked. Harris was opposed to the creation of No. 6 Group RCAF in his words 'for the sole purpose of satisfying a lot of political demands from Ottawa'. In September 1942 Harris wrote to Portal 'I fail to see why we should give these people [Canadians] who are determined to huddle into a corner by themselves on purely political ground, the best of our equipment [Lancasters] at the expense of British and other Dominion crews.'[14] And so the RCAF flew Halifaxes through the most dangerous period of the Second World War. Postwar, the Halifax has been left in the shadow of its more famous counterpart the Lancaster, that is until Karl Kjarsgaard came along.

The first Halifax flight was on 25 October 1939 and entered RAF service on 13 November 1940. Its first combat sortie was the night of 10/11 March 1941 when six Halifaxes bombed the docks and shipping at le Havre in France. The existence of the Halifax was not acknowledged until after on 24 July 1941 and a daylight sortie at la Pallice, France, in which fifteen Halifaxes attacked the German battleship *Scharnhorst*, scoring five hits inflicting extensive damage it took four months in dry dock to repair.[15] I've now learnt that 6,176 Halifaxes were built. As mentioned, Handley Page Limited was the manufacturer. Sir Frederick Handley Page founded his company on 17 June 1909. In Bomber Command they carried out 82,773 combat sorties in which 1,884 Halifaxes were lost.[16]

Karl Kjarsgaard tells me that, by the end of 1943, No. 6 Group (RCAF) was almost entirely equipped with Halifaxes, using them 71 per cent of the time in the war. No. 4 Group was equipped entirely with Halifaxes, and continued using them throughout the war. At its peak, Bomber Command operated a total of seventy-six Halifax squadrons.[17] Early model Halifaxes, the Mk I and II with Merlin 22 engines of 1,390hp, had significant deficiencies. In 1943 the Halifax Mk III and later models were upgraded with more powerful 1,650 hp Bristol Hercules XVI

---

14 *Reap The Whirlwind*, p15
15 Wikipedia *Handley Page Halifax*
16 Karl Kjarsgaard, Curator, Archives - Bomber Command Museum of Canada
17 Wikipedia *Handley Page Halifax*

radial engines, rounded wing tips and hydromatic propellers. This culminated with the Mk VI having the most powerful 1800 hp Hercules 100 engines.

A feature aircrew appreciated was that the Halifax was significantly easier to bale out of, due to better placement of crew emergency exits. On average 25 per cent of Halifax crews successfully baled out from damaged aircraft, while only 15 per cent of Lancaster crews did.[18] The significant disadvantage of the Halifax was having a smaller bomb bay with lower bomb payload and much less versatility in what it could carry, thus depriving it of the flexibility that larger Lancaster bomb bays offered. The Halifax with its more robust airframe was more versatile in what it could do – such as towing gliders. Lancasters were focused on the task of finding targets, dropping bombs, and getting away.

There are only three Halifaxes on display worldwide today. They are Halifax HR792 at the Yorkshire Air Museum in Elvington, North Yorkshire; Halifax W1048 at the RAF Museum, Colindale, London; and Halifax NA337 which was rescued from Lake Mjosa in Norway by Karl Kjarsgaard and his colleagues. It is now on display at the National Air Force Museum of Canada in Trenton, Ontario.

In 1994, Ian Foster[19] of Scotland founded the charitable organization Halifax 57 Rescue[20] which Karl Kjarsgaard took over for Canada and now leads. Its inspiring Proclamation is Appendix III of this book. As mentioned, Karl Kjarsgaard was the project manager for the recovery of Halifax NA337, the Halifax bomber recovered from Lake Mjosa, Norway in 1995. The second rescue was in Belgium in 1997 of RCAF Halifax LW682 with aircrew bodies aboard. The present rescue is in the Baltic Sea south of Falsterbo, Sweden of 405 Squadron Pathfinders Halifax HR871, again led by Karl Kjarsgaard.

3. MOSQUITO

*It makes me furious when I see the Mosquito.
I turn green with envy.... They* [the British]
have the geniuses and we have the nincompoops
Reichsmarschall Hermann Göring[21]

*In the daytime, too, we have more alerts now,
even in Berlin. The English accomplish*

---

18   Wikipedia *Handley Page Halifax*

19   Karl Karlsgaard Project Manager Halifax 57 Rescue Canada Posted an Update on *'Support the Recovery of a RCAF Halifax Bomber'* 4 November 2018 www.fundrazr.com/stories/dE0w36

20   Maggie Macintosh Recovering 'the greatest airplane in all 110 years of flight in Canada' costs $120K CBC News posted 2 July 2019, updated 8 July 2019

21   Stephan Wilkinson *The Miraculous Mosquito* HistoryNet www.historynet.com/the-miraculous-mosquito.htm

WARPLANES

*this with their small Mosquito machines
which are exceedingly hard to hit… .*

Joseph Goebbels, Diary 21 May 1943

The 'Wooden Wonder' was amazing. We could have used more of them. This twin-engine multi-role bomber-fighter aircraft was also known as the 'Mossie'. In total, 6,710 were built for Second World War service. Most de Havilland Mosquitoes were built in Britain, but 1,134 were built in Canada and 202 in Australia. The Mosquito first flew on 25 November 1940, and entered service on 15 November 1941. However, its existence was not made public until 26 September 1942, the day after the Mosquito raid on the Gestapo building in Oslo, Norway.[22] Mosquitoes were built mostly of a wood composite – plywood. The fuselage was a frameless shell of plywood – balsawood sandwiched between sheets of sitka spruce and birch. The wings were wooden as well. It had a crew of only two – pilot and navigator/bomb aimer. Its two engines were also Merlin V-12 engines. The Mosquito was the fastest Allied propeller aircraft for most of the war, flying in excess of 400 mph (640 km/h). It could carry the same bomb load as the heavily-armed four-engine B-17 Flying Fortress.[23] It functioned as both a bomber and a fighter and was increasingly used by the Pathfinders.

While British and Canadian heavy bombers favoured dark nights, the increasingly numerous Mosquitoes flew their nuisance raids even on bright moonlit nights. The Institute says that in twenty-two nights in March 1944, more than 1,400 Mosquitoes were counted. Germans spoke of 'the plague of Mosquitoes'. Mosquitoes often timed their attacks on Luftwaffe night-fighter airfields in Belgium and Germany to coincide with major bomber raids so that they could harass German fighters as they took off and landed.[24] The Mosquito intruder version was fitted with a range of 'homers' to home in on Luftwaffe aircraft by No. 100 Group Bomber Command in its electronic-warfare-countermeasures. In 1944-45, 100 Group destroyed 258 Luftwaffe aircraft for an RAF loss of seventy. Constant harassment by Mosquitoes also reduced the morale and confidence of Luftwaffe pilots, resulting in many Luftwaffe crashes in fast landings to avoid Mosquitoes. Luftwaffe aircrew called this '*Moskito Panik*'.[25] Two Second World War RAF pilots I write about in this book, Colin Bell and Peter Middleton, both flew Mosquitoes. My Uncle Bruce MacKenzie told me he would have gladly traded his Spitfire for a Mosquito.

---

22 Wikipedia de Havilland Mosquito
23 Birrell, pp. 171-2
24 Institute Vol. VII, p. 306
25 Wikipedia, No. 100 Group RAF

4. WELLINGTON

The Vickers Wellington was affectionately known as the Wimpy, a nickname attributed to J. Wellington Wimpy of the Popeye cartoons. The Wellington superficially looks like a Lancaster, but smaller and with only two engines. It is the only Bomber Command aircraft that flew from the first day of the war until the last. It was principally designed by Barnes Wallis, and 11,461 were built. It was named after the Duke of Wellington, victor against Napoleon at the Battle of Waterloo on 18 June 1815.[26] Canada was given Wellingtons along with Halifaxes when 6 Group RCAF became operational in January 1943. By 1943, the Wellington had become a poor choice for combat sorties. However, it worked well as an anti-submarine aircraft; my Uncle Warren Irvine flew one in that role. Best of all, the RCAF discovered Wellingtons were singularly useful for mine-laying ('mining'). By 1944 the RCAF was the leading authority on effective mining. More on that in my chapter on Bomber Command's War at Sea.

As a concluding note concerning the success the RCAF had with both the Halifax and the Wellington in the final two years of the Second World War, I should mention an unofficial motto of the RCAF: 'flexibility is key to airpower'.[27] The RCAF in the Second World War demonstrated this in spades with its innovations such as with the Halifax and Wellington. Necessity is the mother of invention.

---

26 Wikipedia, Vickers Wellington
27 Canadian NORAD Region Public Affairs *NORAD Agile Airpower Seminar Goes Viral* Winnipeg, MB 23 June 2020

Chapter Ten

People

The one thing people who know anything about Bomber Command know is that it had horrendous casualties. Of the 125,000 aircrew, 80,000 were casualties, and of these almost 58,000 died. Although aircrew were primarily from the UK and the Commonwealth Dominions of Canada, Australia and New Zealand, Paul Robinson tells me airmen from sixty-two nations flew with Bomber Command, and it had the highest casualty rate of any formation of the Allied forces in the Second World War.

Winston Churchill Parker of Okotoks, Alberta starts out his personal journey in Bomber Command by stating point blank 'In the early part of the war, the average life cycle of an Allied airman was only twelve trips because of the sheer number of German fighters and defences stacked up against us.'[1] My Dad notes in his logbook 'Through Adversity to the Stars – six weeks of life in Bomber Command 1 in 3 chance to survive'. So Winston Churchill Parker, my Dad and pretty much every other volunteer for Bomber Command knew how dangerous bomber combat was. It meant a high likelihood that they would die. In April 1942, on his thirteenth combat sortie, Winston Churchill Parker was shot down over Germany and so had to endure three years as a PoW, including the dreadful forced march in freezing cold in early 1945 in which his German guards tried to evade the Allies.

A stark, deeply moving, picture of Bomber Command aircrew life continually facing death both at the air base and inside the aircraft on combat sorties is Don Charlwood's 1956 Bomber Command autobiography *No Moon Tonight*. Don flew with 103 Squadron at Elsham Wolds only six miles (10 km) from Kirmington. Both bases used Barnetby-le-Wold by as their railway station. Charlwood says:

> These wayside stations were the first thing a new arrival saw and, if he survived, they were the last thing he saw as he departed. When he was setting out on leave … he would see the station as a gateway to the gaiety of London or Lincoln. It would beckon him with its promise of escape to places where time did not exist. But when he returned he would see the same station darkly, as a gateway to fear and tension. Such a station was Barnetby Junction.[2]

---

1 Parker, *Saddles & Service*, p. 107.
2 Charlton, *No Moon Tonight*, p. 44

BOMBER COMMAND

One constant in I have seen Bomber Command books is that bomber boys were brave. They fought one of the toughest battles in history, with historically high casualties. On 18 May 2021 my mentor David Freeman e-mailed me from California with an audio of internal communication of aircrew aboard Lancasters on combat sorties, accompanied by paintings of Lancasters, including in the inferno of combat, and a video documentary of Bomber Command. This package was so moving that I immediately circulated it among my friends, Bomber Boy families and Bomber Command contacts. It sparked amazing, heartfelt responses. Several specifically admired how calm and professional the Bomber Boys were in combat. Two particularly powerful replies were from RAF Wing Commander Tony Lark in England, and Bomber Boy daughter Sharan Gainor of Nicaragua. Her Dad, Frank Selman, was shot down while returning from a combat sortie at Dusseldorf and survived to be betrayed and captured. Here is what Tony and Sharan said:

--------- Original Message ----------

From: **RAF WC Tony Lark**
Date: Friday, 21 May 2021
Subject: LANCASTERS Aircrew Voices & Video Documentary
To: Roddy MacKenzie

Roddy

Just listened to the recordings. I find it so moving that even though they were in harm's way and could be shot down at any moment they were so calm. It highlights the professionalism and above all the bravery of those airmen.

Roddy, your Dad was one of those airmen. He must have been a brave man too. All of them were magnificent. We must never forget!

Tony

---------- Original Message ---------

From: **Sharan Gainor**
Date: Tue, 18 May 2021
Subject: LANCASTERS Aircrew Voices & Video Documentary
To: Roddy MacKenzie
Cc: Beverely Selman Smith, Marilyn Woolf, Gordon Selman

Oh my, thank you. These tugged at my heart, especially seeing the ones going down on fire, and thinking of my Dad jumping out of one! Humbling, and so grateful he 'made it'!

Thanks
Sharan

PEOPLE

Bomber Command consisted of 125,000 aircrew, supported by 'a million men and women' in groundcrew, the Women's Auxiliary Air Force (WAAF), Air Transport Auxiliary (ATA), Auxiliary Territorial Service (ATS) in which Princess Elizabeth served, and Navy, Army & Air Force Institutes (NAAFI). The overwhelming majority came from the UK and Commonwealth.[3] My understanding is that the Royal Family, and perhaps also the Government, opposed young Princess Elizabeth joining the wartime armed forces. But the princess, who is now our Queen, with her quiet determination, at age 18 politely insisted and prevailed, as she always does. Her instincts were perfect – as they always are.

Paul Robinson describes the situation best, defining Bomber Command support groups as follows:[4]

- aircrew: 125,000, all volunteers;
- groundcrew: first-line trades like airframe and engine fitters, riggers, mechanics, armourers and so on – the squadron personnel who serviced the bombers;
- technicians: the second-line maintenance and repair personnel, often not on a squadron but at the base; and the people who maintained the station's communications, air traffic control, and so on;
- logisticians: those overseeing the movement of people and goods, purchasing, inventory management and warehousing. Paul's mother was a WAAF 'equipment officer'; and finally
- support personnel: a really broad range, from intelligence officers through air traffic controllers, firemen, met (meteorological) forecasters, administrators, padres, RAF police, cleaners, caterers and mess staff (many were local women).

Regarding groundcrew, centenarian Colin Bell who flew fifty combat sorties over Germany, including thirteen over Berlin, responded to a question about his view of ground crew when he was speaking about Pathfinders at the 22 July 2021 RAF Club Dinner by saying

> Oh, fantastic! They were heroes. They worked in appalling conditions, night-long freezing conditions. They made certain, as far as it was possible to do so, that the aircraft were fit for operations. I have no criticism whatsoever of the support staff, the groundcrews. As I say, they were heroes and they didn't get decorations but they deserved them.

Colin's enthusiastic observation triggered my choice of cover for this book. I wanted to recognize groundcrew, as per Colin's concluding sentence.

---

3 International Bomber Command Centre www:internationalbcc.co.uk

4 e-mail to author, 29 June 2020

BOMBER COMMAND

Paul advises me that each airfield had between 2,000-2,500 personnel, so they were big business for Lincolnshire: 60,000 people at any one time. He says, imagine what Lincoln was like on nights of no flying. Paul told me Lincoln ladies, now in their nineties, say they did not have to buy a drink for five years. Paul sums up by saying each squadron of two dozen bombers needed 1,000 first-line personnel consisting of forty-four air and groundcrew times twenty-four bombers. That totals 1,056 people. In addition these squadrons needed those in the second line and other supporting people cited above. In short, in Paul's words, Bomber Command was 'quite some organization'.

I had a personal experience with this on 5 May 2021 while reading in our local neighbourhood newspaper[5] the obituary of Archibald Thomas Kay, age 101. He came from Scotland to British Columbia in 1950 to find and marry a woman here who had briefly visited Scotland. He found her, married her, and stayed here. I never met him but I was curious regarding what he did in the Second World War. It turns out Archie's service was very interesting, as his obituary reports:

> As a young man Archie was Apprenticed to a Heating and Ventilation company in Glasgow where he worked until the outbreak of World War 2 when he was posted by the UK Ministry of Defence to the Royal Aircraft Establishment at Farnborough, Hampshire. Because of his expertise in HVAC he was soon attached to a research group assigned to find a way for the RAF fighters and bombers to fly higher than their normal ceiling of 30,000 ft. without the pilots becoming starved of oxygen or half frozen to death. The Axis fighter planes could already fly much higher giving them a great military advantage. Over the course of the war Archie and his colleagues overcame all the technical barriers and got to fly on many of the test flights to observe first-hand their handiwork.

How is that for someone essential to Bomber Command? The net of those supporting Bomber Command was very wide indeed.

And, impressive as Archie's obituary is, it gets even better. It goes on to say 'One special project was to design and build a special pressurized pod that Prime Minister Winston Churchill could be accommodated in so that the plane carrying him could safely fly at a high altitude to his summit meetings in America and Russia with Presidents Roosevelt and Stalin.'

---

5 Archibald Thomas Kay, *North Shore News*, North Vancouver, Canada nsnews.com 5 May 2021 p. A49

PEOPLE

Command Chain for Bombing Targets

The best description I have encountered of this process is from Bomber Command's most famous pilot, Guy Gibson VC. Here is how he tells it:[6]

- Harris and his advisory staff, 'all of whom have done their fair share of duty over Germany,' study the weather and choose their target
- Harris speaks to all his group commanders in a telephone broadcast
- Each group commander gives the information to their group operation officers
- This information is then passed to the RAF stations
- RAF stations advise their squadrons
- Each squadron commander meets with his two flight commanders
- On each airfield there is soon the roar of Lancasters as each takes off for a thorough thirty-minute air test in which everything is tested including the wireless, guns, navigational instruments and bomb doors – sometimes bombs are dropped for practice
- The squadron commander briefs the aircrews in tonight's operation including the target (e.g. the centre of a cluster of factories making Daimler-Benz engines), the number of bombers participating (e.g. 700), the bomb loads, the weather, Pathfinder timing, and bombing height (e.g. 21,000 feet)
- The navigation officer gives a briefing including zero-hour timing, Pathfinder flare locations and colours, aiming point (e.g. 15 miles/from target) timing to the second at which each bomber must be at the target
- The squadron commander gives his final orders such as 'Now don't forget chaps, once you have reached the preliminary target indicator you turn onto a course of 135 degrees magnetic and hold it for four minutes. You are to take no evasive action, but to keep straight on past the target. Once you have dropped your bombs, you may weave about slightly and gain speed by going down in a gentle dive. The Pathfinders will drop a cluster of green and red flares thirty miles beyond the target, and you are to concentrate on these, and return home in a gaggle. Now don't forget, no straggling.'
- Paul Robinson adds that the station commander would conclude (or in some cases commence) the briefing with some general wise words about how important the target was.
- Time between briefing and take-off is not pleasant – aircrew do not know what to do while waiting. Time passes slowly. Minutes seem like hours.
- The group commander's office phones to confirm the full number of aircraft from each Squadron
- Then comes take-off, Gibson says for the layman 'a thrilling sight' as at exactly the right time each Lancaster takes off
- The Lancasters reach their operational height and set their course to converge on their rendezvous point at exactly the right time

---

6 Gibson, *Enemy Coast Ahead* pp. 213-

BOMBER COMMAND

- At their rendezvous point, all navigation lights go out simultaneously and the bomber force, sometimes of hundreds of bombers, plot their course and fly in formation following a common track and timing often in pitch black and heavy clouds to the target.
- The scope is awesome. Guy Gibson says: 'But imagine a glass brick two miles across, twenty miles long and 8,000 feet thick, filled with hundreds of Lancasters, and move it slowly towards the Dutch coast, and there you have a concentrated wave on its way.'
- German alarm bells ring as the bomber force is detected approaching the Dutch coast – Germany's air defence forces are warned, powerful German searchlights and flak batteries are at the ready, and Luftwaffe night fighters in Holland are airborne – the battle begins.

Regarding Guy Gibson's first point of target selection, on 12 April 2022, Paul Robinson elaborated, telling me that

> in general, the Bomber Command HQs (both British and American) selected the targets, and co-ordinated the raids. After the POINTBLANK directive this was done jointly. Harris' staff would choose the targets and aiming points for the groups, and co-ordinate the pathfinders and 100 Group RCM and night-fighter support. The groups would then write detailed plans for their squadrons and pass them down by 'battle order' to the stations, which managed crew lists, weather and intelligence briefs et cetera.

Regarding Guy Gibson's seventeenth point about the awesome scope of hundreds of Lancasters flying in concentrated waves, Canadian Warplane Heritage Museum CEO Dave Rohrer described it to Rick Mercer on CBC's 2015 coverage of Mercer's flight on the CWHM Lancaster, the only one that flies in Canada. Dave is one of the very few pilots accredited to fly this Lancaster. On that 2015 CBC programme, which is available on YouTube, he told Rick that sometimes 700 to 800 Lancasters flew in formation in the dark with no lights and no communication in an armada ten miles (16 km) wide and thirty miles (48 km) long. Just imagine what a massive accomplishment doing that was by all those young pilots and navigators as they flew in silence and darkness towards what was death for too many of them.

It is not surprising then that Don Charlwood tells us Bomber Command aircrew partied hard – footsteps on the ceiling, furniture turned upside down so aircrew could fling themselves over it, copious amounts of beer. Don has an amusing anecdote regarding a wing commander at Elsham Wolds who visited Kirmington. Don tells it as follows[7]

---

[7] Charlton, p 47

So the Wingco goes to the Kirmington party. There he is, blind as a bloody newt, and what do they do? Whip his bags off! Send him home in his underpants! The sequel to this came shortly before lunch. A Wellington flew low overhead; a parachute appeared and, suspended from it, the wing commander's trousers. The wing commander, we heard, took a poor view. Someone or other at Kirmington was going to be posted.

Bomber Command Women

WAAF were not aircrew, but some ATA pilots were women. From 1943 they received the same pay as men. This male-female equal pay for equal work was a first for the British government.[8] These women flew every kind of aircraft. Paul Robinson tells me about an attractive young wartime female pilot who solo delivered a Wellington to an operational base. When she emerged from the cockpit, they could not believe she had done this, so they searched the Wellington for the real aircrew they assumed must be hiding.

Women assisting Bomber Command did everything except front-line combat fighting, from essential clerical work to packing parachutes, driving tractors towing the trolleys carrying the bomb loads, and with medical assistance. Paul tells me it was tradition that, if you used your parachute, you tipped your parachute packer five pounds. This money was often sent from a PoW camp. Romances started that way. It is said that one airman, surviving PoW camp, became an insurance salesman postwar. One day the door he knocked was opened by his WAAF parachute packer. They married shortly thereafter.

In addition, women were the majority among the codebreakers at Bletchley Park whose work was essential for Bomber Command. The grandmother of Catherine, Duchess of Cambridge, served in Bletchley Park. Also, women serving in Bomber Command stations could be killed during air raids or by fuel or ammunition fires or explosions. These were primarily WAAFs.

Bomber Command Composition

Bomber Command was composed of 126 Squadrons, ninety-two which were British (RAF), fifteen Canadian (RCAF), eight Australian (RAAF) and two New Zealander (RNZAF). In addition to the Commonwealth squadrons, there were four Polish squadrons, two Free French and one Czech; these were all RAF squadrons, bearing numbers of the 300-399 series.

These Canadian, Australian and New Zealander squadrons were created by Article XV of the British Commonwealth Air Training Plan as required by

---

8 Wikipedia Air Transport Auxiliary

Mackenzie King. He did not want Commonwealth air forces to disappear inside the RAF. Article XV squadrons helped but, as it turns out, only a little. And so, at the insistence of Mackenzie King, on 25 October 1942 the Royal Canadian Air Force formed No. 6 Group RCAF Bomber Command. This was the only non-RAF group in Bomber Command. This was an enormous milestone for the RCAF, compliments of a determined Canadian prime minister.

Bomber Command's operational groups were No. 1 Group in which my Dad flew, No. 2 Group, No. 3 Group, No. 4 Group of which Harris had been AOC-in-C in 1937-38, No. 5 Group of which Harris had been AOC-in-C in 1939-40, No. 6 Group (RCAF), No. 8 Group (Pathfinders) and No. 100 Group (Bomber Support). Bomber Command also had Nos 7, 91, 92 and 93 Groups; these were bomber training units. Bomber Command's 126 squadrons mostly had mixed-nationality aircrew. The biggest non-British component was Canadian. I am told almost a third of RAF aircrew were Canadians, such as my Dad, seconded to the RAF by the RCAF. In fact, more Canadians flew in the RAF than flew in the RCAF.

A unique feature of Bomber Command composition was the way heavy bomber aircrews were formed. Canadian pilot Murray Peden, who flew in 214 Squadron RAF, described this 'crewing-up' process at the OTU (Operational Training Unit):[9]

> The instructors and admin officers, who wasted no time getting hold of us, organized the group into classes and laid out our syllabus. They dropped the word that within about ten days we would be teamed up in crews of five, each consisting of a pilot, bomb-aimer, navigator, wireless operator and air gunner. Equal numbers of each of these trades had been brought together to form our course at Chipping Warden, and we were told that if any five could agree amongst themselves that they wanted to form a crew and fly together, the Air Force would oblige and crew them up officially. But at the end of the ten-day period all those who had not made their own arrangements would be crewed up arbitrarily by the staff; and probably, we guessed, by purely random selection.

Peden pragmatically added, 'The reason for anyone wishing to crew up and fly with certain other selected individuals was generally self-preservation pure and simple; you wanted to have crew members with you who were good at their jobs and who could perform them efficiently under the grinding stress of operational conditions.' And even more pragmatically, Peden concluded, 'Choosing a pilot could be a much more critical decision than choosing a wife. A bird-brained wife might still make life worth living, and an object to cherish. A bird-brained pilot was likely to kill everyone who flew with him, soon.' Sir Arthur Harris said about Peden's book 'I consider it not only the best and most true to life "war" book

---

9 Peden, *A Thousand Shall Fall*, pp. 166-7

I've read about this war, but the best about all wars of my lifetime.'[10] Postwar, Peden became a securities lawyer and, in 1968, the first chairman of the Manitoba Securities Commission. He died on 6 January 2022 at home in Winnipeg. He was no bird-brain.

Life in Bomber Command Was About Death

Whatever else we know about Bomber Command, we know it was a place of death for Allied airmen. Casualties were astronomical. Paul Robinson tells me overall 45 per cent of bomber aircrew were killed. Of those joining their first squadron, 55 per cent were killed during their first tour of thirty operations (say three months). Of the remainder, three would be wounded by the time their aircraft made it home, fourteen were shot down but survived (twelve became PoWs, two were evaders), and the remainder like my Dad carried out instructor duties or second op tours, sometimes as Pathfinders.

Putting that in human terms, I refer to my Dad's 166 Squadron which flew from January 1943 until April 1945 – two years and three months. In that single Squadron in only twenty-seven months, 944 aircrew were killed, average age 23. Of these, 155 were Canadians, sixty-five were Australians and eleven were New Zealanders.[11] In addition, 166 Squadron lost 114 Lancasters and thirty-nine Wellingtons.[12] Think about these figures. They stagger me. A single squadron of two-dozen heavy bombers would have 168 aircrew. For 944 aircrew in that squadron to be killed, the entire squadron would have to be wiped out 5.6 times. For 166 Squadron, flying only twenty-seven months, the entire squadron aircrew would have to be killed every five months.

My Dad arrived on 1 April 1944. There he learned that 45 per cent of the entire squadron had been killed in the preceding month. That percentage is so high, that death rate so horrendous, it is for me almost impossible to comprehend. Given how depressing, indeed terrifying, RAF Kirmington was, it is particularly impressive that Dad's DFC citation says in part 'On the ground, as Deputy Flight Commander, he has shown willingness and enthusiasm which have been an inspiration to the whole squadron'. What an accomplishment that Dad helped raise morale, given that death was the overriding reality of life in Bomber Command.

RAF Station Kirmington

For most of my life, I had never heard of Kirmington, or of 166 Squadron. Now I know RAF Kirmington was a Second World War air base near the village of

---

10 Back cover statement by Harris recommending *A Thousand Shall Fall*
11 Wright, *On Wings of War*, Appendix 7
12 Otter, *Lincolnshire Airfields*, p. 156

Kirmington, population 365.[13] My knowledge of RAF Kirmington is primarily through the following five sources: authors Pat Otter,[14] Don Feesey,[15] and Jim Wright;[16] the diary of 166 Squadron Flight Sergeant Dennis Eastcott (Appendix IV); and what I learnt during my four visits to Kirmington (24-25 July 2017, 14 May 2018, 31 August to 2 September 2018 and 4 May 2019). My research reveals RAF Kirmington was opened in January 1942, but was not operational until nine months later. In October 1942, it officially became a satellite of RAF Elsham Wolds, and 150 Squadron was the first to move in. However, 150 Squadron was soon replaced by my Dad's 166 Squadron, which was reformed in January 1943 from detachments of 142 and 150 Squadrons.

Dad's 166 Squadron, having first been formed in April 1918, was first re-formed in November 1936 until April 1940, primarily as a training unit. It was then re-formed a second time on 27 January 1943 as an operational night-bomber squadron located at RAF Kirmington for the duration of the war. It commenced combat sorties immediately and, just over a month later, was immersed in Bomber Command's 'Battle of the Ruhr' from 5 March to 31 July 1943. Bombing the Ruhr was difficult and dangerous because the Ruhr Valley was so heavily defended. In September 1943 at 166 Squadron, the first Lancasters replaced Wellingtons. By the time Dad arrived on 1 April 1944, 166 Squadron was flying state-of-the-art Lancaster Mk IIIs that had just emerged from factories in March 1944. Dad took command of 166 Squadron's AS-L for 'Love' Lancaster Mk III ND757, likely as a brand-new aircraft.

In my imagination, partly from movies, I used to think the one redeeming feature of fighting the Second World War in Bomber Command, until you were killed of course, is that you returned to Britain after each sortie. I imagined in Britain Bomber Boys being wined and dined by appreciative locals for heroism, and being well looked after by enthusiastic women having special ways of showing their appreciation. It is true some of this happened, and some Bomber Command air bases were impressive, particularly for officers, such as the glorious Petwood Hotel at Woodhall Spa. But my research reveals most Bomber Command air bases were not nice places, and RAF Kirmington was one of the worst. Here's what 166 Squadron navigator Don Feesey tells us: 'My first impression of Kirmington is very poor. In fact, to think that it is to be our permanent home from now on, makes me shudder.' Worse, 'the buildings were detestable'.[17] Kirmington was located in the wilds of northern Lincolnshire, at that time way off the beaten track. It was even several miles from Barnetby, the nearest railway station. RAF Kirmington had no entertainment, no amenities, and nothing except The Chopper nearby. During leave, it was hard to get anywhere from Barnetby, and one had the considerable challenge

---

13   2011 Census

14   Otter pp. 151-9

15   Feesey, *The Fly By Nights*, pp. 74-5

16   Wright, *On Wings of War*

17   Feesey, *The Fly By Nights*, writing to his girlfriend, and future wife

of getting back in time to avoid AWOL. Don Charlwood captures the situation poetically, saying the road from Barnetby to the airbase 'led to comradeship, fear and death' while the road from the airbase to Barnetby led to 'relief, safety and, I think, loneliness'.[18]

Building dispersal was a major problem at RAF Kirmington. Buildings were so dispersed that aircrew were issued bicycles, but these were in terrible shape and short supply. Kirmington's only redeeming feature still thrives there today – the Marrowbone and Cleaver Pub, lovingly called The Chopper, of which I wrote in my chapter on my growing awareness of Bomber Command.

10 April 1944 – An Unforgettable Day at RAF Station Kirmington

Dad flew his first two combat sorties the same day, 10 April 1944, although the first of the two commenced the preceding evening. The second of these two sorties featured an unusual accident on the runway. The story of that accident warrants telling. To do so, I'm relying on the accounts of 166 Squadron's Jim Wright[19] and *Lincolnshire Airfields* author Patrick Otter.[20] The picture painted by combining their stories is powerful. So here goes.

On 10 April 1944, 166 Squadron Lancaster AS-F for Freddie blew a tyre while among the 166 Squadron's twenty-two Lancasters taking off. Their combat sortie was to bomb the railway marshalling yards in Aulnoye, France. It was the major junction between the Paris-Brussels railway line and the Calais-Lille line. Jim Wright says the first four Lancasters, including Dad's, were already airborne, but the remaining seventeen were unable to take off. The airborne four successfully bombed their target, then, returning, were diverted because Kirmington's runway was wrecked. Dad's logbook reveals he was diverted to land at No. 1 Group's RAF North Killingholme.

And so, what are the details of this accident? Two-thirds of the way down RAF Kirmington's runway, as mentioned, AS-F for Freddie blew a tyre. The Lancaster swung badly, 'skittering down the runway in a shower of sparks'. As it screeched to a halt, it burst into flames. Fortunately, 166 Squadron Commander Frank Powley arrived almost immediately with the fire tender. Freddie's seven aircrew fled the burning Lancaster, shouting 'The bombs! The bombs!' A member of ground crew remarked he had never seen aircrew move so fast. Wing Commander Powley took the hose from the fire tender and ordered everyone clear. Moments later, nine of AS-F for Freddie's fourteen 1,000 lb (454kg) bombs exploded, creating a huge 50-foot (15 metre) wide crater in Kirmington's runway. Thankfully, there were no casualties. However, this situation being so unusual, senior RAF officers arrived

---

18 Charlwood, p. 45

19 Wright, p. 68

20 Otter, pp. 155-6

to see for themselves how much damage a fully bomb-loaded Lancaster does exploding on its runway. RAF Station Kirmington's commanding officer, Group Captain Graham, had a hundred men furiously shovelling 500 tons of soil into the 15-foot (4.6-metre) deep crater. By 10.00 am the next day, Kirmington's runway was deemed 'useable', but it took another ten days before the runway was declared 'operational'. Airfield buildings were also damaged, including doors to a T2 hangar which was buckled by the force of the blast. The blast also reputedly smashed every window within a mile (1,600 metres) of Kirmington airfield.

A slight dip remains even today in the runway – it is called 'Gibbons' Gulley' after the pilot of AS-F for Freddie, Pilot Officer Dudley Gibbons. He had further adventures. On 22 June 1944, flying 166 Squadron Lancaster AS-W, Gibbons and his aircrew lost all their bombs. Due to an electrical fault, their bombs were automatically released when they opened their bomb doors.[21] On 12 July 1944, while bombing railway yards with my Dad at Revigny in France, Gibbons' Lancaster AS-W was shot down. Gibbons survived with five of his aircrew, evaded capture and managed to get off the continent and back to RAF Kirmington in September to complete his tour of thirty combat sorties.[22]

But what was day-to-day life like for aircrew at RAF Kirmington? For those who served in the military, the following is already well known. But most of my friends and I are among the 'baby boomers' who were the first in their families to go to university, but were also completely disconnected from the military. In 1968 Canada's shutting down of the COTC (Canadian Officers' Training Corps) in Canadian universities created a wide gulf between university students and the military. That continues today. And so, for we who were never in the military, I have attached as Appendix IV the diary kept by 166 Squadron airman Dennis Eastcott. For me his Diary is an eye-opener regarding the realities of life in Bomber Command in the Second World War.

Lodgings

And then there's lodgings. As mentioned, the finest Second World War lodgings for Bomber Command officers I have seen were at the luxurious Petwood Hotel at Woodhall Spa, home of the Dambusters' Memorial. Petwood for a while housed the officers of the famed 617 'Dambusters' Squadron RAF. Their NCO aircrew were, however, miles away in Nissen huts. This division between officers and NCOs in heavy bomber aircrew was as mentioned a source of friction between Canada and the UK, Canada saying all aboard a heavy bomber should be commissioned as officers. The Petwood Hotel is a gorgeous building beautifully situated on elegant grounds in Woodhall Spa, a half-hour's drive east of Lincoln. In May 2019, I had a lovely lunch at Petwood Hotel hosted by RAF Wing Commander Tony Lark

---

21 Wright, p. 86
22 Wright, pp. 91-3

PEOPLE

on the 13th, an interesting visit with New Zealand Bomber Command enthusiast Barbie Hunter and her husband Ken at their Woodhall Spa home on 16 May, and several pleasant hours including lunch with my sons Ruaridh and Guy Roland MacKenzie at Petwood on the 19th. I love the Petwood Hotel. Paul Robinson points out that prewar stations such as Waddington, Coningsby and Scampton had good aircrew accommodation, as opposed to the more austere facilities of wartime-build ones.

RAF officers at Kirmington had what appears to be the best of a bad situation – they were housed in brick-built huts much nearer the airfield, while NCOs were housed 'in cold, damp unheated mice-infested Nissen huts'[23] about a mile (1,600 metres) away. The Sergeants' Mess was in the middle. This dispersal of buildings was awful. Someone decided to locate RAF Kirmington's accommodation far from the airfield for safety if the Luftwaffe ever attacked, which the Luftwaffe never did. Having accommodation far away from the airfield caused terrible problems including people getting killed rushing to and from the airfield in the pitch-black darkness of blackout. Such was the reality of wartime life at RAF Kirmington, one of so many Bomber Command airfields hastily thrown together in the Second World War.

The Dedication of Bomber Command Aircrew

Something no one disputes is the dedication of Bomber Command aircrew. Given that Bomber Command's 125,000 aircrew were all volunteers, and 80,000 of them became casualties, it is a wonder that throughout the war there was no shortage of volunteers. Why, one might ask, would so many volunteer when casualties were so high? The answer lies in the conviction that what these young men were doing in Bomber Command was vital to victory. They were right. Airmen dedication is powerfully articulated by 'An Airman's Letter', published anonymously on 18 June 1940 in the London *Times*. It was written to his mother by an unknown airman. The letter struck such a nerve that, within a month of its publication, over half a million requests for copies were received from all over the British Commonwealth. It articulates why all these earnest young airmen volunteered for Bomber Command in spite of its appalling casualty rate. This unknown young airman said in part:

> Dearest Mother, Though I feel no premonition at all, events are moving rapidly, and I have instructed that this letter be forwarded to you should I fail to return from one of the raids which we shall shortly be called upon to undertake .... First, it will comfort you to know that my role in this war has been of the greatest importance .... Today we are faced with the greatest organized challenge to Christianity

---

23 Feesey, *Fly By Nights*

and civilization that the world has ever seen, and I count myself lucky and honoured to be the right age and fully trained to throw my weight into the scale .... I firmly and absolutely believe that evil things are sent into this world to try us .... But with the final test of war I consider my character fully developed. Thus at my early age my earthly mission is already fulfilled and I am prepared to die ....[24]

On 18 February 1981, it was learnt from his mother's obituary that this anonymous airman, her only child, was Vivian Alan William Noall Rosewarne. He was killed in action during the evacuation of Dunkirk. This letter articulates the incredible sense of purpose, in the face of such high probabilities of being killed, that Bomber Command aircrew had to endure. Likewise, Canada's Gordon Ritchie DFM,[25] a tail gunner on 429 (Bison) Squadron of No. 6 Group RCAF wrote 'For many of us, the services offered the opportunity to get involved in ridding the world of Nazi Germany led by Adolf Hitler. I think the whole country was united in those days as at no other time in our history. We knew what had to be done and we set out to do it.'[26]

LMF: Lack of Moral Fibre

The Institute says Strategic Bomber Offensive aircrew faced an additional challenge, namely 'The nervous strain of flying through flak and of the very frequent damage caused to their aircraft by it – could not fail to affect the morale of the bomber crews .... Some of them were suffering from depression.'[27] And that brings us to LMF – Lack of Moral Fibre. LMF is still controversial. Paul Robinson tells me this 'is a wretched subject' which I've 'dealt with well'. He points out there's a real difference between cowardice and battle fatigue. He says everyone he knows or has read about has been scared about combat flying, although even more scared about failing their friends than dying. However, he points out that to fly 200 hours in unreliable, dangerous training aircraft, followed by service on an operational squadron being shot at, must grind down the strongest individual, especially when they have other issues such as responsibility for a wife and young family. Paul says youngsters don't mind sticking their heads in the lion's mouth, but people with personal responsibilities think twice. We all know those who shirk. That's different, and they don't deserve our sympathy. Paul concludes by saying I am 'spot on' about whole generation being affected by their experience of combat. He says we

---

24 McNeil, *Voices of a War Remembered*, pp. 13-15
25 The Memory Project Veteran Stories: Gordon Ritchie www.thememoryproject.com/stories/265:gordon-ritchie/
26 McNeil, p. 16
27 Institute, Vol. VII, p. 129

didn't cut them enough slack. But then, we didn't understand the trauma they'd been through – until it was too late.

So what happened? The RAF and RCAF, assisted by military medical corps of both nations, used LMF to brand post-traumatic stress disorder as cowardice. Horrendous casualties expose the nightmare Bomber Command aircrew experienced. Men returned from sorties shaken to their core. Their bone-deep trauma was dismissed as cowardice to discourage others from refusing to fly. While LMF afflicted the RAF, and to a lesser extent the RCAF, I am told both the American and Australian air forces were more enlightened, featuring extensive use of psychiatric services and rest camps.[28] However, in reality the harsh LMF was seldom imposed – just the knowledge of it kept many airmen in line. But the consequences of suppression, the lack of recognition of what we now call post-traumatic stress disorder, did an enormous disservice to airmen postwar, and to their offspring, people like me. And suppressed PTSD can rear its ugly head years, or even decades, later.

For example, by the mid-1980s, four decades after he flew combat sorties, my Dad developed a paralyzing fear of flying even as a passenger on an airliner jet. It took considerable courage for him to board flight in Calgary an Air Canada on 7 February 1985 for the 75-minute nonstop trip to Vancouver to attend the celebration dinner that evening on the top floor of the Hyatt Regency for the 100th birthday of his father and my grandfather, Roderick M. MacKenzie. Although Dad and I talked about it by telephone that morning, with me saying 'we will never live it down' if he skips Grandpa's 100th birthday, I did not know whether Dad would come from Calgary to Grandpa's centenary dinner until I saw Dad stepping out of an airport taxi and into the Hyatt at about 4.30 that afternoon.

In November 2020, IBCC Digital Archivist Dan Ellin published an article in the *British Journal for Military History*[29] in which he re-examines LMF in RAF Second World War culture and then considers how and why LMF is remembered by veterans and popular history postwar. Dan says the term LMF was first used at a meeting on 21 March 1940 regarding increasing numbers of airmen who refused to fly. Dan says 'Lack of moral fibre' (LMF) was a metaphorical 'dreadful stick' intended to deter aircrew refusals to fly and displays of 'cowardice' during the Second World War. Cases were rare, but there are tales of humiliating parades; offenders were publicly stripped of their 'wings' and rank and marched away.

Dan points out LMF was never a medical diagnosis, but instead an executive process to reduce the number of aircrew who refused to fly. However, LMF was mixed with medical understandings which in the Second World War concerned the fibre of the individual, that some people 'were simply the wrong type', but since the 1980s is seen as PTSD arising from traumatic events to which anyone can succumb because we all have limits to our endurance. Dan also says LMF is now shrouded in

---

28 Dunmore and Carter, *Reap the Whirlwind: The Untold Story of 6 Group Canada's Bomber Force of World War* II, p. 254.

29 Ellin 'A 'Lack of Moral Fibre' in Royal Air Force Bomber Command and Popular Culture,' *British Journal for Military History* Abstract and pp. 42-65.

myths which have been amplified over the past seven decades. Dan concludes 'that tales of LMF were embellished and circulated verbally throughout the RAF, during training and on operational stations. Many aircrew who were assumed to be LMF may have been posted away for medical or other reasons.' He argues that 'for many airmen, witnessing the humiliating ritual was not necessary; rumours of LMF were as effective and made a lasting impression on them.'

One of the only war stories my Dad told me was, as I remember it:

> A young, inexperienced pilot returned from a bombing sortie totally traumatized. Instead of recognizing this, the RAF hierarchy forced him back into the cockpit of his Lancaster the following night. While our Lancasters were flying in tight formation, this young pilot lost his nerve and yanked his joystick. His Lancaster surged upwards, ripping out the belly of the Lancaster above him. In the ensuing chaos, several Lancasters crashed, all because of the RAF's insane policy of LMF.

Paul recalls a mid-air collision involving six Lancasters. This might have been the incident Dad heard about. If so, 'rumour control' failed, resulting in the spread of altered information. Paul says

> on 23 June 1944 (i.e. when your Dad was there), six 97 Squadron Lancs were practising close formation flying when the No. 4 (piloted by Flight Lieutenant Van Raalt RAAF) got caught in a slipstream, pitched up and hit another Lanc. Both crashed; one man baled out. Van Raalt's crew had flown twenty-two missions on 97 and were experienced Pathfinders. There was no hint of LMF. However, it was the crew's first sortie after returning from leave the day before. It's likely Van Raalt was rusty: close formation in four-engine bombers must have been pretty tricky at the best of times, let alone when you hadn't flown for a week.[30]

Regarding LMF Paul adds:

> Incidentally, I've heard other stories about aircrew who got the 'twitch'. Yes, they had to be dealt with it to discourage others from giving up too easily, but those who had proved themselves in battle and had been worn down by stress over a period of time were treated reasonably. For example, one pilot was grounded, sent for medical treatment then appointed as an admin officer on a non-flying station. It must have been difficult to get the balance right.

During our Naval Officers Association lunch on 27 February 2019, it struck me for the first time that the medical profession was complicit in LMF. The speaker was

---

30 Robinson's e-mail to the author, 21 January 2020

PEOPLE

a military medic whose topic was trauma. When I mentioned Bomber Command, he quickly pointed out he knows only of physical trauma such as broken bones, not emotional trauma. He seemed anxious to separate himself from LMF, and indeed anything emotional arising from that war. Another anecdote: Don Charlton tells us that, when he first arrived at Elsham Wolds to fly combat sorties with 103 Squadron 'I lay on my bed, thinking involuntarily of a man our instructor had spoken of that day. Over the target he had screamed. He was ashamed and apologetic, but they had taken him off ops immediately. Probably, we were told, he would be classed as 'lacking in moral fibre'.[31]

Postwar costs were enormous. First, aircrew labelled LMF were immersed in shame. Second, to avoid the shame of LMF, many traumatized aircrew avoided getting any professional assistance, and so instead returned home, often without physical injuries, but suppressing deep emotional scars they passed on to their offspring, such as me, through what I call the Big Three:

- weak ability to connect emotionally
- perfectionism and
- anger issues.

The descendants of Bomber Boy children, such as mine, also pay for this. On point, in England on 14 May 2018, I met an Australian woman seated facing me on my train from London to Lincolnshire. As soon as I sat down, she asked where I was going and why. I replied Lincolnshire for Bomber Command. I told her about my Dad, and what I was learning about how horrific serving as Bomber Command aircrew was. Then she said:

> My grandfather served in Bomber Command. He returned to Australia without physical injuries, but with anger and alcohol issues my grandmother found intolerable, so she divorced him and ordered our family to shun him. I wasn't born until 1958, so I never met him. But I have found in these past few years I think of him with increasing unease that we wronged him. Now that I hear from you about Bomber Command, I'm ashamed of how my family treated my grandfather.

Sadly, when talking with her I did not know I would be writing this book, so I neglected to obtain her name and contact details.

No. 166 Squadron navigator Don Feesey wrote:

> I suffered a breakdown in my health, shortly after my tour of ops. It took the form of a severe depression … . Once the war in Europe was over, I become completely negative. I was unable to concentrate

---

31 Charlton, p. 49

for long, and I lost interest in nearly all activities. My appetite was gone, and I was nearly always tired, and yet I slept badly. My weight fell by nearly two stones, and I was easily upset. Often, I was close to tears and day after day, I had agonizing headaches, frequently followed by retching and vomiting. The unhappiness is difficult to imagine for those who have not experienced it.[32]

Regarding 166 Squadron, Don Feesey says:

The insignia of 166 Squadron was a fierce-looking bulldog above the word 'TENACITY'. Our crews who pressed on with missions when under severe attack, or with damage to their aircraft, certainly lived up to the emblem of their squadron. Out of 199 Lancaster aircraft which served the squadron, 149 either crashed or were registered as missing. Nearly 1,000 lives were lost, and some survivors were left physically disabled.[33]

And that is where my Dad fought for us in the Second World War! While about 70 per cent of Bomber Command personnel became recognized casualties, many of the remaining 30 per cent came home deeply damaged emotionally. And this had consequences. For example, while perfectionism aided survival in Bomber Command, it was terrible within family relationships. The suppression of emotions was passed on to the next generation. The LMF concept of suppression of feelings did much damage, and keeps on giving even today.

One of the world's most famous and admired people who endured the trauma inflicted on those risking their lives in the Strategic Bomber Offensive was much-loved American actor Jimmy Stewart. He was four years older than my Dad, having been born on 20 May 1908 while Dad was born on 21 April 1912. Unlike our Canadian MacKenzie forebears who, before the Second World War, had no military connections I know of since our arrival in Canada in 1779, Jimmy Stewart hailed from an American military family. Both of his grandfathers fought in America's Civil War, and Stewart's Dad fought for America in the First World War. In 1940, Stewart was rejected for service because he was 32, and was too underweight for his height. Stewart circumvented both problems with persistence – his weight problem by getting his doctor to write that his low weight was genetic, not ill-health, and his age problem was countered by his pilot's licence and skill of flying. His personal aircraft was a military trainer. Stewart even took a trip to Europe in late 1939 to 'get the lay of the land' in the war Britain and Canada were already fighting. Stewart was admitted into the US Army Air Forces in 1941 as a private. In just four years he rose from private to colonel – an unusual accomplishment.[34]

---

32 Feesey, p. 158

33 Feesey, p. 159

34 Wikipedia Jimmy Stewart

PEOPLE

Commanding officers and movie moguls wanted to keep Stewart stateside during the war making propaganda movies, but Stewart circumvented them just as he did his initial rejection in 1940. And so, in November 1943, just five months after my Dad was seconded to the RAF and transferred to England, Stewart, too, was transferred to England – in his case, to the 445th Bombardment Group in the Mighty Eighth.

On 24 February 1944 Stewart was at their base when twenty-five bombers departed to bomb Gotha in Germany. Thirteen of the twenty-five were shot down. The next day, Stewart led the 445th to Fürth about six miles (10 km) from Nuremburg. They were part of a major bombing offensive with twenty groups of Mighty Eighth fighter aircraft and twelve squadrons of RAF Spitfires for protection. With their bomb bays open at 18,500 feet, it was 40 below zero outside. German flak pierced through the centre of Stewart's B-24 Liberator 'Dixie Flyer'. For a moment 'Dixie Flyer' was filled with smoke as it violently ascended. A two-foot (60 cm) hole was created by enemy firepower close to Stewart's boot. He could see the ground below. It was Stewart's tenth combat mission as a squadron or group leader. Bombers around Stewart were shot down, German fighters were swarming and 'Dixie Flyer' was badly damaged. They somehow escaped, and limped back to England, having lost two of their four engines before seeing the English coast. While landing, 'Dixie Flyer' literally broke apart with a crack ripping from the bulkhead to the cockpit. David Crow reports that no one said Major Stewart was 'flak happy' (American slang for PTSD), but his commanding officer kept him on the ground and sent him for treatment, knowing the pressure of leading, and seeing so many of his men killed, was overwhelming. So Stewart 'had to just do what a lot of them did, which is go off into the country, take sodium amytal, and just chill and get re-programmed. They'd sit, and they'd talk to you, and they would give you perspective and they'd calm you down. Then they send you back online.'[35] Stewart's biographer, Matson, sums up saying:

> Combat fatigue and shell shock were the terms of the day for what eventually became known as post-traumatic stress disorder, but whatever the name, Stewart suffered along with millions of other combat veterans who had returned to homes the world over, to friends and family who couldn't understand what they had experienced ... . What could he say about B-24s being shot to pieces beside him in formation or colliding in a fireball over Tibenham? How could he convey how it felt when so many ships [bomber aircraft] hadn't come home from Gotha? Or write all those letters home, especially when he knew that the men he was telling mothers and fathers and wives about were dead?[36]

---

35 Matzen, *Mission: Jimmy Stewart and the Fight for Europe*
36 Matzen, pp. 309-10

General Hap Arnold personally recognized how traumatized Jimmy Stewart was, and so quietly ensured Stewart would never again fly a combat mission. Stewart was, however, showered with honours by America for his contribution to the success of the strategic bombing offensive. America admires The Mighty Eighth. David Crow concludes 'Jimmy Stewart rarely talked about his World War Two experience after returning from the service, but intense air force battles left lifelong scars'. Postwar, Stewart remained in the Air Force Reserve until mandatory retirement in 1968. In 1959, he was promoted to brigadier general. In 1985, President Ronald Reagan promoted Stewart to major general on the US Air Force retirement list.

I speak of Stewart's experiences because he is famous, he is loved, and his story demonstrates that the air war was just as horrific for the Mighty Eighth as it was for the RAF and the RCAF in Bomber Command. But America bombing by day and Bomber Command bombing by night kept Nazi Germany under attack round the clock. And Jimmy Stewart was just as vulnerable to what we called LMF as every other Bomber Boy, be he from America, Australia, Britain, Canada, New Zealand or over sixty other nations whose young men fought in Bomber Command.

And finally I must mention a young Canadian pilot in the First World War who was spared the humiliation, and potentially terrible penalties such as for 'cowardice', for his refusal to fly after he had completed his training as a pilot with the Royal Flying Corps. Some reports say he survived a plane crash. What we know for sure is that, before becoming a pilot, he had served as a volunteer stretcher-bearer as a private in the Canadian Army Medical Corps in Greece.[37] It is well known that his service in the First World War came to an end when in the confusion of an air raid he was hit by a bus in England, and so was sent home to Canada to convalesce. What is generally not known is the real reason his service concluded was because he was too terrified to fly. It was Dr John Blatherwick who enlightened me. And so, returning to Canada in honour instead of disgrace, he was able to serve Canada as a diplomat in London and Washington DC in the Second World War. And there's more. Postwar he won the Nobel Peace Prize for helping sort out the Suez Crisis in 1956, and in 1963 was elected prime minister of Canada. His name? Lester 'Mike' Pearson. Toronto's Pearson International Airport is named to honour him.

Conclusion

Thus concludes my commentary on Bomber Command people, of whom there were over a million, and the crippling stress inflicted on all Strategic Bombing Offensive Aircrew. These people were among the greatest heroes of the war.

---

37 Library and Archives Canada, Lester Bowles Pearson (1897–1972) www.bac-lac.gc.ca

Chapter Eleven

Training

My Dad volunteered to join the RCAF having neither military nor flying knowledge. He was a banker. How was he transformed by the RCAF and RAF into having the expertise to fly Lancasters at war? I needed to know. Advisors encouraging me to learn all I could about my Dad at war culminated on 5 November 2019 in the Canadian War Museum in Ottawa. There I spent a very helpful afternoon with the CWM's Senior Second World War Historian, Jeff Noakes. Jeff told me I must research and then weave the narrative of my Dad into this book, or I will end up with a textbook, and 'nobody reads a textbook'.

I felt helpless because I had virtually no information and my Dad was dead. Then a lightbulb went on in my head. I do have Dad's Logbook. Perhaps experts can teach me how to read it. Coupled with everything else listed below, perhaps Dad's logbook would serve as my 'Rosetta Stone', which was of course the 196 BC decree in three languages discovered in 1799 that enabled historians to read Egyptian hieroglyphics. Much later Dad's RCAF Record of Service finally arrived from Ottawa, but it, too, was filled with codes and acronyms needing interpretation. Dad's logbook and record of service were modern-day hieroglyphics for me.

Deciphering Dad's Second World War RCAF Service

Does this sound simple? It wasn't. To figure all this out, I faced the monumental task of creating into one seamless whole as a compelling narrative the following:

- Ottawa's almost impossible to read tiny handwriting of 26 April 1945 on 'RCAF OFFICER Record of Service Airmen' ('Record of Service') for Dad – it reveals dates and places where Dad was trained in the Plan but is crammed full of acronyms, rendering it a major challenge for a layman like me
- Dad's immaculately written logbook, again filled with acronyms
- The 19 November 2019 e-mail of RAF Air Vice – Marshal Paul Robinson bringing Dad's logbook to life with compelling clarity
- Editor Peter Wheeler's above-mentioned October 2018 *New Zealand Bomber Command Association Magazine*'s superb record of the Plan's air training schools across Canada, many of which were on our flat prairies.

- The Royal Bank of Canada's insightful history of Royal Bankers in the Second World War, including Dad's RCAF accomplishments in the Plan
- Guidance in reading Dad's logbook from Royal Air Force pilots Mike Matthews, Jack Miles and Paul Robinson.

New Zealand's Bomber Command Newsletter helped me in a second way. It opened for me my first door into Dad's logbook. When listing the Plan's air training schools in Canada, Peter thankfully included their initials, their numbered names, their category of school within the Plan and location in Canada. This enabled me for the first time to read parts of Dad's logbook. For example, it now tells me that Dad commenced training on 21 September 1941 at No. 2 MD (Manning Depot) in Brandon, Manitoba. He completed his participation in the Air Training Plan, first as a pupil and thereafter a flight instructor on 31 May 1943 at Claresholm, Alberta. Then for Dad it was across Canada to Halifax by train, followed by across the Atlantic to Britain by ship, to fight as a pilot in Bomber Command.

His logbook tells me that on 11 September 1942 at No. 4 Service Flying Training School in Saskatoon Dad was assessed as 'Above Average' as a pilot, and '*Average Plus*' as a pilot-navigator by No. 4 School Chief Instructor A.E Thompson. He also says Dad had, as a 'Grand Total for All Service Flying', 103.45 hours as 'Dual', 136.05 hours as 'Pilot' and 29.20 hours as 'Passenger'.

Dad's logbook further tells me that, on 6 December 1942, Dad was awarded a 'Temporary School Diploma' from No. 2 Flying Instructors' School at Vulcan, Alberta. Dated the following day, Dad's logbook has a stamped notation of No. 2 Flying Instructor School in Vulcan with a handwritten note: 'A conscientious type of pupil, who should make a valuable instructor with experience.'

So Dad became first a pilot, and then a flying instructor. But his logbook tells so much more, once I found those who could read it, the best being Paul Robinson, whose own logbook is identical to Dad's.

My Dad's Character Revealed

As my quest for answers deepened, I gave copies of extracts of Dad's logbook to a pair of Royal Air Force officers I admire – Mike Matthews and Paul Robinson. I needed to know what Dad's logbook reveals to them regarding his character. So who are these officers, and what do they say?

Mike Matthews was President of the Air Force Officers of British Columbia of which I am a member. It was Mike who, after hearing me speak about Bomber Command to the Royal Commonwealth Society, convened a meeting of his Air Forces Officers Board to reconfigure their formal dinner on 30 March 2019 celebrating the RCAF's 95th Anniversary to make me their speaker about Bomber Command. Mike has followed me every step of the way with this book.

TRAINING

Paul Robinson was an RAF Harrier jump-jet pilot who rose to become an air vice-marshal. He came into my life at the 1 September 2018 RAF Kirmington Ceremonies for Dad's 166 Squadron. The following spring, he joined Allen Packwood and David Freeman to be my three greatest mentors in my quest.

On 19 February 2020 Paul proposed me for affiliate membership in London's RAF Club 'for sustained, significant and active involvement undertaking activities which provide demonstrable support to the RAF Family by actively contributing to promoting the interests of the RAF'. On 24 February 2020 Air Marshal Sir Christopher Coville seconded that proposal. On 18 March 2020 the Board of Trustees elected me into membership. Sadly, the Covid-19 pandemic lockdown immediately kicked in, delaying my ability to travel to London to celebrate this marvellous milestone in my Bomber Command quest until 21 September 2021 when I arrived from Vancouver for twenty-eight days residing at the Club to work on this book.

Here's what Mike and Paul tell me about my Dad, thanks to Dad's logbook. Mike says Dad 'was obviously a gifted pilot, but also a man of great courage. It is a remarkable insight into his coolness in carrying out attacks on such a wide variety of targets – despite anti-aircraft fire and German fighters. No wonder he was decorated with the DFC!' Paul is focused on Dad being graded 'above average' and so 'creamed off' to become a flying instructor. Paul says 'That's quite a compliment to his maturity and flying ability'. Encouraged by this, I sent both men scanned copies of Dad's logbook while he was flying in Britain from 15 September 1943 to 1 October 1944, plus the two back pages listing his air bases and aircraft. This opened the floodgates. Here is what they said:

Mike started by saying 'It has been a stirring experience to read your father's log book. Thank you for the opportunity'. Mike drew my attention to Dad being 'above average'. Then Mike noted Dad's flight with a CFS (Central Flying School) pilot must have gone well that day because Dad wrote in his logbook on 11 May 1943 that 'This ride should get me into Bomber Command'. Mike concludes, 'He was a fine pilot, brave, determined and successful!' For me Dad's note is astonishing – he actually wanted to get into Bomber Command with its horrendous casualty rate. For an untutored civilian such as me, Second World War Bomber Command logbooks were essentially meaningless codes, initials and numbers. But it is amazing what they reveal to Mike Matthews, Paul Robinson and Jack Miles.

In 1995, four years after my Dad died, his younger sister, my Aunt Thelma Irvine, published a book called *What Did You Do In The War?*[1] All seven of Dad's siblings were younger than Dad. Sadly, there is virtually nothing about my Dad in my aunt's book because no one knew anything. Her book has a section succinctly entitled 'A Summary Roland MacKenzie' which includes eleven entries from his logbook, plus a letter Dad wrote in 1975 to the Royal Bank's *Quill & Ledger* newsletter, and two photos. One is of Dad's aircrew. The second is of 'a Lancaster'

---

1 Irvine, *What Did You Do In The War?*, Riftswood Publishing, 896 Shorewood Close, Parksville BC, 1920/8/4395

BOMBER COMMAND

which I now discover was Dad's. Compare that to one of Dad's younger brothers who got twenty-nine pages, and the other who got forty-four.

Here are the eleven entries from my Dad's logbook, which I'd never seen. As I was an untutored civilian, the following meant pretty much nothing to me.

Under her heading of 'Record of Service', these entries as she wrote them are:

#16	EFTS	Edmonton, Alberta	14/3/42	24/4/42
#4	SFTS	Saskatoon, Sask.	24/5/42	11/10/42
#2	FIS	Vulcan, Alberta	11/10/42	6/12/42
#15	SFTS	Claresholm, Alberta	8/12/42	14/6/43
#14	(P) AFU	Banff, Fraserburgh Scotland	24/7/43	17/8/43
#1518	BAT	Edzell, Scotland	17/8/43	28/8/43
#14	(P)AFU	Banff, Scotland	24/8/43	20/9/43
#30	DTU [sic]	Hixon, Staff.	28/9/43	18/1/44
#1656	CU	Lindholme, Yorks.	18/1/44	2/4/44
#166	SQDN	Kirmington, Lincs.	2/4/44	4/9/44
#82	DTU [sic]	Ossington, Notts.	4/9/44	8/1/45

And that's it. No attempt to explain anything. Just numbers, names and codes. Nothing to edify, or even arouse interest in, a Bomber Boy's son who had been shut out regarding his Dad's life, especially during the war. Fortunately, my Aunt also included the 1975 letter Dad published in the *Quill & Ledger*, the Newsletter of the Royal Bank of Canada. It concerned a single combat sortie he flew on 24 April 1944. The letter reveals a lot, now that I have more Bomber Command knowledge. I review Dad's letter when discussing that combat sortie, and I have included his letter in its entirety as Appendix II of this book.

Then I went to England as young backpacker, I was departing Calgary for my first visit to the UK and Europe. I was travelling solo, with no itinerary. Mainly I stayed in youth hostels. I asked Dad where I could visit in England and Scotland that had some connection with his wartime service overseas. He replied that there was nowhere. That has now proven to be so untrue, and it set me back a half century in understanding both him and Bomber Command. I did not learn until 2017 what I could have learnt in 1969. Dad did not even mention generalized RAF locations such as Runnymede or St Clement Danes Church or Hendon. He simply said 'nowhere'.

I say all this because I am learning that other children of Bomber Boys had similar experiences. When emotional connections are weak, and family communication is both poor and potentially dangerous, you do not learn much about wartime service. What I now know is that the man who departed Canada in 1943 to wage war in Bomber Command was different from the one who returned to Canada in 1945. General silence about Bomber Command, coupled with inaccurate sensationalism that so-called experts wrote or broadcast about Bomber Command, made the whole problem worse. Bomber Boys' offspring also paid for what Bomber Command aircrew had to endure postwar – indifference or hostility.

TRAINING

Dad in the Plan

Now, with lots of help, I had cracked the code, and realized how informative my Dad's logbook is. Then it struck me – the best way to demonstrate how the Plan worked, and the enormity of it, is by using Dad's experience as a specific example. But this shone light on a significant problem. Dad's logbook is silent prior to March 1942. Is that when Dad joined the RCAF? I had a nagging feeling in the back of my mind that Dad joined the RCAF in 1941, not 1942. If so, what happened to Dad in the RCAF before anything appeared in his logbook?

Then I struck gold. On 5 March 2020, nineteen months after my formal request as his only son for my Dad's RCAF record of service, and just days before the Coronavirus pandemic locked down everything, two dozen selected pages reached me from Ottawa. I know not what is in Dad's record of service file beyond those documents 'selected for release' to me. But those two dozen pages tell quite the tale, and hugely help me to bring to life my Dad's experiences in the Plan.

In a single sentence, I discovered Dad entered the Plan on 21 September 1941, first as a pupil,[2] and thereafter as a QFI (Qualified Flying Instructor), concluding his involvement with the Plan eighteen months later on 31 May 1943 to fight overseas.

When Dad entered the Plan, he was 29 years old, and had been an RCAF volunteer recruit for less than three months, since 3 July 1941. His flying experience was nil. His record of service further reveals Dad's enthusiasm for the RCAF was so great that he was happy to accept any rank. His reward for his candour was the RCAF making him AC2 (Aircraftsman 2nd Class), the entry level of all recruits.

RCAF Saskatoon 11 September 1942

But everything changed in Saskatoon on 11 September 1942 – on that day, the RCAF:

(1) promoted Dad from lowly LAC to commissioned officer
(2) awarded him his wings
(3) acknowledged that he again graduated at the top of his class
(4) indeed, with the highest marks the Saskatoon School had ever awarded, and
(5) identified Dad as a promising candidate for Flight Instructor School.

How is that for a day to remember? It was exactly sixty-nine years before 9/11.

Likewise, Dad's graduation on 7 December 1942 as a qualified flying instructor was exactly one year after Japan attacked Pearl Harbor. Thereafter, Dad taught recruits to fly until May 1943. That June he was transferred overseas to fight.

---

2 The Plan uses the word 'pupil'. At Chief Crowfoot Elementary School in Calgary we were callepils, but I think at Queen Elizabeth High School, and definitely at the University of Calgary, we were called students.

BOMBER COMMAND

Dad and the Plan

To understand Dad's RCAF record of service, two important acronyms are TOS [taken on strength] and SOS [struck off strength], so I'll use both. They make Dad's record of service a tour de force of the Plan in Canada

[1] 03 July 1941 RCAF Calgary: Dad arrived at the RCAF Recruiting Centre to volunteer to serve with the RCAF, was interviewed, and then TOS. On 20 September Dad was SOS in Calgary and transferred 700 miles (1,100 km) east to Brandon, Manitoba of Calgary so took his leave of employment with the Royal Bank of Canada until April 1945

[2] 21 September 1941 RCAF Brandon: Dad was TOS at No. 2 Manning Depot (MD). What on earth happens at a 'manning depot' I wondered.

My answer came from an unlikely source – Gord Johnsen of Arizona whom I met in Kamloops in July 2019. Gord was in Kamloops with a Second World War B-17 Flying Fortress and B-25 Liberator. Sadly, that day the cloud cover was too low for either plane to fly, so I did not get a ride. But what I did get was Gord as a friend. In April 2020 Gord sent me his review of the service of RCAF Flying Officer Donald McKay of Oyen, Alberta, the details of which Gord had published in their hometown newspaper.[3] McKay had volunteered for the RCAF in Calgary on 17 June 1941, just sixteen days before Dad. McKay was then granted 'Leave of Absence Without Pay' from 18 June until 2 August 1941, so perhaps that was Dad's status from 3 July until 21 September 1941. If so, that would have enabled Dad to continue work at RBC in Calgary and visit with his parents and friends in Stettler.

In any event, McKay was ordered to report back to Calgary on 2 August 1941. There he was SOS and immediately transferred to the manning depot at, you guessed it, none other than Brandon, Manitoba. McKay arrived in Brandon on 3 August 1941, just forty-nine days before Dad's arrival on 21 September. McKay remained at Brandon until 14 October 1941, so perhaps he and Dad met during their twenty-three-day overlap there.

Gord Johnsen in his write-up of McKay describes the manning depot in Brandon as the place where trainees commenced their military careers. In Brandon they learned 'to bathe, shave, shine boots and polish buttons, maintain their uniforms and otherwise behave in the required military manner'. Each day included two hours of physical education. In addition, every day they 'received instruction in marching, rifle drill, foot drill, and other routines'. I doubt Dad liked that. I have trouble imagining my 29-year-old banker father enjoying any of that much. They were also given the RCAF classification test. It was an aptitude test. Then a RCAF Selection Committee decided whether the recruit would be trained as aircrew or groundcrew. Dad and Donald McKay were both selected for aircrew.

---

3 *The Oyen Echo - Serving Oyen & District Since 1969*, Vol. 49, No. 42 Oyen Alberta Front Page 6 November 2018

TRAINING

On 12 November 1941 Dad was SOS at Brandon, then transferred 30 miles (50 km) east to Carberry Manitoba.

[3] 13 November 1941 RCAF Carberry: Dad was TOS at No. 33 Service Flying Training School (SFTS). Jack Miles, who was also at Carberry about the same time, tells me Dad would have commenced ground school there. On 21 December 1941 Dad was SOS and transferred west 250 miles (400 km) to Regina, Saskatchewan.

[4] 22 December 1941 RCAF Regina: Dad was TOS at what Jack Miles tells me would have been further ground school at No. 2 Initial Training School (ITS). Gord McKay says ITS was for pilot aircrew candidates, and that at ITS they studied 'navigation, theory of flight, meteorology, duties of an officer, Air Force administration, algebra and trigonometry' and a psychiatrist interviewed them. Tests included academics, a 'pitiless and tough' four-hour M2 physical exam, time in a decompression chamber, and a 'test flight' in a Link Trainer.

On 14 March 1942 Dad was SOS and transferred 500 miles (800 km) to Edmonton.

[5] 15 March 1942 RCAF Edmonton: Dad was TOS at No. 16 Elementary Flying Training School (EFTS). There Dad was taught how to fly. The first entry in Dad's Logbook is 16 March 1942. His instructor was Mr E. Owen. Dad's logbook reveals he was trained to fly almost exclusively on a Tiger Moth. He even taped a photo of one into his logbook. It was a biplane. I've seen several in various Canadian and British museums. Dad notes in his logbook under 'DUTY' on 16 March 1942: 1. Air experience. 1. A Familiarity With Cockpit Layout. 2. Effect of Controls. 18. Action in Event of Fire. 18.A Abandoning an Aircraft. How's that for Day One of one's logbook in intense training to become a combat pilot fighting in the war? Gord Johnsen says in his McKay write-up that 'the single engine de Havilland[4] Tiger Moth was the foremost training plane of the military and civilian pilots' used for training in the Plan.

Edmonton jogged my memory that I have a sterling silver cigarette case I've never used because I've never smoked. My Dad's initials are engraved on it. It had not been opened in decades, so it took me half an hour of careful exploration before I managed to open it without damaging it. Inside appears the following engraving:

Presented by
Edmonton Flying
Training School
for Highest
General Standing
Course No. 51
22-5-42

---

[4] Actresses Olivia de Havilland and her sister Joan Fontaine were paternal cousins of Sir Geoffrey de Havilland (1882-1965), the aircraft designer who founded the de Havilland Aircraft Company Limited in 1920.

[6] 24 May 1942 RCAF Saskatoon: on Queen Victoria's birthday, which is still a national holiday in Canada, Dad was TOS and commenced further flight training at No. 4 Service Flying Training School (SFTS).

As I wrote earlier, Saskatoon became one of the great milestones of Dad's Air Force career. In reviewing Dad's Royal Bank of Canada file, I found a copy of the 14 September 1942 letter the RBC Manager in Saskatoon wrote to the RBC supervisor in Calgary regarding Dad graduating first in Saskatoon's RCAF No. 4 Service Flying Training School. He said 'you will no doubt be interested to learn that his marks were the highest that have been recorded at No. 4 School since its inception.'

On 9 October 1942 Dad was SOS and transferred south-west 375 miles (600 km) to Vulcan, Alberta.

[7] 10 October 1942 RCAF Vulcan AB: Dad was TOS and commenced training at No. 2 Flying Instructors School (FIS) to become Flight Instructor. On 6 December 1942 VULCAN AB: Dad received a Temporary School Diploma from No. 2 FIS Vulcan. This means Dad graduated as a QFI (Qualified Flying Instructor). As mentioned, the squadron leader wrote on 7 December 1942 in Dad's logbook within the No. 2 Instructor Flying School Stamp (categorized 'C' (T.E.)) 'A conscientious type of pupil, who should make a valuable instructor with experience'.

Dad was then SOS and transferred south-west only 50 miles (80 km) to Claresholm, Alberta.

[8] 7 December 1941 RCAF Claresholm AB: On this, the first anniversary of Pearl Harbor, Dad as a QFI commenced teaching others to fly at No. 15 SFTS. Somehow he survived. And then, on 31 May 1943, Dad was SOS, then transferred east 3,000 miles (4.900 km) across Canada to Halifax, thus concluding his involvement with the Plan. In Halifax the RCAF seconded Dad to the RAF and he was transferred overseas, aboard what ship, when, or to which British port I know not. Dad's logbook then picks up his story in wartime Britain.

Dad's Sent Overseas to Fight

Getting back to 1943, that June the RCAF mercifully ended Dad's flying instructor career and transferred him to Halifax. There Dad was seconded by the RCAF to the RAF and on 22 June was shipped overseas to the UK where he remained until 8 January 1945. The majority of Canadians in Bomber Command were seconded by the RCAF to the RAF but some served directly with the RCAF in No. 6 Group. Dad's RCAF record of service is silent from 22 June 1943 until 8 January 1945 because Dad was overseas with the RAF. In the UK, Dad had heavy bomber flight training, then combat duty for thirty-four sorties, and concluded presumably with instructor duties training others to survive flying heavy bombers. More on that in my Chapter on Dad's combat sorties.

TRAINING

Dad's logbook reveals that his final Canadian flight entry is 24 May 1943 and his first British flight entry is 30 July 1943. The back of his logbook says Dad's last day at No.15 SFTS, Claresholm was 14 June 1943, and his first day at No. 14 (7) AFU at Fraserburgh, Banff, Scotland was 24 July 1943.

RAF Postings in Britain

Dad's logbook tells me that, while in Britain, he had the following postings preceding and then following his thirty-four combat sorties with 166 Squadron:

[9] 30 July 1943 RAF Banff, Scotland: Dad arrived at No. 14 (7) Advanced Flying Unit (AFU) and was there at Banff until 20 September flying in Oxfords until 15 September, plus an Anson on 3 September, in Course 54 of Unit 14(P) AFU. Paul points out Dad was probably doing a six-week 'Europe Familiarization Course', as he did not fly as first pilot. On 19 September, he graduated with proficiency as pilot 'Above the Average'.

* * * * *

Mysterious Insertion in Dad's Logbook: Next comes an undated inserted foolscap lined page having taped at the top 'MacKenzie making steady recovery' from what I know not – it looks like a newspaper clipping headline. Underneath on the foolscap Dad wrote 'Through Adversity to the Stars – 6 weeks of life in Bomber Command 1 in 3 chance to survive'. So Dad knew exactly what Bomber Command combat meant. Dad also wrote a mysterious two-part notation of (1) 'W/C Guy Gibson – Dam Busters VC' and (2) 'Air Marshal Arthur Harris X bad guy. Head Air Force.' I have no idea when or why Dad wrote any of this, but I do recall he took a dim view of the RAF hierarchy which perhaps Harris may have symbolized for him. Dad's dim view may also have reflected friction between the RAF and the RCAF which arose from the differing perspectives of Churchill and Mackenzie King. But Dad's been dead since 1991; he never said anything to me about Harris, and everyone who knew Dad as a wartime pilot is also dead, so sadly I guess we will never know.

* * * * *

[10] 17 to 22 August 1943 RAF Edzell, Scotland: Dad was on a Link Trainer at No. 1518 Beam Approach School in Course No. 73 from which he graduated on 22 August. The RAF Hixon course included a comprehensive course on a Link Trainer for instrument-flying and base landings in poor weather – Paul was surprised to learn from Dad's logbook that they were so sophisticated in 1943. His assessment was average. By car nowadays, Edzell and Banff are 85 miles (137 km) apart. Paul advises that 'Beam Approach' was the bad weather instrument landing system in use at the time. The Link Trainer was a simulator.

BOMBER COMMAND

[11] 29 September 1943 RAF Hixon, Staffordshire: Dad went to No. 30 Operational Training Unit (OUT) where, commencing on 16 October, he flew twin-engine Wellingtons until 11 January 1944. Paul says this means Dad was posted to bombers. OTUs were equipped with Wellingtons. There pilots, navigators, bomb-aimers, wireless operators and gunners were formed into crews of five in which they stayed for the remainder of their training and on to their combat squadrons. The names Dad enters in his logbook are Lefkowitz, McReadie, Murphy and Green. After that Dad just calls them 'Crew'. The syllabus included night-flying, bombing and long-range navigation. RAF Hixon was seven miles (11 km) east of Stafford. It was a No. 93 Group Bomber Command unit, which fed aircrews to No. 1 Group squadrons such as 166. OTU aircrews were sent on sorties to French targets to 'blood' them. Dad's 20 Decemeber 1943 sortie is written in red ink – all 'operational sorties' were. This was a 'Nickel' drop of leaflets. On this flight, McReadie was 'washed up', meaning he failed and was withdrawn from the crew. The RAF Hixon course concluded on 18 January 1944. Dad had flown eighty-three hours. That's a high number in British winters. And he was graded 'above average'.

* * * * *

MacKenzie Family Folklore: A popular story in our MacKenzie family, which I first heard around the campfire at a MacKenzie family reunion a year or so after Dad's death in 1991, arises from a training flight in which Dad was piloting a bomber. As the story goes, flying in bad weather, they were supposed to be over the Atlantic Ocean on the west side of the Isle of Skye. There they were about to practise dropping bombs. A new navigator was aboard. Dad instinctively felt they were not where the navigator calculated they were, so he declined to drop their bombs. Moments later the clouds lifted, and in front of them was Eilean Donan Castle in Loch Duich. It was the first of Clan MacKenzie's twelve castles, and is reputedly the most photographed castle in Europe. That meant they were immediately east of the Isle of Skye, instead of west of it. If this story is true, Dad's instincts saved him from a lifetime of ridicule and contempt as the MacKenzie who bombed our most beloved Clan castle, something he would never have lived down. My impression is Dad's respect for his instincts saved not only our beloved castle, but also saved his life, and that of his crew, on several occasions while bombing Nazi Europe.

* * * * *

[12] 18 January 1944 RAF Lindholme, Yorkshire: Dad and his crew were then sent to RAF Lindholme in South Yorkshire to learn to fly a Halifax on C Flight, then a Lancaster on A Flight. Both heavy bombers had a crew of seven, so they picked up a flight engineer and another gunner. Dad went to No. 1656 Heavy Conversion Unit where, starting on 18 February, he flew Halifaxes until 14 March.

TRAINING

[13] 27 to 31 March 1944 RAF Lancaster Finishing School: Dad and his crew then entered the co-located No. 1 Lancaster Finishing School for a short course from 27 to 31 March 1944 of ground training and four sorties, the first being on 27 March when Dad flew, presumably for the first time, aboard a Lancaster. On his 27, 29 and 30 March flights, he was an observing second pilot. The course consisted of circuits and landings (including a double engine failure to practise flying and landing on two engines only), navigation, bombing and defensive manoeuvring/practice gunnery against a fighter. sorties (eleven hours) to learn the Lancaster's different handling qualities, technology and interior layout. On the third sortie, the instructor departed the Lancaster after only fifty minutes, leaving Dad and his crew to fly 'solo' for the next three hours. Then, on 31 March, he was the pilot. He graduated on A Flight No. 1 Lancaster Finishing School on 1 April 1944. Dad again was graded 'above average'.

COMBAT SORTIES

[14] 1 April to 2 September 1944 RAF Kirmington, Lincolnshire: Dad was sent to RAF Kirmington where he flew his thirty-four combat sorties with 166 Squadron RAF from 9 April until 11 August 1944. They are the next chapter in this book. In Dad's logbook for this period, Paul particularly enjoyed Dad's phrases such as 'The kitchen sink came up but missed us' and 'Wizard prang'; and that Dad saw the D Day invasion fleet in the Channel on the night of 5/6 June 1944. And on his last combat sortie, on 11 August 1944, Dad wrote in his logbook 'Waited a long time for this. Only 3 engines. Went thro target 3 times.' I enjoyed Paul's comment regarding that final sortie that 'going round 3 times, on 3 engines, on your last op, must have tested the nerves somewhat! I concur! Dad was assessed 'Above Average' yet again.

On 2 September 1944 at RAF Kirmington, Wing Commander Donald Garner, officer commanding 166 Squadron, signed a 'Summary of Flying and Assessments' for 1944 in Dad's logbook which declares Dad as a pilot was 'Above the Average' and there was no 'point in flying or airmanship that should be watched.' This form says Dad had 207-40 hours dual, 931-30 hours as pilot and 50-40 hours as a passenger. It also says on ME (Multiple Engine) aircraft Dad had 45.05 hours day flying and 142.50 hours night flying.

Poetic Inspiration -- Dad's Special Poem of Inspiration 'High Flight'

I discovered that Dad kept the following special poem of inspiration in his cockpit:

> Oh! I have slipped the surly bonds of earth
> And danced the skies on laughter-silvered wings;
> Sunward I've climbed, and joined the tumbling mirth
> Of sun-split clouds – and done a hundred things

BOMBER COMMAND

You have not dreamed of – wheeled and soared and swung
High in the sunlit silence. Hov'ring there
I've chased the shouting wind along, and flung
My eager craft through footless halls of air.

Up, up the long delirious, burning blue,
I've topped the windswept heights with easy grace
Where never lark, or even eagle flew –
And, while with silent lifting mind I've trod
The high unsurpassed sanctity of space,
Put out my hand and touched the face of God.

(RCAF Pilot Officer John Gillespie Magee Jr
Killed Flying Spitfire 11 December 1941, aged 19)

On 15 May 2019, RAF Air Vice-Marshal Paul Robinson took me to Scopwick to visit Magee's grave. Paul was moved when I told him Dad kept Magee's poem in his cockpit.

POST COMBAT RAF and RCAF SERVICE

[15] 4 September 1944 RAF Ossington, Nottinghamshire: Dad served as an instructor to No. 82 OTU at RAF Ossington. There he flew Wellingtons for his six final flights between 12 and 17 September 1944 – three as second pilot, followed by three as pilot. The final flight entry in Dad's logbook is piloting a Wellington on 17 September 1944. Paul tells me by then the training system had proved so effective that the demand for new crews had declined dramatically, and it may be that the OTUs didn't need the number of instructors available. In fact, No. 82 OTU ceased training bomber crews completely three months later.

What Dad did with the RAF from 17 September 1944 until his departure for Canada on 8 January 1945 I know not. Silence reigns in his logbook. Perhaps Dad was doing some kind of instructing that did not involve flying. Paul concludes by telling me Dad's logbook says he finished flying with 1,202 hours 20 minutes, of which 177 hour 40 minutes were on combat sorties.

GOODBYE RAF and RCAF

Dad Comes Home

On 22 January 1945 Dad was back in Canada with the RCAF.

TRAINING

[16] 22 January 1945 RCAF Lachine: Dad was TOS at Lachine (Montreal). What he did I know not. On 1 February 1945, Dad was SOS and transferred west 1,400 miles (2,300 km) to Winnipeg.

[17] 2 February 1945 Winnipeg: Dad served in the RCAF in Winnipeg from 2 February to 23 March 1945. What he did there, I know not. On 23 March, he was SOS and transferred west 800 miles (1,300 km) to my hometown, Calgary.

[18] 23 March 1945 Calgary: Dad was with the RCAF in Calgary from 23 March until his discharge on 2 April 1945.

Many mysteries continue. For example, what ship brought him back across the Atlantic. What was he doing in Lachine, Winnipeg, Calgary and elsewhere from his arrival at Halifax until his discharge in Calgary? Dad mentioned once he spent his first night in Alberta from Britain in 'The Mac', which today we call the Fairmont Hotel MacDonald in Edmonton. Since 1915, The Mac has overlooked the Saskatchewan River Valley from the cliff at the edge of downtown Edmonton. I've often thought of how pleasing that night must have been relaxing in luxury in one of Canada's finest hotels, after all Dad endured in the war. This thought of Dad overnight at The Mac is part of my lifelong love of Canada's magnificent 'Castles of the North'.[5] He then told me that, a day or so later, he took the train from Edmonton to Stettler to visit his parents and family. What a re-union that must have been, especially for my awesome grandmother. But none of this shows up in his logbook. So much that happened to him does not appear in his logbook, and anyone who knew anything is now dead. So all I know is that, on 2 April 1945, three years and nine months after he was TOS by the RCAF in Calgary on 3 July 1941, Dad was SOS in Calgary by the RCAF. He then resumed civilian life in Calgary with the Royal Bank of Canada. More on that later. Now to war.

---

5 Chisholm, editor, *Castles of the North: Canada's Grand Hotels*, Lynx Images, 2001

Chapter Twelve

Dad at War

Air Vice-Marshal Paul Robinson tells me Dad flew what could be regarded as thirty-five combat sorties, the first being a Nickel. It did not count because, while it was a sortie over enemy territory, it was to drop leaflets, not bombs, just to 'blood' the crew.

Dad's Aircrew: I knew nothing until, for my 50th birthday, seven years after Dad's death, I received from his younger brother, my Uncle Jack MacKenzie of Calgary, a model of Lancaster AS-L. He said it was my Dad's aircraft in 166 Squadron. The base of the model pedestal holding up this Lancaster has an engraved bronze plaque saying Dad's crew members were W. 'Bill' Barrin, L. Green, R. Jones, 'Lefty' B. Lefkowitz, Charles 'Spud' Murphy and Cliff Smithhurst. About these six men I know nothing, not even their roles aboard Dad's Lancaster. I wonder who they were, where they came from, whether they survived the war, and what they did postwar. Sadly, pretty much anyone who knew those details is dead.

Dad's Aircraft: I have discovered Dad flew Lancaster Mk III ND757 AS-L-Love. The Mark IIIs commenced flying March 1944.[1] Dad presumably took command of this one on his arrival at RAF Kirmington on 2 April 1944.

Dad's Sorties: The question of what Dad did is enormous for me. What was he bombing? It was a challenge finding out, requiring reference to multiple sources to interpret and amplify Dad's logbook notes. Dad's logbook discloses that his thirty-four combat sorties were from 9 April to 11 August 1945. They began with a dramatic baptism of fire because his first two were both on 10 April 1944, although the first commenced on the night of 9 April. Dad's second 10 April sortie began with the most dramatic event I know of in the history of RAF Kirmington. The details are included as part of Sortie 2. Here are his sorties:

[1] 9/10 April 1944, Villeneuve – Saint-Georges Paris: On this, Dad's first combat sortie, just eleven days short of his 32nd birthday, he was accompanied by ten Lancasters from his 166 Squadron[2] which joined the main force of 107 other RAF

---

1 Wright, *On Wings of War*, Appendix 4, p. xiii
2 Wright, p. 68

Dad in 1924 as a 12-year-old Boy Scout, in Kindersley, Saskatchewan.

RCAF 1941. This elderly volunteer, aged 29, is my Dad, Roland MacKenzie, in Alberta. His rank was Leading Aircraftman 2nd Class. LAC2 was the lowest rank in the RCAF in the Second World War.

Above: The MacKenzie brothers in Alberta volunteer to serve – my Uncle Jack (Army), my Uncle Bruce (RCAF) & my Dad (RCAF). Uncle Bruce was ten years younger than Dad but earned his wings first. He flew Spitfires.

Left: RCAF pilot and commissioned officer, my Dad, Roland MacKenzie, Stettler, Alberta. Fall, 1942.

Roland MacKenzie's aircrew and aircraft in Spring 1944 at RAF Kirmington Lincolnshire. Dad's aircrew were, in alphabetical order: W. 'Bill' Barrin, L. Green, R. Jones, 'Lefty' B. Lefkowitz, Roland MacKenze (Pilot), Charles 'Spud' Murphy & Cliff Smithurst. I know neither their full names, nor their ranks, nor their roles aboard their aircraft. Their aircraft was a Lancaster Bomber call letters AS-L. AS was 166 Squadron. L was for Love.

Dad's 166 Squadron Lancaster Mark III ND757 AS-L.

The cockpit of Dad's Lancaster. Although the aircraft was officially 'L' for Love, they called her 'Luftwaffe Lulu'.

My Calgary Lancaster in The Hangar Flight Museum at Calgary Airport. I'm with The Hangar's Executive Director Brian Desjardins on 10 September 2020.

My Nanton Lancaster. Bomber Command Memorial and Museum of Canada Curator Karl Kjarsgaard took this photo of me in the pilot's seat on 28 August 2020.

Above left: Canada's Bomber Command Memorial in Nanton Alberta. I'm with Curator and CEO Karl Kjarsgaard. Calvin Pocock took this photo on 28 August 2020.

Above right: Canada's longest serving Prime Minister William Lyon Mackenzie King near the entrance to the House of Commons in the Parliament Buildings, Ottawa. My wife Ka Hyun MacKenzie Shin took this photo on 5 November 2019.

RAF Kirmington 166 Squadron Memorial Service 1 September 2018. My sons Ruaridh and Guy Roland MacKenzie and I had just laid the Canada Wreath in memory of the 155 Canadian aircrew who were killed flying in 166 Squadron. From left to right: Lord Lieutenant of Lincolnshire, Member of Parliament, Mayor, RAF Air Vice-Marshal Paul Robinson, the Priest, the Three MacKenzies and RAF Air Marshal Sir Christopher Coville. Martyn Wright took this photo.

RAF Kirmington The Lancaster Mural in the Marrowbone & Cleaver pub. This popular pub is often called 'The Chopper'. Tony & Ann Lark are on the left. Proprietor Sally Martin and I are on the right. This pub was the brightest place in Kirmington for 166 Squadron crews and remains today a veritable Museum of 166 Squadron with awesome traditional food and wonderful ambiance.

RAF Elsham Wolds Doreen Burge of Australia is the daughter of Don Charlwood who wrote 'No Moon Tonight' about his service in Bomber Command. Doreen was the special guest at the 75th Anniversary of the disastrous Mailly German Panzer Military Camp Bombing 03/04 May 1944 sortie. I did not know then that my Dad flew that sortie and miraculously survived when so many Bomber Boys did not.

Above: My photo of the Bomber Command Memorial Spire on Canwick Hill overlooking Lincoln with the names in the panels below of all aircrew killed in Bomber Command. I drew tremendous inspiration from that spire and those names during the three weeks in May 2019 in which I stayed at the Premier Inn across the road writing this book.

Left: RAF AVM Paul Robinson's photo of me at the grave of John Magee Jr. RCAF at Scopwick Lincolnshire. Magee wrote the poem 'High Flight' which my Dad kept in the cockpit of his Lancaster. Magee, age 19, was killed in his Spitfire on 11 Dec 1941.

Above left: RAF College Cranwell where AVM Paul Robinson, my sons Guy Roland & Ruaridh and I had the campus ourselves because it was in lockdown between terms. Assistant Librarian Tim Pierce took this photo and introduced me to Germany's Research Institute for Military History work on Bomber Command.

Above right: RAF Scrampton. I'm seated at Dambuster Guy Gibson's desk, complete with Gibson's famous black Labrador dog. My sons were photographed in the cockpits of RAF Red Arrows.

Right: Churchill College Archives Cambridge University. My mentors Archives Director Allen Packwood and AVM Paul Robinson and I are admiring an Archives' cigar partially smoked by Sir Winston Churchill.

Imperial War Museum Duxford near Cambridge is Britain's largest Aviation Museum. I'm standing by a Dambusters' Bouncing Bomb under the Duxford Lancaster, 15 Oct 2019.

'Just Jane' is one of only two Lancasters worldwide where all four engines work but the Lancaster is not yet airworthy. The other is my Nanton Lancaster. My sons are viewing 'Just Jane' at the Lincolnshire Aviation Heritage Centre in East Kirkby, 31 Aug 2018.

RAF Coningsby Battle of Britain Memorial Flight Lancaster. It's one of only two that fly. The other is at Canada's Hamilton Airport at Port Hope ON. I'm in this 13 May 2019 photo with former RAF personnel Richard Tillotson-Sills and his Commanding Officer Tony Lark.

RAF Coningsby Lancaster Cockpit Mascot is designed to recognize Australian, New Zealander and Scottish aircrew aboard. I took this photo on 13 May 2019.

Above left: Bomber Command Memorial in Green Park London. These are the seven aircrew of Lancasters and Halifaxes. My wife Ka Hyun took this photo. The ceiling is from an RCAF Halifax. Queen Elizabeth II unveiled this Memorial on 28 June 2012.

Above right: The Strand London. This is my photo of Marshal of the RAF Sir Arthur Harris in front of St. Clement Danes, the Central Church of the RAF. The statue was unveiled by The Queen Mother, 31 May 1992.

Left: RAF Club London. I'm admiring a portrait of Marshal of the RAF Sir Arthur Harris.

Right: London. Westminster Hall when Lord Boateng gave Ka Hyun and me a tour of the House of Lords. He made a speech to 5,000 Churchillians praising me and this book. On 14 Sep 2022, I was back in Westminster Hall paying my respects to Queen Elizabeth II after walking 30,000 steps in a nine-hour queue.

Below: RAF Club London. Second World War Bomber Command veteran Colin Bell age 101 with Allen Packwood & me with a painting of Queen Elizabeth II and an RAF Colour parade in background. This photo was taken on 7 Oct 2021 at the Opening Reception of the International Churchill Society 2021 Annual Meeting Allen organized at which Colin spoke.

Above: RAF Museum London at Hendon. This RAAF Lancaster flew the second highest number of combat sorties in Bomber Command in the Second World War.

Below: London. My 'Allies' photo of FDR & Churchill with my wife Ka Hyun, June 2022. I know Julia Holofcener, the widow of the sculptor of this piece, Lawrence Holofcener.

RAF Club London. My photo of a portrait of Sir Winston Churchill in his RAF uniform. In front are Churchill's Granddaughter Celia Sandys with my wife Ka Hyun MacKenzie Shin, 01 June 2022.

Washington DC. Ka Hyun's photo of me at the Franklin Delano Roosevelt Memorial. My mother was also in a wheelchair from polio from 1952 until her death in 1970.

Washington DC. My mentors Allen Packwood of Churchill College Archives Cambridge University and David Freeman, Editor of *Finest Hour* and Director of Publications of the International Churchill Society at California State University in Fullerton.

DAD AT WAR

bombers, plus 107 RCAF bombers. They bombed Paris, but they did not destroy the Eiffel Tower. Instead, they bombed railway marshalling yards at Villeneuve-Saint Georges, on which they inflicted 'considerable damage'.[3]

[2] 10 April 1944, Aulnoye France: Weather conditions were good, so 166 Squadron ordered Dad airborne again just a few hours later on that fateful 10 April. His was among twenty-three Lancasters of 166 Squadron sent to attack railway marshalling yards, this time at Aulnoye. It was the major railway junction of the Paris-Brussels and Calais-Lille railway lines. But on take-off at RAF Kirmington, there had been great drama. All Dad says in his logbook notes is 'Damned sticky – Landed North Killingsholm'. And then Dad added 'Gee u/s.' (u/s means unserviceable)

* * * * *

As I describe in great detail earlier in this book, the RAF Kirmington drama arose when Lancaster AS-F-Freddie, which Jim Wright tells us was fifth in line of the twenty-three Lancasters in the process of taking off, blew a tyre. AS-F-Freddie swung badly, part of its undercarriage collapsed and, as it skidded to a halt, burst into flames. The aircrew fled the aircraft, then part of the bombload exploded. That created a huge crater in the runway which prevented the remaining Lancasters from taking off, or those already airborne, including Dad's, from landing when they returned from this combat sortie. Dad was diverted to North Killingsholm.

* * * * *

[3] 18 April 1944 Rouen, France: After several days being stood down by bad weather, Dad's was among the eighteen Lancasters in 166 Squadron to bomb Rouen's marshalling yards. All aircraft bombed the primary target, and returned safely.

* * * * *

Rouen – Joan of Arc and Kriegsmarine: She was burned at the stake at Rouen on 30 May 1431. The *Kriegsmarine*, Nazi Germany's navy, had its HQ in the château. Postwar, it became the Rouen Business School.

* * * * *

[4] 20 April 1944, Cologne, Germany: This was Dad's first combat sortie to the homeland of the Third Reich. Dad's was among two dozen 166 Squadron Lancasters. While seven enemy fighters were sighted, no 166 Lancaster was damaged, thanks in part to thick cloud cover. Dad's squadron was among the main

---

3 Dunmore & Carter, *Reap the Whirlwind*, p. 241

force of 357 Lancasters and twenty-two Mosquitoes – twenty-two were RCAF Lancasters. Dad's logbook note says 'The Kitchen Sink Came Up But Missed Us'.

* * * * *

Ed Moore, Navigator aboard an RCAF Lancaster, later recalled 'a remark by a well-known writer that the Allies had deliberately refrained from hitting the Cologne Cathedral despite the bombing of St Paul's by the Germans.'[4]

* * * * *

[5] 22 April 1944, Dusseldorf, Germany: Dad's second combat sortie (after Cologne) to the Ruhr was challenging. He was among twenty-seven Lancasters from 166 Squadron. One of his squadron's Lancasters failed to return – it was AS-S-Sugar, on its third sortie.[5] Almost 600 main force Bombers took part, including 136 from the RCAF.[6] However, German night fighters intercepted the bomber stream, and shot down twenty-nine bombers, including eight RCAF aircraft. Dad's logbook note says 'Searchlights – Con Trails – No Asi'.

[6] 24 April 1944 Karlsruhe Germany: Dad's third combat sortie to the Ruhr was as part of the main force of 500 RAF and 137 RCAF Bombers. RCAF Flight Sergeant (later Pilot Officer) James Patrick Durkin about whom I write in Remembrance was on his tenth combat sortie. Terrible weather included icing, static electricity, rain and high winds. Nineteen aircraft, including six RCAF bombers, were lost. Dad's logbook note says 'Sticky Weather – No ASi – Saw First Fighters'.

* * * * *

Dad's taciturn entry is but the tip of a very large iceberg. In 1975 Dad published a letter in the Royal Bank of Canada's *Quill & Ledger* Newsletter that tells quite the tale about this sortie. To my knowledge, this letter is all Dad ever wrote about Bomber Command combat. Dad's letter reveals so much, not only about this sortie and how complicated, difficult and important it was, but also about preparations for and return from combat sorties. It also shows how horrible conditions could be, and how split-second Bomber Command aircraft bombing had to be. It is an amazing story, and well written, so I have included it in its entirety as Appendix II of this book. You will be amazed how much my father tells you.

* * * * *

---

4 Dunmore & Carter, p. 243

5 Wright, p. 68

6 Dunmore & Carter, p. 243

DAD AT WAR

Today's Karlsruhe: The vast 'ZKM Centre for Art and Media' is housed in a former weapons factory.

* * * * *

[7] 27 April 1944, Friedrichshafen, Germany: Located on the shore of Lake Constance deep in southern Germany, even deeper than Nuremberg, which was a disastrous raid four weeks before. Worse, it was a bright moonlit night in which bombers are sitting ducks. A large number of night fighters attacked the bomber main force. Four of the two dozen 166 Squadron Lancasters were lost. This sortie was the most accurate of all Allied bombings of that city.[7] Dad's logbook says 'D.R. Compass u/s – Flak Damage From Zurich'.

* * * * *

Friedrichshafen: It had Ferdinand von Zeppelin's dirigible factory at the end of the nineteenth century. The Nazis made it into a major industrial centre. Its factories used hundreds of thousands of concentration camp prisoners as slave labourers. They were also forced to dig tunnels to protect production sites from repeated bombings.

* * * * *

[8] 30 April 1944, Mantenon Amunition Dump, near Rouen, France: Fifteen 166 Squadron Lancasters including Dad's attacked the ammunition dump at Mantenon near Rouen. This raid was exceptionally successful – columns of black smoke rose up to 7,000 feet and fires and explosions could still be seen from the French coast on the return flight. All aircraft returned safely to RAF Kirmington, and Jim Wright says every crew was enthusiastic about the success of this sortie.[8]

* * * * *

Change of Command: Wing Commander Frank S. Powley was succeeded by Wing Commander Donald A. Garner as commander of 166 Squadron. Frank Powley was later killed on a mine-laying sortie. Donald Garner was CO for the remainder of Dad's tour. As of 30 April 1944 the 166 Squadron strength was forty pilots, 240 other aircrew, 342 ground crew and thirteen presumably very popular WAAFs.[9]

* * * * *

[9] 3/4 May 1944, Mailly German Panzer Military Camp in France: This sortie was a tragedy, and a massacre. The details are below. All Dad's logbook succinctly

---

7 Wikipedia Friedrichshafen

8 Wright, p. 72

9 Wright, *On Wings of War*

says is 'The Chopper Fell as We Orbited'. The good news arising from this tragedy is that, once it commenced, the bombing was accurate and successful, inflicting heavy damage on Germany's Panzer Military Camp. My personal good news is that, somehow my Dad survived, so four years later I was born.

* * * * *

Panzer Military Camp Massacre: Sortie [9] was a tragedy. On 4 May 2019, I was an invited guest at the 75th Anniversary Memorial Wreath-Laying Ceremony of Remembrance at RAF Elsham Wolds, at which Doreen Charlwood Burge of Australia was the guest of honour. I remember how pleased, indeed moved, Doreen was that Australia's flag flew there that day. Until attending that ceremony, I had known nothing of that 1944 tragedy. It was not until long after the ceremony that I learnt Dad had been in the thick of it, but miraculously survived. What happened is that the Master Bomber's radio frequency was inadvertently usurped by an American Army Air Forces music broadcast, so he could not signal to commence bombing. This forced our Lancasters to keep circling over the target while night fighters from four nearby Luftwaffe air bases arrived to massacre them. Forty-two Lancasters, including three from 166 Squadron, each with a crew of seven young volunteers, were shot down because of a communication foul-up.

* * * * *

[10] 7 May 1944, Rennes St Jacques, France: Dad's and a dozen additional 166 Squadron Lancasters attacked the airfield and ammunition dump. All returned safely to RAF Kirmington. Dad's logbook says 'Dummy Run – Flak Damage'.

[11] 10 May 1944, Dieppe, France: At Dieppe, the scene on 19 August 1942 of Canada's worst military disaster of the Second World War, Dad's and seven other 166 Squadron Lancasters bombed German Atlantic Wall coastal defences. Everyone returned safely. Dad's logbook note says 'Piece of Cake'.

[12] 12 May 1944, Mining Heligoland Bight: 'Mining', the laying of mines, is also known as 'Gardening'. Dad's and five additional 166 Squadron Lancasters dropped mines in the shipping lanes off Heliogoland, a small German North Sea archipelago. This was a complete success, with no losses, although mining could be very dangerous. Dad noted in his logbook 'Monotonous – Weather Poor'.

[13] 19 May 1944, Orleans, France: Dad's and eighteen additional 166 Squadron Lancasters bombed the railway marshalling yards. AS-N Lancaster was shot down near Paris en route to the target. The remainder returned safely. Dad notes in his logbook 'Good Prang', RAF for good flight. In the RCAF, prang meant crash.

DAD AT WAR

[14] 21 May 1944 Duisburg Germany: Dad's fourth combat sortie to the Ruhr was with twenty-five additional 166 Squadron Lancasters which formed part of the main force of 500. Eleven aircraft were lost, including two from 166 Squadron. Dad notes in his logbook 'Back Ruhr Bashing'.

* * * * *

Duisburg: A wartime major Ruhr logistics centre with chemical, steel and iron industries. It may have been the most heavily bombed city in the war. This sortie did the most damage of any bombings of Duisburg until then.

* * * * *

[15] 22 May 1944, Dortmund, Germany: Dad's fifth and final combat sortie to the Ruhr was with twenty-three other 166 Squadron Lancasters which formed part of the main force of 375 Bombers, including twenty-seven RCAF aircraft. Eighteen Lancasters were shot down, including two 166 Squadron and three RCAF.

* * * * *

[16] 27 May 1944, Aachen, Germany: This combat sortie was to destroy the grid-iron of railway lines surrounding the two railway marshalling yards, and was highly successful although the target was heavily defended. Dad's squadron lost two Lancasters. Dad notes in his logbook 'High Speed Effort – Bags of Flak'.

* * * * *

Aachen: It was the first German city the American Army attacked in the Second World War. The nineteen-day Battle of Aachen, 2-21 October 1944, featured 13,000 Germany soldiers and 5,000 local militia holding off 100,000 American soldiers for almost three weeks – giving the Allies a taste of how effective and determined Germans would be in defending Germany. To Germans, the symbolism of this heroic defence was enormous because Aachen was the capital of Charlemagne, whom Germans say founded 'The First Reich'. And what's more, now that the German Army was fighting for the first time on German soil, one German officer said 'Suddenly we were no longer the Nazis, we were German soldiers'.[10]

* * * * *

[17] 2 June 1944, Calais, France: Dad's was among twenty 166 Squadron Lancasters sent to attack the railway-gun positions at Calais. One Lancaster failed to return. Calais was heavily bombed to disrupt German communications, and to convince Hitler that the Pas-de-Calais, not Normandy, was the location of the

---

10 Wikipedia Battle of Aachen and Ambrose (1998), pp. 146-7

invasion. Dad's was among the six Lancasters who had to abandon the bombing because the 9/10th cloud cover had closed to 10/10th over the target, resulting in the danger of missing the target and instead accidently bombing elsewhere. Dad notes in his logbook simply 'Weather Bad'.

[18] 5/6 June 1944, Cherbourg, France: Returning to base in the early morning of what is now regarded by many as the single most important day for Canada in the twentieth century, Dad's logbook succinctly says 'Invasion fleet was worth seeing.'

* * * * *

Bomber Command – D Day 1944

Bomber Command had more combat sorties on this fateful 5/6 June 1944 evening before and early morning of D Day than on any other night in the Second World War – over 1,200 sorties, of which 230 were by the RCAF.[11]

Dad's logbook says he was piloting his AS-L-Love Lancaster to 'Cherbourg' but Jim Wright's 166 Squadron history[12] doesn't mention Cherbourg – instead it speaks only of the gun batteries at nearby St Martin-de-Varreville (sixteen Lancasters) and Crisbecq (nine Lancasters). By car these gun batteries were about ten minutes apart, but they were both a forty-minute drive from Cherbourg. However, official RAF records disclose that RAF Wing Commander Donald A. Garner, commander of 166 Squadron, like Dad, flew to Cherbourg that night.

At 5:00 am on D Day, the commander of the Crisbecq battery was the first to see the invasion fleet. He immediately notified *Kriegsmarine* HQ in Cherbourg, which triggered the alarm throughout the Atlantic Wall. At 5:52 am the Germans ordered Crisbecq battery to fire on Allied ships that were only eleven miles (17 km) away. At 6:30 am, the battery fired on the American destroyer USS *Cory*, and sank it.[13]

At Cherbourg Dad was, as mentioned, part of the successful ruse to convince Hitler that Pas-de-Calais, not Normandy, was the location of the invasion. Canadians writing about No. 6 Group RCAF Bomber Command say 'moreover, a brilliantly successful ruse put the non-existent First US Army Group in supposed readiness across the Channel directly opposite the Pas de Calais, with none other than the feisty General George S. Patton in command. Weeks before D Day it became apparent that the ploy had worked.'[14]

* * * * *

---

11 Dunmore & Carter, p. 274

12 Wright, p. 85

13 Wikipedia Crisbecq Battery

14 Dunmore & Carter, p. 271

DAD AT WAR

MacKenzies at War – D-Day 1944!

As mentioned, to the best of my knowledge, my MacKenzie ancestors had no military connections for the first five generations they lived in Canada. All that changed with the sixth generation, of which my Dad was the senior member. Dad and two of his younger brothers went to war. As mentioned, D Day 1944 is regarded by many as the most important day in the twentieth century for Canada. Canadians landed on the beaches of Normandy as a full partner of our British and American Allies. The British took Sword and Gold Beaches, the Americans took Utah and Omaha Beaches, and Canada took Juno Beach. While 14,000 Canadian soldiers were fighting their way onto Juno Beach, and incurring major initial casualties, in support were 110 ships and 10,000 sailors of the Royal Canadian Navy offshore, and fifteen squadrons of the Royal Canadian Air Force in the air.[15]

So, what were my MacKenzies doing? While Dad was bombing in the ruse which fooled Hitler, one of his younger brothers, my Uncle Jack MacKenzie, a Captain in the Canadian Army, was aboard the liberty freighter, the MT2 *Sambut*. She was shelled twice by German 16-inch guns of the shore batteries at Cap Gris Nez. Uncle Jack was wounded by the first shelling, and *Sambut* disabled by the second shelling, so all were ordered to abandon ship. Uncle Jack in a raft was saved by an RAF rescue craft which loaded as many men as it could, swung about, and headed at high speed to Dover. Uncle Jack and seven other wounded in his unit were the first invasion casualties to reach England. It was noon on D Day.[16] Post-war Uncle Jack served as chair of the Calgary Public School Board while I was a student at Calgary's Queen Elizabeth High School.

Meanwhile, my Dad's youngest brother, my Uncle Bruce MacKenzie, flew two patrols over the invasion beachhead in his Spitfire in 441 Fighter Squadron RCAF. His first patrol was at dawn, so Uncle Bruce, like Dad, was among the first to see the invasion fleet. Bruce's second patrol later that day enabled him, in his words, to 'see the whole procedure, the tank battles unfolding, the shelling from the ships, and to note the successful progress'. He saw no enemy fighters.[17]

* * * * *

[19] 14 June 1944, le Havre, France: Dad was among twenty-six Lancasters of 166 Squadron which formed part of the main force of 221 Lancasters with an escort of Spitfires to bomb in daylight the docks to disable the fast German motor torpedo boats (E-Boats) and other German light naval forces threatening shipping off the Normandy beaches. All 166 Squadron Lancasters returned safely. Dad noted in his logbook 'Flak Damage – Bang On'.

* * * * *

---

15 Foot, 'D-Day and the Battle of Normandy' *The Canadian Encyclopedia*

16 Irvine, *What Did You Do In The War?* pp. 26-31

17 Irvine, p. 81

BOMBER COMMAND

German E-boats (Motor Torpedo Boats: E-boats had a top speed of 40 knots. They were faster and more agile than British or American similar fast-attack torpedo boats. E-boats sank over forty warships, including twelve destroyers, and over a hundred Allied merchant vessels.[18] The E-boat threat to Normandy shopping was almost completely destroyed by this combat sortie, thanks in part to several 'Tallboy' bombs scoring hits on the pens and one penetrating the concrete-covered E-boat pens roof.[19]

* * * * *

[20] **16 June 1944, Sterkrade, Germany:** Dad's was among twenty-three Lancasters from 166 Squadron which formed part of the main force of 221 RAF and 100 RCAF bombers. The target was the synthetic-oil plant at Sterkrade in Oberhausen in the Ruhr. Eight bombers were shot down. Dad notes in his logbook 'Weather Sticky – Flak Bad – Jones Sick.'

[21] **17 June 1944, Aulnoye, France:** Dad was among twenty-one Lancasters of 166 Squadron sent to bomb a railway bridge. Visibility dropped to 10/10th cloud cover, so the Master Bomber instructed twenty including Dad not to bomb, and instead return to RAF Kirmington. Dad notes in his logbook 'Couldn't get below cloud'.

* * * * *

Frustrations of Standby, Then Being Scrubbed: For the next five nights, 166 Squadron was instructed to stand by, but then each operation was scrubbed. Jim Wright advises that 'The aircrew found these situations very frustrating. After going through all the build up and tensions, briefings, donning flying kits, transporting out to the aircraft and carrying out all the ground checks and after many hours of waiting, the complete anti-climax when the signal came to cancel the operations.'[20]

* * * * *

19 June 1944, 'SCRUBBED': Dad's logbook note says '13,000' [lbs] jettison (was I MAD)" I'm thinking it was Dad to whom Jim was referring when he wrote: 'In one instance the aircraft had already taken-off when the 'scrub' signal was received and aircraft had to be recalled.'

* * * * *

---

18 Birrell, *Johnny – Canada's Greatest Bomber Pilot*, p. 174
19 Wright, p. 86
20 Wright, p. 86

DAD AT WAR

[22] 24 June 1944, Fleur: Dad's logbook says 'Another piece of cake. Konow as 2nd Dickie'.

[23] 27 June 1944, Château Bernapre, France: Dad took part in 166 Squadron's attack on the V1 rocket site at Château Bernapre. Dad's logbook notes 'Coned in searchlights. Bomb doors u/s.' (they would not open.)

* * * * *

166 Squadron Lancaster AS-E Crash: Its seven aircrew are buried in the churchyard cemetery at Belleville-sur-Mer in France. To the consternation of French locals, all seven bodies were buried in the same box because 'military authorities of occupation [Germans] decided all should be together'.

* * * * *

[24] 30 June 1944, Oisemont/Neuville, France: Dad took part in the 166 Squadron daylight bombing of northern French flying-bomb sites. Everyone returned safely. Dad noted in his logbook 'Nice Trip But Hot Work'.

[25] 4 July 1944, Orleans, France: Dad was among twenty-one Lancasters of 166 Squadron attacking the railway yards at Orleans. All returned safely to RAF Kirmington. Dad noted in his logbook 'Longer Than Last Trip – Good Prang'.

* * * * *

The RAF No. 13 Base Senior Intelligence Officer reported that 166 Squadron's bomb plots were the best in No. 1 Group Bomber Command, a singular distinction.

* * * * *

[26] 6 July 1944, Foret-Du-Croc, France: Dad was among twenty-two Lancasters of 166 with a Spitfire fighter escort. All twenty-two returned safely to RAF Kirmington. Dad notes in his logbook 'Bombed on Instruments'.

[27] 12 July 1944, Revigny-Sur-Ormain, France: Dad's was among twenty-nine Lancasters of 166 Squadron sent to attack the railway marshalling yards and rail junction. Dad noted in his logbook 'Chopper Trip – Cloud Down to 1,500 ft – Landed Wittering' My understanding is the Master Bomber sent them home.

* * * * *

No Sortie Was Safe. This reality was brought home at Revigny. It was a fine summer evening, so all twenty-nine crews walked or cycled down to the airfield to attend the briefing for that raid. Jim Wright reports 'Although Revigny was not considered a particularly dicey [dangerous] target, they all knew the easiest target could be lethal given the wrong set of circumstances.'[21] And that is what happened. Four 166 Squadron Lancasters were shot down that night, and seventeen of their twenty-eight aircrew were killed. Dad was among the ten Lancasters the Master Bomber ordered to bring their bombs back because clouds moved in obscuring the target before they were ready to bomb, making accuracy impossible. Weather was often an implacable Bomber Command foe.

* * * * *

[28] 20 July 1944, Wizernes, France: Dad was among twenty-three Lancasters of 166 Squadron to join a main force of 345 Bombers for an attack on six flying-bomb launching sites being constructed at Wizernes. The sortie was successful for reducing the number of V1 'doodlebug' attacks on London. All 166 Lancasters returned.

[29] 23 July 1944, Kiel, Germany: Dad was among two dozen 166 Squadron Lancasters in a main force of 587 RAF Bombers and forty-two RCAF bombers. All 166 Squadron Lancasters safely returned to RAF Kirmington.

* * * * *

Kiel Germany, First and Second World Wars: Kiel was the first major RAF raid on a German city in more than eight weeks, and this was the heaviest raid on Kiel in the Second World War. Kiel was the site of Germany's 4 November 1918 'Sailors Munity' which sparked the German Revolution towards the end of the First World War. This resulted in the Kaiser's abdication, creation of the ill-fated Weimar Republic and, fourteen years later, the election of Adolf Hitler as chancellor. In the Second World War, Kiel was a major naval base and shipbuilding and submarine building centre using slave labour for local industry. This raid was particularly successful, with only four Lancasters lost, because the Luftwaffe were spoofed into attacking a decoy instead of the main force bombing Kiel.[22]

* * * * *

[30] 2 August 1944, le Havre, France: Dad bombed a flying-bomb launching site. He notes in his logbook 'Another Good Prang'.

[31] 3 August 1944, Trossy, France: Dad bombed a flying-bomb storage site. He notes in his logbook 'Deadly Trip – Good Results'.

---

21 Wright, pp. 92-3
22 Wikipedia, Kiel

DAD AT WAR

[32] **5 August 1944, Pauillac (Bordeaux), France:** Dad was among twenty-two Lancasters from 166 Squadron to bomb an oil plant. Visibility was excellent. It was a heavy concentration of bombing. Fires and explosions seen at the target.

* * * * *

RAF Kirmington Lancaster Collision: No Lancasters from 166 Squadron were lost on this sortie, but two 166 Lancasters collided just after take-off from RAF Kirmington. The tail unit and rear turret of Lancaster AS-J2 were sliced off. It plunged into the sea, exploding on impact. There were no survivors. The mainplane of Lancaster AS-V was badly damaged, but it managed to return to RAF Kirmington.

* * * * *

[33] **7 August 1944, 'Western Front', Fontenay le Marmion, Normandy, France:** All Dad's logbook says is 'Western Front'. Dad was I assume among the twenty-three Lancasters from 166 Squadron attacking enemy troop and heavy armour concentrations to support our Allied armies. Visibility was hazy, and accurate bombing essential for the safety of our troops. Part way through the attack visibility worsened, so the master bomber called off the attack and directed all aircraft who had not bombed to return to base. Eight 166 Squadron Lancasters brought their bombs back.

[34] **11 August 1944, Douai, France:** This was Dad's final combat sortie of the Second World War, and the one for which he was awarded the Distinguished Flying Cross. In his logbook he wrote 'Have waited a long time for this. Only 3 engines. Went through target 3 times.' This means Dad's Lancaster was badly shot up, including the loss of an engine. In spite of the damage, he flew over the target three times to ensure a direct hit before releasing the bombs. Then he somehow managed to get his aircraft and crew back to England. Dad once commented dryly to me that 'higher ups' seemed happier to retrieve the Lancaster than the crew. Family lore says, by the time Dad managed to get back to RAF Kirmington, they had already stowed his stuff and assigned someone else his bed. They thought he was dead.

* * * * *

Dad's Final Sortie: Dad's final combat sortie at Douai is confusing because the 166 Squadron history discloses twenty-two Lancasters from 166 Squadron bombed the marshalling yards at Givors, with no mention being made of Douai. Givors is a long way south of Lyon, while Douai is up north only twenty miles (32 km) from Vimy Ridge. Douai's coalfield was the richest in northern France.

Dad's DFC: Adding to this final sortie confusion, Dad's DFC citation erroneously dates his Douai sortie 16 August instead of 11 August. In the heat of the war, hastily written documents were, on occasion, inevitable and erroneous. My guess is Dad's logbook is correct, and not the official records. I have included Dad's DFC citation in its entirety as Appendix I. On 18 July 1945, to the day exactly three years before I was born, his DFC was sent to Dad by registered mail. I'd have preferred King George VI presenting it in Buckingham Palace with photographers.

102 Sorties of Three Airmen

One way of looking at what Bomber Command was doing is by reviewing actual sorties. I had access to the following three sets of tours totalling 102 combat sorties. They demonstrate the focus on military and economic targets, not mindless bombings as some say. These three tours, each of which was for thirty-four sorties, are:

1. My Dad's thirty-four sorties from April to August 1944 in 166 Squadron RAF compiled by me from Dad's logbook coupled with Jim Wright's book *On Wings of War*:

   9 sorties bombing railways and their marshalling yards
   7 sorties bombing flying-bomb bases
   5 sorties bombing enemy troop locations to assist our armies
   5 sorties bombing synthetic oil plants and ammunition dumps
   5 sorties bombing the Ruhr[23]
   1 sortie bombing industrial city – Friedrichshafen
   1 sortie bombing an E-boat base
   1 sortie bombing the naval port at Kiel

2. Navigator/author Don Feesey's thirty-four sorties of October 1944 until April 1945 in 166 Squadron RAF compiled by me from Don's book *Fly By Nights* coupled with Jim Wright's book *On Wings of War*:

   9 sorties bombing enemy troop locations to assist our armies
   7 sorties bombing railways and their marshalling yards
   7 sorties bombing synthetic oil plants and refineries
   6 sorties bombing the Ruhr[24]
   3 sorties bombing armaments, coking & benzol plants
   1 sortie bombing U-boat base
   1 sortie bombing a coal mining area

---

23 Cologne, Dortmund, Duisburg, Dusseldorf and Karlsruhe
24 Cologne (three times) Dortmund, Duisburg and Dusseldorf

3. Pilot Officer James Patrick Durkin's thirty-four sorties of March to November 1944 in 424 Squadron RCAF, compiled for me by my friend and word count editor RCAF Colonel (Retd) Patrick Dennis from P/O Durkin's logbook:

11 sorties bombing the Ruhr[25]
7 sorties bombing railway marshalling yards
6 sorties bombing guns & ports, including guns at ports
2 sorties bombing communication centres
2 sorties laying mines (gardening)
2 sorties bombing V1 launching base
1 sortie bombing industrial city – Friedrichshafen
1 sortie Dutch coast diversionary attack
1 sortie sea search
1 sortie troop support to assist our armies

Comparing these three sets of combats sorties is informative because they span the final year of the Second World War from March 1944 to April 1945 – this is when Bomber Command was most effective. Also, sixty-eight of these combat sorties were flown by 166 Squadron RAF while the remaining thirty-four were flown by 424 Squadron RCAF – yet they look similar. And finally, Dad's thirty-four sorties were flown under the direct command of SHAEF's General Eisenhower through his deputy, Air Marshal Sir Arthur Tedder, while Don's were flown under the direct command of the RAF through Harris; and P/O Durkin's were a combination of the two.

These 102 sorties show Bomber Command was not mindlessly carpet bombing cities of no military relevance as some wrongly say. Instead, Bomber Command conducted a concerted attack on Nazi Germany's ability to wage war. This was not mindless terror bombing of civilians that Adolf Hitler erroneously thought for far too long it was. Instead, this was military and economic bombing that Albert Speer failed to convince Hitler of until it was too late.

---

25 Bochum, Cologne (twice), Dortmund (twice), Dusseldorf (twice), Essen, Homburg, Oberhausen and Sterkrade

Chapter Thirteen

Weaknesses into Strengths

The primary engines of the Bomber Command controversies are four-fold – Dresden, ethics, media and bombing accuracy. Each is worthy of examination. All reflect Bomber Command's evolution from weaknesses into strengths.

> 'As a synonym for the indiscriminate bombing of the German population, attacks on Dresden have had spun around them a a web of a great amount of legend, speculation and myth.'
>
> Germany's Research Institute for Military History[1]

Dresden is what too many people first think of when they hear the words Bomber Command. As the Institute observes, Dresden is buried in a mountain of myths. So much so that I feel I must address Dresden first. Dresden produced two of Reich Propaganda Minister Joseph Goebbels' biggest lies – a pair of lies so big and resilient that both are believed by too many today, three quarters of a century later.

Goebbels' First Lie was that 200,000 were killed. Dresden authorities told Berlin about 20,000 died. Goebbels simply added a zero to make it 200,000. This number grows. Some Neo-Nazis and Holocaust deniers now say over a half million were killed. Others actually compare Dresden to the Holocaust in which Germans killed over six million. However, the 'Dresden Commission of Historians for the Ascertainment of the Number of Victims of the Air Raids on the City of Dresden on 13/14 February 1945' has estimated the likely death-toll at around 18,000 and definitely not more than 25,000.[2] And one must remember those killed included German soldiers desperately manoeuvring to stop the Soviet Red Army, and war factory workers, which leads us to Goebbels' second lie.

Goebbels' Second Lie was that Dresden was not a military target, but instead just a picturesque medieval town. In fact, Germany's 1942 official guide to Dresden described it as 'one of the foremost industrial locations in the Reich'. In 1944, the German High Command's weapons office listed 127 medium-to-large factories and workshops in Dresden supplying the Army.

---

1 Institute, Vol. IX, Part 1, p. 471
2 Taylor, *How Many Died in the Bombing of Dresden*? Spiegel Online International 10/02/2008

WEAKNESSES INTO STRENGTHS

So much of what is written about Dresden is not true. For example, the Institute says 'The reports of low-level strafing ... and of phosphorus "raining down" from the sky, like those of the number of refugees in Dresden during the raids, prove after critical examination to be speculation and exaggerated accounts, mistakes, or even the product of the imagination.'[3] The fact is, bombing Dresden was needed by Stalin's approaching Soviet Red Army, which was vulnerable. Dresden's communications centre and railway-marshalling junctions were being used in a frantic effort to re-supply and manoeuvre the German army to stop the Soviets.

America's reaction to Dresden: America participated fully in bombing Dresden, but has the opposite view to Britain and the Dominions. Americans are proud of the Mighty Eighth. To counter a 17 February 1945 Associated Press speculative report that bombing Dresden was 'deliberate terror bombing', General of the US Army George Marshall issued a statement that Russia requested the Dresden bombing. This ended Dresden as a controversy in America.[4] Sadly, Churchill was silent.

For decades I believed both of Goebbels' lies. I was astonished when, in February 2015, German Chancellor Angela Merkel said the true number of deaths was not 200,000, but in fact was below 25,000. She added that she's amazed that we actually believed the Nazis. In spite of many credible sources refuting both Nazi lies, they are still believed by too many people today. They are fake news on a massive scale. Goebbels was expert at both creating fake news and suppressing the truth.

So, what really happened at Dresden? The facts are that from 13 to 15 February 1945 Dresden was bombed by 719 British, 527 American and seventy-seven Canadian bombers.[5] Ten of the RCAF bombers were Pathfinders. Days before Dresden, Roosevelt, Churchill and Stalin met in Yalta between 4-11 February. The meeting was not a success. FDR was dying, Churchill depressed and Stalin demanding. Stalin asked for the bombing of Dresden. A British interpreter at Dresden testified that this happened although it does not appear in the record. Stalin's chief spokesman at Yalta, General Aleksei Antonov, asked for air attacks[6] to prevent Germans moving troops from other theatres to the Eastern Front[7] and because the Soviets wanted German lines of communications destroyed.[8] It is interesting to note that General Antonov, at Yalta Deputy Chief of Staff of the Soviet Army, was promoted to Chief of the General Staff later that month. Richard Overy says Antonov and Stalin developed 'the most effective working relationship of the war'.[9]

---

3 Institute, Vol. IX, Part 1, p. 471
4 Bishop, *Bomber Boys – Fighting Back 1940-1945*, p. 347.
5 Bashow, *No Prouder Place*, p. 389.
6 Cooper, *Target Dresden*, p. 247
7 Harris, *Bomber Offensive*, p. 319
8 Johnson, *Churchill*, pp. 133-4
9 People Pill, *Aleksei Antonov* www.peoplepill.com

Accordingly, Dresden 'was an Army support operation, aimed at easing the Soviet advance, and Harris was simply following instructions.'[10] Just as Bomber Command had assisted western Allied armies, the USSR's Red Army was now in need, and was our Ally. In short, Stalin wanted Dresden bombed. FDR and Churchill concurred and ordered it. Paul Johnson says Dresden also arose from 'the desire of Churchill and Roosevelt at Yalta in January [sic] to prove to Stalin that they were doing their best to help the Russian effort on the Eastern Front. The Russians had particularly asked for Dresden, a communications centre, to be wiped out. When Harris queried the order, it was confirmed direct from Yalta by Churchill and Air Chief Marshal Peter Portal.[11] My Dad had been repatriated back to Canada on 22 January 1945, but his 166 Squadron helped bomb Dresden. Aircrew were told in the 166 Squadron pre-briefing that the primary purpose of bombing Dresden was to assist the Red Army.[12]

Bomber Command critics complain that the war was almost over anyway, some thought as early as D Day, so why were the bombers still flying? The war was not over. No less an authority than General George Patton, commander of Third US Army, warned in January 1945, 'We can still lose this war. Anything was possible.'[13] Germans in Italy and elsewhere showed great skill at defensive fighting. No country knows that better than Canada. In Ortona, Italy (Canada's Stalingrad), from 20 to 28 December 1943, our division in the Eighth Army fought the Germans building to building and room to room, a process called 'mouse-holing'. Ortona is where Seaforth Highlander Ernest 'Smokey' Smith of New Westminster won the Victoria Cross. I had the pleasure of chatting with Smokey several times, including with the Seaforth in The Netherlands in May 2005. I attended his Full Military Funeral in Vancouver on 13 August 2005. He was 91. His was Canada's first Full Military Funeral in a half a century since Billy Bishop VC in 1956.

Getting back to Yalta, the British had a report that the Second World War could drag on another year if we didn't help the Soviets. The Soviet Army was only seventy miles (113 km) from Dresden, but its supply lines were dangerously overextended. It was vulnerable and Germany was showing no signs of surrender. Instead, Germans were digging in for a hard-fought fight, hopefully to keep a vicious defensive war going longer than the Allies cared to fight. Roy Jenkins[14] who served as UK Minister of Aviation, and then Chancellor of the Exchequer, and is a noted biographer of UK leaders, tells us that Churchill's decision to intensify area bombing was founded on Churchill's belief that so doing would shorten the war. Britain wanted this war to end, and so did America. Through its 'Germany-First' policy, America had two-thirds of its fighting force in Europe,

---

10   Bishop, *Air Force Blue*, p. 357
11   Johnson, *Churchill*, pp. 133-4
12   Feesey,. *The Fly By Nights*.
13   Hampton, pp. 327-8
14   Jenkins, *Churchill – a Biography*.

and only one-third fighting Japan.[15] It was time to transfer to the Pacific. In addition, relations with Stalin were deteriorating. From all this, Germany had reason to believe that, if it dug in as it had in Italy, it could conduct a defensive war long enough for the western Allies to negotiate peace. However, devastating blows inflicted by the strategic bombing offensive in 1945 destroyed the German ability to keep fighting.

Bombing Ethics

The question of the ethics of bombing arose from the reality that most German heavy industry was located inside certain cities – and so *ipso facto* were the workers. Given the Allies' demand at Casablanca for 'Unconditional Surrender', the only way to defeat the Nazis was to destroy Germany's ability to wage war. What would have been unethical was either losing the war, a very real possibility especially in the early years, or the large-scale massacre of Allied soldiers as happened in the First World War. Britain, for example, lost three times as many soldiers in the first war as it did in the second. The strategic bombing offensive achieved its primary objectives of saving the lives of hundreds of thousands of Allied soldiers and shortened the war, as it did, according to Harris, by at least two years.[16] Also, the majority of Bomber Command's 955,044 wartime bomb tonnage was dropped on military targets away from cities – 524,747 tons of a 955,044 total, being 54.9 per cent.[17] Postwar authors found rich markets for sensationalist books condemning Bomber Command for bombing cities, and thereby killing civilians, but the biggest casualty of these books has been the truth.

Regarding British leadership, America's counterpart to Harris, Lieutenant General Ira Eaker says:

> I can testify to the fallacy of this anti-humanitarian charge against British leadership, political and military ... . Never at any time did he [Churchill] propose or encourage wanton attacks on civilians. No bomber strike was ever scheduled which was not aimed at an important element of the enemy's war making capacity.[18]

America's postwar investigation of bombing results in Europe estimates about 300,000 were killed, including German soldiers and workers in the factories that supplied the means for making war. A USAF 1953 report says, for example, that 50,000 war factory workers lived in Dresden.

---

15 Roberts, *Masters and Commanders,* p. 468
16 Harris, *From the Horse's Mouth*
17 www.nucleus.com/twright/bc-sats/html
18 Peden, *A Thousand Shall Fall*, pp. ix-x

Germany killed about seventeen million, including six million in the Holocaust and over three million PoWs. Of the 5.7 million Soviet PoWs taken by the Nazis, 3.3 million died in captivity.[19] Paul Robinson points out that the Soviet Union lost about twenty million civilians, primarily to starvation and atrocities. My awareness of Germany's Holocaust started of course with Anne Frank, whose diaries I've read several times, and whose hiding place in Amsterdam I've visited several times. Since then, I've paid my respects at several Holocaust Memorials worldwide, including The World Holocaust Remembrance Centre in Jerusalem, the United States Holocaust Memorial Museum in Washington DC, and the Canadian Museum of Human Rights, Winnipeg. I've read extensively and watched documentaries and movies. My son Ruaridh paid his respects at Auschwitz.

In 2005 Ruaridh and I visited the Dutch Nazi Camp at Westerbork which Adolf Eichmann, a major architect of the Holocaust, took control of from the Dutch on 1 July 1942. Postwar he escaped to Argentina. The Mossad captured him there on 11 May 1960. I watched his trial in Israel on television. He was executed in Israel by hanging on 1 June 1962. Westerbork has 102,000 stones – one for each Dutch inmate, including Anne Frank, deported from Westerbork to horrific deaths in Germany or Poland.[20] Camp Westerbork was liberated by the Canadian 2nd Infantry Division on 12 April 1945. Of 102,000 inmates, only 876 were still there – 98,000 perished in the German death camps.

And then there's Japan. It is estimated Japan murdered about six million civilians and PoWs[21] although other estimates range as high as ten million. Most were Chinese. My awareness of Japanese atrocities arose from Anne de Ridder, the mother of my life-long friend Eric de Ridder. She and her husband Ben were Dutch imprisoned by Japan in Indonesia. Camp conditions were inhumane. Over the decades from my boyhood until her death at age 97, Mrs de Ridder told me much about their horrific captivity. A powerful point she stressed was that, had President Truman delayed even a month in dropping the atomic bomb, most of the Dutch including the de Ridders would have died. She told me that the British liberating her camp were so appalled by what the inmates told them about the sadistic camp commander that they assembled the Dutch and, in full view of everyone, executed him so that no one would wonder whether he returned to a postwar happy life in Japan.

In December 2016 I participated in the 75th Anniversary in Hong Kong at Sai Wan War Cemetery of the disastrous 8-25 December 1941 Battle of Hong Kong. Two Canadian battalions, the Winnipeg Grenadiers and the Royal Rifles of Canada from Quebec City, suffered 100 per cent casualties of killed or captured. Captured Canadian soldiers were treated inhumanely. Japan had no regard for international

---

19 HISTORY TV Channel *Prisoners of War* A+E Networks AETN www.history.co.uk/history-of-ww2/prisoners-of-war

20 *Herinneringscentrum Kamp Westerbork* www.kampwesterbork.nl/en/

21 Rummel, *Statistics of Democide*, Chapter 3, Statistics of Japanese Democide Estimates, Calculations and Sources www.hawaii.edu/powerkills/SOD.CHAPS3.HTM

law. In December 2011, Toshiyuki Kato, Japan's parliamentary vice-minister for Foreign Affairs, apologized for the mistreatment to a group of Canadian veterans of the Battle of Hong Kong.[22] But the Emperor remains silent.

Media Portrayal

Another significant source of Bomber Command controversy has been its portrayal in the media. Media during the war and in the decades since has in various ways either supported Bomber Command or trashed it. One of the greatest supports has been movies and documentaries about the now famous Dambusters. One of the worst of these trashings was the January 1992 CBC/NFB broadcast of 'Death by Moonlight' in 'The Valour & the Horror' series which I mentioned earlier. A challenge with Bomber Boy movies is, while the Fighter Command Battle of Britain story is relatively straightforward and therefore easy to make movies about, Bomber Command's Second World War work was far more complex.

The Dambusters movie on television when I was a teenager was my first exposure to Bomber Command. Then circa 1995 I by chance saw at the airport in Gander, Newfoundland what was described as being the RAF's only documentary on a 'Day in the Life of Bomber Command Aircrew'. My memory of its contents is poor because it was shown in black-and-white on a small-screen television, and its authenticity of actual wartime footage was so perfect that it was boring. I did not know then that boredom was a major challenge for Bomber Command aircrew waiting for sorties. What I remember most was seeing a long line of Lancasters on the tarmac preparing to take off. The narrator droned on that none of the pilots of those Lancasters was old enough to qualify for a driver's licence. The exhibit at Gander Airport said that this was one of only two places in the world where this documentary could be seen. I know not where the other place was.

And then in August 2021 I discovered Simon MacKenzie's 2019 book *Bomber Boys on Screen*. His book is so deeply researched that some chapters seem to have almost as many pages of endnotes as text. His book is described as the first in-depth study of how and why the Bomber Boys have been portrayed as they have in the media during the Second World War, and in the decades after. He devotes a chapter to the war, and to each decade thereafter. He points out that, during the war, the emphasis was on bombing success and that its achievements resulted from teamwork, not individual heroics.[23] The earliest films, such as *The Lion Has Wings,* fairly quickly became outdated because of changes in Bomber Command tactics. The movie he pays great attention to in the 1950s is *The Dam Busters* in 1955. It continues to be relevant today. For the 1960s, what caught my eye was the 1962 *Canada at War* series. I remember watching the whole series on television

---

22 Wikipedia Battle of Hong Kong
23 MacKenzie, *Bomber Boys on Screen*, p. 1

that year. Regarding the Bomber Command component of that series, Professor MacKenzie says:

> Bomber Command in general and 6 Group (RCAF) in particular were shown to be grinding down the enemy war effort by bombing the Ruhr industries, setting back the Nazi rocket programme at Peenemunde, helping prepare for D-day through 'precision bombing' and striking heavy and presumably effective blows at cities like Hamburg and Berlin. Aircrew losses and fear are touched on in the script written by Donald Brittain and Bud Knapp, but concerning the loss of civilian life and property, blame is placed entirely on Hitler.[24]

In the 1970s I remember watching the *World at War* about the Second World War on a global scale. It consisted of twenty-six episodes narrated by Laurence Olivier. Professor MacKenzie focuses on the twelfth episode *Whirlwind* on 24 January 1974 on strategic bombing, the sixteenth episode *Inside the Reich: Germany 1940-1944* on 20 February 1974 on the Hamburg firestorm, and other big raids, On 3 April 1974 *Nemesis: Germany February-May 1945,* including reference to Dresden, was broadcast.[25] This series, however imperfect, had a major impact on thinking at that time and for some still today.

For the 1980s I learnt about *Fireraiser,*[26] which Professor MacKenzie politely calls 'a highly partisan piece of filmmaking'. It targets Hugh Trenchard, Anthony Eden, Sir Winston Churchill and, of course, Sir Arthur Harris. Channel Four, created in that decade to provide alternative perspectives from ITV and BBC, was going to broadcast *Fireraiser* in February 1988 on the anniversary of Dresden. Fortunately, Channel Four's new chief executive, Michael Grade, viewed it first. He was astonished by how unfair it was to Harris, and so thankfully ordered that under no circumstances was *Fireraiser* ever to be shown on Channel Four. I wish Canada had someone of his calibre stop CBC's broadcast of *Death by Moonlight* in *The Valour and the Horror* series in 1992. However, BBC aired *Bomber Harris* on 2 September 1989. It was evidently more palatable to supporters. On 3 August 1994, in spite of the intervention of the Queen Mother as Patron of the Bomber Command Association, Channel Four in the UK broadcast CBC's *Death by Moonlight*. I echo Andrew Roberts' thundering reply in the *Daily Mail* that 'Goebbels could not have made a better job of this travesty of the truth.'[27]

Canadians furious with *Death by Moonlight* including former Canadian National Defence Minister Barney Danson created a new documentary *No Price Too High* to counter it. It was premiered on a Canadian cable channel in the summer of 1995, picked up by Canadian border stations of the US Broadcasting System in 1996 and

---

24 MacKenzie, pp. 71-2

25 MacKenzie, pp. 96-7

26 MacKenzie, pp. 110-12

27 MacKenzie, p. 128

finally was broadcast across Canada in 1998. I had never heard of it until reading Professor MacKenzie's book in September 2021. It correctly declares, as military historian Terry Copp so aptly puts it, 'the bomber offensive was one of the decisive factors in the defeat of Nazi Germany'.[28]

Professor MacKenzie advises the new millennium produced a host of books and documentaries to either support or condemn Bomber Command 'and even attempts to strip away some of the myths around the targeting and bombing of Dresden'.[29] His details regarding all this are impressive. He concludes[30] by saying that what sets Bomber Command apart from Fighter Command or the American Eighth Army Air Force 'is not a relative paucity of titles but rather divergence of perspectives'. The Battle of Britain, in spite of some uncomfortable truths that have now come to light, remains a classic David and Goliath conflict, while Americans continue to view the Mighty Eighth as a clean and precise campaign, even though it was in fact highly inaccurate. Bomber Command continues to be controversial for both morality and effectiveness. My hope is what I have discovered in my quest brings clarity to what really happened. *Bomber Boys on Screen* is filled with movies, documentaries, television shows and other media which supports or condemns Bomber Command in many ways. The depth of the research is phenomenal. I have only touched on points that jumped out at me. For those interested in rich detail, Professor MacKenzie is your man.

Then on 8 September 2021 I received from Doreen Charlwood Burge in Australia news of the Australian Series *Wings of the Storm – Documentary of Australians in Bomber Command*[31] which her father helped make and in which her mother was featured. As I've mentioned, Doreen's dad was Second World War Bomber Command navigator Don Charlwood, author of the iconic *No Moon Tonight*, which has now been in continuous print for over sixty-five years, and his autobiographical *Journeys Into Darkness* written almost a half-century later.

And yet, misinformation about and marginalization of Bomber Command continues. The TV mini-series four episode *Winston Churchill's War*[32] in its third episode *A Perfect Unity*, originally aired on 21 March 2021, portrays Bomber Command as marginal to the war effort and focused on area bombing to spread terror and kill civilians, with Harris himself shown in a dark light, although it concedes Churchill used Bomber Command to try to mollify Stalin's demands since 1941 for a second front in the West. Its fourth and final episode *Deliverance*, originally aired on 28 March 2021, is even worse. It deals with 1944 and 1945. Bomber Command is never mentioned. How is that possible? Canada is never mentioned either, not

---

28 MacKenzie, p. 130

29 MacKenzie, p. 143

30 MacKenzie, p. 162

31 www.ww2talk.com/index.php?threads/wings-of-the-storm-documentary-of-australia

32 Winston Churchill's War Wild Bear Entertainment and Sky H History Narrated by Liam James and Directed by Production Manager Edmond Duff Broadcast by BBC 2021 and Knowledge Network 2022

even on the beaches of D Day. It beggars belief that televised *Winston Churchill's War* could completely miss vitally important information.

I conclude with news of accurate media portrayal. On 9 March 2022 Netflix released outside Denmark the Danish movie *The Bombardment* (also known as *The Shadow of My Eye*). It had been released in Denmark on 28 October 2021. It is based on the true story of Bomber Command, under intense Danish pressure to do so, bombing the Gestapo Headquarters in Copenhagen on 21 March 1945. Through torture, the Gestapo was on the verge of learning enough to crush the Danish Resistance. Tragically, several of the participating Mosquitoes bombed a nearby school by mistake. The movie captures the intensity of the pressure Bomber Command was under from Denmark to carry out this bombing, how difficult and dangerous it was, the toll on terrified aircrew, and the tragedy on the ground when some bombs went astray. *Rotten Tomatoes* gives it an audience score of 93 per cent.

Bombing Accuracy

The *Bombardment* movie brings me to bombing accuracy. My research reveals an enormous negative myth, still believed by too many today, that Bomber Command's bombing was highly inaccurate.[33] While in the early years of the war bombing was inaccurate, this myth stuck long after increasingly impressive technology was invented and used. Two sources of this myth were the 18 August 1941 Butt Report and the 14 February 1942 British Area Bombing Directive. Churchill the pragmatist was focused on what was strategically desirable and tactically possible.[34] Bombing early in the war was shown by David Butt of the War Cabinet secretariat on to be highly inaccurate. Lord Cherwell (physicist Frederick Lindemann), Churchill's scientific advisor and close friend, had ordered Butt to evaluate accuracy by studying aircrew logs and target photos.[35] The results suggested significant weaknesses in bombing accuracy, so much so they questioned the viability of Bomber Command.

Paul Robinson points out that, in France in May 1940, the RAF Advanced Air Striking Force bomber squadrons of obsolete Bristol Blenheim twin-engine and Fairey Battle single-engine British light bombers flown by the RAF, RAAF (the Fairey) and RCAF were destroyed by German flak and fighters. This rendered RAF daylight bombings unsustainable without air superiority, so the RAF returned to night bombings where loss rates were high, but sustainable. However, the navigation/bombing systems were so primitive that finding targets at night was difficult. The Butt/Lindemann studies found, for example, that

---

33 Hastings, *Winston's War – Churchill 1940- 1945*, New York NY, Borzoi Book Published by Alfred A. Knopf, 2009, p. 208

34 Hastings, *Bomber Command*, Michael Joseph Ltd, 1979, pp. 68-9.

35 Dunmore & Carter, p 5

WEAKNESSES INTO STRENGTHS

during Ruhr attacks in 1941, only 10 per cent of bombers got within five miles of their target.

The Butt Report, while disputed by the RAF as highly questionable, shocked Churchill. With Lord Cherwell's encouragement, the result was Churchill's 14 February 1942 'Area Bombing Directive to Bomber Command' which declared that 'operations should now be focused on the morale of the enemy civilian population, and in particular, the industrial workers. The immediate aim is, therefore, twofold, namely, to produce (i) destruction and (ii) fear of death.' Paul Robinson points out that the targets of this directive and its amendments were towns and cities that hosted German war industries. This was total war, and nothing the Germans had not already done. That directive remained in force for a year until replaced on 4 February 1943 by the 'Casablanca Directive' with America which remained in force until 17 April 1944. The Casablanca Directive articulated the strategic bombing offensive objective of 'The progressive destruction and dislocation of the German military, industrial and economic systems, and the undermining of the morale of the German people to a point where their capacity for armed resistance is fatally weakened'. Harris was appointed Air Officer Commanding-in-Chief of Bomber Command on 22 February 1942, a week *after* the directive for which he has too often been blamed.

Pathfinders and Bomber Aircraft Support

A major step forward on improving accuracy happened on 15 August 1942 when several elite Bomber Command squadrons were formed into what was called the Pathfinder Force (PFF) to locate and mark targets with flares. For the remainder of the war, the Pathfinders AOCin-C was the Australian Air Commodore Donald C.T. Bennett, 'one of the world's best navigators'.[36] The Pathfinders were originally within No. 3 Group but, on 8 January 1943, were reformed into their own No. 8 Group.[37] Theirs was dangerous work – they flew 51,053 sorties in which 675 aircraft were lost[38] and 3,727 Pathfinder airmen were killed.

Bombing accuracy was further aided by protecting Bomber Command bombers. To this end, on 11 November 1943, Bomber Command formed No. 100 Group (Bomber Support). Its purpose was electronic warfare and countermeasures. Its motto was 'Confound and Destroy'. It countered the considerable force of radar-equipped Luftwaffe night fighters with a range of electronic 'homers' fitted to radar-equipped Mosquitoes, like Serrate and Perfectos. This enabled Mosquitoes to 'home in' on night fighters to either shoot them down or disrupt their sorties. In 1944-45, No. 100 Group shot down 258 Luftwaffe aircraft at a cost of seventy Mosquitoes. To further disrupt German radio

---

36 Birrell, *Johnny*, p. 92
37 Chorlton, *The RAF Pathfinder*, p. 16
38 Chorlton, p. 161

communications and radar, No. 100 Group used thirty-two devices, most of which were developed at the Telecommunications Research Establishment (TRE). These included the Airborne Cigar (ABC) jammer, Airborne Grocer jammer, Carpet jammer, Corona spoofer, Jostle jammer, Lucero homer, Mandrell jammer, and Pipe-rack jammer. These countered Luftwaffe Freya, Lichtenstein and Wurzburg air-defence radars.

Erik Nielsen flew thirty-three combat sorties with 101 Squadron, an ABC unit of No. 1 Group which Paul Robinson points out provided support jamming to all groups, not just its parent. Nielsen earned the DFC for 'courage and devotion to duty'. Surviving the war was notable for Erik because 101 Squadron reputedly had the highest casualty rate in Bomber Command. The ABC, a top-secret radio-jamming system, was the reason for its high casualty rate. ABC was operated by an eighth aircrew member known as a 'special operator' (spec op or SO) who spoke German. He sat behind a curtain towards the rear of the Lancaster to locate and jam German fighter-controller broadcasts. He would also pose as a German controller to spread disinformation to the enemy. This forced his Lancaster to break radio silence, thereby rendering it vulnerable to being tracked and attacked by Luftwaffe fighters, the result being the highest casualty rate.[39] The first Operation MANNA sortie to feed the Dutch was flown by 101 Squadron, Bob Urquhart's aircrew.

Postwar, Erik rejoined the RCAF in 1946 as a legal officer while earning his law degree at Dalhousie University in Halifax. Then he opened his law practice in Whitehorse, capital city of the Yukon. In 1957, he was elected to Parliament. There he served as a Yukon MP for three decades. On 17 September 1984, Erik became Deputy Prime Minister of Canada. He was only the third person to ever hold that office. Erik Nielsen Whitehorse International Airport is named in his honour. Erik's younger brother, much loved actor Leslie Nielsen, was an RCAF aerial gunner still in training when the war ended.[40]

What was the German perspective? The Institute points out that searchlights and poor winter weather made bombing Berlin even more difficult, and navigation was a major issue because H2S radar didn't work as well over Berlin, given Berlin has fewer natural features to fix on. In addition, while Bomber Command had the advantage of OBOE and 'Window' in its battles of the Ruhr and Hamburg, Germany had developed night-fighter defence methods to offset those advantages by the time of the Battle of Berlin. Also, German night fighters were no longer as easily taken in by British diversionary and feint attacks, even though German night fighters were once more fooled by the RAF on 26 March 1944 over Essen.[41]

---

39 Wikipedia No. One Group RAF, and 101 Squadron

40 Wikipedia Erik Nielsen, and Leslie Nielsen

41 Institute Vol. VII, p. 90

WEAKNESSES INTO STRENGTHS

Bomber Command Navigation for Dummies Like Me

Most Bomber Command commentary on navigation leaves me bewildered. Fortunately, Paul Robinson has done wonders to make it understandable. He organizes the subject in the following helpful way: [42]

- GEE, OBOE and H2S transformed night, all-weather navigation
- 'Beam Approach' systems enabled bombers to return to base in bad weather
- Bomb sights, like the Mk XIV my Dad would have used, were improved. They culminated in the SABS (stabilized automatic bomb sight)
- VHS radios enabled bomber aircraft to communicate clearly with each other, thus enabling the use of Master Bombers

Paul says SABS could put a Tallboy bomb within a 100-yard circle from 15,000 feet. The Mk XIV equivalent accuracy was 200 yards (183 metres). In addition, the bomb-aimer no longer had to tell the pilot where to fly during the bombing run. The correct course was fed automatically to the pilot's instruments, and he could feed it to the autopilot. The bombs would be released automatically, and the bombs could be aimed via H2S radar, so automatic bombing through a cloud cover became possible. The bomb-aimer became a radar operator.

By chance at RAF Metherington Airfield Visitor Centre at Westmoor Farm at Martin Moor in Lincolnshire on 11 May 2019, I met RAF Squadron Leader (Retd) Andy Marson of Aviation Heritage Lincolnshire. Andy was also able to explain to me the evolution of accuracy with clarity. His approach was to remind me that, in the early years of the war, it was decided to bomb at night because aircraft and aircrew casualties were too high in daylight. This led to significant navigation problems, visual sight being no longer applicable except on cloudless, moonlit nights which were too dangerous for bombers, and dead reckoning being inherently inaccurate. The result? The Butt Report. Andy told me Bomber Command's four-engine heavies, primarily Halifaxes and then Lancasters, made 'blind navigation' essential. This led first to GEE, then to H2S, and finally, as mentioned, to OBOE. These aids enabled accurate navigation and timing. With each aircraft navigating individually to a track, height and time over target, the bomber stream could be compressed and German defences overwhelmed. Then the Pathfinders were created, using experienced crews and the most up-to-date equipment. Andy said they preceded the bomber stream and marked the target with coloured flares, akin to laser marking of today, and controlled the bombing VHF radio, adjusting the aim of the main force as required.

Andy also told me about ECM (electronic countermeasure) aircraft from No. 101 Squadron (Erik Nielsen's squadron) at RAF Ludford Magna. It was only twenty-one miles (34 km) north-east of Lincoln and sixteen miles (26 km) south of RAF Kirmington. ECM aircraft were implanted in the bomber stream to protect our aircraft from attack. The German speaking eighth crew member I wrote of

---

42 Robinson, 21 January 2020 e-mail to author

concerning Erik Nielsen was aboard to spoof enemy ground controllers on German radio frequencies, known as Airborne Cigar (ABC) jammers, i.e., noise jamming with microphones by aircraft engines. Paul Robinson says Tinsel was used; and Window, strips of metal foil, were dropped to cause false reflections on German radar screens. Andy introduced me to interdictor Mosquitoes harassing German night fighters at their home airfields. Paul observes that these were No. 100 Group Mosquitoes attacking with bombs and guns. If they saw a night fighter, they would attack it. They had their main air-intercept (AI) radar removed so a set would not fall into German hands. This rule was lifted after D Day, after which these Mosquitoes went hunting German night fighters in earnest. Andy also spoke of OCU and HCU aircraft flying decoy raids in enemy territory to confuse German controllers. All that Andy and Paul told me helped me understand a complex topic. Just as Andy hugely helped my understanding of the evolution of Bomber Command navigation, Paul did likewise for the evolution of precision bombing and bombsights in both Bomber Command and The Mighty Eighth.

In his own words, Paul tells me 'The evolution of US and UK strategic bombing strategy is shared heritage': both nations developed policies of strategic deterrence during the 1930s. If deterrence failed, the slaughter of the First World War could be avoided by a strategic bombing campaign that would cripple an enemy's industry and economy and persuade his leaders and population to surrender without recourse to invasion. However, neither nation initially had the technology and numbers of platforms to deliver this: neither the Germans nor Japanese were deterred from expansionism, and bombers could not deliver the strategic effect required to encourage surrender.

The strategy could only be successful if attacks could be delivered with the accuracy and payloads required to achieve the effects required: i.e. small numbers of powerful weapons delivered precisely (precision bombing: cheaper), or large numbers of less-powerful weapons delivered less accurately (area bombing: expensive). The UK, being earlier into the Second World War, was forced down the latter pathway by circumstances (strong German defences/night operations for survival/poor navigation aids and weapons accuracy = night area bombing), while developing the tools required for precision bombing.

America tried to leap-frog straight to precision bombing. The Norden bombsight was a key component of this policy, enabling (relatively) accurate bombing from high level. However, the other components were not in place when The Mighty Eighth began its B-17 daylight ops over Germany. First, the B-17 carried a small bomb load; many aircraft were required to achieve the desired effects. Second, German fighter defences by day were significant (as the RAF had found). Third, B-17s had to fly in non-manoeuvrable close formations to provide mutual defensive firepower. Unfortunately, this meant individual B-17s could not aim their own bombs. When flying in a defensive phalanx only the lead bombardier could exploit his Norden sight, with the rest of his bomb group (perhaps twenty-four aircraft) releasing their bombs when they saw the lead aircraft's bombs falling. This inevitably led to poor accuracy. Also, the phalanx was very vulnerable to flak.

The advent of long-range Mustang and Thunderbolt escort fighters in 1943/44 reduced the German fighter problem, and jammer escorts like Mandrel disrupted

WEAKNESSES INTO STRENGTHS

flak accuracy, so The Mighty Eighth's results improved in 1944-45. However, the Pacific Theatre was different. Bombers were unescorted until the Americans had captured islands relatively close to Japan. General Curtis LeMay, who had flown in Europe, realised that to achieve the strategic aim he would need to operate at night (when, despite the Norden sight, target acquisition and weapon accuracy was poor). So, he adopted night area bombing, and napalm was ideal for creating firestorms in (wooden) Japanese cities. As soon as he had fighter bases close enough to Japan, he changed to daytime, escorted precision operations. Ultimately, the 1930s bomber deterrence/no invasion strategy became possible with the advent of nuclear weapons. Arguably, it's kept the world safe(ish) for the last seventy years.

Now bombsights. Both the RAF and The Mighty Eighth strove to develop accurate bombsights throughout the 1930 and 1940s. Norden started to develop his bombsight in the late 1920s for the US Navy. It was gyro-stabilized and worked by tachometry: you kept a cursor on the target as the bomber flew towards it, and the sight's computer measured the rate of change in angle (a so-called angle-rate bombsight). The aircraft's height and speed were also automatically fed into the computer, which calculated the correct position to release the bombs, which it would do automatically. An allowance for windage was also calculated automatically, and steering instructions could be fed directly into the aircraft's autopilot so, in effect, the bomb aimer 'flew' the final phase of the attack run. Its circular-error probability (CEP) was around 200 yards from 15,000 feet. During tests, the Norden demonstrated a CEP of 80 yards, but in combat it was well over 300 yards. This disappointing performance was one reason LeMay introduced the 'phalanx' formation: he had the best bombardiers fly in the lead B-17s.

The RAF developed two gyro-stabilized bombsights. One was developed from the non-stabilized bombsight family. With these, the pilot had to keep 'wings-level' during the final approach to the target, or the bomb-aiming symbology moved like a pendulum. The gyro-stabilized sights kept steady as the bomber manoeuvred. By 1944 most Lancasters had the Mk XIV. The computer drove a continuously-computed impact point sight which indicated where the bombs would hit. The bomb-aimer 'flew' the aircraft until the CCIP was over the target, then released the bombs. It was pretty good; about the same accuracy in combat as the Norden, although the windage had to be set manually and it could not be connected to the autopilot. However, it could drive a 'fly left/right' indicator in the cockpit for the pilot to follow, and it could be linked to the ground-mapping radar (H2S) that some (mostly Pathfinder) Lancasters carried, and it only required the bomber to fly a 10-second steady approach. It was excellent for general day and night bombing, and 166 Squadron Lancasters would have had them.

The other RAF gyro-stabilized sight was SABS – the Stabilized Automatic Bomb Sight. Its technology was very similar to the Norden, using tachometric 'angle-rate' aiming, which automatically allowed for windage and auto-release. It was more accurate than the Norden and Mk XIV, with a combat CEP of 120 yards. Only produced in limited numbers, it equipped 617 Squadron whose 'Tallboy' and 'Grand Slam' bombs required the greater accuracy that SABS would bring. The other two Tallboy squadrons used the Mk XIV. SABS was further developed to equip the RAF's postwar bombers. It was apparent that the aptitude and skill of the bomb-aimer was a major factor with all these bomb sights. Ironically, the RAF wanted to buy the Norden in 1939, but the US Navy/USAAF wouldn't sell it 'in case it fell into enemy hands'.

Paul concludes by saying 'Hope this helps, Roddy.' It certainly does. It would have been virtually impossible for me to figure this out.

Andy summed up by saying that, in the final stages of the war, Bomber Command flew well-co-ordinated integrated packages, as per today, and was an extremely effective fighting formation.[43] This included my Dad's thirty-four combat sorties. To this, Canadians Spencer Dunmore and William Carter add that the results of Bomber Command at night 'were on occasion significantly more successful than the USAAF's daylight bombing, thanks to a high degree of experience and accuracy with the blind-bombing aids Oboe and H2S, the Air Position Indicator (API), the Group Position Indicator (GPI) and the improved Mark XIV gyro stabilized automatic bombsight (SABS)'.[44] I am told this is the source of the GPS we use to guide us in our vehicles today – although not the same technology, but the same requirement: accurate navigation.

So what does Harris say? By way of preamble, commencing in March 1944, bombing in France in preparation for D Day required highly accurate bombing of the railways to avoid French casualties as much as possible. My Dad's first two combat sorties were bombing Paris, but not the Eiffel Tower. Both times, Dad was bombing railway marshalling yards. About this, Harris wrote:

> Railways are extraordinarily difficult and unrewarding targets for air attack. Main lines can be repaired in a few hours, and through lines in wrecked marshalling yards in a few days .... But what if the repair organization itself could be attacked? That, in effect, is what it was decided to do.[45]

Harris also says that, in addition to the Pathfinders:

> some targets were also marked by No. 1 Group [in which my Dad flew] which developed a variant of the Pathfinder Force technique for precision bombing.... Our attacks on the marshalling yards proved to be astonishingly accurate; never before had there been such concentrated bombing ... [and] Bomber Command's night bombing, from this point onwards, proved to be rather more accurate, much heavier in weight, and more concentrated than the American daylight attacks ....[46]

---

43 Andy Marson, e-mail to author, 13 May 2019
44 Dunmore & Carter, p. 462
45 Harris, *Bomber Offensive*, p. 197
46 Harris, pp. 202-3

WEAKNESSES INTO STRENGTHS

Aircraft, Bombs and Defences

Bomber Command aircraft and bombs steadily improved as the war progressed, and so did the defences. An important reason why both bombs and aircraft improved was Sir Barnes Neville Wallis. Regarding aircraft, Sir Barnes developed the Wellington twin-engine bomber with his light but strong geodetic airframe. He also developed the prewar R100 airship and the postwar Swallow supersonic design.

Regarding bombs, Sir Barnes created the bouncing bombs (codenamed Upkeep) for the Dambusters, and in 1944 the 12,000 lb (5443 kg) Tallboy and 22,000 lb (9979 kg) Grand Slam deep-penetration 'earthquake' bombs which destroyed German military installations, bunkers and underground factories previously thought 'bombproof'. James Fyfe wrote, 'The only regret was that these awesome additions to its armoury did not become available until fairly late in the war ... . Yet delivery to the enemy of Tallboys and Grand Slams would have been quite impossible at any time without the superlative lifting qualities of the faithful Lancaster.'[47] My research reveals that, to carry a Tallboy Bomb, the armour plating behind the pilot's chair was replaced with plywood and only half the ammunition was taken – even then their Lancaster's take off was slow. At the end of the runway their pilot retracted the landing gear and they climbed very slowly, hitting bushes and treetops on their way up.

Speaking of which, the enormous advantage Bomber Command had over the Luftwaffe were our four-engine heavy bombers, known as the 'heavies', especially Lancasters and Halifaxes. As Paul points out, the 'heavies' were more reliable (they could continue flying on two of their four engines), and carried a disproportionately heavy payload of weapons, equipment and fuel. This meant our bombers could fly further faster, defend themselves better, and drop more bombs. Fortunately for us, the Luftwaffe failed to see the importance of heavy bombers until it was too late, and so the Luftwaffe was essentially a tactical air force while ours were both tactical and strategic.

Accuracy was further improved by Bomber Command's development of better defences for its aircraft which Paul sums up as:

- Lancasters were given radar (Monica and Fishpond) to detect German night-fighters
- Specialist Squadrons of 101 Group and 101 Squadron 1 Group (Erik Neilsen's squadron) carried equipment to identify and jam German air defence and flak radar and fighter control communications
- Some squadrons had Lancasters, including those built in Canada, that had improved armaments – 0.5 inch rather than 0.303 Brownings[48]

---

47 Fyfe, *The Great Ingratitude*, p. 259
48 Browning, Basic Bomber Aircraft Machine Guns originally designed by John M. Browning

- 'Village Inn' automatic tail turrets were developed that located a target, identified it as hostile and opened fire automatically. No. 101 Squadron used these. Infra-red lights and detectors were installed to tell friend from foe.

Accuracy: Bomber Command and The Mighty Eighth

Another myth my research reveals is that Bomber Command was highly inaccurate with its strategic night-time 'area bombing', but The Mighty Eighth was incredibly accurate with its daytime 'precision bombing'. The following highlights how wrong this myth is. This story stars yet again in my book none other than America's beloved actor Jimmy Stewart. As mentioned, by 1945 Private Stewart of 1942 had risen to be Colonel Stewart. He became commander of the Second Combat Wing of the Mighty Eighth's Second Bomb Division. In June 1945, Colonel Jimmy Stewart was presiding officer in the court martial of a pilot and co-pilot who, on 4 March 1945, led six Mighty Eighth B-24 Liberator four-engine heavy bombers to bomb Zurich in Switzerland by mistake, instead of Freiberg in Germany as ordered. As Stewart biographer Robert Matzen, who refers to Jimmy Stewart as 'Jim', tells this story:

> The circumstances were all too familiar to Jim – bad weather, inoperative Mickey equipment, and misidentification of terrain by the lead navigator who was convinced he was over Freiberg, Germany, as the formation looked for a target of opportunity. The navigator even compared wooded terrain, marshalling yards, and a stream with an aerial photo of Freiberg to confirm he had the right target …. The jury of twelve officers found both pilots not guilty.[49]

Poor visibility in daylight led to the bombing not only of the wrong target, and not only the wrong city, but even the wrong country, by the Mighty Eighth in daylight while instrument bombing at night ever increased accuracy.

Accuracy: The View of a Child of the Third Reich

I can think of no better way of concluding the subject of bombing accuracy than with an eyewitness account of 11-year-old Irmgard Hunt. She was born on 28 May 1934 and raised on 'Hitler's Mountain' – Berchtesgaden – as a child of the Third Reich. When three years old, she even sat on Hitler's lap, to the delight of her parents and the disgust of her grandparents. Albert Speer Jr was one of her classmates. She says 'Prussian obedience, order, and discipline as

---

49 Matzen, *Mission: Jimmy Stewart and the Fight for Europe*, pp. 301-3.

WEAKNESSES INTO STRENGTHS

well as blind submission to Nazi ideology'[50] were the pillars of her education. Until 25 April 1945, the war never came to Berchtesgaden, but people living there knew of it from deaths on the fronts of relatives and neighbours. Irmgard's dad was drafted into the German Army and killed in France. They also noticed ever increasing shortages of everything, and transportation issues such as it took Irmgard's family two-and-a-half days instead of an afternoon to travel by train to visit her dying grandparents.

But what young Irmgard and millions of other German civilians really noticed were the bombers. Irmgard says, 'By 1943 the hours we spent in the town shelter had increased dramatically, due mostly to overflights by Allied bombers going after strategic targets to the south.'[51] Most German air-raid shelters were dreadful. But children of the Nazi elite, such as Irmgard's classmate Albert Speer Jr, were rushed by limousines from school to luxurious safe shelters on Obersalzberg near Hitler's villa. Such glaring discrimination was rankling Germans. However, what antagonized German citizens most was the inability of the German military to determine where Bomber Command would actually bomb. That inability forced the sounding of air-raid sirens for all communities en route. This meant for example that Berchtesgaden children spent hours in air raid shelters forty-eight times from January 1945 while Bomber Command passed nearby en route elsewhere.

Then came 25 April 1945, the only time Bomber Command bombed Berchtesgaden. Dad's 166 Squadron participated in that combat sortie but he of course was back in Canada. The purpose of the bombing was to ensure Hitler's mountain headquarters could become neither an immortal last stand for fanatics nor a postwar shrine for fascists. Irmgard says:

> On the deceptively clear spring morning of April 25, 1945, like a final thunderclap after a violent storm, British warplanes came swooping into the valley ... . The hellish explosions were followed by an enormous storm-like wind that would have blown me off my feet had I not gripped the rough bark of the nearest spruce and pressed myself against it ... . The earth shook, and the air was filled with the rumble of airplane motors, the whistle of falling bombs, the detonations, and the wind that followed ... we fully expected that the entire valley had been laid to waste. Where was the tack tack tack of the anti-aircraft guns, and why was Obersalzberg no longer shrouded in the usual acrid [camouflage] fog? The answer was simple: the chemicals for the fog had run out weeks ago; the guns had run out of ammunition and, perhaps, the soldiers to fire them. Yet when it was finally over we found that at least our immediate neighbourhood was undamaged. The very lack of fog cover had apparently allowed the

---

50 Irmgard Hunt, *On Hitler's Mountain*, p. 120
51 Hunt, p. 131

enemy pilots to be extremely accurate. The bombs had destroyed most of the Nazi settlement on the mountain, but left us and the town untouched.[52]

Irmgard then tells us that, after Bomber Command's visit, SS soldiers garrisoning Berchtesgaden begged townspeople for civilian clothes in which they could vanish. On 3 May 1945, the mayor sent a messenger from house to house instructing everyone to hang white sheets from their balconies or windows, and to open their homes without resistance to any foreign soldier who wanted to enter. The following day was one of great drama. That afternoon, the first American tank rolled into town. Irmgard, now eleven, had never seen an American, but says she had been taught they were uncultured barbarians run by Jews. She says:

> I decided that I must see the first Americans with my own eye … . They looked fierce but to my surprise just as young and handsome as our soldiers had been … . I found the Americans to look more human than I had thought possible … . It dawned on me then that we were no longer at war, the guns and bombs were silenced, and I would grow up in a world totally different from the one that Hitler had so forcefully instructed us to believe in.[53]

Irmgard grew up to become an international environmental consultant for clients such as the World Bank and USAID. She developed a preference for downhill skiing in Rocky Mountain powder snow. Hers is a powerful testament to Bomber Command accuracy. And it resulted in America taking Berchtesgaden without firing a shot – compliments of Bomber Command.

---

52 Hunt, pp. 193-4
53 Hunt, pp. 211-13

Part III

GERMANY'S PERSPECTIVE

Chapter Fourteen

Germany's Research Institute for Military History

My Biggest Breakthrough of My Bomber Command Quest

You may have noticed my references to Germany's Research Institute for Military History. I did not know what it was, or even that it existed, until Saturday 18 May 2019 at RAF College Cranwell in Lincolnshire with my sons Guy Roland and Ruaridh and RAF Air Vice-Marshal Paul Robinson. That day at Cranwell opened me to my biggest breakthrough in my quest to discover what Bomber Command actually accomplished in the Second World War. At Cranwell I learned from Assistant Librarian Howard ('Tim') Pierce of an important German source, the *Militargeschichtliches Forschungsamt* (Germany's Research Institute for Military History) of the Bundeswehr.

So what is this Institute? It began as separate entities in East and West Germany in 1958. They were merged in 1994 as the Military History Research Office (MGFA). In 2013 MGFA was combined with the German Army Social Sciences Studies Centre to become the Centre for Military History and Social Sciences of the Bundeswehr. It employs about sixty historians, political scientists and sociologists, supported by seventy other employees, some being military and others civilians.[1] My focus is a series of volumes headed *Germany and the Second World War* edited by Germany's Militargeschichtliches Forschungsamt (Research Institute for Military History), which I will refer to as the 'Institute'.

How did this breakthrough happen? It began a week earlier on Saturday 11 May 2019 while Graham Brett as my Bomber Command expert and Stu Altoft at the wheel were touring me around Lincolnshire to see Second World War Bomber Command sites. That fateful afternoon, Graham and Stu took me to the Cranwell Aviation Heritage Museum. It had just closed, but I told Angela Riley, the person closing it, about my Bomber Command quest. She invited the three of us to come in for half an hour. After I had inspected her Museum and was chatting with her, Angela told me something which turned out to be extremely important – that I should contact Tim Pierce at nearby RAF College Cranwell. It was now raining,

---

1. Wikipedia *Center for Military History and Social Sciences of the Bundeswehr*

but Stu and Graham complied with my request that we drive by the College. Looking at it from outside through its impressive wrought-iron fencing, its main building was grand indeed. So back at my hotel I e-mailed Tim.

On 14 May 2019 Tim replied saying that unfortunately RAF College Cranwell was in lockdown because it was between terms. But then Tim made the most marvellous offer – he was willing to organize my entry and personally show me Cranwell College Library. I could scarcely believe my good fortune. And more good fortune followed. The weekend we visited RAF College Cranwell, my London sons Ruaridh and Guy Roland were with me on my Bomber Command quest for their grandfather Roland W. MacKenzie DFC. So they came too. And, best of all – my mentor RAF Air Vice-Marshal Paul Robinson chauffeured us.

Saturday 18 May 2019 opened a whole new world to my sons and me, the world of the RAF's elite College. Cranwell in lockdown meant that, once we were processed through heavy security, we had the whole campus to ourselves. Tim's thoughtfulness on 18 May even included having on prominent display in the Library the *Gazette* entry of my Dad's Distinguished Flying Cross, and an informative write-up on RAF Kirmington, the RAF station from which Dad flew all thirty-four of his combat sorties in the Second World War.

And our time at Cranwell got off to the best possible start. Once we were inside the campus, Paul parked his vehicle beside the Cranwell College polo grounds. I had never seen polo played before, except in movies. It was our great good luck that, in the mist of that morning, a game was in progress between the RAF and a Reserve Army Team. Although it appeared to be a friendly Saturday morning get together rather than any form of league game, it was clear both teams wanted to win. The versatility and speed of polo ponies fascinated me. Given my love of horses, it was unforgettable.

Tim and Paul gave my sons and me the definitive tour of RAF College Cranwell. On 1 April 1918 the RAF became the world's first independent air force. My Finnish friend Pekka Moisio tells me that the Finnish Air Force was founded three weeks earlier on 6 March 1918, but it is not independent like the RAF; rather, the Finnish Air Force is a branch of the unified Finnish Defence Forces, just as the RCAF, which thankfully was independent in the Second World War, is now a branch of the unified Canadian Armed Forces. For many years the RAF was also the world's largest air force. And so, as befits the RAF being the world's first and largest air force, College Cranwell is housed in the elegance one would expect.

The highlight of the day, and indeed the whole month, was in Cranwell College Library when Tim showed me the fateful volume in the College's library of the Germany's Research Institute for Military History entitled *Germany and the Second World War*. And Tim had good news for me. Cambridge University, where I was headed next, has the volume. That was wonderful. On my arrival at Cambridge, Churchill College Head Librarian, Annie Gleason, told me they do not have that volume, and Cambridge Colleges do not exchange books, but she would find it for me. And find it she did – it turned out to be in Cambridge's main library. Annie arranged for me to be approved for admission there, a process that took about forty-five minutes. As soon as I was admitted, I found my volume waiting for me at the front entry desk. Eagerly I located a lovely desk at which to examine it in a quiet wood-panelled place with a lovely view. And guess what I discovered? It was part of a series of volumes.

Back to the front desk I went. A Cambridge librarian there did a search and found them for me. The two of us crowded into the tiniest ancient wooden elevator and clacked our way up into the narrow tower rising above the centre of the library. What we found there astonished me. We found the full set of thirteen volumes – a definitive statement on the Second World War. The series is entitled *Das Deutsche Reich und der Zweite Weltkrieg* – Germany and the Second World War. It's published by the Deutsche Verlags-Anstalt.

These thirteen volumes took the military academics of the Institute thirty years to finish. Fortunately, the Clarendon Press (an imprint of Oxford University Press) began publishing English translations of this series in 1990 and by 2014 ten of the thirteen volumes had been published at a rate of one every two years. There was a long delay between publishing Volumes IX, Parts One and Two because of the death of the main translation editor. I'm assuming but uncertain this was Derry Cook-Radmore in July 2010, aged 81. He twice held office as chair of the Translators Guild. He was the translation editor of Volumes V Part II, Volume VII and Volume XI, Part I, all of which I have reviewed. I also reviewed Volume II, the translation editor for which was P.S. (Paul Stephen) Falla, and Volume VI, the translation editor for which was Ewald Osers. Fortunately, Cambridge University Library had all thirteen volumes for me to inspect.

I raced through them, looking closely at the volumes which deal most deeply with Bomber Command. And what a story these volumes of the Institute's *Germany and the Second World War* series have to tell. Here are highlights.

Destabilized Nazi Leadership

During the Second World War, Hitler's position as Führer was unchallenged, albeit there was an unsuccessful attempt to murder him on 20 July 1944. But the Third Reich's Heir Apparent, Göring, had his reputation ridiculed by Bomber Command. This Institute tells us that this destabilized the Nazi leadership by opening the field to jockeying to replace him – most prominently by Himmler, Goebbels, Bormann and, of course, Speer. Each took steps to weaken his opponents that concurrently weakened the Reich's ability to wage war more effectively.

Let's look at Speer to see how this worked. The Institute says Speer was expert at withholding needed parts that frustrated the ability of his competitors to meet goals established for them by Hitler in Germany's failed fight against Bomber Command. This escalated internal machinations by Reich officials trying to make themselves look good, and their rivals look bad, regardless of how this might adversely affect Germany's ability to conduct the war.

But then, in January 1944 Speer fell ill. The Institute points out that a critical point in this rivalry, and the Reich's wartime material production, was Speer's hospitalization for almost four crucially important months from 18 January to 8 May 1944. The Institute says this was 'a tragic stroke of fate for him that had far-reaching consequences'.[2] Speer attempted to keep relevant by sending missives to Hitler from his hospital bed. But the Institute observes that his apparent fall from grace in hospital arose from Speer having provoked his rivals. Worse, Speer aroused Hitler's nascent mistrust through Speer's meteoric rise in 1943.[3] However, here again Bomber Command plays a major role, this time saving Speer through strengthening Germany's need for an 'armaments miracle'.

Armaments Miracle

A steadily repeated theme of the Institute, and also Albert Speer, is the enormous role the fixation on miracle weapons played in Germany losing the war. As Bomber Command damage escalated, Hitler indulged increasingly in the search for a quick fix – a miracle weapon. This diverted badly needed German labour and supplies from producing weapons essential for Germany's survival. While miracle weapons became an increasingly important topic in Germany as the war situation worsened, the concept in Germany was active from the outset of the war.

The Institute reports that British interest in German development of such weapons may well have arisen through Hitler's 19 September 1939 speech referring to 'a secret weapon against which there was no defence'. Speer managed to recover both from his illness, which at one point was thought by Hitler to be fatal, and his loss of influence arising from his absence in hospital. The Institute states: 'The intrigues by Speer's enemies failed ... due, ultimately, to the dramatic situation in air armament. Once again Speer managed to attract himself all Hitler's hopes for an "armaments miracle".'[4] As the war progressed, being saved by an 'armament miracle', sometimes referred to as a 'miracle weapon' or even a 'magic weapon', became increasingly important to Germans generally, and Hitler in particular. This concept seriously hurt Germany, because it accelerated Hitler's erratic and ultimately ruinous changes in priorities.

For the Allies, this was wonderful, because the Institute advises that Hitler's changes in armament priorities created increasingly catastrophic consequences to overall output. What Germany needed was focused output on a small number of essential products, enabling factories to produce just one item each to maximize economies of scale and mass production. Changing priorities forced factories to quickly retool, and produce items needed for several projects concurrently. In addition, this wasted enormous quantities of increasingly scarce raw materials. Best

---

2 Institute, Vol. V, Part 2, p. 411

3 Institute, Vol. V, Part 2, p. 409

4 Institute, Vol. V, Part 2, p. 418

of all, these continuing changes in priorities wrought havoc with the Luftwaffe's ability to cope with Bomber Command. The Nazis were ultimately trapped by this concept of an armaments miracle, which gave continuing hope to many Germans well into 1945.

So what's a specific example of this? The jet-engine V1 and the V2 rocket. Albert Speer says that, from the end of 1943 onward 'our tremendous industrial capacity was diverted to the huge missile known as the V2 ... the whole notion was absurd'.[5] Bomber Command's 1944 campaign against the V1 launch sites which my Dad participated in, coupled with the costly Bomber Command bombings of the rocket development centre at Peenemunde on 17/18 August 1943, and in October on the V1 manufacturing site at Kassel, effectively blunted the limited impact of these missiles. However, had these weapons been available in quantity on D Day, bombs raining down on the embarkation ports and the massed invasion fleet could have been catastrophic for the Allies.[6]

However, the Institute reports that Speer wrote in his memoirs[7] 'that the takeover of the air armament industry had been a 'minor matter compared with the havoc being wrought in Germany by the enemy air forces'.[8] On 24 August 1944 Speer told a meeting of the heads of the aviation industry and his armaments staff that his aim was 'by boosting fighter production to succeed in finally fending off the greatest danger that faces us, that of armament here in our homeland being brought to its knees'.[9] However, the Institute concludes with this damming comment:

> Speer's own personality, and his scheming for power, stood in the way of the move begun a whole year earlier to bring the diverse sectors of armaments together by means of a planning office. His juggling with reckless promises, priorities and partial successes was bound sooner or later to bring him crashing down.[10]

The Institute further advises that 'the ability to produce arms was increasingly cramped by the Allies' air war' and that 'the unceasing air raids targeting key points in the German war economy must have been even for Speer an unmistakeable signal that the armaments miracle would soon be over'.[11]

---

5 Speer, *Inside The Third Reich*, p. 367
6 Bashow, *No Prouder Place*, p. 470
7 Speer, p. 349
8 Institute, Vol. V, Part 2, p. 430
9 Institute, Vol. V, Part 2, p. 430
10 Institute, Vol. V, Part 2, pp. 430-1
11 Institute Vol. V, Part 2, p. 436

GERMANY'S RESEARCH INSTITUTE

Oslo Report and Peenemunde

In November 1939 the British received the 'Oslo Report', an anonymous seven-page document which an unknown person dropped off at the British embassy in Norway. Decades later it was revealed that a telecommunication scientist at Siemens, Professor Hans Ferdinand Mayer, wrote the Oslo Report on a business trip to Norway on 1/2 November 1939. The Institute says he used his hotel's typewriter, and then personally placed his report into the British embassy letterbox, because he opposed the Nazis. Later he was put into a concentration camp.[12] The Institute says the Oslo Report spoke of both rocket development and flying bombs, and was the first to mention Peenemunde in this context. The Institute then says 'As Germany was way ahead of Britain and America in the development of liquid-fuel rockets, the British lacked any yardstick of comparison and for a long time disbelieved the report.'[13]

The Institute reports that the British later learned about German long-range rockets from bugging a conversation between PoWs Wilhelm Ritter von Thoma and Ludwig Crüwell, a pair of German generals. The Institute says Churchill then ordered Duncan Sandys (his son-in-law and Diana Churchill's husband) to learn whether such rockets existed, and to propose counter-measures. In May 1943 a British WAAF aerial photographic interpreter discovered a V1 flying bomb. Also that month, Sandys' work resulted in the creation of the Crossbow Committee which led to the August 1943 to May 1945 Operation CROSSBOW, the Anglo-American campaign against German long-range weapons. In mid-June 1943 a Mosquito obtained new aerial photographs of Peenemunde which revealed rockets. Sandys requested Churchill to order the bombing of Peenemunde."[14]

Peenemunde from Canada's Perspective

Given its importance, I should share what I have learned about Bomber Command and Peenemunde from the Canadian perspective. Bomber Command first bombed Peenemunde in Operation HYDRA on 17/18 August 1943 with 596 heavy bombers, of which sixty-two were RCAF No. 6 Group bombers. That bombing began Operation CROSSBOW, in which for the first time Bomber Command used a master bomber to direct the main force. Thereafter, master bombers became mainstays of large-scale raids. Using radio instructions, they directed bombers to a series of target indicators, and sent the remaining bombers home if they deemed they were no longer needed or conditions such as cloud cover had changed,

---

12 Institute Vol. VII, p. 446
13 Institute Vol. VII, p. 447
14 Institute, Vol. VII, p. 447

rendering them ineffective. That's what happened to my Dad on his twenty-first combat sortie on 17 June 1944 over Aulnoye, France.

Peenemunde reveals Bomber Command internal conflict, colourfully described by Dunmore and Carter as follows:

> Harris himself had commanded 5 Group early in the war. Now its leader was the autocratic and opinionated Air Vice-Marshal the Honourable Ralph Cochrane, the bitter rival of the equally autocratic and opinionated Donald Bennett, AOC 8 Group, the Pathfinders. Cochrane wanted his Group to handle Peenemunde alone. It was just the sort of pinpoint job his crews had been trained for. Harris said no; if it failed, the element of surprise would be lost and the Germans would bring in untold numbers of flak batteries and searchlights and put God only knows how many fighter units on permanent readiness. Any second attempt would be suicidal.[15]

Bennett selected RAF Group Captain John Searby, CO of 83 Squadron, as master bomber for the Peenemunde sortie on 17/18 the August 1943. His deputies were Canadian Wing Commander Johnny Fauquier, CO of 406 Squadron, 'Canada's Greatest Bomber Pilot', and Wing Commander John White, a flight commander of 156 Squadron.[16] 'The contribution of the Master Bomber and his Deputy (sic) was of inestimable value over Peenemunde. The Main Force crews held these exceptionally brave airmen in the highest esteem.'[17] Fortunately for the Allies 'Peenemunde's defences were extraordinarily slow to react, perhaps because of orders to hold their fire until they received permission from a suitably elevated authority; the secrecy which enshrouded every aspect of life at the establishment worked on that night to the advantage of the attackers.'[18]

Having said that, Bomber Command still lost 215 aircrew and forty bombers (most in the final wave) while Germany lost twelve nightfighters. However, V2 rocket scientist Walter Thiel (von Braun's engine designer) and Chief Engineer Walther were killed; prototype V2 rocket launches were delayed two months; and evidently the morale of German survivors of the bombing was severely affected. Among the survivors was the now famous Wernher von Braun, the former Nazi who became an American hero. He joined the SS Horseback Riding School on 1 November 1933, the Nazi Party on 12 November 1937, and Himmler's notorious SS in 1940. He became a leader in Nazi military rocket technology, and especially the V2 rocket at Peenemunde. Postwar, through Operation PAPERCLIP, von Braun was secretly taken to America where he became a leader in developing America's rocket and space technology.

---

15 Dunmore & Carter, p. 146

16 Dunmore & Carter, p. 146

17 Dunmore & Carter, p. 150

18 Dunmore & Carter, p. 149

In 2006 Adam Tooze called the bombing of Peenemunde 'highly successful' and said the resulting transfer of 12,000 A4 missiles (which von Braun helped create) to Thuringia was a 'Herculean task'.[19] On 19 April 1944, General Eisenhower, at the request of the British War Cabinet, ordered that Operation CROSSBOW targets have priority. As a result, seven of my Dad's thirty-four combat sorties from April to August 1944 were bombing rocket-launching and flying-bomb bases. The last V1 rocket launched from Occupied France was on 1 September 1944. Four days later, on 5 September 1944, the V1 threat from France vanished because the 3rd Canadian Infantry Division laid siege to, and froze, Germany's military in the Nord-Pas de Calais area. Those Germans surrendered on 30 September 1944.

Nazi Party at War

The Institute points out one result of the Allied strategic bombing offensive was a million German soldiers being pinned down defending the Fatherland instead of fighting on the fronts. And increasing numbers of civilians were likewise forced to fight the air war. For example, on 29 May 1942, after the Lübeck bombing, Hitler ordered that flak batteries should be in future operated by civilians as well. And then there's Göring. Since spring 1942, Göring sought more help from Germany's Nazi Party. In December 1942 Hitler ordered the Nazi Party to facilitate 'in every respect' the Luftwaffe's growing need for personnel for the *Heimatflak* batteries. This meant that thereafter the Nazi Party was recruiting the people needed to operate the ever-increasing number of anti-aircraft guns needed.[20] And then the women. On 17 July 1943 Hitler abandoned his opposition to women in the military, and approved female Luftwaffe auxiliaries. Their duties included operating searchlights, predictor equipment and radar sets in the fire-control units of heavy batteries.[21]

The scale of escalating Nazi Party recruitment of workers necessitated by Bomber Command was enormous. The Institute advises that by 30 September 1944, 13,535,300 men had become war workers. Through the *Volkssturm* (the National Militia created by Hitler), the Nazi Party had access to more workers than the Wehrmacht had soldiers with its 11.2 million troops.[22] And there arose many indirect results. For example, the thousand bomber raids in Hamburg in July 1943 wiped out a whole year's furniture output. People needed furniture, but they needed food more. The Institute says people needing feeding increased in five years from 79.2 million to 88.8 million. The Nazis could do nothing to halt this.[23]

---

19 Tooze, *The Wages of Destruction: The Making and Breaking of the Nazi War Economy*, Allan Lane, London, 2006 pp. 621-2
20 Institute, Vol. IX, Part 1, pp. 188-9
21 Institute, Vol. IX, Part 1, p. 190
22 Institute, Vol. IX, Part 1, p. 199
23 Institute, Vol. V, Part 2, p. 522

Nazi Slave Labour

On 19 July 1940, following the fall of France, Hitler made a number of promotions including General Erhard Milch to the rank of field marshal, and, as mentioned, Hermann Göring from field marshal to reich marshal. Hitler also named Milch director-general of air armament. To produce aircraft, Milch turned to the SS for slave labour of PoWs and civilians from concentration camps. In March 1944, Milch and Speer oversaw *Jagerstab* (fighter staff) to increase fighter plane production, partly by moving production facilities underground with SS slave labour. As the Second World War progressed, so did Nazi Germany's use of and abuse of slave labour. These people were foreign workers, prisoners of war and concentration-camp inmates. Their uses included endless digging out of the dead and wounded from ruins, clearing rubble and putting out fires.[24]

Behind all this was Bomber Command. On point, the Institute reports:

> Where on questions of supplies of machine tools, and of construction, [the Luftwaffe] had to rely on Speer, the Allies' heavy bombing raids – which touched Hitler on a raw nerve – lent enough emphasis to ensure that Milch's demands were met ... . They [Milch and Speer] were soon close and inseparable friends ... .[25]

Göring meanwhile in vain tried repeatedly to persuade Hitler to give aircraft the same priority as tanks. The Institute says:

> Above all else it was a power-struggle between Göring and Speer for the crown-prince role and for command of the war economy. And as 1943 was turning into 1944, Speer was winning ... Speer was able to make use of the order to build underground aircraft factories to get Göring to hand over the Luftwaffe's construction service to him. The turning point came with the heavy raids on German air armaments factories in the spring of 1944 ....[26]

Allied Pointblank Directive

The Institute's review of Allied bombing policy in 1942 and into 1943 culminated with the Anglo-American Chiefs of Staff 14 May 1943 'Combined Bomber Offensive from the United Kingdom'. It became the 'Pointblank Directive' to both bomber forces on 19 June 1943. That directive was written by Ira Eaker, commander of the US 8th Army Air Force, but was agreed to by Portal and Harris. However, the

---

24 Institute, Vol. IX, Part 1, pp. 401-2

25 Institute, Vol. V, Part 2, p. 419

26 Institute, Vol. V, Part 2, p. 422

Germans conclude: 'The real main target remained, as in the Casablanca Directive, the progressive destruction of sources of German power and the sapping of the will to resist.'[27] The Institute reports that 'The British-American strategic bombing offensive intensified in 1943 ... . Not only was fear spreading, but also a wish for early retaliation for the attacks.' In addition, 'The population has no sympathy for crashed enemy airmen being treated as prisoners of war.'[28]

The Institute says German hatred of the English was escalating, but so was German fear of the Russians. Escalating hatred of England and fear of Russia was another source of internal German pressure on the Third Reich to find miracle weapons, an ultimately fruitless task that diverted much from the production of weaponry essential for the Third Reich's survival. On 19 February 1942 Hitler ordered the shifting of prisoners of war and workers from the building sector into arms manufacture. This and 'other large-scale projects drastically reduced the capacity available for the priority programme as the war continued. From 1942 the fortifying of the Atlantic Wall and building of U-boat pens alone absorbed substantial resources from the construction industry and manpower administration.'[29]

The Institute says 1943 was the pivotal year. It began with Hitler appointing Goebbels as chair of the ILA (Inter-ministerial Committee on Bomb Damage) that January. The ILA gave Goebbels great power. This was demonstrated following the 22 October 1943 bombing of Kassel in which about 6,000 died and as many as 120,000 were bombed out of their homes.[30] Kassel convinced Goebbels that constant watch and defence preparations against air attacks were now needed throughout the Reich.[31] Goebbels persuaded Hitler to create a Reich Inspectorate for Civil Air. In December 1943 Hitler ordered its creation and put Goebbels in charge. The ILA and Reich Inspectorate became central authorities for the Reich's air defence.

Daily Life for Germans under the Bombs

The Institute explains how deep and widespread the Allied strategic bombing offensive was in disrupting German society, and tying down so many Germans in defending the Fatherland from bombing. Bombing brought war not only to the German military, but also to Nazi officials, civilians and slaves, which the Nazis called foreign workers. From 1942 all aspects of daily life were affected by bombing. The physical and psychological burden grew greater as bombing intensified from

---

27 Institute, Vol. VII, p. 14
28 Institute, Vol. VII, pp. 369-70
29 Institute, Vol. IX, Part 1, pp. 412-13
30 Institute, Vol. IX, Part 1, p. 407
31 Institute, Vol. IX, Part 1, p. 407

1943 onward. Social and family life were being lost by bombing.[32] And all this exposed serious shortcomings in air-raid protection for civilians, including:

- Building bombproof shelters petered out two years into the war because of shortages of labour and raw material;
- A plan for providing short-term accommodation for those bombed out of their homes was incapable of meeting the need created by bombing;
- Evacuating cities from the summer of 1943, including the expanded children's evacuation scheme (the KLV), and total war measures imposed in 1944 placed heavy burdens on the population.[33]

Germany had divergent classes of air-raid bombing protection – luxurious, virtually impregnable ones for the elite; and cellars, slit trenches, awful bunkers and tunnels for other Germans. Slaves had much worse. From 1942 onwards, life moved increasingly into horrible air-raid facilities.[34] As bombing became increasingly effective, these differences generated increasing resentment.

After the RAF bombed Berlin on 26 August 1940, Hitler ordered the building of bombproof shelters in major cities, but the Institute says that what was actually built was much less, because the materials and workforces needed to build more were not available.[35] On 10 October 1940 Hitler ordered the 'Führer's Priority Programme' – the building of 'bomb-, debris- and splinter-proof protection premises' including underground bunkers, surface shelters, tower bunkers and shelter tunnels to protect people and cultural treasures. Kurt Knipfer, since 1933 head of the Civil Defence of the Reich Aviation Ministry, said these 'bombproof' constructions would become 'a kind of new West Wall built of steel and concrete' that would be beyond the reach of the bombers.[36] How wrong he was.

The Institute states that throughout the war providing every *Volksgenosse* with bombproof shelters was 'no more than wishful thinking'. As well, even concrete bunkers could not withstand direct hits. And so, the Institute says, 'The inadequate number of bunkers and shelters for the public led, in the last months of the war, to vociferous criticism.'[37]

To avoid the high cost of surface bunkers, tunnel shelters were constructed using local labour and state monies. The two largest Reich shelters for civilians were both tunnels – the *Schlossberg* in Graz for about 50,000 people and the city centre tunnel in Dortmund for 20,000. The Dortmund tunnels began in 1937 for a planned underground railway.[38] It had nineteen entrances and was about 15 metres

---

32 Institute, Vol. IX, Part 1, p. 371
33 Institute, Vol. IX, Part 1, p. 372
34 Institute, Vol. IX, Part 1, pp. 409-10
35 Institute, Vol. IX, Part 1, p. 410
36 Institute, Vol. IX, Part 1, p. 410
37 Institute, Vol. IX, Part 1, pp. 413-14
38 Institute, Vol. IX, Part 1, p. 416

(50 feet) below ground. On 4 November 1943 Göring's edict to Reich defence commissioners 'expressly emphasized that the building of tunnel shelters is one of the most important measures for protection against the terror raids'.[39]

And the Institute reports that another serious problem arose in bunkers, saying 'As the Allied air raids increased after the spring of 1943, however, life in a bunker became more and more of a torture. Even regulations and appeals for maintaining hygiene and cleanliness could do nothing to prevent vermin and infectious diseases'.[40] And so, the Institute concludes:

> For most Germans ... so-called 'shelters' gave no effective protection against the massive bombing raids that began from 1943 on. Yet towards the end of the war even the deep tunnel shelters and surface regarded as being 'bomb-proof' did not offer absolute safety, as a number of direct hits on them were to show.[41]

Britain's Bletchley Park

This difference in command structure between the totalitarian Axis and democratic Western Allies comes up time and again in my research. On 31 May 2019 I visited Britain's famous Bletchley Park, home of the brilliant British wartime breaking of German codes. Wartime work there was of astonishing quality, especially that of Alan Turing, whose postwar suicide on 7 June 1954 for being gay is reason for us all to hang our heads in collective shame. What most astonished me at Bletchley Park was being told that the Germans were also devastatingly effective at breaking our codes. Where we parted company with Germany is the democratically governed Western Allies maximized use of what we learned about Germany, while Germans, hobbled by their autocratic form of government, made far less effective use of information they obtained about us.

An interesting Bletchley Park anecdote is that a young woman named Valerie Glassborow served there in the Government Code and Cypher School during the war.[42] In 1946, Valerie married RAF pilot Peter Middleton. Their granddaughter is Catherine, Duchess of Cambridge. Valerie died in 2006.

Municipal Administration Destruction

Given my expertise as a lawyer acting for municipalities, I was particularly interested to discover from the Institute how much damage Bomber Command

---

39 Institute, Vol. IX, Part 1, p. 416
40 Institute, Vol. IX, Part 1, p. 426
41 Institute, Vol. IX, Part 1, p. 416
42 *Daily Mail*, Mailonline, 15 Nov 2019

did to German municipal administrations. Commencing in 1943 in 'air war crisis areas', bombing created enormous problems for local government, including destruction of their official buildings, their equipment and records, as well as a lack of staff. Local government continued, however, to try to appear to be fully servicing defence efforts against the bombing. This was increasingly a mirage. In April 1943 the Essen city treasurer tells that what was really happening was 'The administration ... is finished. We're muddling along, both with inadequate and incompetent staff and in what we received, since when it comes down to it we're very often after a long and laborious process having to tell the homeless that.'

The Institute says that the inability of local authorities to cope with bombing forced intervention by the Nazi Party, SA rescue squads, Hitler Youth, HJ fire brigades and Luftwaffe and Heer troops.[43] For example, when the municipal administration in Hamburg collapsed under the bombing, the Nazi Party intervened massively.[44] Personnel were also needed from Organization Todt, the Civil and Engineering Organization in Nazi Germany named after Fritz Todt. Industrial firms, the Reichsbahn and the Reichspost who had created their own air-raid protection units, co-operated closely with the civil defence police.[45]

Judicial System Destruction

Even though I am a lawyer, an aspect of bombing I had not considered until reading the Institute's volumes was how deeply it damaged Germany's judicial system. The judiciary was in trouble from the outset. On 5 September 1939 the Nazis created 'special courts' to prosecute 'enemies of the people ordinances' against looters; 'radio broadcasts ordinance' against those listening to 'enemy transmitters'; and 'malicious conduct' against such issues as political jokes and rumours. Gestapo terror was exercised by special units ruthlessly attacking 'gangs' and 'undesirable elements' in Germany. Armed teenage gangs challenged the Gestapo. The Gestapo and civil police were both controlled by the SS.[46] However, bombing significantly weakened the judiciary by expanding the Gestapo's scope, in part through new offences such as 'spreading rumours about the air war' and 'looting after air raids'. Death sentences rose from ninety-nine in 1939 to 5,363 in 1943.[47]

As the war progressed 'special courts' executed 'tens of thousands'. Looters were particularly harshly dealt with by a German Justice Ministry decree following the famous thousand-bomber raid on Cologne of 30 April/1 May 1943. That decree empowered superior district court presidents to create summary special courts to pass judgement on looters 'on the spot'. Someone suspected of looting was almost always executed,

---

43 Institute, Vol. IX, Part 1, p. 400

44 Institute, Vol. IX, Part 1, p. 385

45 Institute, Vol. IX, Part 1, pp. 401-2

46 Institute Vol. IX, Part 1, p 402

47 Institute Vol. IX, Part 1, pp. 402-3

regardless of protests by the public or even the SS. The process was merciless. An example the Institute cites is Ilse Mitze, age 19. Accused of stealing some underwear after the 1 October 1943 bombing of Hagen, and in spite of all points for her, she was beheaded as a looter.[48] Trials and executions for looters were fast. The Institute mentions Kasimir Petrolinas, age 69, from Lithuania. After the Essen bombing of 5/6 March 1943, he found three worthless damaged metal bowls he needed. Essen's special court sentenced him to death, and he was executed by firing squad a few hours later. The Institute says this was 'done with a speed that made the trial a farce'.[49] And it got worse. In early 1944, the Reich Justice Ministry declared that anyone who used enemy air raids, blackouts or other circumstances of war to enrich themselves committed a breach of trust against the *Volksgemeinschaft*.[50] Bombing had led to increasing disintegration of what had been close-knit and united communities in Germany.

On 15 February 1945 the Reich Justice Minister allowed creation of summary courts 'at the approach of the enemy'. Coupled with the military court system and 'flying courts martial', these special civilian courts were nothing more than a 'legalized means' of mass murder to stiffen Germany resistance. The Institute mentions Major Erwin Helm. His 'flying court martial' in his grey Mercedes from the Rhine to the Sudetenland executed so many that 'the number of his "court's" victims in southern Germany alone is now impossible to tell'.[51] The Institute says executing Germans and foreigners ultimately became one of the Gestapo's main activities.[52] In the final seven months of the war, the Gestapo carried out mass murders in western Germany as they had been doing in occupied territories for the duration of the war. These mass murders continued until just hours before the arrival of Allied troops.[53]

Third Reich Destruction

Under the heading 'The Bombing War Draws to its Close', the Institute say:

> The finale of the bombing war was being played out. And the effects it was having put everything that had happened before in the shade .... Towards the end of the war the good mood and attitude in large parts of the population, maintained by the Nazi leadership since 1943, often by only dint of propaganda and a great many other measures, had sunk to rock bottom .... Saturation raids ... were aimed at paralyzing the fire, civil defence, administration, and air defence

---

48 Institute Vol. IX, Part 1, p. 403-4
49 Institute Vol. IX, Part 1, pp. 404-5
50 Institute Vol. IX, Part 1, p. 402
51 Institute, Vol. IX, Part 1, p. 405
52 Institute, Vol. IX, Part 1, p. 402
53 Institute, Vol. IX, Part 1, pp. 401-2

services .... The repeated air-raid warnings and spoof indications of an impending large-scale attack, given by dropping target-markers were an irritant to the German night fighters, and lured them away from the real targets. For the population, on the other hand, the repeated air-raid warnings at night meant sleeplessness that put them under both physical and mental strain.[54]

The Institute goes on to report:

> Though the raid on 3 February by more than 1,000 American bombers did have two marshalling yards in the Reich capital as its target, it hit most of all the inner city. More than 100,000 were bombed out of their homes, and the water and electricity supplies were cut off for a long time. For the Berliners this was the costliest raid of the whole war .... [it] was however to be surpassed by a two-day raid by the 8th USAAF on Nuremberg. Screened by hundreds of escort fighters, a total of more than 2,000 four-engined aircraft attacked the 'city of the Party rallies' on 20 and 21 February. This two-day raid was aimed at bringing about 'transportation chaos' in southern Germany.[55]

The Institute also says:

> 12 March saw the heaviest attack flown against any European city during the Second World War: this was on Dortmund. During March, the industrial area of the Rhineland and Westphalia was to be bombed into a state where it was 'ripe for ground attack', and cut off as far as possible from all transport links with the rest of the Reich.[56]

The Second World War Was Not Over Until It Was Over

It was certainly not the case that the war was effectively over with the success of D Day, and Bomber Command still had a vital role to play, and Germany demonstrated in Italy and Aachen its extraordinary ability to fight defensively. Germany in 1944, while surrounded, was not on the verge of collapse. The Institute reports 'On 21 October 1944 Aachen was the first major city to fall into Allied hands, and the "fight to the end" put up there gave the Allies a foretaste of what they could expect

---

54 Institute, Vol. IX, Part 1, p. 468-9
55 Institute, Vol. IX, Part 1, p. 469-70
56 Institute, Vol IX, Part 1, pp 472-73

in the Reich's other big cities.'[57] The Allied military set back in failing to seize its final objective at Arnhem in MARKET GARDEN (17-26 September 1944) which condemned the Dutch to suffer their horrible 1944-45 *Hongerwinter* under Nazi control in which over 20,000 Dutch starved to death is another example of how hard the Germans intended to fight.

My overview of the Institute led me to examining leading German warmongers, including Albert Speer and Joseph Goebbels. From this, the Institute overview led me into a close look at all four wars Bomber Command fought – the air war, the sea war, the war assisting Allied armies and, most decisive of all, the war to destroy Germany's ability to make war.

---

57 Institute Vol IX, Part 1, p 458

Chapter Fifteen

German Leaders – Especially Speer

Albert Speer was astonished that all the Allies' books on the Second World War seemed to have overlooked the fact that the bombing of Germany had actually brought about its defeat.[1]

The Allies Never Really Knew What Bomber Command Accomplished

It was difficult for the Allies to determine what Bomber Command accomplished. Photos taken of bombing sites did little more than confirm the aircraft was there, and not just unloading its bombs somewhere over the North Sea. After the war, researchers climbing through rubble, whether they were three from Britain or 3,000 from America, were likewise unable to determine the scope of what was accomplished. The *United States Strategic Bombing Survey* did, however, produce 208 volumes, and called the Allied strategic bombing 'decisive' in winning the war.[2] With the Nuremberg trials looming, frightened German leaders willingly told them whatever they wanted to hear. Ulterior motives reigned. And then, almost by magic, West Germany quickly became our friend and Russia our enemy. Allied apologies started creeping in, further muddying the waters, while reconstruction rapidly erased evidence of Bomber Command accomplishments. Worst of all, criticism of Bomber Command became fashionable, particularly in academia.

All of this obscured what Bomber Command accomplished. And so, after reading over 200 Bomber Command books unclear on accomplishments, I've turned to the Germans. They knew best what Bomber Command accomplished. Here's what they say, especially Armaments and War Production Minister Albert Speer.

---

1 Cooper, *Target Dresden*, p. 240 Speer at Home in Heidelberg in Conversation With Alan Cooper 1980

2 Wikipedia *United States Strategic Bombing Survey* was released on 30 September 1945

GERMAN LEADERS – ESPECIALLY SPEER

What German Leaders Say

Leading German military leaders say it was Allied air supremacy and bombing that destroyed Germany's ability to continue fighting the Second World War.

That sentiment is best captured by Field Marshal Erwin Rommel telling Hitler face-to-face, 'If you can't stop the bombing, we can't win the war.'[3]

Hitler, as mentioned, declared, just days before his suicide 'The real cause of Germany's defeat was the failure of the German Air Force.'[4]

Albert Speer summed this up in the inscriptions he wrote in his books he sent to Harris. Speer told Harris that, in all the war books Speer had ever read, and he had read a lot of them, 'The effect of the strategic bombing of Germany is always under-estimated,' and that 'The strategic bombing of Germany was the greatest lost battle for Germany of the whole of the war, greater than all their losses in all their retreats from Russia and in the surrender of their armies in Stalingrad.'[5]

Here's a sampling of what other German leaders and historians say.

Gotz Bergander, a German historian distinguishes private morale and war morale in the Third Reich. He says the former was not broken (protecting family, surviving) but the latter was severely damaged, and that:

> In reality, the air raids on cities and industries shook the foundations of the war morale of the German people. They permanently shattered their nerves, undermined their health and shook their belief in victory, thus altering their consciousness. They spread fear, dismay and hopelessness. This was an important and intentional result of the strategic air war, of this warfare revolution.[6]

Horst Borg, chief historian of the German Research Institute of Military History, said at the RAF Staff College, Bracknell, in March 1993 'The judgement that the British area attacks were ineffective can no longer be supported. For a proper assessment, we have to look at indirect effects. Had there been no bomber offensive things in Russia might have developed differently.' Borg notes over a million men were kept in Germany manning anti-aircraft guns. They could have served Germany better in Russia, or in factories. He dispels the myth of continued high morale under bombing. He defines morale as 'The will to continue to work for the war effort'. Political surveillance and Gestapo terror meant doing what you're told and not shirking while others can see you.[7]

---

3 *Straight From the Horse's Mouth*
4 Overy, 'World War II: How the Allies Won', BBC.co.uk, 17 February 2011
5 Harris, *From the Horse's Mouth*
6 Probert, *Bomber Command*, p. 337
7 Bashow, p. 468

BOMBER COMMAND

Josef 'Sepp' Dietrich, formerly Hitler's chauffeur, and afterwards a general, said that the Ardennes 'Battle of the Bulge' was lost because Bomber Command destroyed the supply lines, thereby cutting off ammunition and petrol supplies.[8] He died on 21 April 1966 (my Dad's birthday); 6,000 attended his funeral.

Adolf Galland, the one-time Luftwaffe *General der Jagdflieger*, about whom I write and who flew 705 combat sorties, said:

> The combination of the Pathfinders' operations, the activities of No. 100 Group, the British advantage in radar, jamming and Window techniques, combined with intelligent attacking tactics, as well as the bravery of the RAF crews, have been remarkable. We had our severe problems in trying to defend Germany in the air.[9]

The German Steel Syndicate said that Allied bombing reduced German steel production from 20 million tons a year in 1942 to almost nothing by 1945.

Hermann Göring attributed Germany's defeat to the successful invasion and the 'irresistible' superiority of Allied air forces and that, if it were not for the Allied air forces, Germany could have quickly brought reinforcements to Normandy and made full use of armoured units to resist the D Day invasion.

Edouard Houdremont, a professor and Essen Krupps works controller who had 50,000 employees in the Essen district, while looking at the shambles of the Krupps works, said Allied bombing shortened the war by at least two years.

Albert Kesselring Field Marshal of the Luftwaffe, who some regard as Germany's best Second World War General, said Allied strategic bombing behind German lines and attacks by low-flying Allied aircraft were why Germany was defeated.

Karl Koller, Chief of the General Staff and Head of Luftwaffe Operations, said Germany lost the war through failure to attain air supremacy.

Erhard Milch, the Field Marshal who oversaw the development of the Luftwaffe, said Pathfinder ability to find and mark targets vastly exceeded the German system against Britain and the German army was defeated by destruction of the railways; lack of fuel; lack of lorries, all caused by Bomber Command. Regarding guns, Milch told senior RAF officers:

---

8 *Inside the Third Reich* pp 417-18.

9 Wikipedia, *No. 100 Group, Bomber Command*; Iveson, Tony DFC and Brian Milton, *Lancaster – The Biography* London Andre Deutsch 2009

If we had in the East all the 8.8 to 12.8 mm guns required at home then the Soviets would have been incapable of carrying out their successful tank attacks and the results would have been disastrous for them. Of the 19,713 guns produced from 1942 until the end of 1944 only 3,172 of them went to the Army because the rest (84%) had to be diverted to the defence of the German cities against the bombing.[10]

Field Marshal Gerd von Rundstedt, Commander-in-Chief in the West, and a commander in the Ardennes offensive (Battle of the Bulge) said Allied bombers were decisive in his downfall at the Battle of the Bulge and the downfall of the Reich. He said 'Air power was the first decisive factor in Germany's defeat; lack of petrol and oil the second; and the destruction of the railways the third.'[11] All three were compliments of Bomber Command.

Albert Speer the Nazi Enigma

> Albert Speer was happy to tell his captors about the war machine he had built. But it was a different story when he was asked about the Holocaust.[12]
>
> Gilbert King, The Smithsonian's History Blog

Albert Speer was an enigma to me. For most of my life, I believed the two enormous lies he so skilfully wove in the Nuremburg trials to avoid death. On reflection, it is a good thing he told those lies, because the books he later wrote give invaluable insights into how the Third Reich was governed at the highest levels. He had the intelligence and introspection ideal for writing these books, unlike his criminal colleagues who unquestioningly took as much advantage as they could of being at the centre of one of the world's most horrific regimes. He also had extraordinary access for so many years to Adolf Hitler on a personal level. They were friends. Understanding Hitler is essential to understanding the Third Reich and the war.

The two lies Speer told to save his life at Nuremburg were that he was not a Nazi, but instead an innocent young architect patriotically serving his country and that he was unaware of the genocide his regime was carrying out, even though he was working hundreds of thousands of the victims to death. More on that in a moment.

---

10 Fyfe, *The Great Ingratitude*, p. 321; Brookes, 'An Interview With "Bomber" Harris 8 September 1975', *Royal Air Force Historical Society Journal* No. 74, 2020, p. 58
11 *Target Dresden*, p. 223
12 King, Smithsonian.com, 8 January 2013

My Growing Awareness of Albert Speer

But first, I feel I must speak of my personal growing awareness of Speer and of the value of his knowledge of what Bomber Command accomplished. Speer caught my attention in a serious way when I learned that he said that no Allied book about Bomber Command that he had seen, and he had seen a lot of them, comes even close to articulating what Bomber Command actually accomplished.[13]

This amazing news from the Nazi leader best placed to know it aroused in me two thoughts. First, what did Bomber Command accomplish? Second, why has no Allied book come close to articulating what Bomber Command accomplished? The answer to my second question is that the Allies never really knew. Then it dawned on me that for this book I must look to German sources, starting of course with Speer.

Speer doesn't pull punches. Instead, he declares that Bomber Command did more damage to the German war effort than all the disasters in Russia, including Stalingrad. Speer says Germany's failure to defeat Bomber Command was the greatest lost battle of the war, because Bomber Command increasingly damaged, and ultimately destroyed, the means needed for the Reich to make war.[14]

These are extraordinary statements by someone singularly well placed to make them. Speer spurred me on to pursue German sources, because I know I must be cautious relying only on Speer, given he had proven himself to be an accomplished liar on a grand scale. Having said that, he was central to creating and supplying the German war machine that Bomber Command was dedicated to destroying, and Speer says Bomber Command succeeded.

As I deepened my focus on who Albert Speer was, and what he did, I discovered he had a unique relationship of intimacy with Hitler which gave him invaluable insights, and enormous power. And I discovered that he was a dedicated Nazi from the get-go, having applied for membership in January 1931 and being admitted as a member in March 1931, many months before Hitler gained power as chancellor, and ultimately Führer, of what became the Third Reich.

I also discovered that Speer used what he preferred to call 'foreign labour' or 'forced labour', but was in reality 'slave labour' on a monumental scale for his war machine. In doing this, Speer worked closely with one of history's most odious figures, Heinrich Himmler. Speer needed workers from Himmler's concentration camps. To the extent Speer pushed for more humane treatment of these slaves, it was to slow their death rate so that he wouldn't be forced to replace them so often.[15] Speer showed no concern for the extreme inhumanity of how he treated them in their hundreds of thousands, possibly millions. Small wonder that, post-war, his son Albert Speer Jr, also an accomplished architect, said he 'tried his whole life to

---

13 Harris, *From the Horse's Mouth*
14 Harris, *From the Horse's Mouth*
15 Speer, *Inside the Third Reich*

separate himself from his father'.[16] Albert Jr was 'one of the few children of Nazi leaders to recognize the wrongs of their parent'.[17]

Albert Speer was a Brilliant Leader of a Monstrous Regime

We tend to forget nowadays just how inhumane the Third Reich was. We were fighting the Second World War, not just to defeat, but to destroy, one of history's most horrific evils. Speer himself was convicted of war crimes and crimes against humanity in the Nuremberg trials from September 1945 until 1 October 1946. As mentioned, Speer was spared the death sentence largely due to the lies he was able to weave, saying he was a patriot instead of a Nazi and was unaware of Nazi atrocities in the death camps. He was, however, imprisoned for twenty years. On 18 July 1947 (exactly one year before my birth), Speer was transferred to Spandau Prison in Berlin to serve his sentence. Interestingly, Speer's father, who died in 1947, despised both the Nazis and Hitler himself, while Speer's mother loved socializing with Hitler. Speer was released from Spandau at midnight on 1 October 1966. He wrote *Inside the Third Reich* and *Spandau: The Secret Diaries*. Later he wrote about Himmler and the SS. He died on 1 September 1981, aged 76.

Speer was brilliant at manipulating statistics to make himself shine. To do this, he was also expert at taking credit for the work of his predecessors and colleagues in the building of what is now known as the 'Speer Myth'. That myth is that he virtually single-handedly accomplished miracles in German war production. Keeping up the appearance of astonishing accomplishments in the latter part of the war required a combination of Speer's criminal use in horrific conditions of many hundreds of thousands of Eastern European conscripts, concentration camp inmates and PoWs as slave labour, and steadily reducing quality to keep up quantity. This was prompted in part by the monthly telephone calls Speer was required to make to Hitler full of statistics showing what a fine job he was doing.[18]

Speer Becomes Minister of Armaments, 8 February 1942

Speer refers to fuel shortage problems as early as 1941, particularly in the production of the Luftwaffe's Ju.88 medium-range bombers for which he had to build factories as part of his responsibility for erecting buildings for the army and air force. Speer says

---

16 Ewing, 'Albert Speer Jr, Architect and Son of Hitler Confident, Dies at 83' *New York Times* 27 September 2017

17 Albert Speer Jr, Wikipedia

18 Speer, *Inside the Third Reich*

From the autumn of 1941 on, however, our work was hampered by the shortage of fuel .... By January 1, 1942, to a sixth of our needs .... Along with this, repair of the bomb damage in Berlin and the building of air raid shelters, had been turned over to me. Without suspecting it, I was thus preparing for my duties as Minister of Armaments.[19]

That fateful day came sooner than expected. The single most important day in Albert Speer's life was 8 February 1942. That morning, Dr Fritz Todt, the creator of autobahns,[20] roadbuilder, head office for technology, builder of the West Wall, builder of U-boat shelters along the Atlantic, Minister of Armaments and Munitions and brigadier general of the Luftwaffe,[21] was killed in a mysterious plane crash. Speer was scheduled to be aboard, but had begged off at the last minute because he had been with Hitler until 1:00 am that morning and so was exhausted.

On 8 February 1942, Speer was summoned as Hitler's first caller of the day at the unusually late hour of 1:00 pm. Here's how Speer describes their meeting. 'In contrast to the night before, Hitler received me officially as Führer of the Reich. Standing, earnest and formal, he received my condolences, replied very briefly, then said without more ado: "Herr Speer, I appoint you the successor to Minister Todt in all his capacities". I was thunderstruck.'[22]

But it didn't stop there. Speer was one to strike while the iron is hot. On 21 March 1942 Speer had Hitler sign a decree that Germany's economy must be 'subordinated to armaments production', giving Speer dictatorial power over the whole economy. That's when Speer proceeded with his 'comprehensive plan of industrial self-responsibility' now known as the 'Speer Myth'. It was based on principles Milch and Todt had already adopted. The real creator was Walther Rathenau, the Jew who organized Germany's economy in the First World War.

Speer reveals a great deal about himself when he summed up his situation as 'Reverence for Hitler, a sense of duty, ambition, pride – all these elements were operative. After all, at thirty-six, I was the youngest member in the Reich.'[23] Having said that, Speer was extraordinarily competent at both manoeuvring his way through byzantine Nazi politics at the highest level, and producing the necessities for making war. As a result, Speer knew better than anyone just how huge a problem Bomber Command increasingly became as the war progressed. Here's what I've gleaned from Albert Speer.

Bomber Command cancelled Hitler's Victory Parade

One of Speer's earliest Bomber Command references was his interesting anecdote on 25 June 1940, the day Hitler paid his only visit to Paris. Speer accompanied him.

---

19   Speer, p. 182
20   Speer, p. 193
21   Speer, p. 196
22   Speer, pp. 194-5
23   Speer, pp. 206-9

GERMAN LEADERS – ESPECIALLY SPEER

They arrived at le Bourget airfield at 5:30 am. Hitler and his chauffeur sat in the front of a large Mercedes sedan with Speer on the jump seat behind them. By 9:00 am Hitler's tour of Paris was over, so they headed back to the airport. Here's the anecdote. Speer says Hitler raised the issue of a victory parade in Paris, and then decided against it. 'His official reason for calling off the parade was the danger of its being harassed by English air raids.' [24]

Havoc Wrought on Germany Railways

Speer turned to young state secretary Albert Ganzenmuller to modernize production of locomotives and eliminate train back-ups 'until the systematic air raids of the fall of 1944 once again throttled traffic and made transportation, this time for good, the greatest bottleneck in our war economy.'[25]

Germany Fixation on Finding 'Magic Weapons'

Speer repeatedly refers to another adverse effect damaging Germany by the work of Bomber Command – the growing need in the minds of both the German population and Adolf Hitler himself for 'magic weapons' to solve their problems. The resulting search for 'magic weapons' caused erratic changes to German war production, and massive amounts of labour and material were poured into projects that fizzled. Speer observes succinctly regarding the most famous of the 'magic weapons' production facilities, saying 'Peenemunde was not only our biggest but our most misguided project.'[26] Peenemunde was Germany's top secret and heavily-defended Army Research Centre famous for Second World War development of guided missiles and rockets. They killed people in the last year of the war, but had no impact on the war's outcome. Had the time, effort and money devoted to them been instead on massive numbers of additional fighter aircraft and anti-aircraft guns to destroy Bomber Command, the war could have ended quite differently.

List of Speer's Bomber Command Problems

By 1944 Bomber Command had finally come into strength in numbers of aircraft, quality of bombs, accuracy of navigation and to commence the delivery of crushing blows to the Third Reich. The statistics then became devastating to Germany. Here's the list I have compiled of Bomber Command problems for Speer.

---

24 Speer, pp. 171-2
25 Speer, pp. 223-4
26 Speer, p. 228

BOMBER COMMAND

Air Raid Shelters: This problem arose early in the war, and steadily increased. He knew about this because building of air-raid shelters was turned over to him.[27]

Atlantic Wall: Bomber Command prevented completion of the Atlantic Wall, because workers were diverted to repairing Bomber Command damage. In addition, Field Marshal Erwin Rommel, who in 1943 was Germany's Inspector of Coastal Defences, and so was responsible for the Atlantic Wall, told Hitler 'If you cannot check the bombing, all the other methods will be ineffective, even the barriers.'[28]

Atomic Bombs: Speer tells us Hitler ruled out atomic bombs partly because 'Hitler occasionally referred to nuclear physics as 'Jewish physics' – citing Lenard as his authority for this.'[29] In addition, however, Speer says 'The increasing air raids had long since created an armaments emergency in Germany which ruled out such an ambitious project.'[30]

Fuel Shortages: Speer says 'From the autumn of 1941 on, however, our work was hampered by the shortage of fuel … . By January 1, 1942, to a sixth of our needs.'[31] Speer then says, 'I asked Hitler for power to declare a total mobilization of all our resources.' Hitler objected because he prioritized tanks. Speer replied tanks will be useless if they haven't enough fuel. Hitler gave consent. The situation steadily worsened as the war progressed and Bomber Command acquired better bombs, better aircraft and better navigation aids.

Luftwaffe Fighter Aircraft: Bomber Command activated a major fight for Hitler's ear on increased production of Luftwaffe fighter aircraft, and their use. Speer was demanding 2,000 fighters for homeland defence, especially of hydrogenation plants, against Bomber Command. But Hitler and Göring persisted in sending fighters to the front where they were destroyed by the Allies.

Magic Weapons: Speer says erratic research fuelling the increasingly desperate need of them wrought havoc with supplies and manpower needs for essential war production, and with priorities because each new dream overrode everything.

Plants for Aviation Fuel: By 22 June 1944, Speer advises 'nine-tenths of the production of airplane fuel was knocked out … . On July 21 … we were down to one hundred and twenty tons daily production – virtually done for. Ninety-eight per cent of our aircraft fuel plants were out of operation.'[32]

---

27 Speer, p. 182
28 Speer, p. 353
29 Speer, p. 228
30 Speer, p. 229
31 Speer, p. 182
32 Speer, pp. 349-50

GERMAN LEADERS – ESPECIALLY SPEER

Plants for Chemicals: Speer says 'The many attacks had taken such a toll on the piping systems in the chemical plants that direct hits were no longer required to do extensive damage. Merely the shock of bombs exploding in the vicinity caused leaks everywhere. Repairs were almost impossible.'

Plants for Hydrogenation: Speer reports that, because of Bomber Command 'a hundred and fifty thousand workers had been assigned to rebuilding the hydrogenation plants. A large percentage of these constituted skilled workers whose labour was indispensable for armaments production. By the late fall of 1944 the number had risen to three hundred and fifty thousand.'[33]

Transportation: Speer recognized a key component of Germany's ability to wage war was transportation, especially of troops and supplies to the fronts, and of materials factories needed for war production. As early as 21 May 1942, Hitler identified transportation problems as capable of losing Germany the war. Ultimately Bomber Command destroyed Germany's transportation, thereby eliminating Germany's ability to continue waging war.

U-boats: Speer's incredible statement regarding U-boats is that 'We would have been able to keep our promise of delivering forty boats a month by early in 1945, however badly the war was going otherwise, if air raids had not destroyed a third of the submarines at the dockyards.'[34]

Germany's Research Institute for Military History Takes on Speer

The Institute says:

> Speer had to recognize that the ceaseless bombing was putting clear limits on his initial optimism. In his report on the tour (submitted to Hitler) he did note an unflagging determination among the population – 'in spite of the constant heavy air raids, in spite of the hours of air-raid warnings by day and night, in spite of the problems with food and transport, in spite of the lack of water and electricity', given the enormous damage done by the raids, and its lasting consequences, however, he could only hope for a miracle.[35]

---

33 Speer, pp. 350-1
34 Speer, p. 274
35 Institute, Vol. IX, Part 1, p. 463

The Institute goes on to report

> Speer then turned to the 'miracle weapons', and urged an immediate concentrated use of the new Me.163 rocket-propelled fighter and the Me.262 jet fighter over this region, in particular to shoot down the Allied Pathfinder aircraft but also 'to boost the low morale of the population, who feel themselves defenceless'. He further asked Hitler to make available 100,000 to 150,000 workers for clearing the bomb damage to railway yards and industrial works in west German cities.'[36] Speer's mid-March 1945 comment perhaps tells all. He said 'My office was without window panes; we no longer bothered replacing them, since they were blasted out by bombs every few days.'[37]

Speer's Summation

And so, to conclude where I began, I'll simply say Third Reich Minister of Armaments and War Production Albert Speer sums up saying:

> Germany's failure to defeat Bomber Command was Germany's greatest lost battle of the whole war. The strategic bombing offensive did more damage to the German war effort than losing every battle in Russia, including the surrender of Stalingrad, because bombing continuously damaged with ever-increasing ferocity, and then ultimately destroyed, Germany's ability to produce the means necessary to make war.[38]

---

36 Institute, Vol. IX, Part 1, p. 463

37 Speer, p. 428

38 *From the Horse's Mouth*

Chapter Sixteen

Joseph Goebbels

If you repeat a lie often enough, people will believe it,
and you will even come to believe it yourself. And

A lie told once remains a lie, but a lie told a
thousand times becomes the truth, but

There will come a day when all the lies will collapse
under their own weight, and truth will again triumph.

Joseph Goebbels[1]

Joseph Goebbels' Multiple Titles and Ignominious End

For most of my life I erroneously thought that Propaganda Minister Joseph Goebbels was simply the mouthpiece of Adolf Hitler. In 2019 my research in German sources revealed to me he was far more than that, both in titles and in fact. He was a serious force to be reckoned with and, ultimately, he was Minister for Total War.

First, his titles. Goebbels' most famous title was that of Reich Minister of Public Enlightenment and Propaganda. He held that position from 14 March 1933 until 30 April 1945, virtually the entirety of the twelve years of the Third Reich. Goebbels was also gauleiter of Berlin, and for even longer. He was gauleiter from 9 November 1926 until his suicide on 1 May 1945. My research reveals that the gauleiters were a political force that Hitler had to accommodate throughout the war. They were party leaders of regional branches or administrative regions of the Nazi Party. Theirs was the second highest Nazi Party paramilitary rank. During the war, one became a gauleiter only by the direct appointment of Adolf Hitler.

On 23 July 1944 Goebbels really came into his own. On that day he became the Third Reich's very first, and only, Reich Plenipotentiary for Total War. Now why, I asked myself, would the Reich wait until 23 July 1944, almost seven weeks after D Day, to finally put someone other than just Hitler in charge of 'Total War'?

---

1 www.azquotes.com/author/5626-Joseph_Goebbels

The answer, my research reveals,[2] is that Hitler tried to minimize demands placed on Germans in the war for as long as possible. This was the exact opposite of Churchill, FDR and Mackenzie King, who looked for massive commitment. Hitler's fear of pushing Germans arose from the revolution through which Germans overthrew the Kaiser towards the end of the First World War. And Germans did not want war. So, for as long as he could in the Second World War, Hitler kept assuring Germans victory was near, and the costs would be minimal. By the summer of 1944, when the Nazi regime faced catastrophe, realities had to be faced: hence Goebbels' appointment. Goebbels final title was Chancellor, compliments of Hitler's will. Goebbels lasted in that position only one day. Hitler committed suicide on 30 April 1945. On 1 May 1945, as his sole act as Chancellor, Goebbels wrote a letter for delivery under a white flag to Soviet Eighth Guards Army commander, General Vasily Chuikov, requesting a ceasefire. Goebbels' request was rejected.

That evening Goebbels and his wife Magda murdered their six children. Helga, the eldest, fought hard to resist. Soviets report her body had black and blue bruises, and that her jaw may have been crushed, indicating she struggled with her killers. Earlier, Magda Goebbels had refused the offers of Albert Speer and others to take the children out of Berlin. Joseph and Magda were so committed to Hitler they could not imagine their children living in a Germany not ruled by Hitler. Then, with all six children dead, at 8:30 pm on 1 May 1945, Joseph and Magda left the bunker, walked up to the garden of the Chancellery, and committed suicide. It was an ignominious end for a monstrous leader of a murderous regime.

The Secret Diaries of Joseph Goebbels

But miraculously at least some of Goebbels' diaries survived. I say miraculously, because the Soviet method of reviewing Reich records was to empty the filing cabinet contents in the Reich Chancellery and elsewhere on the floor to see whether anything interesting fell out. This resulted in mountains of paper being randomly scattered everywhere. Luckily for us, Goebbels used exceptionally expensive and difficult to obtain paper on which to write his diaries. An amateur junk dealer found this fine paper scattered in the courtyard of Goebbels' ministry papers. Somehow, it escaped being burned. He salvaged some binders and about 7,000 loose sheets of paper. Among these were many of Goebbels' papers, including some concerning his personal finances and even a pile of birthday greetings. The expensive paper on which his diaries were typed was of fine water-marked quality rare in Germany, so a customer bought the expensive papers for their value as scrap paper. Fortunately, after several others had dismissed them as nothing more than expensive scrap paper, they came to the attention of Frank Mason, the former military attaché at the American Embassy in Berlin. He recognized them as being fragments of Goebbels' diaries. The pages were unnumbered, making it all far more difficult. However,

---

2 Albert Speer, *Inside the Third Reich*, p. 214

examination by Louis Lochner, former chief of the Berlin bureau of the Associated Press, confirmed their authenticity.[3]

Duly published, they were so popular they became a 'Book of the Month Club' selection. During my boyhood, my parents subscribed to the Book of the Month Club, so I grew up reading many of them. I did not see Goebbels' diaries, however, until researching for this book. And when I finally did read them, guess what? Goebbels' diaries often say the exact opposite of what he said publicly. Worse, the Allies actually believed some of what he said publicly; examples include his pair of gigantic lies about Dresden. What renders these diaries particularly important is their honesty. Goebbels wrote them to himself. I doubt he ever thought they would survive to be read by us.

Extracts from Goebbels' Secret Diaries in 1943

The evolution of the air war in the pivotal year 1943 gave leaders of the Third Reich an increasingly clear view of what lay ahead. Until 1943 Bomber Command had been hobbled by unsatisfactory aircraft, bombs and navigation aids. In 1943, all that changed. In addition, as mentioned, in January 1943, Germany faced three Allied air forces instead of just the RAF; the RCAF and the Mighty Eighth joined the fray. Here are extracts I have chosen of Goebbels' diary entries on the war in the air in 1943:

7 March 1943: 'During the night Essen suffered an exceptionally severe raid. The city of the Krupps has been hit hard ... . If the English continue their raids on this scale, they will make things exceedingly difficult for us ... . Our anti-aircraft guns arc inadequate ... . As we lack a weapon for attack, we cannot do anything noteworthy in the way of reprisal.'[4]

15 March 1943: 'Now that air raids on German cities are increasingly frequent we are naturally getting shorter and shorter on artisans and materials for even partly repairing the damage. We are already being forced to transfer to Essen or Munich companies of skilled workers whom we have sent, for example, to Duisburg ... . We should by no means believe that the worst is already over. The worst is yet to come.'[5]

16 March 1943: 'The dropping of forged food-ration cards from English planes is causing a lot of trouble. I had a press notice published in the provinces affected, stating that the use of forged food-ration cards will be punished severely, in certain cases even by death.'[6]

---

3 Gibson, Publisher, *The Goebbels' Diaries 1942-43*, pp. v-ix
4 *Goebbel's Diaries*, p. 277
5 *Goebbels Diaries*, p. 299
6 *Goebbels Diaries*, p. 301

BOMBER COMMAND

9 April 1943: Goebbels 'with a large entourage' arrives in Essen to confer with Milch 'who spoke in terms of sharpest criticism' about Göring for the failure of the Luftwaffe against Bomber Command. New planes are needed but large-scale production takes time. Goebbels writes: 'Until then the English can lay a large part of the Reich in ruins' and Göring's prestige 'has suffered very much.'[7]

10 April 1943: Goebbels tours Essen on foot because driving is impossible. The damage inflicted by the last three air raids is 'colossal and indeed ghastly' and city building experts say normally it would take twelve years to repair the damage. Goebbels writes: 'I believe Essen today is the city hit hardest by the English raids' and that 'The construction of bunkers and bombproof shelters is the most urgent problem.'[8]

10 May 1943: 'The painter Gerhardinger has refused to let the Munich Art Exposition have his canvasses because he fears they might be destroyed by air raids. The Führer ordered that he be punished very severely. It just won't do for an individual painter to arrogate to himself the right of avoiding part of the national risk .... Things would come to a pretty pass if behaviour like this went unchallenged and the artists were allowed to shirk their national duty.'[9]

15 May 1943: 'Air raids are becoming more frequent again. During the night the Skoda works near Pilsen were hard hit. Among other targets the drafting room was destroyed. This is naturally quite a setback for us. However, the number of planes we shot down is colossal. Within forty-eight hours the English lost seventy-eight four-engine bombers.'[10]

18 May 1943: 'Air raids the past night inflicted heavy damage on us. The attacks of British bombers on the dams in our valleys were very successful. The Führer is exceedingly impatient and angry about the lack of preparedness on the part of the Luftwaffe.'[11]

19 May 1943: 'The English and Americans discuss practically nothing but air warfare. Their successful raid on the German dams created a great sensation both in London and in Washington. Of course they know exactly what they achieved by this attack ... from a Jew who emigrated from Berlin .... I feel certain that treason was involved in this whole attack, for the English were so absolutely in the know,

---

7 *Goebbels Diaries*, p. 320
8 *Goebbels Diaries*, p. 322
9 *Goebbels Diaries*, p. 365
10 *Goebbels Diaries*, p. 379
11 *Goebbels Diaries*, p. 382

and after their attack had such exact knowledge of what damage was done, that it is hardly to be presumed they ascertained this solely by air reconnaissance.'[12]

21 May 1943: 'The English at present are making a sport of driving as large sections of our population as possible out of their beds by air alerts … . In the daytime, too, we have more alerts now, even in Berlin. The English accomplish this with their small Mosquito machines which are exceedingly hard to hit ….

We cannot just stand air warfare indefinitely. We must try as fast as possible to develop counter measures, especially reprisal attacks … . Otherwise sooner or later air war will become unbearable for us.'[13]

25 May 1943: 'The night raid of the English on Dortmund was extraordinarily heavy, probably the worst ever directed against a German city … . Reports from Dortmund are pretty horrible. The critical thing about it is that industrial and munition plants have been hit very hard. One can only repeat about air warfare: we are in an almost helpless inferiority and must grin and bear it as we take the blows from the English and the Americans … received reports from Bochum and Dortmund indicating a new low in morale … we must recognize people in the West are gradually beginning to lose courage. Hell like that is hard to bear for any length of time, especially since the inhabitants along the Rhine and Ruhr see no prospect of improvement … . The fact is that the Royal Air Force is taking on one industrial city after another and one need not be a great mathematician to prophesy when a large part of the industry of the Ruhr will be out of commission.'[14]

27 May 1943: 'The English are giving sensational publicity to their successes in the air. They exaggerate a lot, but unfortunately much of what they claim is true. Their attack on Dortmund, especially, is praised as a great accomplishment of the Royal Air Force. As a matter of fact we do have extraordinary difficulties to overcome there.'[15]

28 May 1943: 'Our supremacy in the air was wrested from us by the English not only by a tremendous expenditure of energy on the part of the RAF and the British airplane industry, but also because of a number of unfortunate circumstances and negligence on our part … . It seems to me that air warfare ought to be regarded as one of the most important phases of war and that it ought to be conducted quite independently of developments in the East.'[16]

---

12 *Goebbels Diaries*, pp. 383-4
13 *Goebbels Diaries*, p. 387
14 *Goebbels Diaries*, pp. 393, 397
15 *Goebbels Diaries*, p. 399
16 *Goebbels Diaries*, p. 400

25 July 1943: 'The results of the English air raids are gradually becoming evident. Our textile industry has been pretty badly hit. We are not in a position to meet our obligations about the Reich textile coupon card ... letters keep asking why the Führer does not visit the distressed air areas, why Göring isn't to be seen anywhere, and especially why the Führer doesn't for once talk to the German people to explain the present situation.'[17] Again, this behaviour is the exact opposite of that of the Allied leaders of America, Britain and Canada.

26 July 1943: 'During the night an exceptionally heavy raid on Hamburg took place, with most serious consequences both for the civilian population and for armaments production. This attack definitely shatters the illusions that many have had about the continuation of air operations by the enemy .... Unfortunately only two days previously Colonel General Weise[18] took the heavy anti-aircraft guns away from Hamburg to send them to Italy. That was the last straw! ... The eastern section of Altona was particularly hard hit. It is a real catastrophe .... Air warfare is our most vulnerable point.'[19]

29 July 1943: 'During the night we had the heaviest raid yet made on Hamburg. The English appeared over the city with 800 to 1,000 bombers .... A city of a million inhabitants has been destroyed in a manner unparalleled in history. We are faced with problems almost impossible of solution. Food must be found for this population of a million. Shelter must be secured. These people must be evacuated as far as possible. They must be given clothing. In short, we are facing problems there of which we had no conception even a few weeks ago .... [We have] begun moving 300,000 loaves of bread into Hamburg ...

A great deal of unrest has been created in Berlin by the manner in which the evacuating of certain Berlin public offices has been handled .... The Berliners therefore believe that in case more serious air raids were to occur, the government could be the first to run away. Naturally there can be no thought of that. I have therefore started propaganda by word of mouth to offset it.'[20]

NOTE: On 23 August 1943 America bombed Berlin. It was reported the fires were visible two hundred miles away. The Nazis decided they had to evacuate all non-essential people from Berlin. The next day, Hitler replaced the elderly Wilhelm Frick with the terrifyingly sadistic Heinrich Himmler as the Reich's Minister of the

---

17 *Goebbels Diaries*, p. 404

18 I am guessing that Goebbels is referring to Luftwaffe General Hubert Weise. He could, however, have misspelt the name and is referring to German General Friedrich Wiese, commander of Nineteenth Army.

19 *Goebbels Diaries*, pp. 404-5

20 *Goebbels Diaries*, pp. 419-21

JOSEPH GOEBBELS

Interior. Himmler concurrently continued to head the Gestapo and the SS, both of which he now used ruthlessly 'to curb rising unrest within the Reich'.[21]

10 September 1943: 'Unfortunately the English raids on Peenemunde and on our OT work in the West have thrown our preparations back four and even eight weeks, so that we can't possibly count on reprisals before the end of January. The Führer places great hopes in rocket bombs. He believes that through them the whole picture may possibly change as regards England ... .'[22]

7 November 1943: 'Air raids at home also cause deep concern to the troops. Hatred against England exceeds all bounds. For the present, however, it is an impotent hatred. The troops would naturally like to know something about our plans for retaliation. But we can't oblige them about that.'[23]

24 November 1943: 'I just can't understand how the English are able to do so much damage to the Reich's capital during one air raid ... utter desolation. Blazing fires everywhere ... . Transportation conditions are still quite hopeless .... Once it no longer functions, business soon stops, supplies cease to move, and difficulties increase by the hour ... . The English fly in bad weather ... all the way to Berlin; but the German pursuit planes can't rise from the ground in Berlin because weather prevents! ... Again it was a major, grade-A attack ... . They destroyed everything around the Potsdamer Platz [Berlin's busiest square]. The pressure was so strong that even our bunker, though constructed deep underground, began to shake ... . Devastation is again appalling in the government section ... . Hell itself seems to have broken loose over us ... . The government quarter is nothing short of an inferno. One can hardly recognize the Wilhelmplatz ... . This is one of the worst nights of my entire life.'[24]

25 November 1943: 'The [second] heavy air raid equalled the first in intensity ... . Conditions in the city are pretty hopeless. [At Goebbels' home] there is no heat, no light, no water. One can neither shave nor wash ... . The streets must be cleared before repairing the worst damage. For this, however, the man power is not sufficient. The Wehrmacht ... promised within twenty-four hours to furnish me two-and-a-half divisions, or 50,000 men. These 50,000 men are to do nothing except to clear the main traffic arteries of the Reich .... About 400,000 people in Berlin are without shelter ... . Contrary to expectations the number of people killed is, thank God, quite low. During the first air raid we registered 1,500 and during

---

21 *Goebbels Diaries*, p. 423
22 *Goebbels Diaries*, pp 435-6
23 *Goebbels Diaries*, p. 499
24 *Goebbels Diaries*, pp. 521-4

the second about 1,200 dead .... I was able at last to make a tour of some of the destroyed sections of the city .... What I saw was truly shattering.'[25]

26 November 1943: 'The English are achieving nothing with their attempts to unload the responsibility for air warfare on us. Everybody in Germany knows that the English started it and that the blood guilt falls on them .... At last I have got the Führer to the point that we may give two types of alert in Berlin: one, a genuine alert, when bomber formations are on their way here, and the other a mere warning in the case of a few nuisance planes. This is necessary, for I don't want to throw a city of four-and-a-half million into a panic every night merely because of two Mosquitoes.'[26]

27 November 1943: 'The diplomatic quarter along the Tiergarten looks like one gigantic heap of rubble. One can hardly pass through the streets, as they are covered in debris .... [Tonight the bombers appeared to be heading to Frankfurt] But that was merely a camouflage manoeuvre ... cleverly to mislead our pursuit planes .... Once again a major attack descended upon the Reich capital. This time ... [the target was] chiefly the large munitions plants in Rinickendorf .... The news that the Alkett plant was on fire was especially depressing. Alkett is our most important factory for the production of fieldpieces. There we produce one half of our entire output of these guns, amounting to 200 pieces .... This is a heavy blow. The Führer, too, is very much depressed .... The situation has become even more alarming in that one industrial plant after another has been set on fire. The main damage, however, is at Alkett ... .'[27]

28 November 1943: 'This time the munitions industry was especially hard hit. The Alkett works received a blow from which they won't recover easily. At Alkett 80 per cent of our fieldpieces were produced, of which there will now be a shortage. At Borsig's also tremendous destruction took place. It must be remembered that Borsig produces a large percentage of our gun output and has 18,000 employees. Naturally everything is being done to get munitions production started again. But that is more easily said than done ....

London reports that more than a million people met their death in Berlin. That, of course, is arrogant nonsense, for the total number of fatal casualties owing to three heavy air raids totals between three and four thousand. But I don't issue a denial of these exaggerations.'[28]

29 November 1943: 'The Berlin munition industry is still in bad shape. Alkett is almost completely destroyed and, worst of all, valuable and virtually irreplaceable

---

25 *Goebbels Diaries*, pp. 525-9
26 *Goebbels Diaries*, pp. 529-30
27 *Goebbels Diaries*, pp. 533-4
28 *Goebbels Diaries*, pp. 535-6

tools and machines have been put out of commission. The English aimed so accurately that one might think spies had pointed their way ... .'[29]

5 December 1943: 'Unfortunately the air raid on Leipzig [the seat of Germany's supreme court] last night was exceedingly severe and fateful. The city was not prepared ... . The fire department was not adequate. Almost all public buildings ... have either been completely destroyed or seriously damaged ... . About 150,000 to 200,000 people are without shelter.'[30]

6 December 1943: 'In the spring, after the German cities have been reduced to ruins, the English allegedly want to start the invasion. Of course chills run down their backs even at the use of this word. They want, above all, to intensify their air offensive against us during January because that is the coldest month and it is expected that air raids will then affect German morale more adversely.'[31]

NOTE: The 9 December 1943 entry, which does not mention the air war, was the last found among these Goebbels papers.[32]

Conclusions Regarding Goebbels

To conclude, I must mention, in a salute to the strategic bombing offensive, that Roosevelt famously said 'When Hitler built Fortress Europe, he forgot to put a roof over it.'[33]

Germany's Military Institute for Research History chimes in by saying Goebbels also spoke of that roof:

> For Goebbels personally the air war over Germany and above 'Fortress Europe', whose 'roof' he saw as 'unprotected', gave the gravest concern. Not only was it the most important and decisive 'problem of problems' in domestic policy, the cardinal problem, but it was also the subject that overshadowed all other topics of conversation. This is where the real weakness of our conduct of the war lies', he correctly diagnosed, 'a weakness that causes a kind of intellectual and psychological paralysis among the German leadership'.'[34]

---

29 *Goebbels Diaries*, p. 537
30 *Goebbels Diaries*, pp. 542-3
31 *Goebbels Diaries*, p. 543
32 *Goebbels Diaries*, p. 547
33 President Trump quoted FDR making this famous statement in his D Day Speech in Normandy on 6 June 2019
34 Institute, Vol. VII, p. 371

The Institute Describes Goebbels' Enormous Influence

The Institute says two organizations,

> the ILA and the Reich inspectorate, substantially increased Goebbels's influence. Through his control via these two bodies he played, from 1943, a central role.
>
> Both organizations in almost every measure were involved with the air war at civilian level. At the same time, he had an overview of the whole broad sweep of what was happening in the air war, unequalled by any other leading Nazi politician except perhaps Albert Speer.[35]

The Institute then says 'This means that Goebbels can be described as the most important key figure on the home front; for he not only had the fullest information on developments in the bombing war, but enjoyed close contact with the leading personalities and bodies involved – even down to the municipal level.'[36]

On 23 July 1944, Hitler made Goebbels Reich Commissioner for Total Mobilization of Resources for War. The Institute says that 'This made him, when the bombing war was at its peak, one of the Reich's most powerful politicians and decision-makers.'[37]

Through all of this the Institute says 'Goebbels penetrated, in 1943/4, Göring's existing work and organizational structures as commander-in-chief of the Luftwaffe, as well as those of Himmler, who as Reich minister of the interior and chief of the German police was also in charge of the entire fire protection and ARP police system.'[38]

Goebbels was indeed one of the most powerful, and best informed, Reich leaders. And his diaries in 1943 reveal the strategic bombing offensive which were now the combined air forces of America, Canada and Britain with Australia and New Zealand terrified him.

---

35 Institute, Vol. IX, Part 1, p. 409

36 Institute, Vol. IX, Part 1, p. 409

37 Institute, Vol. IX, Part 1, p. 409

38 Institute, Vol. IX, Part 1, p. 409

Chapter Seventeen

Luftwaffe Leaders

To understand Bomber Command's war in the air, I felt I needed some understanding of the Luftwaffe Leaders, who they were and how they affected the Luftwaffe's response to Bomber Command. A comprehensive look at Luftwaffe Leadership is beyond the scope of this book, so I restricted my research to the following three whose participation helps me understand the challenges they posed for Bomber Command. My first discovery was that Luftwaffe leadership meant first and foremost Hermann Wilhelm Göring.

Hermann Göring – Supreme Commander of the Luftwaffe

In many movies, Göring is portrayed as fat, greedy, pompous and stupid, almost a cardboard cartoon caricature. The truth is more complex. US Army Air Forces General Carl Spaatz wrote that Göring 'despite rumours to the contrary, is far from mentally deranged. In fact he must be considered a very "shrewd customer", a great actor and professional liar.'[1] Of greatest importance, Göring was Hitler's heir apparent, so he warrants a closer look

Hermann Göring was born in Bavaria, the second son of the second wife of Heinrich Ernst Göring, Germany's consul general in Haiti. He had been Germany's first governor-general of South West Africa, now Namibia which my wife Ka Hyun and I visited in 2019. Hermann was raised in a small castle, Veldenstein, near Nuremburg, the city where on 15 October 1946 while waiting trial he committed suicide. The castle's owner, Hermann Ritter von Epenstein, was a Jew who, until their falling out in 1913, was Göring's mother's lover. He was also the godfather of her children, including Hermann.[2] Yes, you read right. Göring's godfather Hermann Ritter von Epenstein was a Jew. So was Hitler's paternal grandmother, Maria Anna Schicklgruber.

In 1912, Göring was commissioned as an officer of Crown Prince Wilhelm's Regiment (112th Infantry) in which he entered the First World War. His request for transfer from it to what became Germany's 'air combat forces' was turned down.

---

1 Larson, *The Splendid & the Vile*, p. 51
2 *Encyclopedia Britannica* www.britannica.com/biography/hermann-goring

BOMBER COMMAND

Encouraged by his friend Bruno Loerzer, Göring transferred himself and began flying as Loerzer's observer. Goering was saved from prison for his self-transfer when his relationship with Loerzer was made official. They flew bombing and reconnaissance missions. Crown Prince Wilhelm invested both with the Iron Cross First Class. Göring was invalided for a year to recover from a serious hip wound in aerial combat. Returning to combat in February 2017, Göring was credited with twenty-two victories as a fighter pilot. RAF postwar examination of loss records reveal that only two of Göring's 22 victories were doubtful. Of the remaining twenty, three were possible and seventeen were certain or highly likely.[3]

Göring was furious with the shabby postwar treatment civilians gave veterans in Germany, and fervently believed the 'stab in the back' myth that Germany did not lose the war on the battlefield, but was betrayed by civilian leadership, Jews, Marxists and Republicans who toppled the kaiser. Postwar, Göring became a civilian pilot in Scandinavia, where he married into the nobility. He met Hitler in 1921 and also met and became infatuated with Baroness Carin von Rosen in Sweden. The infatuation was mutual, so she divorced her husband in December 1922 and married Göring on 3 January 1923. She was a wonderful hostess for him, and Goebbels used their love story to boost Nazi popularity throughout Germany. A great blow to Göring was Carin's death on 17 October 1931. It resulted from the heart attack she had the day after attending her mother's funeral in Sweden; she was 42. Göring named his famous palatial hunting lodge north of Brandenburg Carinhall in her memory.

In late 1922 Göring joined the small National Socialist German Workers' Party, the Nazis. About Göring, Hitler said 'I liked him. I made him the head of my SA. He is the only one of its heads that ran the SA properly. I gave him a dishevelled rabble. In a very short time, he had organized a division of 11,000 men.'[4] Then came the 'Munich Beer Hall Putsch' of 8/9 November 1923. Göring was shot in the groin during the Putsch while marching with Hitler to the war ministry. With his wife Carin's help, he was smuggled to Innsbruck and then Italy for medical assistance to recover. Göring's recovery featured something fortuitous for the Allies in the Second World War. To deal with his intense pain from his groin wound, Göring became addicted to morphine.

The failure of the Beer Hall Putsch put Hitler in prison with a five-year sentence of which he served only part. There he wrote his autobiographical manifesto *Mein Kampf* (*My Struggle*). It was published on 18 July 1925 which in 1948 became my date of birth. Although Hitler was Führer of the Nazi Party from 29 July 1921, he did not take office as Chancellor of the German Reich until 30 January 1933. In the July 1932 election, the Nazis won 230 seats in the Reichstag and, on 30 August 1932, Göring became President of the Reichstag. That was the first of many positions he held until 23 April 1945. No party won a majority in the elections

---

3 Kilduff, *Herman Göring, Fighter Ace: The World War I Career of Germany's Most Infamous Airman*, pp. 165-6 Wikipedia Hermann Goering

4 Adolf Hitler (1988) *Hitler's Table Talk 1941-44*, p. 168

of July and November 1932. Under great pressure to restore stability, albeit with reluctance, Weimar Republic President of the German Reich Marshal Paul von Hindenburg appointed Hitler Chancellor on 30 January 1933. What a mistake that was! Hitler's first priority as Chancellor was to take control of the German police. Göring oversaw creation of the Gestapo which he ceded to Heinrich Himmler in 1934. Here are more Hitler appointments for Göring, all lasting until April 1945:

10 April 1933	Minister President of Prussia
27 April 1933	Reichsminister of Aviation (police aircraft being lawful)
01 March 1935	Supreme Commander of the Luftwaffe
18 October 1936	Reich Plenipotentiary of the Four-Year Plan
30 August 1939	Chairman, Ministerial Committee for Reich Defence

The Reich plenipotentiary appointment far exceeded four years, and indeed lasted until April 1945. It empowered Göring to mobilize every sector of the economy for war, including giving him control over numerous government agencies. Hitler's most important appointment for Göring happened on 1 September 1939. After invading Poland at dawn, Hitler spoke that day to the Reichstag. In his speech, Hitler declared Göring his successor and deputy in all offices. And there is more. After the fall of France, Hitler made Göring Reichsmarschall on 19 July 1940, the Reich's highest ranking military officer in the Second World War. Göring was then at the peak of his popularity. People liked him. One can see from all this how devastating it was inside the German hierarchy when Bomber Command reduced the gigantic Reich hero Göring to a figure of ridicule.

Galland, Beppo and Kammhuber

Erik Larson's entertaining book *The Splendid and the Vile* introduced me to a pair of interesting characters – Luftwaffe fighter ace Adolf Galland and General Joseph ('Beppo') Schmid. The latter was commander of the Luftwaffe's Military Intelligence Branch until 24 June 1943, the date for which the 'General of Germany's night fighters, Josef Kammhuber, attracted my attention.

First let us look at German pilot Adolf Galland. In 1932, he was one of 20,000 applicants for training to be a pilot in what is now Lufthansa. Twenty were chosen, including Galland. By the end of 1932 Galland had earned his preliminary flying certificate. He was among five of the twenty summoned in secrecy to Berlin to be invited to take a secret course on how to fly military aircraft – secret because, as mentioned, the Treaty of Versailles prohibited Germany from having an air force. The law of unintended consequences was reflected in German hatred of that treaty, causing so many Germans to vote for Hitler. All five pilots, including Galland, agreed to take this secret course and were transferred to Munich for training.

There Galland was thrilled to meet Göring, who was secretly building Germany's air force. In December 1933 Galland was invited back to Berlin to join Göring's still secret Luftwaffe, and was posted to its first fighter squadron. He was among the Luftwaffe fighter and bomber pilots of Germany's 'Condor Legion', sent in secrecy to Spain to fight for Franco in the Spanish Civil War. In Spain, Luftwaffe pilots learnt much about combat, while Göring and Hitler got the idea that bombers do not need fighter escorts. That was true in Spain, but they later learned at great cost it was not true over Britain.

The Condor Legion was required by the Third Reich, so its members returned to Germany as heroes, unlike the soldiers of Canada's Mackenzie-Papineau Battalion fighting against Franco. Parliament enacted the Canadian Foreign Enlistment Act in April 1937 to prohibit Canadians from fighting in foreign wars. In July 1937 this was formally applied to Spain. And yet, in spite of this, Canadians with strongly-held beliefs still fought in Spain in the Mackenzie-Papineau Battalion, and also in America's Abraham Lincoln or George Washington battalions. Except for France, no nation had a greater percentage of its population fight in Spain than Canada. Almost half of those fighting in the Mackenzie-Papineau Battalion were killed. Canada's Dr Norman Bethune, later a legendary hero in China, was one of the few Canadians to be recognized for his service in Spain. But times change. Monuments to the Mackenzie-Papineau Battalion were unveiled in Queen's Park Toronto on 4 June 1995, in Victoria British Columbia on 12 February 2000 and in Green Island Park Ottawa in 2001.

Larson says the average age of Battle of Britain RAF pilots was 20, while for the Luftwaffe it was 26. Galland was 28.[5] As the war progressed, the British Commonwealth Air Training Plan in Canada steadily increased the quantity and quality of Allied aircrew while the reverse was happening to the Luftwaffe. Galland says one of Göring's major deficiencies was not seeming to understand that aerial warfare had changed enormously since the First World War. Galland also said 'Göring was a man of almost no technical knowledge and no appreciation of the conditions under which modern fighter aircraft fought.'

A second major problem hampering the Luftwaffe was the lack of meaningful numbers of heavy bombers. This arose from Hitler continually questioning Göring about the number of bombers being produced for the Luftwaffe, without being specific. Göring found he could far more easily produce numbers that pleased Hitler if he built smaller two-engine bombers like Britain's Wellingtons, instead of the much bigger four-engine bombers which took far longer to make. This Göring subterfuge to please Hitler was one of many in which Göring misled him. The best recognized German twin-engine bomber was the Heinkel He 111 of which Germany built 5,656 from 1939 until 1944.[6] The Heinkel He 177 Greif was regarded as a long-range heavy bomber, but it also had only two engines, and its use was significantly delayed by problems with its engines and frequent changes

---

5 Larson, pp. 140-1.
6 Nowarra, *Heinkel He 111: A Documentary History*, Janes Publishing London, 1980, p. 233

LUFTWAFFE LEADERS

to its intended uses. Although 1,169 were built, by the time they had a useable design it was too late in the war to play an important role.[7] The Luftwaffe also flew the twin-engine Dornier Do 17, known as the 'Flying Pencil' because of its slim fuselage, of which 2,139 were built. Its use was curtailed by the end of 1941 because its bombload and range were limited.[8] Germany's most important aircraft was the twin-engine multi-role Junkers Ju 88, of which 15,183 were built. It was used as a bomber, dive-bomber, night fighter, torpedo bomber, reconnaissance aircraft, heavy fighter and, at the end of the war, as a flying bomb.[9]

The Luftwaffe was also burdened with a third major problem – massive communication confusion. And that leads us to Josef 'Beppo' Schmid. He was a significant source of that confusion. In the Battle of Britain, Beppo said RAF pilots were weak and dispirited. About this, Larson succinctly says 'What Beppo Schmidt's reports depicted, however, was very different from what Luftwaffe pilots were experiencing in the air … . German pilots found no hint of [British] diminished strength or resolve'.[10] In addition to gross inaccuracies about RAF pilot morale, Beppo told Hitler that the RAF was losing many aircraft it was unable to replace, so much so that soon the RAF would have no aircraft at all. Beppo had not reckoned with Beaverbrook. Antony Beevor calls Beppo the 'most disastrous intelligence officer the Wehrmacht ever produced'.[11] To this, Galland adds that hiring Beppo was Göring's 'worst error', and that 'Beppo Schmid was a complete wash-out as an intelligence officer, the most important job of all'.[12] My research reveals this Luftwaffe command pattern of information distortion and blockage, coupled with all power being held by Hitler, Göring's increasing tendency to lie to please Hitler and Göring's ignorance of the technicalities, increasingly damaged the Luftwaffe as the war progressed.

Beppo continued with Luftwaffe Command Intelligence until, on 24 June 1943, something remarkable happened. Josef Kammhuber, GOC XXII Air Corps infuriated Hitler that day by telling Hitler that America was building 5,000 military aircraft a month. The Luftwaffe war diaries say Hitler responded 'It's absolute nonsense. If the figures were right, you'd be right too! In that case I should have to withdraw from the Eastern Front forthwith and apply all resources to air defence. But they are *not* right. I will not stand for such nonsense!' So Kammhuber was replaced by Beppo. The Allies were blessed by Hitler's temper tantrum on 24 June. Kammhuber retained his title as General of the Night-Fighters until mid-1943 when he lost all further influence. The Luftwaffe war diaries conclude by saying

---

7   Wikipedia Heinkel He 177 Greif
8   Wikipedia Dornier Do 17
9   Wikipedia Junkers Ju 88
10 Larson, p. 153
11 Beevor, *Ardennes 1944*, p. 90
12 Larson, p. 51

about Kammhuber that 'The man who had been responsible for the whole build-up of the night-fighter arm found himself posted to Norway'.[13]

I was interested to discover that, for the defence of the Reich against our strategic bombing offensive, Kammhuber created a chain of radar stations with overlapping coverage in three layers of zones known to the British as the 'Kammhuber Line'. Our bombers when crossing it would be illuminated by searchlights and then attacked by night-fighters. To counter this, a brilliant young RAF physicist Dr. Reginald V. Jones about whom I write in the next chapter suggested that Bomber Command send all of its bombers in a 'bomber stream' carefully positioned to fly down the middle of a cell. His tactic was hugely successful.[14] Bomber streams overwhelmed the Kammhuber Line.

Galland also fell from favour with Hitler. On 20 January 1945 the Luftwaffe war diaries report about Hitler that:

> Where the Luftwaffe was concerned, he listened only to talk of offensive action; to the need for air defence he was deaf. When, as late as August 1944 Speer and Galland personally expressed to him the crying need for German fighter strength to be concentrated on the Defence of the Reich, Hitler merely threw them out, shouting that they should obey his orders. Next day, he proclaimed that the whole fighter arm was disbanded, and instructed Speer to switch from fighter production to flak guns.

Also on 20 January, by which time Galland had already been suspended from any active role as *General der Jagdflieger*, Hitler reduced Galland to commander of a squadron of Me.262 jet fighter aircraft. The Luftwaffe war diaries conclude: 'So it was that Galland, who had started the war in 1939 as a squadron commander with the rank of first-lieutenant, ended it as a squadron commander again, though with the rank of lieutenant-general.'[15]

Hitler was running amok.

---

13 Bekker, *Luftwaffe War Diaries*, pp. 331-2
14 Wikipedia Josef Kammhuber
15 Bekker, pp. 357-9

Part IV

BOMBER COMMAND ACCOMPLISHMENTS

Chapter Eighteen

Air War

> The Navy can lose us the war but only the Air Force can win it. Therefore, our supreme effort must be to gain overwhelming mastery in the air. The Fighters are our, salvation, but the Bombers alone provide the means of victory.
>
> Winston Churchill[1]

> The real cause of Germany's defeat was the failure of the German Air Force.
>
> Adolf Hitler, days before his suicide[2]

We call the air war the strategic bombing offensive. Germans call it their defence of the Reich campaign. The three longest battles of the Second World War were the Battle of the Atlantic, the strategic bombing offensive, and the Allied blockade of Germany's Fortress Europe. All three were decisive Allied victories at enormous cost. Bomber Command was deeply involved in all three. The air war ran the duration of the Second World War from the day Britain declared war on Germany on 3 September 1939 until the day Germany unconditionally surrendered on 7 May 1945. The numbers speak for themselves – of Bomber Command's 125,000 aircrew, 80,000 were casualties. The United States Army's Eighth Air Force in Britain, 'The Mighty Eighth', suffered similar casualties. My purpose here is to discover what the 'air war' was, and what it accomplished. Here is what my research reveals.

Under Hitler and Göring, Germany started preparing the Luftwaffe in secrecy for this air war as early as 1933 in violation of the 1919 Treaty of Versailles' prohibition on Germany having an air force, although the 1926 Kellogg-Briand Pact did allow Germany to have police aircraft. It is well known that Churchill spent the 1930s in the political wilderness warning that Germany was arming while the Allies were not. And so, when war was declared in 1939, Britain and the Dominions were unprepared.

---

1 Birrell, *Johnny*, p. 30
2 Overy, 'World War II: How the Allies Won,' BBC.co.uk, 17 February 2011

AIR WAR

I am surprised to discover just how unprepared we were. Bomber Command's most famous pilot, one that even I knew of, was Guy Gibson VC of Dambusters fame. Gibson joined the RAF on a short service commission in November 1936. He was commissioned as an acting pilot officer on 31 January 1937, received his wings on 24 May 1937, and in June 1939 was promoted to flying officer. The first three words of his report, which I have *underlined*, say it all about the state of British air defences when Britain declared war on Germany on 3 September 1939.[3] Gibson wrote:

> *We were unprepared*; only last week I had been flying in our summer home defence exercises. Twice we had 'raided' London from the direction of Holland. On neither occasion had we seen any 'enemy' [i.e. British] fighters, and had flown on another 150 miles [240 km] to 'flatten' the English Air Force Headquarters at Abingdon.

Not only were we unprepared, but I also discovered how seriously we underestimated the evolution of German fighters and flak. The assurance Prime Minister Stanley Baldwin gave, while he was still just Lord President of the Council, in a speech to Britain's parliament on 10 November 1932 that 'the bomber will always get through' was not accurate in the first years of the war.

Allied and Axis Air Forces

Through Churchill and Trenchard, Britain, Australia, Canada and New Zealand had seem the air force as a long-range strategic offensive bomber force since the First World War. This fact brought me to wondering about the other air forces fighting the Second World War. Harris says the long-range bombing status of these Air Forces was:[4]

France: The French believed the only use of bombers was as long-range artillery for the Army. They were vague as to how this would happen. In any event, they had no bombers, so left it to Britain to support their Army.

Germany: The Germans completely subordinated their whole Air Force to the land operations of their Army. General Walther Wever, the Luftwaffe's first Chief of Staff, was Germany's most fervent advocate of long-range strategic bombers.[5] Fortunately for the Allies, he died in an air crash on 3 June 1936.

---

3 Gibson VC, *Enemy Coast Ahead*, p. 23 (this doesn't tally with the pagination in my copy)
4 Harris, *Bomber Offensive*, p. 53
5 Bashow, p. 469

Soviet Russia: The Russians never seriously attempted strategic bombing in their wars against Germany or Finland. They had neither the knowledge nor the productive capacity to equip a heavy bomber force. In addition, their pilots were not successful flying British heavy bombers.

Japan: The Japanese entirely subordinated their air force to the operations of their Army and Navy.

America: The United States had not originally envisioned the use of aircraft in any but a close strategical-tactical role, although Paul Robinson tells me US Generals Hap Arnold and Carl Spaatz between the wars were advocates of strategic bombing. Harris says America took the main idea of the strategic use of air power from the RAF and America's incredibly efficient industrial capacity enabled production of strategic bombers in time to fight in the latter part of the war against both Germany and Japan.

The Ultimate Battle – War in the Air to Control the Skies

Pretty much every leading German military official says Germany's loss of control of the skies cost Germany the war.[6] Luftwaffe Field Marshal Erhard Milch points out that the RAF took control of its own skies before massively bombing Germany. He says the Luftwaffe's failure to keep control of German skies 'in the end dealt us the death blow'. But the Institute advises the Luftwaffe was in the impossible position of Germany needing 50 per cent armament for the army and 50 per cent for the Luftwaffe to hold the Russian front while to defend the homeland from the strategic bombing offensive the Luftwaffe needed 100 per cent of the armament effort.[7] That priority to defend Germany proved disastrous for Germans fighting in Russia. Paul Robinson points out that Germany had 900 aircraft tied up fighting our bombers, as well as a million men reconstructing bomb damage. In addition, Germany had a serious problem arising from its form of governance – a totalitarian Nazi state. Of this the Institute says:

> Trapped between the demands of attack and defence, the Luftwaffe's high command failed to switch soon enough from an offensive to a defensive conduct of the air war; when they did so, it was for far too long only half-heartedly, at the same time arming themselves to undertake bomber offensive in the east and west when they were not even masters of their own airspace. In the totalitarian Nazi state they were, however, not free to take their own decisions.[8]

---

6 Cooper, *Target Dresden*, pp. 221-8.
7 Institute, Vol. VII, p. 291
8 Institute, Vol. VII, p. 291

AIR WAR

In the opening stages of the Second World War, the Luftwaffe was immersed in internal challenges similar to those of the RAF – finding its place distinct from the Army and Navy, neither of which wanted a third separate service. They wanted instead an air arm of their own two services. However, Germany and Britain both began with support where it mattered most – Hermann Göring for the Luftwaffe, and First Lord of the Admiralty Winston Churchill for the RAF.

Changes worked to the advantage of both air forces in 1940. For the RAF, the biggest advantage occurred on 10 May, when King George VI elevated Churchill from First Lord of the Admiralty to Prime Minister. For the Luftwaffe, the biggest advantage occurred on 19 July, when Hitler elevated Göring to the especially created highest position of *Reichsmarschall*. That gave Göring seniority over all other officers in the German armed forces. And he was Hitler's heir apparent.

Bomber Command and the Battle of Britain

I was astonished to discover Bomber Command lost more aircrew in the Battle of Britain than did Fighter Command. I was first alerted to it when Erik Larson pointed out that, in keeping track for the public which side lost what each night during the Battle of Britain 'The score also omitted British bombers shot down or damaged during raids over Germany. On Friday night, August 16, for example, RAF Bomber Command despatched 150 bombers and lost seven.'[9] I then discovered that, in the Battle of Britain, Bomber Command flew 9,180 combat sorties. This forced some German fighters to defend their air bases instead of attacking Britain.[10] I also learned that, during the Battle of Britain, 520 were killed in Fighter Command, and over 700 aircrew were killed in Bomber Command.[11]

While RAF Fighter Command dogfights of Hurricanes and Spitfires fighting Messerschmitts were seen first-hand in British skies by those below, and so captured the public's imagination, Hitler was more concerned about Bomber Command destroying his planned embarkation ports and, worst of all, Bomber Command with the Royal Navy sinking his invasion fleet in the Channel. He decided he could not invade Britain until Germany controlled the skies. An interesting anecdote is told by Hauptmann Zimmerman, chief air raid warden at the port of Bremen, when commenting that stores of food, petrol, spares and ammunition for the invasion of England were being destroyed by Bomber Command. His anecdote was that supplies intended for Germany's invasion in the summer of 1940 were burnt, presumably at Bremen, in a single Bomber Command attack which set Germany's supply organization back several months.[12] This information was not well received in Berlin.

---

9 Larson, *The Splendid and the Vile*, p. 172
10 Correll, 'How the Luftwaffe Lost the Battle of Britain,' *Air Force Magazine* 1 August 2008 www.airforcemag.com
11 Aftermath – The Battle of Britain/NZ History, New Zealand History Online www.nzhistory.govt.nz
12 Cooper, p 227

A turning point for Bomber Command was 24 August 1940. A group of German bombers got lost searching for aircraft factories and an oil depot in the east end of London. By mistake, they dropped their bombs in central London. Damage was minimal, and casualties few, but public indignation massive. This accidental attack on London gave Churchill the justification he needed for attacking Berlin.[13] The next day the RAF bombed Berlin for the first time – its targets being Tempelhof airfield where I landed when I first flew to Berlin in 1969, and Siemens' factories in Siemenstadt. RAF accuracy was so poor that Hitler, infuriated, erroneously jumped to the conclusion the RAF was deliberately bombing indiscriminately. Then Hitler compounded his error with three mistakes that deeply damaged Germany's air war. Hitler's first mistake was ordering reprisals in Britain through massive indiscriminate bombing, especially of London. That effectively repealed Goering's 30 June 1940 general order that 'The war against England is to be restricted to destructive attacks against industry and the air force targets which have weak defensive forces ... . It is also stressed that every effort should be made to avoid unnecessary loss of life amongst the civilian population.'[14] Hitler's second mistake arising from his emotional change of direction was diverting the Luftwaffe from the destruction of RAF airbases and other essential facilities. One could say Hitler's temper tantrum saved the RAF. Hitler's third mistake was misunderstanding what Bomber Command was really doing until it was too late for Germany to take proper defensive action. More on that later.

Radar and Beam Guidance Navigation

A major factor in the RAF Battle of Britain win was radar and the integrated system it was part of. Sir Henry Tizard was the Air Ministry's trusted scientific advisor and patron of radar. Radar and defence electronics eventually employed some 3,500 high-grade scientists and technicians.[15] Fred Glueckstein tells us:

> The British pioneer of RDF [Radio Direction Finding] and radar technology was Robert Watson-Watt, a scientific civil servant. Churchill recognized that Watson-Watt had the foresight to apply the concept of radar to a military system. Watson-Watt's scientific contribution of RDF was a major factor in winning the Battle of Britain and ultimate victory.[16]

---

13 Larson, pp. 187-9

14 Wood & Dempster, *Strategic Bombing During WWII*, p. 117

15 Nahum, 'The PM and the Boffins – Churchill and His Scientists,' *Finest Hour* No. 195 First Quarter 2022, p. 9

16 Glueckstein 'An Extraordinary Advantage – Winston Churchill, Robert Watson and the Development of Radar', *Finest Hour* No. 195 First Quarter 2022, p. 22.

Germans failed to take radar seriously, in spite of swarms of Spitfires and Hurricanes inexplicably finding many German bombers and fighters in heavy cloud cover which the RAF then shot down. The Luftwaffe would knock out the occasional radar tower, but it would be replaced within hours, and Göring evidently lost interest in what the RAF was doing with radar. My first father-in-law, and my children's grandfather, Guy Winter, was an early RCAF radar specialist. He even fought with the RCAF in the 23 October to 4 November 1942 desert war Battle of El Alamein which Montgomery won.

In addition, the Luftwaffe under-utilized its beam-guidance system because, even though 'Germany's beam-navigation technology had reduced the Luftwaffe's dependence on moonlight', Larson explains that 'its pilots remained wary of the new system and still preferred attacking in clear weather over a landscape agleam with lunar light.'[17] However, pilots who preferred eyesight views, which of course required cloudless skies lit by sun or moon, were extremely vulnerable. Radar was not precise enough at night, so if the Germans had made better use of their navigation aids they would have been far safer when attacking at night.

RAF's R.V. Jones to the Rescue

Erik Larson tells compelling stories, that being one reason his books are so often best sellers. This Larson story is about Dr Reginald V. Jones, the 28-year-old RAF Assistant Director of Intelligence (Scientific) and physicist from the Royal Aircraft Establishment Farnborough about whom I wrote in my previous chapter. Jones made an important discovery in Britain's darkest hour which demonstrates how effectively, and with such blinding speed, Churchill recognized new possibilities and dangers, and acted on them. It also shows how close Churchill and Cherwell were. Indeed, as Martin Gilbert has shown, Lindemann was 'as close to Churchill in thought, proximity and ideas as any other individual'. The two first met in 1921 and formed a professional-political relationship, and in due course a friendship, which endured for more than three decades.[18] And the Jones story illustrates that British ingenuity in which Eisenhower tells us Bomber Command excelled.

Larson's story starts when Jones learned that a captured German airman was overheard telling his German aircrew cellmate in German that, no matter how hard the RAF looked, they would never find 'the equipment'. This piqued Jones' curiosity. All German bombers were equipped with standard Lorenz landing systems. Jones asked the engineer examining a German bomber that the RAF had shot down whether he saw anything unusual about the blind-landing receiver. The engineer at first said 'no'. But then he remembered there was something unusual: the receiver was far more sensitive than was needed for blind landing. Jones immediately told

---

17 Larson, p. 157
18 Ruane, 'The Professor and the Prime Minister – Frederick Lindemann and Winston Churchill,' *Finest Hour*, No. 195 First Quarter 2022, p. 14 and Footnote 2

BOMBER COMMAND

Lord Cherwell. It was Thursday, 13 June 1940, less than a month before the Battle of Britain began. This meant, if the Luftwaffe recognized and harnessed this new technology, it could potentially put an aircraft within 400 yards (366 m.) of a target. That would be 'a startling degree of accuracy'.[19]

Cherwell immediately told Churchill, who instantly recognized the significance. He ordered the Air Ministry to investigate. That resulted in Cherwell and Jones meeting with Air Ministry officials on Sunday 16 June. These Ministry officials were doubtful, indeed sceptical, but Cherwell was convinced, so Churchill issued a directive that this research proceed, and take precedence in materials and men.[20] Also on 16 June 1940 French Prime Minister Paul Renaud resigned, and was replaced by Marshal Phillipe Pétain, who immediately asked Hitler to cease hostilities, and make known his peace terms. France had fallen. Britain, the sovereign Dominions and Britain's Empire now stood alone against evil in Europe.

On Friday 21 June 1940 Jones found himself at 10 Downing Street. If the Luftwaffe was indeed being guided by a new navigational system, the British needed counter-technology immediately. Mistakenly thinking the meeting was a prank, Jones arrived a half hour late. A dozen men, including scientists and RAF brass, were seated, with Churchill between Lords Cherwell and Beaverbrook. Jones sat at the end of the long table, in a no man's land between his RAF colleagues on one side and his patron Lord Cherwell on the other. It was obvious the two sides were divided. When Churchill directed a question at Jones to clarify a detail, instead of answering, Jones asked whether it would help if he told his story from the start. He then told it as a detective story. Hearing from Jones that the Luftwaffe could now possibly bomb accurately in moonless overcast nights was for Churchill 'one of the blackest moments of the war'. Worse, British air intelligence believed the RAF was vastly outnumbered by the Luftwaffe. They were right about that.

What do we do, Churchill asked? Jones, as I mentioned aged 28, replied, use aircraft to determine whether the beams exist; then fly among them to learn their characteristics so Britain could devise counter-measures, including jamming the beams and transmitting false signals to trick the Germans into dropping their bombs too early or flying the wrong course. Churchill ordered the search for these beams to commence immediately. An aircraft was in the air that very evening with instructions to search for transmissions like those generated by a Lorenz blind-landing system. Jones wondered whether he would be proven wrong, and then disgraced in front of the most powerful men in Britain.

The answer came the next day, Saturday 22 June 1940. The pilot attended that meeting in person to advise that yes, they found the beams. Best of all for Jones, the flight also detected a second beam on a different frequency which would necessarily intersect the first shortly before the target, thereby giving the Germans time to drop their bombs. Now counter-measures were essential. The code name for the search was 'Headache'. The counter-measures were called 'Aspirin'. Work was

---

19 Larson, p. 74.
20 Larson, p. 87

to begin immediately but, giddy with relief he was right, and not disgraced, Jones and a colleague walked across to Whitehall's St Stephen's Tavern where I have dined with my sons. It's a hundred yards from the Elizabeth Tower wherein sits Big Ben. There he got drunk.[21] In a lecture to the Royal United Services Institute (RUSI) on 19 February 1949, Jones said identifying and defeating German bomber navigational beams was 'the best fun I ever had'.[22] Jones also said Churchill 'alone among politicians, valued science and technology at something approaching their true worth'.[23]

1942 – The End of the Beginning

For the Allies 1942 was, in Churchill's words on 10 November 1942, 'The end of the beginning' in that it was the final year in which the Allies were on the defensive. Terrible 1942 began the previous December with Pearl Harbor on 7 December 1941, and the Hong Kong surrender on 25 December with 14,000 soldiers including Canada's Winnipeg Grenadiers, the Royal Rifles of Canada from Quebec and the Royal Canadian Army Medical Corps. Then 1942 started with the disastrous Singapore surrender on 15 February of 82,000 Allied soldiers to 36,000 Japanese soldiers. This was followed by the Philippines and Battle of Bataan surrender on 9 April with 76,000 soldiers forced into Japan's Bataan Death March. Tobruk in Libya came next on 21 June 1942 with the surrender of 33,000 Allied soldiers to the Italo-German Panzerarmee Afrika. But then the tide of war finally swung towards the Allies, especially with America's Pacific victory at Midway on 4 June and Montgomery's African victory at El Alamein in Egypt on 11 November 1942. On 10 November Churchill said this was the end of the beginning.

In the air war, changes in 1942 were for the worse in the Luftwaffe, and for the better in the RAF. In Germany, Göring's reputation as the undisputed heir apparent to Hitler began its downward slide, compliments of Bomber Command. But Britain entered 1942 with good news. The German Research Institute for Military History says the arrival in 1942 of the Lancaster, the usefulness by then of the Mosquito, Bomber Command's development in 1942 of navigational aids and the creation in 1942 of the Pathfinders were all pivotal to the Allies winning control of the air.[24] Best of all, on 22 February Churchill made Harris Bomber Command's new, and as it happens, incredibly effective Air Officer Commanding-in-Chief (AOCinC) for the remainder of the war. Germany had no equivalent, except indirectly Albert Speer. On 8 February 1942 Speer became the Reich's Armaments and Munitions

---

21 Larson, pp. 94-101

22 Nahum, p. 9 and Footnote 4

23 Ruane, p. 14 and Footnote 3

24 Institute, Vol. VI, p. 562 Volumes of Militargeschichtliches Forschungsamt (Research Institute for Military History) Freiburg im Breisgau, Germany, were translated into English by Clarendon Press, Oxford, commencing in 1991

Minister, just as Churchill had been for Britain when the Royal Air Force was created on 1 April 1918. But Speer's personal quest to become heir apparent created conflict with Göring. Their other competitor colleagues included Himmler, Goebbels and Bormann. This power struggle contributed to Speer not supporting the Luftwaffe in several critically important situations. In short, in 1942 Göring falling and Speer wavering while Harris is accomplishing miracles with Churchill's firm support and encouragement gave the Royal Air Force an enormous advantage over the Luftwaffe.

January 1943: One Air Force Becomes Three

In 1943 the Luftwaffe situation worsened. From 1939 to 1942, the Defence of the Reich over Germany was the Luftwaffe versus the RAF. In January 1943 two more air forces bombed Germany – Canada on 23 January and America on 27 January. Although the British still selected the targets, and did that well,[25] the RCAF in No. 6 Group commenced fighting as a separate air force with its own Canadian command structure. The United States created the US Army Eighth Air Force bomber force in Britain, known until the end of February 1944 as VIII Bomber Command. To avoid confusion, I refer to it by its famous nickname, 'The Mighty Eighth'.[26] Fighting three air forces was for the Luftwaffe far different than just fighting the RAF because Americans, Canadians and the British have different ways of fighting. The Luftwaffe was forced to deal with these differences, something it failed to do well. Neither America nor Canada was anywhere near up to speed until towards the end of 1943, but by 1944 both air forces were in full swing with the RAF. That is when the Allied 'strategic bombing offensive' inflicted serious damage from which Germany could not recover. It had become one of the most powerful and lethal weapons the world had ever seen.

Canada remained deeply involved in the RAF, with more Canadians including my Dad seconded by the RCAF to the RAF than flying in the RCAF, even though by 1944 the RCAF had grown to become the fourth largest air force in the world, and the RAAF fifth. The RAF steadily increased its Commonwealth, and especially Canadian, aircrews through the Plan training aircrew in Canada. But Canadian Prime Minister Mackenzie King pushed hard against considerable British resistance to have the RCAF fight as a separate entity. It is true that on 23 April 1941, 405 (Vancouver) Squadron RCAF became the RCAF's first bomber squadron[27] as one of the Dominion squadrons created under Article XV of the British Commonwealth Air Training Plan Agreement that Mackenzie King had insisted on in 1939. However, Article XV Dominion squadrons were virtually invisible in the RAF, so in 1942 Mackenzie King demanded and got a separate bomber group for the RCAF. Over stiff British

---

25 Parker, *Saddles & Service*

26 *The Bombing of Germany Air War From 1939 – 1945* American Experience Public Broadcasting Service USA www.pbs.org/wgbh/americanexperience/features/bombing-air-war-1939-1945/

27 Birrell, p. 31

AIR WAR

objections, No. 6 Group RCAF was formed on 25 October 1942. It was the first, and only, non-RAF group in Bomber Command. The RCAF spent the rest of 1942 organizing its bomber force. America, likewise, spent 1942 building its European strategic bombing capability, although it operated The Mighty Eighth in a limited fashion over France and the Low Countries.

The RCAF commenced 1943 with a pair of mine-laying sorties on 3 and 9 January in the Frisian Islands near the German Bight. Mine-laying was particularly dangerous. The RCAF evolved into being expert at it. On 14 January the RCAF joined the RAF in bombing the Lorient U-boat base. And then, on 23 January, the RCAF bombed Germany for the first time – Esens, about 20 miles (32 km) north of Wilhelmshaven.[28] Just four days later, on 27 January, The Mighty Eighth also bombed Germany for the first time – Wilhelmshaven.

What was the German perspective on the arrival of these Americans? The Luftwaffe war diaries[29] observe that, for the first time since the Battle of Britain two and a half years earlier, German defensive aircraft were forced back into daylight fighting instead of just being night fighters, but now against four-engine bombers. German fighters with sensitive equipment essential for night fighting in darkness were put out of action in daylight by heavily-armed American B-17 Flying Fortresses and B-24 Liberators. Germany could still replace lost aircraft, but was losing the ability to replace highly-qualified airmen expert at night fighting who were now being thrown into daylight battles. This forced the Luftwaffe to make significant changes in defensive tactics but it was not enough. By the end of 1943, the strategic bombing offensive had turned the tables. The tide of the air war now favoured the Allies.

RAF and RCAF Reflect their Prime Ministers

A significant factor leading to a separate RCAF bomber group and what it became was articulated by Dave Birrell:

> The Canadian government did not want its air force to be merely a source of manpower for the Royal Air Force nor its squadrons to be part of Royal Air Force groups. To accomplish this, 6 (RCAF) Group was formed on 25 October 1942, initially with eight squadrons. It was to begin operations on 1 January 1943. The Group would continue to be part of the RAF's Bomber Command but the squadrons would be getting their orders directly from the Canadian Bomber Group's headquarters. At the peak of its strength, 6 Group consisted of fourteen squadrons.[30]

---

28 Dunmore, pp. 19-29

29 Bekker, *The Luftwaffe War Diaries*, pp. 302-3

30 Birrell, p. 84

There continued, however, to be British confusion regarding Canadian status. For example, in 1943, just after 6 Group RCAF became operational, RAF Air Marshal Sir Bertine E. Sutton of the Air Ministry found it necessary to lecture his colleagues that Canada was an independent dominion, not a colony, and as such was entitled to its own air force in Britain. Some shrugged – dominion or colony, what's the difference? They had not reckoned on the steely determination of Mackenzie King that even Churchill could not override. By war's end, the difference was clear to everyone. The RAF and the RCAF had to work out how best to fight this war together while each respected the divergent views of their prime ministers. The result was Allied success at great cost to the Luftwaffe, but it was not always easy.

I discovered an early event that is generally unknown which had a profound impact on the relationship between the RAF and the RCAF. It is sometimes called the 'Canadian Revolt at Cranwell' or the 'Cranwell Mutiny'.[31] These air force details reveal much about the evolution of the complex, evolving, wartime relationship between Canada and Britain. In February 1941 RCAF aircrew were at the RAF's Cranwell College for 'vocabulary, technical, and procedures training'. These Canadian airmen reacted poorly to boot camp activities unrelated to their training, and especially to 'a self-important little flight sergeant' who had them standing on parade in a chilly winter downpour for no apparent reason. Worse, his accent was so strong they could not understand what he was yelling at them. So they abandoned him, and trudged through the rain back to their barracks. Running after them, 'Voice throbbing with outrage, he at last made himself understood,' calling them 'bloody Canadians', 'savages', and, even worse, 'colonials'. He ordered them all to scrub the privy, and to wash and polish the floor. They ignored him. A succession of disciplinary corporals arrived. The Canadians laughed at them. Later, a routine march turned into a disaster, with Canadians breaking up into small groups and wandering away. Then came a major mistake. A British disciplinary corporal, furious with the smile on the face of a good-natured Canadian airman from Timagami, Ontario, grabbed him. That Canadian airman, 'still smiling, delivered a single, highly effective punch.'

The corporal lost interest in any further contact, and disappeared. The Canadians strolled back to their barracks, threw every stick of furniture onto a pile, and burned the lot. The situation rapidly deteriorated. An RAF air vice-marshal, whom I will not name, rushed from the Air Ministry to Cranwell. He called a parade where, wagging his finger at them, he told the Canadians that the RAF knew how to handle 'mutineers'. He referred to the Canadians as 'mutinous colonials'. That did it. The Canadians again broke ranks, abandoned the air vice-marshal, convened a meeting, and sent two of their members AWOL to London. They returned with an RCAF squadron leader despatched personally by Canadian High Commissioner Vincent Massey. On 18 February 1952 Massey became the first Canadian Governor

---

31 *Reap the Whirlwind*, pp. 154-8

AIR WAR

General of Canada. With the arrival of Massey's squadron leader, the 'Canadian Revolt at Cranwell' was quickly resolved through agreement that Canadians were to have their own organization, commanded by the RCAF rather than the RAF, and even Canadians who like my Dad were seconded to the RAF, were still to be treated by the RAF as RCAF airmen. Bottom line? The Royal Canadian Air Force was in Britain to help, but not to serve, the British.

Australia's Don Charlwood, flying out of RAF Elsham Wolds, has what for me is a sequel to this story. It happened in autumn 1942 when RAF Squadron Leader Fox was speaking to new aircrew, Don being among them. As Don tells it, 'Fox sat casually on the table and said 'I would like to have a yarn with you chaps who have just come to the squadron. I see that most of you are from Australia and one or two from Canada. I know that ideas of – uh – discipline are not quite the same in the colonies.' Beside me Geoff was on his feet. 'Excuse me sir, we come from the Dominions!' Fox looked at him disconcertedly. 'I – Yes, I had forgotten. You chaps do prefer the term 'Dominions', don't you.'[32] 'Geoff' was Geoff Maddern, Don's Australian pilot in Bomber Command.

Another example. On 20 April 1943, 405 (Vancouver) Squadron RCAF, the only RCAF Squadron in No. 8 Group Pathfinders, arrived at its new No. 8 Group station, RAF Gransden Lodge. This it shared with 8 Group's Navigational Training Unit (NTU), making it convenient for training. RCAF Wing Commander Facquier of 405 (Vancouver) Squadron soon found his Squadron in conflict with the RAF station commander on rules and regulations. To settle matters, Facquier told the station commander, 'This is my squadron. We are a Canadian squadron. We are here to help you. My rules are not yours. You look after your babies and I'll look after mine.'

Battle of the Ruhr

In the early days of the war, Germany quite rightly recognized that the RAF was unable to conduct effective bombing because it had neither the aircraft nor the bombs it needed.[33] But the Institute recognizes that as the war progressed the RAF succeeded in creating both a powerful bomber fleet and much more accurate navigation and target-finding. That brings us to the Ruhr, which the Institute refers to as the 'Vulcan's Forge' of the Reich for building tanks, artillery, U-boats and air armaments, and mining coal needed to produce Germany's steel.[34] The Battle of the Ruhr commenced on 5 March 1943 with Bomber Command bombing Essen. It ran from 5 March to 31 July 1943. The Allied aircrew nickname for the heavily defended Ruhr was 'Happy Valley'. Targets included Barmen, Bochum, Cologne,

---

32 Charlwood, *No Moon Tonight*, p. 60.
33 Institute, Vol. IX, Part 1, p. 377
34 Institute, Vol. IX, Part 1, pp. 379-80

BOMBER COMMAND

Dortmund, Duisburg, Dusseldorf, Elberfeld, Essen, Gelsenkirchen, Hamborn, Huls, Krefeld, Mulheim, Oberhausen, Remscheid, Ruhr and Wuppertal. To prevent Germany from concentrating defences in the Ruhr Valley, during the course of the battle of the Ruhr Bomber Command also bombed Aachen, Berlin, Frankfurt, Friedrichshafen, Hamburg, Kiel, Munich, Munster, Nuremberg, Pilsen, Stettin (now Szczecin) and Stuttgart.

On 8 May 1943 Hitler told Field Marshal Milch, the successor to Luftwaffe *Generaloberst* (Colonel General) Ernst Udet as chief of procurement and supply, that either the Luftwaffe's tactics or technology was lacking. Goebbels that day blamed Göring and Udet. Göring had also tried to blame Udet for losing the Battle of Britain. Torn between loyalty and truth, and being forced by Göring to lie to Hitler, as well as realizing the Russian invasion would end in catastrophe for Germany, but failing to convince Hitler of this, Udet had a nervous breakdown. On 17 November 1941, while on the phone with his girlfriend, Udet committed suicide by shooting himself in the head. The Nazis kept his suicide secret and lauded him as a hero at his funeral, even burying him beside Manfred von Richthofen, the First World War fighter pilot ace best known as the 'Red Baron' who, at age 25, was killed on my Dad's sixth birthday, 21 April 1918. After meeting Hitler on 8 May 1943, Goebbels wrote 'The technical failure of the Luftwaffe results mainly from useless aircraft designs. It is here that Udet bears the fullest measure of blame.'[35]

Tooze[36] says Bomber Command severely disrupted German production, and its impact was underestimated in later accounts. The Ruhr was Europe's most important source of coking coal and steel, and the main source of components. Bombing the Ruhr disrupted production all over Germany, and even forced a large cut in ammunition production. Tooze concludes that in the Ruhr 'Bomber Command had stopped Speer's armaments miracle in its tracks'. In spite of losing 640 bombers and most of their crews, Bomber Command increased in size between February and August 1943 due to increased output of British aircraft.[37]

The Institute says the Ruhr Battle created for the first time in the war a serious threat to Germany's economy. The massive destruction inflicted by bombing the Ruhr forced Germany to find more raw materials and use increasing numbers of 'foreign workers'[38] most of whom were slaves. A highlight of the Ruhr battle was the Dambusters' spectacular Operation CHASTISE on 16/17 May 1943 breaching German dams. The Institute says their bombing created serious water shortages that prevented Germans from adequately fighting the many large fires that broke

---

35 Cooper, p. 62
36 Tooze, *The Wages of Destruction – the Making and Breaking of the Nazi Economy*, Penguin, London, 2006, pp. 59-598 and 602
37 Wikipedia, Battle of the Ruhr
38 Institute, Vol. IX, Part 1, pp. 383-4

out.[39] Albert Speer immediately visited the Ruhr to survey the damage. In his judgement it could jeopardize Germany's whole economic structure, so in August 1943 the 'Ruhr Staff' was created, answering directly to Speer.[40]

Battle of Hamburg[41]

The Institute calls the battle of Hamburg 'the turning point in the air war'. From 25 July until 3 August 1943, Bomber Command and The Mighty Eighth bombed out 900,000 from their homes, totally destroyed 35,000 buildings, and rendered 43 per cent of Hamburg's dwellings uninhabitable. In August 1943 the SD (Security Service of the *Reichsführer*-SS) named the ever-escalating air war as one of Germany's strongest causes of stress. The SD said the bombing of Hamburg, Hanover, Remscheid, Kassel and Heligoland created 'air-raid terror psychosis'. The Institute reports that bombing Hamburg created a 'bomb-site society' in which daily life collapsed. Massive drops of leaflets by the Allies warned of further escalation of the air war. This generated fear in Berliners that they, too, would be bombed that way. When, in August 1943, Goebbels organized the evacuation of women and children from Berlin, the SD monitored a 'mood akin to panic'. Bombing rumours even included lime pits being dug for victims' corpses.

The Hamburg bombings demonstrated to everyone how powerful the strategic bomber offensive of Bomber Command and the Mighty Eighth had become.

Battle of Berlin

Postwar critics question whether Bomber Command's 18 November 1943 to 25 March 1944 Battle of Berlin accomplished much, given the horrendous cost in aircrew killed and aircraft lost fighting it. Berlin is a long way from Lincolnshire. For aircrew, the ten-hour flights combined misery, given how freezing cold Lancasters were, with terror, given having to fly such a vast distance over Nazi-controlled territory gave Germans many opportunities to kill them. However, the Institute reveals the overwhelming importance of Berlin as a target politically, militarily and economically. One can see below from the Institute's information that Berlin was by far the most important target in Nazi Germany. I had erroneously assumed Berlin was essentially a prestige target because it was Germany's capital city. The Institute certainly set me straight on that. When commenting on the Battle

---

39 Institute, Vol. IX, Part 1, p. 381

40 Institute, Vol. IX, Part 1, p. 384

41 Institute, Vol. IX, Part 1, pp. 385-7

of Berlin, the Institute gives the following fifteen reasons why Berlin was the key primary target:[42]

1. Berlin was Germany's seat of power and administrative centre
2. Berlin was also an important industrial centre
3. Berlin had by the end of 1940, the Wehrmacht estimated, 1.27 million workers employed in the city in 276,000 firms
4. Berlin accounted for 14 per cent of the German economy's total turnover
5. Berlin had 57.5 per cent of the manufacturing capacity of the German electronics industry
6. Berlin had a 'sizeable production' of machinery and vehicles, as well as chemicals
7. Berlin produced 95 per cent of all radio sets
8. Berlin produced 75 per cent of all telephones
9. Berlin produced 60 per cent of all field cable
10. Berlin produced 50 per cent of all aero-engines
11. Berlin produced 30 per cent of all airframes
12. Berlin produced 70 per cent of all torpedoes
13. Berlin (including environs) produced all electric U-boat motors
14. Berlin produced more than one quarter of all tanks (but not Panthers or Tigers)
15. Berlin produced half of all German field artillery

From the foregoing, it is obvious why Berlin had to be bombed repeatedly, given how quickly thousands of workers scrambled to repair bomb damage. But why did Bomber Command sustain such horrific losses of aircrew and aircraft? Those losses arose from Berlin's distant location, and Berlin being by far Germany's most heavily-defended city. The Institute says that, by January 1944, Berlin was defended by 104 heavy flak batteries, around twenty-five medium and light batteries, and thirty-five searchlight batteries. No other city in Germany was protected by such extensive anti-aircraft defences.[43] In addition, the Institute describes how difficult Berlin's location made bombing it. The round trip from Britain was over 1,100 miles (1,800 km). This enormous distance meant bombers were exposed to German night-fighter attacks for far longer than when raiding Hamburg or the Ruhr. Also, German night fighters and flak were concentrated along approach paths to Berlin.

The Mighty Eighth

In this air war, I encountered two surprises: the RCAF in Bomber Command was more independent than I had assumed, and the Mighty Eighth was closer to Bomber Command than I had assumed. Americans bombing by day, while the RAF and

---

42 Institute, Vol. VII, p. 89
43 Institute, Vol. VII, p. 89

AIR WAR

RCAF largely bombed by night, was one reason I erroneously assumed the Mighty Eighth operated separately. But now I discover his American counterpart General Ira Eaker saying about Harris 'For nearly two years I had daily conferences with him, concerning features of our joint bombing effort, targets, weather, results of the previous day's attacks, etc.'[44] Daily conferences? Our joint bombing effort? These are powerful words. The more I researched, the closer the Americans became. There was, Harris said, no 'relationship' between Bomber Command and the Mighty Eighth because 'we were one'.[45]

In December 1942 Eaker assumed command of the Mighty Eighth in England, and then became commander of all US Army Air Forces in the United Kingdom.[46] On 1 July 1943 General Fred Anderson was promoted to command the Mighty Eighth under General Eaker as commander of the US Army Eighth Air Force.[47] In December 1943, FDR decided Eisenhower – not Marshall – would be Supreme Allied Commander in Europe.[48] Over RAF Air Chief Marshal Peter Portal's objections, Eisenhower made Eaker Air Commander-in-Chief of the Mediterranean Allied Air Forces. Portal wanted to keep Eaker in Britain. On 6 January 1944, General Anderson left the Mighty Eighth to serve as Deputy Commander of Operations, giving him the job of co-ordinating America's two bomber forces – one in Italy and the Mighty Eighth in Britain. That same day, General Jimmy Doolittle became America's Harris counterpart as commander of the Mighty Eighth until September 1945. He had big shoes to fill. When Doolittle had his audience with King George VI on 4 February 1944, the King echoed Portal by saying 'We're certainly sorry to lose Eaker.'[49] On 13 March 1944, Doolittle was promoted to lieutenant general, the highest rank held by an active reserve officer in modern times.

Doolittle, of course, had already won worldwide fame on 18 April 1942 for leading the 'Doolittle Raid' by sixteen B-25 Mitchell Bombers from the aircraft carrier USS *Hornet* to bomb Japan, including Tokyo. They also bombed Kobe, Nagoya, Osaka and Yokohama on their one-way trip. It was America's first bombing of the Japanese archipelago. They did not have enough fuel to return so, after the bombings, they baled out over China. Doolittle parachuted into a rice *padi*. 'Chinese soldiers and guerrillas scoured the countryside and rescued 69 of the Raiders from thousands of Japanese soldiers, also looking for them .... The Chinese people paid dearly for helping the Americans to safety – the Japanese army destroyed many villages and murdered up to 250,000 Chinese.'[50]

---

44 Eaker's Foreword in Peden, *A Thousand Shall Fall*, p. x
45 *From the Horse's Mouth*
46 US Air Force General Ira C. Eaker/Air Force/ Biography af.mil
47 History of War www.historyofwar.org Major General Frederick Anderson 1905 -1969
48 Wikipedia Dwight D. Eisenhower
49 Air University Press (2015*) Leading The Mighty Eighth* – Jimmy Doolittle, pp. 80-1
50 Kane, 'The Doolittle Raid – 75 Years Later', *Air & Space Power Journal* www.airpower.au.af.mil p 76

BOMBER COMMAND

In Europe, Doolittle changed the policy of fighter escorts having to remain with their bombers at all times, and instead allowed them to fly far ahead to flush out and destroy German fighters lying in wait for the bombers. After the bombers bombed their targets, the fighters were free to strafe German airfields and other 'targets of opportunity'.[51] Doolittle also helped develop and flight-test instrument flying. However, Doolittle had significant morale problems, and so wanted to alleviate Operation CROSSBOW demands so that his bombers would only strike targets confirmed by aerial reconnaissance. Harris supported him. This persuaded British authorities to endorse a plan allowing the Mighty Eighth to strike oil depots rather than German V1 launch facilities. This helped raise the Mighty Eighth's morale.[52]

Bombs may have been part of the Mighty Eighth's 1944 morale problem. Barnes Wallis developed Tallboy and Grand Slam bombs for Bomber Command. They were the only bombs so powerful that they could penetrate the ever-deepening concrete bunkers and underground factories that Hitler felt forced to build to withstand the Allied strategic bomber offensive, including heavily concrete-encased U-boat pens and Germany's biggest canals. Tallboys even sank Germany's mighty battleship *Tirpitz*. The Mighty Eighth had no comparable bombs, and no aircraft that could lift these RAF bombs – only Lancasters could.

To compensate, America undertook Operation APHRODITE in which, loaded with explosives without aircrew, Army Air Forces B-17 Flying Fortresses and Navy PB4Y-1s (Liberators) would be deliberately crashed into their targets by radio controls. The problem was these 'drones' could not take off safely on their own. Instead, they needed a crew of two to take off and reach an altitude of 2,000 feet, at which point the crew would activate the remote-control system, aim the detonators, and parachute from the aircraft. The US Navy portion of this project was called Operation ANVIL. Lieutenants Wilford John Willy and Joseph P. Kennedy Jr were designated as the US Navy's first ANVIL flight crew. Kennedy was JFK's older brother. On 12 August 1944, they took off in their explosive-laden converted PB4Y-1 Liberator. The intended targets were U-boat Pens at Heliogoland in the North Sea. At 2,000 feet, near the North Sea coast, Kennedy and Willy removed the safety pin, arming the explosives. Two minutes later, and well before the planned crew bale-out, the explosives detonated prematurely, destroying the Liberator, and killing Kennedy and Willy. Kennedy had already completed twenty-five combat missions, and so had been eligible to return home when he instead volunteered for Operation ANVIL. The US Navy paused ANVIL, examined what happened, then terminated any further missions.[53] This failed experiment reveals how badly America wanted bombing power equivalent to Bomber Command's Lancasters with Tallboys and Grand Slams.

In any event, regarding Bomber Command and the Mighty Eighth, Harris sums up saying 'We could have had no better brothers-in-arms than Ira Eaker,

---

51 Wikipedia Jimmy Doolittle

52 Air University Press, p. 84; Craven & Cate, *Europe: Argument to VE Day*, pp. 529-30.

53 Wikipedia, Joseph P. Kennedy Jr.

AIR WAR

Fred Anderson and Jimmy Doolittle, and the Americans could have had no better commanders than these three. I was, and am, privileged to count all three of them as the closest of friends.'[54]

Bombing Devastated the Third Reich

In the final year of the war, our strategic bombing offensive was at last operating in full strength. As a result, the Institute reports:

> Very often there were well over 2,000 Allied aircraft operating over Germany, heading for several targets at once. Strategic raids by four-engined long-range bombers alternated with tactical missions by twin-engined machines and fighter-bombers ... . Besides the physical and mental strain from the almost constant attack from the air, the public was beset with further difficulties (arising in part from Goebbels' Total War Measures).[55]

Under the heading 'Air Raids, Every Day, Every Night', the Institute has several pages of interesting commentary, commencing with:

> In the closing phase of the war the Allied air forces concentrated on individual regions and operational hotspots. Between October and December 1944, RAF Bomber Command undertook a second battle of the Ruhr .... In the last two months of 1944 the strategic bomber fleets launched an air offensive against railway traffic and inland shipping in northern, western, and southern Germany .... In Essen the famous Krupp works lay largely silent after a 'double whammy' by more than 1,800 RAF bombers on 23/24 and 25 October ... . After a 'fan-pattern raid' by more than 220 aircraft of 6 Bomber Group [Royal Canadian Air Force] on Braunschweig in the evening of 15 October 1944... over 80,000 were bombed out and on the street ... . In 1944/5 the air war held almost all regions of the Reich in its grasp, especially those in the west, and in its effects can be often likened only to great national disasters.[56]

Turning to the Luftwaffe's fighter aircraft, while the night fighters were more effective against British and Canadian bombers than the day fighters against America, this situation steadily worsened for Germany at night too. There were individual German successes, such as destroying ninety-five of our bombers on 30/31 March

---

54 Harris, *Bomber Offensive*, p. 246
55 Institute, Vol. IX, Part 1, pp. 458-9
56 Institute, Vol. IX, Part 1, pp. 459-61

1944 at Nuremberg, but the Institute says such successes were becoming the exception. Between December 1943 and May 1944, German night fighters lost 407 aircraft and 556 aircrew while destroying 1,100 British and Canadian bombers. German aircrews had been highly skilled but their replacements – lacking flying hours and training – were no longer up to the same standard.[57]

After Bomber Command's Nuremberg loss, the RAF's next large-scale, 1,000-plus bomber raids against German cities were not until 22/23 April 1944 against Dusseldorf and 24/25 April against Karlsruhe. Both attacked Germany's transport network.[58] My Dad piloted his 166 Squadron Lancaster on both of these sorties, and Friedrichshafen (tank-engine gears) on 27/28 April 1944 as well.

In addition, the Institute says Bomber Command's night navigation kept improving in spring 1944, as did its tactics and techniques. For example, in poor visibility, and in strong winds, 'blind marking' using H2S navigation repeatedly set sky marks. In addition, increasing numbers of Allied bombers were equipped with H2S radar so that they could do their own navigation. And, to confuse Germany regarding targets, Bomber Command routed far out over the North Sea and Jutland. This avoided night fighters' areas of operation, and left Germany unsure of the actual intended target,[59] thereby forcing Germany to be ready to simultaneously defend against multiple possible targets every night.

Bomber Command grew steadily more effective at creating counter-measures to defeat the Luftwaffe. For example, Paul tells me the Luftwaffe had '*Schrage Musik*' (Jazz), an upward firing cannon which enabled night fighters to creep under our bombers where they could not be seen by our gunners. As soon as Bomber Command realized its bombers were being blown up without warning, H2S was modified in only three weeks to search the sky below the bomber. That is only a matter of weeks to assess the situation, have scientists improve our radar and install the improvement into our bomber fleet. Bomber Command embraced improvements with breathtaking speed. As Eisenhower wrote to General George Marshall, Bomber Command was 'always seeking and finding and using new ways for their particular type of aircraft to be of assistance'.[60]

As for a German perspective, I will yet again quote Adolf Galland. As *General der Jagdflieger* Galland said:

> The combination of the Pathfinders' operations, the activities of No. 100 Group, the British advantage in radar, jamming and Window techniques, combined with intelligent attacking tactics, as well as the discipline and bravery of the RAF crews, have been remarkable. We had our severe problems in trying to defend Germany in the air.[61]

---

57 Institute, Vol. VII, p. 306
58 Institute, Vol. VII, p. 306
59 Institute, Vol. VII, p. 309
60 Cooper, *Target-Dresden* p. ?
61 Iveson & Milton, *Lancaster – the Biography*, Andre Deutsch, 2009, p. 122

AIR WAR

Strategic Bombing Offensive and Defence of the Reich Statistics

For Germany's defence of the Reich Campaign, Allied belligerents are listed as 'United Kingdom, United States, Canada and other Allies'. Germany, like FDR's America, consistently saw Canada as a separate power with formidable and effective armed forces, a sovereign nation separate from Britain. The defence of the Reich lists as casualties 79,281 RAF Bomber Command personnel and 79,265 American airmen. I was astonished to see that these RAF/RCAF and American casualty numbers are virtually identical – only differing by sixteen airmen.[62]

The defence of the Reich, however, cost Germany dearly.[63] In addition to Luftwaffe airmen diverted to this defensive fight, by mid-1944 Germany had over a million – 1,110,900 to be precise – personnel pinned down manning:

- 2,655 heavy flak batteries
- 10,930 88mm flak guns
- 4,157 105mm & 128mm flak guns and
- 1,612 light flak gun batteries having 30,463 flak guns.

Also, our strategic bombing offensive forced Germany to divert its essential 88mm anti-tank, anti-aircraft guns from destroying Soviet tanks to defending German cities. All this German firepower fighting our bombers[64] forced Germany to produce 160 million rounds of ammunition for shooting down our aircraft instead of blowing up Soviet tanks. This firepower was sorely missed by the German army on all three fronts. The Institute says the Luftwaffe lost 57,405 aircraft in its failed defence of the Reich[65] while Bomber Command lost about 22,000 and the Mighty Eighth lost about 18,000 aircraft. This air war was unique, never having happened before and never happening again. It was one of the most fiercely-fought battles ever. In it our Bomber Boys did us proud.

The Institute states that, in 1944, our strategic bombing offensive was catastrophic for Germany. The Institute's numbers speak for themselves. In the first five months of 1944, we made 223,796 sorties, as compared to 31,672 sorties in the first five months of 1943. In addition, in 1944 Bomber Command had more technically advanced heavy bomber aircraft than in 1943. Bomb tonnage tells the same story. In the first five months of 1943, 86,806 tons of bombs were dropped. In the first five months of 1944, 433,733 tons of bombs were dropped, and they were

---

62 Defence of the Reich, Wikipedia
63 Brookes, 'An Interview With 'Bomber' Harris 08 September 1975', *Royal Air Force Historical Society Journal* 74, 2020, p. 58
64 Defence of the Reich, Wikipedia
65 *US Strategic Bombing Survey Statistical Appendix to Overall Report* (European War) Feb 1947, Table 1, p. X

dropped considerably more accurately.[66] The Institute lists the following statistics for the spring of 1944:

- 13,197 tons of bombs fell on German aircraft factories
- 8,970 tons of bombs fell on German airfields
- 2,500 tons of bombs fell on fuel-producing plants
- 11,826 tons of bombs fell on railways in April and May, and that this 'came as a shock' to Germany
- 91,084 tons of bombs fell on industrial areas, almost double that dropped in the same period in 1943.

The Institute reports that the quantity of bombs the strategic bombing offensive dropped on target groups in France between January and May 1944 is significant: 20,468 tons were dropped on airfields, 48,732 tons on the transport network, 14,100 tons on VI launch sites, and in February and March more than 2,500 tons on aircraft factories.[67] Statistics never tell the full story. I'm reminded that Mark Twain said 'There are lies, damned lies, and statistics' which he attributed to British Prime Minister Benjamin Disraeli. But they lead me to wonder what sorts of things happened on combat sorties, especially with human error among leaders.

Here's an example. One of iconic American actor Jimmy Stewart's strategic bombing offensive stories, as David Crow tells it,[68] is that on 7 January 1944 as a captain he was wing lead of the 445th bombing Ludwigshafen in Germany. As the oldest man in the air at age 35, and with his crystal-clear enunciation, he was a natural leader. On combat missions, Stewart would command as many as 150 bombers. After the bombs were dropped, the 389th, the lead bombing group that day, took a wrong turn en route back to England, having ignored Stewart's radio communication about their error. The error took them over Nazi-controlled Paris. Stewart made the decision to follow the 389th to Paris. That enabled them to keep tight formation, thus avoiding the chaos and isolation of separation in the sky. As Luftwaffe fighters rose from Paris to destroy them, they were saved by their tight formation coupled with American Thunderbolts and British Spitfires racing to their rescue. For his level-headed leadership that day, Stewart was promoted to major.

Paul Johnson says 'The losses in bombers and aircrews were heavy because of Hitler's concentration of fighter squadrons and air defences to defend his cities. On the other hand, without the British bombing these assets would otherwise have gone to the Eastern Front. As a result the Germans lost the war there. By mid-1943, their air superiority had disappeared, and this was a key factor in their losing the ground war too. These facts tend to be forgotten by those who assert that it

---

66 Institute, Vol. VII, pp. 291-2
67 Institute, Vol. VII, p. 292
68 Crow, *Jimmy Stewart and the WW2 Mission That Almost Broke Him*, Den of Geek, 21 March 2021 www:denofgeek.com/movies/jimmy-stewart-ww2-mission-air-force/

AIR WAR

was Russia which really defeated Nazi Germany. Without Churchill's bombing campaign, the Eastern Front would have become a stalemate."[69]

John Martin, a Lancaster wireless operator, was assigned to my Dad's 166 Squadron in January 1944. Martin and my Dad could not have met there because Dad did not join 166 Squadron until April 1944. On his third combat sortie as a 21-year-old, Martin was trapped in a burning Lancaster from which, miraculously, he was thrown. He survived to spend the remainder of the war as a PoW and thereafter write of his experiences. Regarding Germany's air war flying bomb and rocket attacks, Martin says:

> I fully understood what people who had suffered flying bomb and rocket attacks in London meant when they said of the two terrorizing weapons, they would rather have the rockets, even if they were more devastating, because of the terrible nerve-racking seconds between the engine of the flying bomb cutting out, and the explosion upon landing. They had seconds, which would have seemed like an age, to see who was going to get it.[70]

My Dad's thirty-four combat sorties with 166 Squadron included bombing both rocket and flying-bomb bases in German-controlled Europe.

April 1944 was huge for the strategic bombing offensive because Eisenhower, through his Deputy Supreme Commander of SHAEF, RAF Air Marshal Arthur Tedder, took direct control. It was also huge for me, because my Dad flew the first eight of his thirty-four combat sorties that month. Concerning April 1944, Harris said:

> control of the strategic bombing that month had been handed over to Eisenhower for the purpose of making things ready for the invasion. And a vast amount of bombing was done on that score, knocking out the French railways and a still greater amount was done knocking out the flying bombs release platforms and the two sites at Mimoyecques where the Germans were preparing for the V3 long-range guns and also flattening places like the mushroom-growing caves which were the largest of the underground V1 storage sites.[71]

And so, as will be seen in my chapters which follow, at horrific cost in aircrew killed and aircraft lost, our strategic bombing offensive prevailed over Germany's defence of the Reich Campaign. For Germany this was catastrophic, and Hitler knew it, as revealed by his words at the beginning of this chapter.

---

69 Johnson, *Churchill*, p. 133
70 Martin, *A Raid Over Berlin*, p. 118
71 Brookes, p. 62

Chapter Nineteen

Sea War

> For much of the first four years of the war,
> support for the naval war comprised a significant
> portion of the Command's overall effort
>
> David Bashow[1]

What focused me on Bomber Command's sea war was the invitation of the Naval Officers' Association of BC, of which I am a member, to make a presentation about Bomber Command on 25 September 2019. I had not associated Bomber Command with doing much at sea. My research amazed me. I was astonished to discover just how much Bomber Command contributed to winning the sea war.

Churchill's Perspective

In his Victory speech praising the armed forces at the end of the Second World War, Churchill not only omitted reference to Bomber Command, he also omitted reference to the Royal Canadian Navy, instead saying the Royal Navy won the Battle of the Atlantic even though Canada had the world's third largest navy and played an enormous role. Yet, regarding Bomber Command, at Churchill College, Cambridge, on 22 May 2019, I discovered with Archives Director Allen Packwood a telegram Churchill sent to Harris for Bomber Command on 15 May 1945. This largely unknown document discloses Churchill's knowledge of Bomber Command's war at sea. In this telegram, Churchill said in part:

> Your Command also ... made a vital contribution to the war at sea. You destroyed or damaged many of the enemy's ships of war and much of his U-boat organization. By a prolonged series of mining operations you sank or damaged large quantities of his merchant shipping. All your operations were planned with great care and skill; they were executed in the face of desperate opposition and

---

1 Bashow, *No Prouder Place*, p. 459

appalling hazards; they made a decisive contribution to Germany's final defeat.[2]

Churchill's reference to Bomber Command destroying or damaging warships and U-boats, and the destruction of merchant shipping by such extensive mining (also called gardening) was impressive, and important. But I went on to discover that Bomber Command's victory in the sea war encompassed even more.

Luftwaffe and Kriegsmarine Conflicts

Even before the war began, there was competition and conflict between the Luftwaffe and the Kriegsmarine, Nazi Germany's navy. The Institute reveals three early bones of contention: the use of torpedoes, aerial reconnaissance to assist U-boats; and the mine war on the importance of which Admiral Raeder pressed Hitler.[3] However, the Kriegsmarine wanted to wait until sufficient mines and aircraft were available before mining Britain's west coast. Worse for Germany, on 26 February 1940, Hitler decided the Kreigsmarine should wait until the Luftwaffe too was prepared to start dropping mines. From 20 April until 10 May 1940, Germany's Luftflotte IX, planned specifically for mining, together with Germany's naval air forces west, dropped a mere 188 mines in six operations off the south-west coast of Britain and the French Channel coast, sinking only seven merchant ships totalling 14,564 gross registered tons.[4]

The attempted 27 January 1939 'Naval Protocol With the Luftwaffe' between Raeder and Göring for aerial reconnaissance did not work because naval aircraft did not have the range or sophistication to be of use to U-boats searching for convoys and 'The Luftwaffe was more interested in increasing its own sinkings of enemy ships than in flying reconnaissance for the commander of U-boats.'[5] Also, Göring wanted naval air forces to cease using aerial torpedoes while the Kriegsmarine considered torpedoes a weapon of sea war that only naval officers could use effectively.[6] The problem underlying all this was that Göring wanted to prevent creation of an independent naval air arm while Raeder wanted to ensure that the naval air arm was not further downgraded by an inadequate supply of aircraft or their tasks taken over by the Luftwaffe.[7]

---

2 CHAR 20/229, Churchill Archives Centre, Churchill College, Cambridge

3 Institute, Vol. II, p. 174

4 Institute, Vol. II, p. 175

5 Institute, Vol. II, p. 347

6 Institute, Vol. II, p. 348

7 Institute, Vol. II, p. 349

Mining

In the early years of the war, Bomber Command was weakened by the conflicting priorities of the British services. Paul Robinson tells me numerous Bomber Command squadrons in 1941 and 1942 were taken from Bomber Command to fight the U-boat threat. Even Harris was buffeted from all sides. One by one, Harris won these squadrons back, particularly after the value of mining had been established. The enormous difference between the RAF and the Luftwaffe was that, once Harris took control in 1942, Bomber Command was increasingly protected from these problems while the Luftwaffe was increasingly paralyzed by them. The resulting advantages to the Allies, and damage to the Axis, steadily increased as the war progressed.

My research revealed mining's huge contribution to victory in the sea war – 'mine-sweeping duties occupied at least 40 per cent of German naval personnel on a full-time basis.'[8] The major expensive effort by the Kriegsmarine during the war was trying to find and destroy the 30,000 tons of mines Bomber Command laid in every port used by Germany from the Baltic along the whole North Sea coast and south to the Bay of Biscay. That task was enormous. Bomber Command laid more than 22,000 mines in 1944 alone. Much of this was thanks to the Royal Canadian Air Force, using Wellingtons.

Mining was exceptionally dangerous because of the need for low-level flying. Flak was a major threat. In 1942, the RAF lost an aircraft for every thirty-four mines laid. By mid-1943, No. 6 Group RCAF was heavily involved because its two-engine Wellingtons, sometimes called Wellies or 'Wimpys', proved ideal for mining enemy waters. The RCAF became expert in sea-mining. In early 1944, two RCAF Wellington squadrons, 419 and 428, pioneered the use of a new sea-mine that could be dropped from far higher altitudes. These two RCAF squadrons became pathfinders on several mining operations when No. 8 Group Pathfinders were unable to provide aircraft. Paul Robinson tells me mining combat sorties did not use pathfinders unless it was difficult to find the start point of the mining run because a pathfinder would have alerted the defences. The mines dropped were non-contact. Instead, they lay at the bottom of the sea, to be activated by acoustic or magnetic waves. Battery-powered, their useful life was rated to be nine months.[9]

More good news. Those mines, coupled with bombing, virtually annihilated Germany's merchant marine fleet. Bomber Command sank or damaged a thousand ships. Many were ships on which Germany depended for the import of vital ores from Scandinavia. Bomber Command's mining of German-controlled ports yielded huge indirect benefits of pinning down forty German divisions, being one-third of the whole German army fighting the Red Army, that were uselessly holding from the Russians the eastern Baltic where the Kriegsmarine was hiding from Bomber Command. The loss of German control of that area would have paralyzed the German navy. Ironically, these forty German army aivisions in the eastern Baltic

---

8 Dunmore & Carter, *Reap the Whirlwind*, p. 250

9 Dunmore & Carter, pp. 251-2

area contributed virtually nothing to the final defence of the German homeland, and protection of U-boat operations in the eastern Baltic had by then become a moot point.[10]

Australian war correspondent Chester Wilmot sums this up beautifully by saying

> The history of the Second World War affords no more striking example of the interplay of naval, air and land power, or of the interrelation of the Eastern or Western Front, or, for that matter, of the grotesque miscalculations and wild hopes that governed Hitler's strategy. Because the German Air Force was unable to protect the U-boat bases and training waters in the western Baltic, the German Army was obliged to hold the eastern Baltic against the Russians so that the German Navy might build up a new U-boat fleet capable of inflicting a severe defeat on the Western Allies, and especially on the hated British, whose refusal to capitulate in 1940 had made inevitable that war on two fronts, which had already destroyed most of Hitler's empire and was in the process of destroying the Third Reich.[11]

U-boats

I was amazed to discover in preparing my 25 September 2019 naval officers presentation the damage Bomber Command inflicted on German U-boats (submarines). Speer, who Harris points out was responsible for the production of U-boats, says 'We would have kept our promised output of submarines for Admiral Dönitz' U-boat war if the bombers had not destroyed a third of them in the ports'. Harris adds, 'Now, in addition to the third that were destroyed in the ports, quite a number were destroyed by hitting mines. 30,000 tons of mines were dropped and quite a number of U-boats disappeared and sank without trace.'[12] What's more, the German admiral in charge of the training of U-boat crews in the Baltic wrote 'We can't operate U-boats without properly trained crews, and I can't properly train our U-boat crews if you can't keep the Bombers and their mines away from where we train.'

Men who constructed U-boat assembly plants said:

> If you had not bombed Bremen, Hamburg and Kiel, apart from other targets, we would have had so many U-boats that Admiral Dönitz's threat of throwing a ring of steel around the British Isles would have

---

10 Bashow, p. 472

11 Bashow, pp. 471-2; Wilmot, *The Struggle for Europe*, p. 620

12 Brookes, 'An Interview With 'Bomber' Harris 8 September 1975', *Royal Air Force Historical Society Journal* 74, 2020, pp. 57-8

been virtually possible, and we can assure you that your bombs saved the lives of thousands of seamen who would have been threatened by our rapidly progressing submarine production, which was hampered and eventually frustrated by your air force.

Hauptmann Zimmerman, chief air raid warden at the port of Bremen, said U-boat warfare was severely hampered through consistent bombing of the Bremen assembly plants and U-boat pens.[13] Harris said that the Royal Navy 'wanted to pinch all our Lancasters to go looking for haystacks all over the Atlantic – looking for needles in the haystacks', but we who set the pace, decided to instead get the submarines where they came from.'[14]

U-boats were one of Germany's most effective assets, wreaking havoc with Atlantic convoys supplying Britain with essentials. A Canadian admiral in the pulpit at a church parade I attended at a Royal Dutch Army Base in The Netherlands in May 2005 told us that, during the darkest days of the Battle of the Atlantic, German U-boats sank on average one of our ships every hour, twenty-four hours a day for over forty consecutive days. They had to be stopped. It turns out Bomber Command played a major role in stopping them. I at that time had no idea of this.

I now know Bomber Command used its biggest bombs to do even more damage to the U-boats; that's because, given the magnitude of Bomber Command destruction of German ports, Speer decided to construct U-boats in enormous sections inland. This, too, failed. Each section was so big that it could only be moved to ports via a pair of huge canals, the Middle Land and the Dortmund-Ems canals. Bomber Command bombed both, using their newest big bombs, Tallboys and Grand Slams which only Lancasters could carry. Only they were powerful enough to destroy the canals. The result of Bomber Command bombing these seemingly indestructible canals was that prefabricated sections of U-boats being delivered to ports shrank from a maximum of 120 sections per month to zero.[15]

Bomber Command and Germany's Fleet

Germany entered the Second World War with a fleet comprised of eighteen major warships, the big ones being the battleships *Tirpitz* and *Bismarck*. The others were pre-dreadnought battleships, battle-cruisers, heavy cruisers, light cruisers and destroyers, plus S-boats and U-boats as well as converted merchant ships used as commerce raiders. Bomber Command's other challenge was the weather. An example was on 12 February 1942 when bad weather and total cloud cover prevented 405 (Vancouver) Squadron RCAF Wellingtons and other Bomber

---

13 Cooper, *Target – Dresden*, p. 228

14 *Straight From the Horse's Mouth*

15 Brookes, 'An Interview With 'Bomber' Harris 8 September 1975,' *Royal Air Force Historical Society Journal* 74, 2020, p. 58

SEA WAR

Command aircraft from locating a small fleet of German ships. However, battleships *Scharnhorst* and *Gneisenau* suffered damage striking mines while passing through waters mined by Bomber Command.[16]

This is what my research reveals happened to the Kriegsmarine's High Seas Fleet:

1. The Royal Navy sank four:
    a. *Admiral Graf Spee* heavy cruiser, damaged in the Battle of the River Plate on 13 December 1939, was scuttled on 17/18 December.
    b. *Bismarck* battleship was sunk at sea on 27 May 1941
    c. *Karlsruhe* light cruiser was sunk in Norway in April 1940, and its wreck discovered in deep Norwegian waters in summer 2020[17]
    d. *Scharnhorst* was sunk at sea on 26 December 1943

2. The Royal Navy Fleet Air Arm sank *Konigsberg*, a light cruiser on 10 April 1940
3. Norwegian shore defences sank *Blücher*, a heavy cruiser, on 8 April 1940
4. The Mighty Eighth sank the light cruiser *Köln* in shallow waters in March 1945

So what then did Bomber Command do?

5. Bomber Command sank four major warships:
    a. *Admiral Scheer* heavy cruiser was capsized at Kiel on 9 April 1945
    b. *Lutzow* heavy cruiser was sunk in shallow waters in April 1945
    c. *Schleswig-Holstein* pre-dreadnought battleship sank December 1944
    d. *Tirpitz* battleship was, most famous of all, was sunk in the Kaafjord, on 12 November 1944 – Bomber Boy Roy Brand Sr, the father of my friend Roy Brand Jr, took part in that sortie in 617 Squadron with its Tallboy bombs

6. Bomber Command kept three more out of action through severe damage:
    a. *Admiral Hipper* heavy cruiser was severely damaged on 3 May 1945, by which time the war was almost over.
    b. *Emden* light cruiser was repeatedly damaged at Kiel by bombing and so run aground outside the harbour to prevent her sinking in 1945
    c. *Gneisenau* was severely damaged on 26 February 1942

7. The naval mine Bomber Command air-dropped on 3 May 1945 so damaged the *Schlesien* pre-dreadnought battleship that her crew scuttled her.

---

16 Birrell, pp. 48-9
17 Metcalfe, 'Wreck of WWII battleship with Nazi symbol discovered off Norway,' *Live Science*, 11 Sep 2020 www.livescience.com

BOMBER COMMAND

As for Germany's remaining warships, in October 1944, the light cruiser *Leipzig* collided with the heavy cruiser *Prinz Eugen* and was damaged so severely the Kriegsmarine decided full repairs were unfeasible; it was patched up to keep afloat and then used to help defend Gotenhafen from the advancing Red Army in March 1945. It then carried fleeing German civilians, reaching Denmark by late April. Postwar it she was used as a barracks ship for mine-sweeping forces and was scuttled in July 1946.

That left the Kriegsmarine with only two major warships, the heavy cruiser *Prinz Eugen* and the light cruiser *Nurnberg*. Theirs is a strange story. Harris says this story began with the naval liaison officer at Bomber Command headquarters being 'all in a tremble' when Harris returned from a brief absence of just a few minutes. The officer told Harris, 'I had to counter-command the attack on the *Eugen* and the *Nurnberg*.' 'Why?' asked Harris. 'Orders of the Admiralty,' was the reply. To this Harris later said 'Well, of course you could not blame the lad, to a naval officer an order from the Admiralty is one above a direct command by the Almighty.' Unfortunately, fuel limitations rendered it too late to turn around the bombers as Harris had ordered, even though sinking them would have been a dead certainty. Both ships escaped and bombarded Copenhagen.

And so, to sum up, Bomber Command's sea war accomplishments include:

1. destroying a third of Germany's U-boats at their bases;
2. destroying the canals needed to transport prefabricated U-Boat sections to the German ports Bomber Command had already seriously damaged;
3. sinking or disabling half the German fleet, including the *Tirpitz*.

In addition, Bomber Command, notably No. 6 Group RCAF, mined every German port from the Baltic and along the North Sea south to the Bay of Biscay:

4. destroyed Germany's light surface naval forces in the English Channel;
5. sank or damaged about a thousand ships of the German merchant marine, thus depriving Germany of desperately needed essential military supplies;
6. tied up over 40 per cent of Germany's Kriegsmarine naval personnel working on mine-sweeping on a full-time basis; and
7. blockaded every port, creating catastrophic shortages in Germany and also destroying an unknown number of U-boats entering or leaving those ports.[18]

Long story short: Bomber Command achieved astonishing results contributing to winning the sea war.

---

18 Dunmore & Carter, p. 250

Chapter Twenty

Assisting Allied Armies

> In point of fact there was hardly an occasion
> when we did not intervene in the battlefield as soon
> as the Germans built up a really strong position.
>
> Sir Arthur Harris[1]

Harris asks 'How was it that some 30 divisions of British and American troops, totally destroyed double their number of German divisions and drove them from the field every time?'[2] The answer? Bomber Command. Bashow points out 'Also, in the latter stages of the compaign, even attacks against industrial cities were frequently tactical rather than strategic, conducted as they were in support of the advancing Allied land armies. For much of ... 1944, it [Bomber Command] was extensively used in support of the invasion of north-west Europe.'[3]

D Day 1944

It is not generally known but, according to Churchill, the total number of Allied airmen killed in the weeks preceding D Day was greater than the number of soldiers killed in that 'great cross-channel adventure'.[4] After D Day, Bomber Command sustained higher casualties than the British Second Army in Normandy.[5] The night before the D-Day landings, Bomber Command flew more combat sorties than on any other night in the Second World War. For example, Harris says 'on the night of the invasion itself [we despatched] 1,136 aircraft to attack coastal batteries.' Harris reports his incredibly good invasion news as follows – 'Within a few hours of

---

1 Harris, *Bomber Offensive*, p. 212
2 Brookes, 'An Interview With 'Bomber' Harris, 8 September 1975,' *Royal Air Force Historical Society Journal* 74, 2020, p. 59
3 Bashow, *No Prouder Place*, p. 459
4 Hastings, *Bomber Command* p. 83 and Hampton, p. 314
5 Hampton, p. 314

the bombing of the ten coastal batteries we knew how successful the operation had been; only one of these batteries was able to open fire at all, and that ineffectively as the convoys approached the coast of Normandy.[6]

In addition, also on the night of the invasion, Harris organized elaborate three-fold radar and communications diversions which bluffed Germany, and especially Hitler, into thinking the invasion site was elsewhere. These included radar deceptions dropping a special type of Window created especially for this occasion, and having Stirlings and American B-17 Flying Fortresses carrying jamming equipment to limit the range of Germany's early-warning radar. Harris says, 'This was a method of jamming which Bomber Command had not been able to use before, but everything to do with the invasion had such high priority that we were at last able to get and use the equipment; it proved to be very a valuable weapon against the enemy's early warning system in the future.'

Of particular interest to me because Dad flew in No. 1 Group, Harris says:

> A third force of Bomber Command aircraft, Lancasters of No. 1 Group ... carried equipment for jamming the night-fighters' radio-telephone communications with their ground-control stations. Curiously enough, although this was only designed to protect the Window-dropping aircraft and the airborne forces landing in Normandy, the enemy was actually the more inclined to believe that the invasion was taking place in the Pas de Calais because they believed that airborne forces approaching that area were being protected by this Lancaster force.[7]

As mentioned, that night was my Dad's eighteenth combat sortie. He was part of the bluff. The bluff worked. Dad noted in his logbook 'Invasion Fleet was worth seeing'.

Harris reports:

> It was not until much later that we learnt of the success of our jamming and diversionary operations. The enemy, it appears, was completely taken in by the bogus convoys and convinced that the main assault was to be in the Pas de Calais. This, it is now known, caused a definite and vital delay in bringing up strategic reserves to Normandy.[8]

---

6 Harris, p. 207

7 Harris, pp. 206-7

8 Harris, p. 207

ASSISTING ALLIED ARMIES

Pre-D Day

Harris writes:

> It was obvious to me that the heavy bomber offered the only conceivable means of breaching the Atlantic walls, destroying the enemy's interior lines of communications, and thus enabling the army to break out of its beachhead when it had gathered sufficient strength .... The date for this elaborate campaign to begin was March 1944. The plan of the campaign ... was entirely the conception of Tedder, who certainly has one of the most brilliant minds in any of the services ... .[9]

Harris continues[10] 'Besides railways and fortifications, a number of other military objectives were put on the list of priority targets.' During May Bomber Command wrecked the military depots at Bourg Leopold and Mailly-le-Camps. As mentioned, Dad's ninth combat sortie was the bombing of Mailly Panzer military camp on 3/4 May. Bomber Command Lancasters were massacred by German fighters there that night.

> Five of the largest ammunition dumps used by the German army and air force were also blown up during May, and in April we destroyed a large explosive works at St Medard-en-Jalles. Just before the invasion we were required to put out of action three wireless stations and a radar station, which was done.

And Harris has more good news, this time concerning railways and the marshalling yards which my Dad bombed of several times. Harris says:

> The success of the three months' campaign against the railways of North-Western Europe was seen as the two opposing armies began to build up their strength in the battlefield. In this the allies were always well ahead of the enemy, and if the railways had been working normally the artificial port which the allies had constructed and their lavish use of ingenious equipment for landing supplies on the beaches would never have compensated for the immense advantage the enemy would have had from an efficient railway system and interior lines of communication.

---

9 Harris, pp. 196-7
10 Harris, pp. 205-6

Harris sums up by saying: 'After the war almost every German officer who knew anything about the subject said that the bombing of the railways of North-West Europe was the main cause of the success of the invasion.'[11]

Germany's Perspective[12]

The German Research Institute for Military History (the 'Institute') says the strategic bombing offensive against French railways in 1944 was devastating to Germany. In May 1944, the French system was largely crippled; traffic moved only with great difficulty. By late May, movements in northern France were at only 13 per cent of their previous level; in the rest of France, the figure was 50 per cent. Traffic between France and the Reich had dropped to 20 per cent of normal. From March to June 1944, 67,000 tons of bombs were dropped on traffic nodes in France. This caused *Ministerialdirigent* Dr Ebeling of the Reich Transport Ministry to warn 'major operational movements by the Germans on the railways [were] as good as impractical' if the bombing continued at the same intensity.[13] For Germany, Bomber Command just kept providing worse news in spring 1944. For example, along the Rhine between Germany and France, all transit stations were at times out of action. The Duisburg bridge over the Rhine was destroyed. Dr Ebeling also saw the bombing campaign against the transport network, the aircraft industry and aviation and fuel plants as a certain sign of an impending landing in France. However, for the invasion to be successful, the Luftwaffe had to be decisively weakened beforehand.[14]

The Institute emphasizes, with powerful phraseology, the essential role of Bomber Command in the Normandy invasion, saying:

> Gen. Eisenhower was well aware that the role played by the strategic bomber forces would be decisive for the success of the planned invasion in Normandy. They were, he wrote on 1 February 1943, indeed the only weapon that could crucially influence how the operations went, especially during the landings phase. Field Marshal Gerd von Rundstedt, the German C-in-C West, also commented later that it had all been a matter of the Luftwaffe and then again the Luftwaffe. It is thus impossible to overestimate the critical importance of air power on the two sides in deciding the success or failure of the venture. If the fighting ability of the Luftwaffe had not been weakened, and German supplies had not been delayed by the Allied operations in the air, the invasion might well have come to naught.

---

11   Harris, pp. 207-8
12   Institute, Vol. VII, p. 130
13   Institute, Vol. VII, p. 292
14   Institute, Vol. VII, p. 292

I can't think of terminology more powerful than these words of the Institute: 'It is thus impossible to overestimate the critical importance of air power on the two sides in deciding the success or failure of the [invasion].' I had no idea the contribution of my Dad and his colleagues was so central to the Allied success in this most important of all Allied endeavours, the liberation of a continent by the D Day landings in June 1944. It is so sad I knew none of this while my Dad was still alive. Speaking of my Dad, the Institute also observes that 'If the Luftwaffe, and in particular its reconnaissance capability, had not been virtually put out of action beforehand, the elaborately planned and executed spoofing operation [of which Dad was part] to suggest that the main landing was going to be made in the Pas-de-Calais would also have not succeeded.'

Post-D Day

Harris then decided to commence large-scale day bombings with fighter escorts in addition to the night bombings. This maximized what he could accomplish in any given twenty-four hours. The results were devastating to Germany's light surface fleet in the Channel. In addition, on the night of 14/15 June 1944, Bomber Command attacked a great concentration of German troops and vehicles, wiping out everything. On 30 June in daylight Bomber Command bombed the 2nd and 9th Panzer Divisions at Villers Bocage, forcing the Panzer divisions to call off their attack.[15]

Regarding multiple military targets, Harris says:

> Within a few days of the landing we were called upon to take part in a long campaign against German synthetic oil plants in Germany and, as soon as the first flying bombs were launched, to give very high priority to the new flying bomb launching sites and supply depots in the Pas de Calais. Besides this there was an even more urgent call to destroy the enemy's large fleet of E-boats and other light surface naval craft in the Channel which the Navy thought an extremely serious threat to the invading army's sea communications.

Harris says, 'When the enemy began his disastrous retreat from Normandy, Bomber Command was able to demonstrate the dominance of air power even more conclusively than before.' Harris sums up saying:

> Between D Day and the middle of August Bomber Command dropped 17,560 tons of bombs on German troop concentrations in the battlefield; eight separate attacks of this kind were made. It was estimated that at any moment Bomber Command's 1,000 aircraft could put down a barrage which, for the time being, was equal

---

15 Harris, p. 210

in weight to the shells of 4,000 guns. To bring up such a mass of artillery to the required position in any reasonable time would, of course, have been a physical impossibility, but the bombers could strike without giving the enemy any warning on a few hours' notice.[16]

Regarding post-D Day railway objectives, Harris says, 'This campaign against short-term railway objectives was naturally continued after the allies had landed. Up till the end of June, Bomber Command carried out 13,349 sorties against the railways of North-West Europe ... .'[17]

Channel Ports

Germany hoped to deny the Allies the use of the Channel ports, thereby creating insoluble problems of supply and communication and so German soldiers were expected to hold those ports 'to the last man'. But what happened was:

- After seven Bomber Command attacks in a week (of which three, admittedly, were aborted), le Havre which was held by over 11,000 enemy soldiers was captured – in capturing it, we lost thirty soldiers and took 11,000 enemy soldiers prisoner.
- After one Bomber Command attack on St-Martin-Boulogne and Mont Lambert, Boulogne surrendered following an assault spearheaded by 79th Armoured Division, and we took 8,000 enemy soldiers prisoner.
- Brest, Calais, Cap Gris Nez, and the Île de Cezembre, which was essential for the defence of St Malo, were all occupied by the Allies without trouble after attacks by Bomber Command.
- Brest was also attacked by American heavy bombers, then Bomber Command sank several large ships before the Germans could tow them into position to sink them as blockships.

Harris concludes by remarking, 'In past wars, without the heavy bombers, these ports could only have been captured after prolonged siege.'[18]

Battle of the Bulge

Few recognize how important Bomber Command was in defeating Hitler's last great offensive on the western front, Germany's Ardennes offensive in Belgium, often referred to as the Battle of the Bulge. It was fought from 16 December 1944

---

16   Harris, p. 212
17   Harris, p. 204
18   Harris, p. 214

ASSISTING ALLIED ARMIES

to 25 January 1945. On 16 December Germany achieved a total surprise attack against 228,741 Allied soldiers by 406,342 German soldiers.[19] Bomber Command flew to the rescue from Lincolnshire in dreadful weather that initially kept the Mighty Eighth grounded by even worse weather in East Anglia. Field Marshal von Rundstedt, the German commander, said Allied bombers were decisive in his downfall in the Ardennes offensive.[20] General Sepp Dietrich of Sixth Panzer Army said the Ardennes offensive was lost because Bomber Command destroyed the supply lines, thereby cutting off ammunition and petrol supplies.[21] On 18 December 1944 *Westdeutscher Beobachter* reported 'there is the unending terror from an air offensive of a kind never before concentrated in such a small area'.[22] By 16 January 1945 the tide had turned, and now 700,500 Allied soldiers were fighting 383,016 German soldiers. The battle was the bloodiest US forces fought in Europe in the Second World War. The United States Army Centre of Military History's official numbers are 75,000 American casualties and 100,000 German casualties.[23]

Barnes Wallis's Big Bombs

Of supreme importance to Bomber Command effectiveness in the final year of the Second World War was Barnes Wallis, the inventor of the Dambuster bouncing bombs. He created the two biggest bombs of all, the deep-penetration Tallboy and the even bigger Grand Slam. Grand Slams destroyed the Bielefield viaduct between Hamm and Hanover – a key communications German target for which all previous bombings had failed at a heavy toll of aircraft involved. Tallboy sank the *Tirpitz*. In total, Bomber Command dropped 854 Tallboys and forty-one Grand Slams to destroy:

- Flying-bomb installations (often underground)
- Blocks of reinforced concrete as big as houses protecting submarine pens
- Both the airfield and naval base at Heligoland on 1 April 1945: the following day six Grand Slams and twenty-seven Tallboys ensured nothing was left of the island fortress
- Berchtesgaden on 25 April 1945: direct hits by Tallboys severely damaged Hitler's *Adlernest* (eagle's nest) and SS barracks, with the loss of only two, possibly the final two, of the 3,431 Lancasters Germany destroyed since the Lancaster entered service in spring 1942.[24] Bomber Command enabled the US Army to take Berchtesgaden without firing a shot.

---

19 Wikipedia Battle of the Bulge
20 *Target Dresden*, p. 223
21 *Inside the Third Reich*, pp. 417-18.
22 Institute, Vol. IX, Part 1, p. 462
23 Bergstrom, *The Ardennes: Hitler's Winter Offensive 1944-1945*, Casemate Publishers, Havertown, Pennsylvania, 2014, p. 425
24 Fyfe, *The Great Ingratitude*, pp. 262-3

Dresden

American, British and Canadian bombers destroyed military facilities, communications and railway marshalling yards to damage the German army and make way for the approaching Red Army as Stalin had requested at Yalta.

Monty's Thanks!

I conclude this chapter by citing no less an authority than Bernard Law Montgomery, Viscount Montgomery of Alamein, Commander in Chief of Ground Forces on D Day and the Battle of Normandy and Commander of 21st Army Group in 1944 and 1945 which consisted primarily of Second British Army and First Canadian Army. Monty spoke powerfully of Harris in the Battle of Normandy, crossing the Rhine and winning the war.

For the Battle of Normandy, in the early hours of 7 July 1944, just a week after the Panzer bombing of 30 June, Bomber Command received the following:

URGENT REQUEST from First Canadian Army and Second British Army – **HELP!** [25]

These two armies had encountered formidable German tanks and troops. Twenty-nine Lancasters of 166 Squadron joined the relief force of 467 bombers which took to the air that very day to come to the rescue by bombing German heavy tank and troop concentrations threatening our armies. This was 166 Squadron's most devastating attack on German troops in the Second World War. While 166 Squadron Lancasters were arriving back in Kirmington, Monty sent the following signal. Not known for idle compliments, Monty on this occasion could not constrain his enthusiasm.

> The Allied Armies in France would like to thank Bomber Command for their magnificent co-operation last night. We know well that your men were also engaged further afield and we applaud your continual and sustained bombing of German war industries and the effect this has on the German war effort. But we know well that you are always ready to bring your mighty effort closer in when such action is really needed, and when you do this your action is always decisive. Please tell your brave and gallant Aircrews how greatly the Allied Soldiers admire and applaud their work. Thank you very much.

For crossing the Rhine, Montgomery signalled Harris the morning after Bomber Command took out the German defences at the Rhine: 'Thanks for the magnificent

---

25 Harris, p. 213

co-operation in the battle of the Rhine. The bombing last night was a masterpiece and enabled us to take our objectives by midnight.'[26] Harris points out that military planners feared casualties crossing the Rhine could be as high as the 70,000 sustained on the first day of the Battle of the Somme in the First World War. The Rhine was Germany's last geographic defence from the west. But we did not lose 70,000 soldiers. Instead, after Bomber Command destroyed German defences, Montgomery's casualties crossing the Rhine were relatively light. Small wonder Monty uses the words 'magnificent' and 'masterpiece' even though he, unlike me, is not given to hyperbole.

For winning the war, Monty said it best postwar, declaring about Harris, 'I doubt whether any single man did more in winning the war than he did. I doubt whether that is generally realized.'[27] Monty's right. It isn't. But it should be.

---

26 Brookes, 'An Interview With 'Bomber' Harris 8 September 1975,' *Royal Air Force Historical Society Journal* 74, 2020, p. 59

27 Probert, *Bomber Harris*, p. 370

Chapter Twenty-one

Germany's War Machine

> Hitler's greatest miscalculation in the war
> was mistaking as terror bombing what in fact
> was Bomber Command's economic bombing.
>
> Richard Overy[1]

Hitler's Massive Mistake

Unlike King George VI and Churchill who did, Hitler never visited bombing sites, so he did not see the damage, except perhaps from a car window if driving by. In addition, Göring hid from Hitler as much bad news about Bomber Command as he could. This helped lead Hitler into his massive mistake of thinking Bomber Command was conducting terror bombing in an attempt to smash German morale. Hitler was confident that such bombing would only serve to stiffen German resolve. He said, 'The devastation actually works in our favour, because it is creating a body of people with nothing to lose – people who will therefore fight on with utter fanaticism.'[2] Hitler was correct, at least publicly. Nazi Germany was a police state under a reign of terror, so Germans knew that publicly they must appear determined to fight. Privately, an increasing number were developing doubts. The direct result of Hitler's massive mistake was his failure adequately to protect Germany's economic structure from Bomber Command attacks that ultimately destroyed Germany's ability to wage war.

Terror or Economic Bombing – Harris and Speer

Regarding terror bombing, Harris declared in March 1945:

> We have never gone in for terror bombing and the attacks which we
> have made in accordance with my Directive have in fact produced

---

1 Overton. *The Air War 1939-1945*, p. 119
2 Ibid., taken from Irving, *Hitler's War*, p. 574

the strategic consequences for which they were designed and from which the Armies now profit .... Attacks on cities, like any other act of war, are intolerable unless they are strategically justified. But they are strategically justified in so far as they tend to shorten the war and so preserve the lives of Allied soldiers.

In short, the Allied strategic bombing offensive, escalating with ever-increasing ferocity, damaged and then destroyed Germany's ability to produce the means necessary to make war.

'Unconditional Surrender'

With FDR declaring on 24 January 1943 at Casablanca that the Allies would accept nothing less than 'Unconditional Surrender', Nazi leaders had no incentive to surrender, and were quite prepared to fight to the last man – and even the total destruction of Germany. But they discovered they could not do that. And so, on 8 May 1945, they surrendered. Why? Not because they lost a decisive battle such as Napoleon at Waterloo. Instead, because the strategic bombing offensive had eliminated Nazi Germany's ability make war.

Overy uses as an example of Bomber Command effectiveness Hitler's demand that production be pushed underground. Work on that enormous plan began in 1943 when Bomber Command's ultimate power was starting to show. Hitler ordered construction or conversion of over 93-million square feet of underground floor space. In 1944 work began on 71-million square feet, but only 13-million were completed, and that took half a million of Germany's building workers, and enormous quantities of construction and machinery, assets which could have been used on the Atlantic Wall. Much of the completed underground construction was never used. As Overy says, 'The scheme was an economic fantasy; the reality was the diversion of valuable resources to a project of little strategic worth.'[3]

Industrial Decentralization, Parts Supply, Power Supply and Transport

Dispersing factories in the countryside away from Bomber Command target areas created a growing need for vehicles the Reich was unable to produce.[4] Ruhr air raids severely disrupted the parts-supply industry.[5] Hitler decreed in July 1943 that Speer had control over all power-industry facilities which had been failing to meet growing demand. However, Bomber Command's damage to state-owned power

---

3 Overy, *Bomber Command 1939-1945*, pp. 198-9

4 Institute, Vol. V, Part 2, p. 495

5 Institute, Vol. V, Part 2, p. 494

stations went from 3.6 per cent in September 1943 to 7.7 per cent in September 1944 to 23.4 per cent in January 1945. In transport, Bomber Command created two stages of problems – first in bomb-shattered areas where vital supplies had to be transported by makeshift means[6] and second, by autumn 1944, when the transport of even bare essentials was destroyed by bombing.[7]

The Institute says Churchill's 22 June 1941 promise of 'making the German people taste and gulp each month a sharper dose of the miseries they have showered upon mankind' became 'a bitter reality less than a year later'. In March 1942 Bomber Command had opened what Nazi leaders had long feared – a new front. For the remainder of the war, the Institute says 'It was a race between the Nazis' ability to make good the damage suffered by the population and ensure proper supplies, and the annihilating blows being dealt by the Allied bombers.'[8]

Nazi Leadership 'Push-Pull'

'Push-Pull' among the Nazi Leadership generated by bombing was catastrophic for Germany. It led to ruinous erratic changes of priorities which seriously adversely affected war materials production. Bomber Command presented push-pull problems for Nazis early on. For example, as mentioned, on 4/5 September 1940, Bomber Command bombing Berlin generated so much public resentment that Hitler switched Luftwaffe bombing priorities from Fighter Command airfields to London just as, unknown to Hitler, the RAF was in danger of losing the Battle of Britain. Bombing creation of push-pull prevented the Me. 262 fighter jet from potentially winning the war for Germany through delays in its production arising from Hitler's insistence it become a bomber, and erratic pursuit of other priorities generated by bombing diverting Germany from fixing technical problems in the jet's power plants. Had Germany not been paralyzed by bombing push-pull and, had it instead produced the Me. 262 as a fighter even six months earlier then that jet's impact on Allied bomber formations could have been cataclysmic. Bombing generated unforeseen technological responses conducted at breakneck pace, sending German leadership into desperate solutions created by a passionate desire for retribution instead of methodology and logic.[9]

German Morale

German morale was affected as early as 1942, even though significant bombing did not commence until 1943 and was not able to reach its real potential until 1944. Consider the following.[10] American military historian Murray Williamson says:

---

6   Institute, Vol. V, Part 2, p. 495
7   Institute, Vol. V, Part 2, p. 520
8   Institute, Vol. V, Part 2, pp. 521-2
9   Bashow, p. 471
10 Bashow, pp. 464-5

Yet the night bombing campaign's greatest contribution to the winning of the war was precisely what Harris claimed .... Recent scholarship in the Federal Republic indicates that as early as the summer of 1942, the night bombing campaign was affecting German attitudes. In 1943, the heavy bombing caused a dramatic fall off in popular morale.[11]

Williamson adds that being a police state, the Third Reich rendered unrealistic a popular uprising to overthrow the Nazis, but the cumulative effects of the bombing, especially the bombing by night, were intensely demoralizing. On 30 March 1942 Lord Cherwell wrote to Churchill, 'Investigation seems to show that having one's house demolished is most damaging to morale. People seem to mind it more than having their friends or relatives killed.'[12]

Mr Justice John Singleton's 29 May 1942 *Report to the War Cabinet on the Bombing of Germany* expresses similar sentiments in much greater detail, as does the 22 June 1942 report of the US Consul General in Geneva to America's Secretary of State. British Intelligence Report No. 346 of 22 September 1942 states: 'These big raids cause much destruction. In spite of the statements in the Wehrmacht reports, the destruction of war production facilities is fairly considerable. The loss caused by the destruction of food stores and depots is extraordinarily great, as the food cannot be replaced.'

An autumn 1942 British Intelligence *Report on Bombing's Effect on Housing and Division of Effort* adds that Germans losing their homes and possessions is not only one of their most important points of morale, but it also affects the morale of Germany's fighting services. The Chiefs of Staff Committee for the War Cabinet *An Estimate of the Effects of the Anglo-American Offensive Against Germany* of 3 November 1942 reported that bombing was forcing Nazis to tell people they must look after themselves as best they can. This might be tolerable in a democracy, but reflects badly on Nazi governance because it indicates a breakdown in state organization 'in which the Germans have been so carefully taught to place implicit faith ... .'

Workers in areas threatened by bombing suffered long, exhausting hours in cramped air-raid shelters or cellars, and absenteeism increased – for example, at the Ford works in Cologne on any given day in 1944, at least one-quarter of the work force was absent. Slave labour existed in atrocious situations, was only two-thirds as productive as that of free Germans, and was motivated solely by terror.

---

11 Bashow, p. 463; Williamson, *The Luftwaffe – Strategy for Defeat*, p. 223
12 Bashow, *No Prouder Place*, p. 464; Churchill at War, PM's Papers 1940-45, Unit 1, in UK National Archives Prem 3/11/4, 144

BOMBER COMMAND

Severe Disruption to German Society

Richard Overy points out that Allied bombing severely disrupted German society. Nearly nine million citizens were evacuated from German cities, hugely reducing the potential work force and creating enormous problems in providing housing, food and essential consumer goods to evacuees. This forced Germany to divert from the war industries. Given what workers managed to accomplish through all this, Overy says one must wonder what they could have achieved, had they not been faced with a near-constant threat of death from the air.

Destruction of German War Production

One reason for what appeared to be significantly increased German industrial output in the final years of the war is that, for the first three years, Germany was deliberately working nowhere near full war capacity – the nation was still producing only 3 per cent more war output than in peacetime because Hitler was adamant for too long that the military needs not interfere with consumer industries. Hitler expected a *Blitzkrieg* win in Russia of fast powerful attacks using speed, surprise and air superiority.

Air superiority proved impossible because of Bomber Command. This meant massive amounts of personnel and equipment were tied down inside Germany to defend the industrial cities. In addition, Speer says many new and promising battlefield technology improvements had to be shelved to produce more anti-aircraft equipment instead. An example of shortages created by Bomber Command is that one-third of the precision optics Germany produced had to be used for gun-sights for flak batteries even though they were desperately needed at the front.

Had Germany not been so diverted by Bomber Command and instead free to mobilize its manpower and technical resources for total war, Germany might have developed chemical weapons. In addition, Bomber Command prevented reliable delivery systems from being developed. Germany might also have developed biological weapons, including a foot-and-mouth virus Germany was ready to deploy against Britain towards the end of the war, but again reliable delivery systems were not developed. Instead, at war's end, unused by Germany were a half million artillery shells and 100,000 aircraft bombs of Tabun nerve gas that the Allies found in Germany's arsenals because reliable delivery systems had not been developed.

Bombing forced evacuation of much of the Kaiser Wilhelm Institute for Physics research facility's infrastructure from the Dahlem suburb of Berlin to Haigerloch in the Black Forest, creating considerable confusion and disruption in Germany's atomic programme. Bombing curtailment of the V.2 programme was fortunate for the Allies because Germany was developing an advanced version the A.10 rocket which would have used the V.2 as a second-stage booster, thereby enabling German rockets to cross the Atlantic and hit America.

Destruction of the Reich's Economy

> From the autumn of 1944, in the major industrial regions, the Allied bombing brought restrictions on rail, road, and waterborne transport and industrial production: the latter was particularly affected by its indirect effects (power cuts, raw materials supplies, and non-deliver of component parts). The industrial strength on the home front needed to back up the 'fighting spirit' was in danger of being lost.[13]

Hampton reminds us that 'the German industrial machine was second only to that of the United States' but 'the strategic bombing offensive placed a ceiling on it that prevented the full exploitation of the resources of Germany and the occupied territories.'[14]

The Institute sums up saying:

> It was becoming clear that neither bunkers nor miracle weapons could offer any effective protections against the bombs ... the realization that they had been left defenceless against the Allied bombing made a great part of the German public abandon all hope of the final victory that Nazi propaganda was still heralding up to the very last days of the war.

In Berlin on 16 March 1945 Goebbels noted in his diary his impression of the war situation on the home front: 'Our armaments potential and transport system are here crippled to such a degree that it is easy to calculate when the time will come when we so to speak stand on the edge of the void.' The Institute says:

> The plainly approaching collapse of the Ruhr was in fact a clear signal to the population in other industrial regions, and quoted a March 1945 comment from Hamburg saying 'No more raw materials, we can't make anything. When the Ruhr is lost, then it's close-down time.'[15]

The Reich's economy had been destroyed.

And so, in April 1945, Allies on the Western Front took about 1,500,000 prisoners. Also in April, Western Allies captured at least 120,000 German soldiers in Italy. From January to April 1945, over 800,000 German soldiers surrendered to the Soviets on the Eastern Front.[16] Germany's formidable forces surrendered because they no longer had bullets or boots, and their tanks and aircraft lacked fuel. They were starving. Bombing had deprived Germany of the means to make war.

---

13 Institute, Vol. IX, Part 1, pp. 462-3
14 Hampton, p. 318
15 Institute, Vol, IX, Part 1, p. 473-4
16 Wikipedia, 'End of World War II in Europe'

Part V

REMEMBRANCE & CONCLUSIONS

Chapter Twenty-two

Dad Postwar

Remembrance of Churchill postwar requires several books of its own, and indeed many have already been written. In addition, Churchill continues to make news today. Accordingly, I will conclude this book with only two postwar Remembrances – first my Dad, then Bomber Command.

So what became of this 33-year-old bachelor Canadian banker Roland MacKenzie DFC postwar back in Canada after flying thirty-four combat sorties from April to August 1944? First and foremost, from my perspective, he married my Mom, Joyce Lenore Miller MacKenzie, on 11 August 1945 and on 18 July 1948 I was born, all in Calgary. But what else did he become back home in Canada after such a horrific nightmare in Europe? That's a core question which drove me to research Bomber Command and then write this book. Most of what I have learnt about Dad's work at war, and through that about Bomber Command overall, is since 2017. Until 2017, my knowledge was shadowy, piecemeal and, thanks to biased media, just plain wrong, partly rumour, partly unconnected facts, partly lies, and partly family lore, much of which has proven to be largely inaccurate. All frustrating.

But what comes to mind for me now? First is a photo of Dad and Mom celebrating their marriage at a dinner on 11 August 1945 at what is now Calgary's Fairmont Palliser, another of Canada's 'Castles of the North'. Sadly for them, and for me, theirs was not a happy marriage. I had erroneously thought they didn't meet until Dad got back to Calgary in April 1945. Accordingly, I thought their marriage was the classic sad story of my Mom marrying a handsome, decorated RCAF pilot in his smart uniform while Dad was marrying a beautiful vivacious young woman. In reality, they were singularly unsuited for one another.

As mentioned, I was born three years later, among the first of the 'Baby Boomers', on 18 July 1948. That day was auspicious, although we didn't know it then. The day I was born was Nelson Mandela's 30th birthday. The day I was baptised at Calgary's Knox United Church was also auspicious – it was 14 November 1948, the day Prince Charles was born. Then, in the spring of 1952, disaster struck. My Mom contracted polio in the terrifying epidemic that was sweeping across Canada. I remember as a little boy in the hallway of our house overhearing the diagnosis in her bedroom. That tragic news changed our lives in so many ways.

Speaking of which, I recently learned that a girl five years older than me was struck by polio about the same time. She was Joan Anderson, daughter of

DAD POSTWAR

RCAF Flight Lieutenant William Andrew Anderson. She was hospitalized for weeks, but thankfully recovered. However, the lingering effects of polio caused changes in her voice, and caused her to play the guitar in an unusual way. In June 1965 she married Chuck Mitchell. That makes it easy to guess her identity. She is Canada's much-loved, world-famous, iconic songwriter and singer, Joni Mitchell.[1] She felt polio's changes to her voice made her more distinctive. That it is! On 3 April 2022, at age 78, Joni Mitchell became the 2022 MusiCares Person of the Year.

Being only three-years old, my memories of that terrible time are sketchy, and now there is no one alive who knows any more than I do. My memory is that Mom was taken north to Edmonton and put into an iron lung for a prolonged period. For decades I knew virtually nothing about the iron lung, save that it was dreadful. In 2018 for the first time I saw one in a movie. It was even worse than I'd imagined. What a nightmare for my poor mother. I remember going with Dad to Edmonton where he visited Mom in hospital, but I never saw Mom in the hospital. On 10 August 2021, my maternal cousin Trev Lancaster (our mothers were sisters) who is eleven years older than I am, told me he saw my Mom in the iron lung.

Dad and I never spoke about Mom's situation in the iron lung. We never spoke about much else either, on those long, lonely drives north to Edmonton, and afterwards back home to Calgary. Life was indeed lonely in a family devoid of meaningful communication. I remember the day Mom returned to our home in Calgary. She was paralyzed from her waist down, and so confined to a wheelchair for the rest of her life. Calgary in the 1950s and 1960s, while I was growing up, was not a nice place for the disabled. They were called 'cripples'. Some thought they should be kept hidden. On Mom's return to Calgary, we continued living in Mount Pleasant, which really was a 'pleasant' older neighbourhood.

In January 1955 we moved into brand-new St Andrew's Heights on what was then on the outskirts of Calgary, and today is regarded as an inner-city neighbourhood for rich people. In St Andrew's, we were the first owners of our brand-new home. Our family owned it for fifty-four years until 2009. Dad told me once that he'd imagined we'd only live in St Andrew's for about two years. Little did he know he'd spend the rest of his life there. Something memorable happened there in 1965 while I was a high school student. I expressed a strong interest in joining the Royal Canadian Air Force Cadets. My friend, classmate and neighbour on our street Hugh McIntosh had just joined, and looked magnificent in his Air Cadet uniform. Hugh spoke of flying. I was astonished that Dad reacted with horror, saying, 'Absolutely not, Roddy. Your Boy Scout Troop was bad enough. For me even it was too much like the military. I don't want you anywhere near the military.'

---

1 Wikipedia, Joni Mitchell

Dad's Postwar Career

In 2017 I learned for the first time that the Royal Bank decided in 1952 to transfer Dad from Calgary to its headquarters in Montreal. Dad's banking career was about to soar, but Mom got polio. That ended Montreal, and so much else. I now know Bomber Command and polio also affected me deeply. Dad's rise in RBC was severely reduced by Mom's paralysis because of the time and energy needed to care for her. For example, it necessitated Dad coming home from work every day at lunchtime to put her to bed. He was seldom able to work evenings or go on business trips from then until her death in 1970. Fortunately, with each of his bank promotions postwar, Calgary kept becoming increasingly important, so each new promotion was located in Calgary.

This reality was reinforced in 1968 when RBC's Alberta Regional vice-president told me Dad could have become President of the Royal Bank, had it not been for my Mom being paralyzed with polio. He said this in the presence of my University of Calgary colleagues during our Students' Union Executive lunch in his impressive private dining room in the Royal's headquarters downtown. We were the bank's guests because our Students' Union banked with the Royal. I was at that time a vice-president of the University of Calgary Students' Union.

I remember Dad travelling by train, and in later years by plane, to RBC headquarters in Montreal. He told me about staying in what is now the Fairmont Queen Elizabeth. Although it does not look like a castle, it is a modern version of the Castles of the North. It is located above Montreal's train station. RBC's world headquarters were across the street in the four-winged cross-shaped tower of famously beautiful Place Ville Marie. I was amazed to hear Dad say Montreal's train station, the Queen Elizabeth, and RBC headquarters were all accessible by an elaborate set of underground tunnels filled with shops and restaurants. That in those days was a far cry from Calgary, the downtown of which today is connected by an equally elaborate set of Plus-15 overhead indoor walkways.

Dad after Mom's Death

Mom died in February 1970, aged 48. I was halfway through first year law school at UBC in Vancouver. I was awakened by someone in my UBC residence saying my Dad was on the community phone down the hall. He told me my Mom died during the night. Stunned, I was on the plane back to Calgary that afternoon. In 2008 the Minister at Knox United Church, the 'Cathedral of the West' according to the Government of Alberta, told me my Mom's funeral in 1970 was the biggest funeral at Knox ever. Her death, and the death of my grandmother Mary Catherine Gunn MacKenzie a decade later in June 1980, were two of the greatest losses of my life. When Dad stopped our car in the shadow of the Lancaster at the entrance to the terminal at Calgary Airport to drop me off for my flight back to Vancouver after Mom's funeral, he surprised me by saying he had not been sure whether I would

DAD POSTWAR

come back to Calgary for the funeral. I realized at that moment that my Dad hardly knew me. Nothing would have stopped me from coming home for Mom's funeral, but he did not know me well enough to know that. Were we strangers? I wondered that while boarding my plane.

Dad and I spent a bit of time together between Mom's death and Dad's second marriage two years later. I was at law school at UBC in Vancouver from September to April each year, but I was briefly at home for holidays like Christmas, and driving a taxi in Calgary in the springs of 1970 and 1971 before heading to Banff and Jasper to work as a tour guide to finance my education. It was easy to slip into Calgary from Banff for a few hours now and then as well. During our brief encounters while I was at home, Dad and I became a bit closer. Once we even went to a movie together.

Dad insisted I spend those two memorable law school summers giving tours of Canada's Rocky Mountains. I had obtained summer employment with a survey company that paid far more money. But Dad told me he did not want me wasting my final two summers before I became a lawyer isolated in the wilderness living in survey camps. Instead, he wanted me in Banff and Jasper meeting people worldwide, and learning lots about our Rockies.

Dad remained in Calgary working until his RBC retirement in 1972, and remained in Calgary until his death on 24 August 1991. In November 1971 I married, and in April 1972 Dad remarried. His life was in Calgary, mine in Vancouver. Our brief moments together were over.

Dad died on 24 August 1991, at age 79. Dad's death was a side-effect of the cortisone medicine he was forced to take to cope with emphysema arising from his heavy smoking, even though he quit cold turkey in 1959, when I turned 11. I never smoked because continuously overflowing ashtrays in our house in my boyhood made smoking repulsive to me. About three weeks after Dad died, I received a letter from one of his sisters, my Aunt Thelma Irvine. It said in part 'Your Dad loved you Roddy, but I suspect he never told you so.' She's right, he never did.

After Dad's death, my weak interest in his war experiences grew even weaker, given I had virtually no knowledge of anything he did, and bombing was not appealing. I had a dreadful feeling on 19 January 1992 when watching what I now know to be the inaccurate *The Valour and The Horror* on CBC National TV. But what really spurred me was in 2017 when by chance I discovered internet responses for pleas for help I'd posted in 2015 in a brief attempt to learn something about his time at war. Those responses changed everything. I have no idea how I did it, but it turns out somehow I had entered some form of RAF chat group. All I know is that this produced a mother lode of information about my Dad's service while seconded to the Royal Air Force in the Second World War.

This pretty much captures what I knew about my Dad. Sadly, most of my awareness of his wartime service arose since 2017, twenty-six years after his death way back in August 1991. But in 2017, my interest in Bomber Command started to soar, leading directly to my compelling desire, indeed my deep-seated need, to write this book.

Chapter Twenty-three

Bomber Command Postwar

A nation that forgets its past has no future.

Winston Churchill[1]

Our Failure of Remembrance is Unworthy of Us

Canada does not honour Bomber Command. Instead, we either forget it or defame it. Too many older Canadians are misinformed. Too many younger Canadians know nothing. My friend Brother Maximus sadly says for Bomber Command, 'We Canadians have become people who are forgetful, ungrateful and easily deceived.'[2] This situation is somewhat better in Australia, Britain and New Zealand, because their Bomber Command Associations and memorials keep Bomber Command's memory alive. But controversies persist, awash in misinformation. James Fyfe says, 'To denounce or even belittle or underestimate the accomplishments of its leader and its crews would be – regretfully has been and still is – one of the greatest ingratitudes ever inflicted on those who have offered their services in war.'[3] This is a serious problem. I have discovered in my quest that far too many know nothing about Bomber Command, even if their father or grandfather flew in it. And of those who have heard of Bomber Command, what far too many think they know is wrong. All of this is a collective failure of Remembrance. It is unworthy of us. Fyfe[4] points out that Britain fought the war longer than any other ally, and Bomber Command fought longer than any other military service, never stopping from when the war was just minutes old until the final attack by Mosquitoes on Kiel on 2/3 May 1945. James Hampton[5] adds, 'Had Mr Churchill not committed British industry to a major programme for the construction of heavy bombers, there could have been no bombing of the 'V' Weapon

---

1 This truism is often associated with Churchill, but I cannot determine whether he actually said it.
2 Brother Maximus, Westminster Abbey Christ the King Seminary, Mission, BC, Canada, 27 Novem 2018
3 Fyfe, *The Greatest Ingratitude*, pp. 325-36.
4 Fyfe, pp. 325-36. This, of course, was overmatched by the Royal Navy, which fought until the Japanese surrender in August 1945.
5 *Selected for Aircrew*, p. 329

Establishment at Peenemunde in August 1943 and no destruction of the launching sites in 1944.' As well, Hampton points out that, according to Eisenhower, the V weapons would have 'put paid' to the invasion and, without the heavy bombers, transportation in northern France could not have been destroyed. That, too, would have rendered impossible invading Europe.

Bomber Command fighting right up to Kiel 2/3 May 1945 paved the way for the British T-Force led by Major Tony Hibbert to capture Kiel, its port, scientists and canal on 5 May 1945, thus preventing the Soviets from taking the town, and indeed then Denmark in violation of the Yalta Agreement.[6] T-Force was the operational arm of the joint US/UK Armies to secure German scientific and technological targets and key personnel towards the end of the Second World War.[7] Fyfe says Bomber Command:

> suffered, how it had suffered – and anyone arguing that it played no significant part in re-establishing peace in Europe is skating on the thinnest of ice. When the broad spectrum of its achievements are examined, and digested, it might even be questioned whether victory would ever have been possible without it.

Australia, NZ and UK Remember

One fifth[8] of all Australians killed in the Second World War died flying in 300 Royal Air Force squadrons. Of the 10,000 Australians flying in Bomber Command, 4,000 (40 per cent) were killed. To honour those who died for us, the first Sunday in June is Bomber Command Sunday. I am told this has become the third biggest annual military event in Australia. In addition, founded in 1997, Australia has the Bomber Command Association in Australia, Inc., of which I am a member.

As for New Zealand, of the 6,000 New Zealanders flying in Bomber Command, 1,700 (28 per cent) were killed. New Zealand also honours Bomber Command on the first Sunday each June. In addition, founded in 1986, New Zealand has the New Zealand Bomber Command Association, of which I am a member.

In the United Kingdom, Bomber Command is remembered on the last Sunday in June, and London has the Bomber Command Memorial. Sadly, the Bomber Command Memorial and the Canada Memorial, both in Green Park, were vandalized with white paint on 21 January 2019. Also vandalized that night was the FDR and Churchill statue.

---

6 Wikipedia, Kiel, Operation Eclipse, History Learning Site

7 Wikipedia, T-Force

8 Grant. 'The Australians of Bomber Command who helped defeat Nazism were brave, not shameful.' *Sydney Morning Herald*, 2 June 2017.

Contrast all this to Canada doing nothing to thank, or even remember, one quarter of all Canadians in uniform killed in the Second World War – Canada's Bomber Boys.

Bomber Command Memorials

Statue of Sir Arthur Harris on The Strand in London: The Queen Mother unveiled this statue on 31 May 1992. The ceremony was marred by aggressive protestors disrupting Her Majesty's speech by screaming 'mass murderer!' They sprayed red paint on the footpath, and then on some of the 2,000 attendees. That forced police to haul them away from furious veterans. Undeterred, the Queen Mother completed her speech and the unveiling ceremony with dignity. No member of Britain's Cabinet attended, but the ousted Margaret Thatcher did. At the unveiling, Her Majesty said in part:

> As Patron of the Bomber Command Association, I am very pleased to join you today on this memorable occasion … . It is right that we should not forget those dark days of war when we were in grave danger and Bomber Command gave us hope and the means of salvation. Sir Arthur Harris was an inspiring leader who carried a heavy burden of responsibility for more than three years … more than 55,000 [Bomber Command aircrew] died defending our freedom … . We remember them today with pride and gratitude.

Royal Air Force Bomber Command Memorial in London: As mentioned, the Queen brought twenty-three members of the Royal Family to her unveiling of this Monument on 28 June 2012. This was done in the presence of 6,000 aircrew veterans from Australia, Britain, Canada, New Zealand and elsewhere, and family members of those killed. It is one of the finest war memorials in London, and has one of the best locations. Prince Philip, Prince Charles and Prince William wore their RAF uniforms. The Queen said to Marshal of the RAF Sir Arthur Beetham 'You've waited a long time for this. Well done.' The Lancaster flying overhead dropped 55,573 poppies – one poppy for everyone killed in Bomber Command – on Green Park.

Too many politicians blow with the wind. When times are tough, they are fair-weather friends. Successive British governments and the National Lottery[9] pointedly paid nothing for this Memorial, and nothing for the cost of the dedication. Instead, the Bomber Command Association picked up the £6.5 million bill to build the Memorial, and also paid the £700,000 for the dedication.[10]

---

9 Robert Hardman, 'How a Handful of Heroes beat the officials who tried to sabotage the new memorial to Bomber Command,' *Daily Mail*, 26 June 2012.

10 Holledge, 'They Were the Means of Victory,' *Wall Street Journal*, 2 July 2012

BOMBER COMMAND POSTWAR

Maintenance of the Memorial is financed through the Bomber Command Memorial Upkeep Club[11] of donors who contribute at least £1,000 to paying for the Memorial's upkeep. The Club is so named after the famous 'Upkeep' bouncing bombs created by Barnes Wallis and used by the Dambusters to bomb Germany's Ruhr Valley dams in May 1943.

The Memorial is in Green Park on Piccadilly near Hyde Park Corner, across the street from the RAF Club. It was designed by Liam O'Connor and built of Portland stone. The seven bronze 9-foot (2.7m) aircrew are sculpted by Philip Jackson. They appear as though they had just disembarked from their aircraft returning from a combat sortie.

The design of the Memorial's roof incorporates aluminium from Halifax LW682 of Bomber Command's 426 (Thunderbird) Squadron, No. 6 Group RCAF. That RCAF Halifax was shot down on 12 May 1944[12] and crashed into a bog. The bodies of only five of the eight airmen were recovered at the time. Fifty-three years later, in 1997, a Canadian-led recovery team, headed by Karl Kjarsgaard, recovered the Halifax and the remaining three bodies inside. Parts of this Halifax were used to restore Halifax NA337 which is on display at the National Air Force Museum of Canada at Trenton, Ontario. The aluminium was melted down into ingots, some of which the Bomber Command Museum of Canada donated for incorporation into the roof of the Bomber Command Memorial in Green Park.[13]

Bomber Command Memorial Spire in Lincoln was dedicated 2 October 2015 by Earl Howe, Minister of State in the House of Lords for Defence, in the presence of 2,600 guests, including 312 Bomber Command veterans. Perched on Canwick Hill, overlooking the City of Lincoln, this spire is the United Kingdom's tallest war memorial. The spire's dimensions are of the airframe and wings of the Lancaster. The spire represents two Lancaster wing fragments tapering towards the sky, separated by perforated plates similar to those used in a Lancaster's frame construction. The spire's 102-foot (31.09m) height is the span of a Lancaster wing, and its 16.4-foot (5m) wide base is the width of a Lancaster wing. Weathering steel gives the spire a bronzed austere feel, and makes it maintenance free. The names of those killed in Bomber Command, both aircrew and ground personnel, are laser cut into weathering steel panels. The Spire won the 2016 Structural Steel Design Award.[14]

This Spire was an enormous inspiration to me when I began writing this book in April and May 2019. I stayed for three weeks at the Premier Inn across the street.

---

11 Royal Air Force Benevolent Fund Bomber Command Memorial Upkeep Club www.rafbf.org/bomber-command-memorial/upkeep-club

12 Royal Air Force Benevolent Fund Bomber Command Memorial www.rafbf.org/bomber-command-memorial/about-memorial

13 Bomber Command Museum of Canada www.bombercommandmuseum.ca

14 Steel Construction Info – The Free Encyclopedia for UK Steel Construction Information www.steel-construction.info/The_Memorial_Spire

BOMBER COMMAND

I would walk over to the Spire and sit among the names of the deceased. This energized me to keep writing. Compiling these names is the dedicated handiwork of volunteer Dave Gilbert and his colleagues. Dave devoted a day to me as my tour guide and host on Sunday 12 May 2019.

International Bomber Command Centre by the Spire could, with re-worked software, become the definitive articulation of Bomber Command's accomplishments. I hope that happens. It opened informally at the end of January 2018 and was officially opened 12 April 2018. The ceremony was hosted by BBC political commentator John Sergeant and the main speaker was again Lord Howe. The Bishop of Lincoln oversaw the spiritual side. Five thousand from across the world were invited, many having Bomber Command family connections, and over 300 were Second World War Bomber Command veterans aged 92 to 100.[15]

Canadian Bomber Command Memorial was dedicated on 20 August 2005 in Nanton, Alberta in the presence of 4,000 attendees, including Canada's Minister of National Defence Bill Graham and RCAF Brigadier General David Graham. There was a flypast by 408 (Goose) Squadron RCAF and vintage aircraft. This Memorial has five panels of polished black granite on which are engraved the names of 10,673 Canadians killed in Bomber Command. The central panel has the name and purpose of the Memorial, the Bomber Command crest and a photograph of a Canadian Bomber aircrew.[16]

This Monument is beautiful and moving. It is outdoors in front of the Bomber Command Museum of Canada. They have largely avoided controversy because their location is Nanton, Alberta, a town of 2,000 an hour's drive south of Calgary. Most Canadians are unaware of this Memorial and Museum. I am a life member. Karl Kjarsgaard and his colleagues do wonderful work, but the location is a far cry from Ottawa. Contrast Nanton to London, Canberra and Auckland, the locations of the other three Commonwealth National Bomber Command Memorials.

Royal Australian Air Force Bomber Command Memorial was unveiled on 23 July 2005 by Australian Minister of Veteran Affairs De-Anne Kelly. It is in the Australian War Memorial Sculpture Garden in a suburb of Canberra in the Australian Capital Territory. The 54-foot (16.5m) high stainless steel central tower appears as a symbolized searchlight beam with air and ground crew as silhouetted figures and stencils of the eight types of aircraft flown.[17] The Australian War Memorial also has 460 Squadron RAAF Lancaster G-George. This Lancaster's ninety combat sorties is second of the survivors only to RAAF Lancaster S-Sugar in

---

15 Royal Air Force Memorial Flight Official Club www.memorialflightclub/blogm

16 Canada's Bomber Command Memorial, Bomber Command Museum of Canada www.bombercommandmuseum.ca

17 Monument Australia www.monumentaustralia.org.au/themes/conflict/ww2/display/90060-bomber-command

London (137 sorties). G-George is also noted for having brought home alive every aircrew member who flew aboard that aircraft. Most operational Lancasters were shot down before they reached twenty of the 107,085 combat sorties Lancasters flew over Germany.[18]

Royal New Zealand Air Force Bomber Command Memorial was unveiled on 1 March 2009 in the Auckland War Memorial Museum by the Chief of the Royal New Zealand Air Force, Air Vice-Marshal Graham Lintott, in the presence of 200 Second World War Bomber Command veterans, their families and friends, Auckland Mayor John Banks and President Bill Simpson of the New Zealand Bomber Command Association. It is a freestanding bronze sculpture of a Lancaster crew with a Lancaster coming out of the marble background.[19]

Bomber Command and Commonwealth Air Training Plan Memorials on Wellington in the Heart of Ottawa have not yet been constructed, or even proposed, but I deeply hope they will appear in my lifetime to complement the Memorials in Nanton, Alberta and Brandon, Manitoba.

Paradigm Shift of Perception

For me the biggest benefit of my Bomber Command quest is the paradigm shift I have undergone regarding my Dad and his Bomber Command colleagues. My research reveals our Bomber Boys are among the greatest heroes of the war. What they endured is unimaginable, and their shabby postwar treatment is shameful. Imagine being traumatized to the very core of your being fighting for us, and having to suppress all feelings postwar back home while being defamed by books and documentaries, and having to endure the failure of our leaders to defend you. I hope this book will lead others to a similar paradigm shift of perception.

Australia's Bomber Command Families –
An Important Concept

As mentioned, I am a member of the Bomber Command in Australia Association. Until a few years ago, Australian failure of remembrance of Bomber Command was, I'm told, as poor as it remains today here in Canada. However, even though almost all Australian Bomber Boys are now dead, their Bomber Command Association grows stronger each year thanks to their children, grandchildren and great grandchildren unhappy with Australia's postwar failure of remembrance.

---

18   Wikipedia G-George
19   Peter McQuaid, 'Bomber Command Memorial Air Force,' www.airforce.mil.nz/about-us/archive/102/bomber-command

These next three generations, now known as the 'Bomber Command Family in Australia', number a quarter of a million Australians.[20] And those numbers do not include the 'Uncles', meaning those Bomber Boys who died childless, but are, or should be, remembered by their nieces and nephews for all three generations. These must all be included too, because dying while fighting for our freedom in Bomber Command is what caused these uncles to die childless.

Australia's Bomber Command Family has contributed in the past decade or so to a paradigm shift in Australia's perception of Bomber Command. The 2 June 2017 edition of *The Sydney Morning Herald* is an example of this:

THE AUSTRALIANS OF BOMBER COMMAND WHO HELPED DEFEAT NAZISM WERE BRAVE, NOT SHAMEFUL

> From 1942, Australia's main contribution to the war against Germany was made by the RAAF. With 27,500 Australian airmen serving in 300 different Royal Air Force squadrons alongside Brits, Canadians and New Zealanders, experiences were diverse... . Casualties were high, accounting for nearly twenty per cent of all Australian combat deaths of the war... . Bomber Command was the most dangerous service in which Australians served in World War II ... . The allied bombing campaign did not deliver decisive victory, but it damaged Germany's ability to fight. It engaged and destroyed the German air force, and occupied manpower and resources that would otherwise have been deployed against allied forces elsewhere.[21]

My Life is Filled with RCAF Bomber Boy Families

Given the numbers in Australia without uncles, imagine how many Canadians are members of the yet to be formed Bomber Command Family in Canada, including nieces and nephews because so many Bomber Boys died childless.

My Bomber Command quest reveals an astonishing number of my friends are in Bomber Command families. They are below. I must thank Karl Kjarsgaard, the curator of the Bomber Command Memorial and Museum of Canada of which I am a life member. Karl has kindly provided a substantial amount of the following information for those of my Bomber Command families who knew little about their Bomber Boy ancestor. Those families are most grateful to Karl, as am I.

Jim Bartlett: My Kamloops friend is a nephew of Bomber Boy Christopher Smales Bartlett. Jim's Uncle Chris, a wing commander, led 434 (Bluenose) Squadron, No. 6 Group RCAF. He received a DFC and Bar, the latter for his 13 July 1944

---

20 Bomber Command Association in Australia Inc. Newsletter No. 69, Autumn 2019, p 4.
21 Grant, The Sydney Morning Herald, Sydney, Australia, June 2017

sortie over France where he was killed at the age of 26 when his Halifax bomber was shot down over Arras, six miles (10km) from Vimy Ridge). Bartlett Lake in Saskatchewan is named in his honour.

Jim's Dad, Richard Edward ('Dick') Bartlett, Chris Bartlett's younger brother, also warrants mention. In Stalag Luft III Dick built and operated the radio featured in the 1963 movie *The Great Escape*. The movie makers asked Dick to be their technical advisor, but the Royal Canadian Navy declined – the RCN wanted Dick to continue as its Naval Air Attaché to NATO. Jim became a PoW when, as a naval pilot, he was shot down while flying with the Fleet Air Arm off the aircraft carrier HMS *Ark Royal*. The forced march of PoWs by their guards to evade the Allies from January to March 1945 was murderous, but Dick survived.

Frank Borowicz QC: My friend and fellow lawyer since 1977 is the son-in-law of Bomber Boy RCAF Flight Lieutenant Gordon Smith, a Lancaster navigator in 418 Squadron, No. 6 Group RCAF. Intruder squadron 418 was Canada's highest-scoring squadron in the Second World War for air-to-air and air-to-ground kills in both day and night operations.[22] Gordon flew thirty-plus combat sorties. He cherished his Ops Wing confirming completion of his tour. Postwar, Gordon's three children became athletes – Mel played with the Canadian Football League Edmonton Eskimos, Terry played with the National Hockey League Chicago Black Hawks and Frank's wife Marilynn swam professionally for the US Navy before becoming a lawyer and then a judge here in British Columbia.

On 26 April 2021 I received from Frank the assessment Gordon, at age 99, gave him of what Bomber Command accomplished. Here unedited is what Gordon says:

> I believe Bomber Command shortened the war. We won the Battle of Britain. That made it possible to win the Battle of Europe. It was costly, but we saved lives. RAF had control of our targets. They did a hell of a job of that. Guns were firing at us every time. We could see them. It was all about human attitude. Who are we without character and determination? So many did so much.

Roy Brand: My friend and FitFellas exercise partner is the son of Bomber Boy RCAF Flight Sergeant Frederick Roy Brand (Roy Sr), a navigator who served briefly with 50 Squadron RAF. Roy Sr then completed two tours, each of twenty-five combat sorties each, with the elite 617 Squadron (Dambusters) RAF, plus three additional sorties to enable three of his aircrew to complete their tours with him as their navigator. During combat sorties, Roy Sr crashed three times. On one crash he was knocked unconscious briefly and smoke filled the fuselage, so his crewmates had to drag him to safety. Back in Canada, he had to be checked at Sunnyside Veterans Hospital bi-annually for the back problems he incurred. As mentioned in my 'Sea War' chapter, on 12 November 1944 Roy Sr participated

---

22 Wikipedia RCAF 418 Squadron WW2

with Tallboy bombs in the sinking of the mighty *Tirpitz*, one of Germany's greatest battleships. Roy Sr's sorties bombed V.1 flying-bomb and V.2 rocket launching sites and U-boat pens, as did my Dad's. Returning from one combat sortie, Roy Sr and his crew were swarmed by ground crew who were going on leave the minute the aircraft was serviced. These airmen watched in shock the quantity of shrapnel that crashed to the ground, and how close some of it had been to their fuel tanks. When they flew to Murmansk, each member of the crew was given a large tin box of Russian cigarettes which Roy Jr tells me his Dad, to the horror of Roy Jr's Mom, always served postwar whenever members of his crew visited him.

Rochelle Bruce: My Vancouver friend is a cousin of Bomber Boy David Sair, an RCAF Lancaster pilot, aged 21, who flew eleven combat sorties from Yorkshire before being wounded in action and grounded by shrapnel. He lost several fingers.

Doreen Charlwood Burge: My Australian friend is the daughter of Bomber Boy Donald Earnest Cameron ('Don') Charlwood, an RAAF navigator with 103 Squadron at Elsham Wolds, which is only six miles (10 km) from Kirmington. Don wrote *No Moon Tonight* (1956) about which the *Manchester News* wrote 'No finer requiem has been said for the dead of Bomber Command'. Trained in the Plan in Canada, his combat sorties were to heavily defended targets such as Berlin, Bremen, Dusseldorf, Duisburg, Essen and Nuremberg. Don began his detailed notes from diaries, letters and his memory for his book in 1944 'during enforced leisure in a Canadian military hospital'[23] which was right after he married his Canadian bride in Victoria. Don also wrote *Journeys Into Night* (1991), his autobiographical account written with the perspective of almost a half century of hindsight. These two books are regarded as among 'the finest autographical accounts of Bomber Command'[24] although Don regarded *No Moon Tonight* as a memoir, not an autobiography. Both books have had many editions. To me Don is a Bomber Command giant whose writings are worthy of enormous respect. They give life to Bomber Boys in a way that enriches us all. Don died on 18 June 2012.

Ernie Davis: My friend since boyhood whose daughter-in-law, Rebecca Walker, is a great niece of Bomber Boy Sergeant John Patrick ('Pat') Rothera. Rebecca's Great Uncle Pat was a bomb-aimer in 207 Squadron, No. 5 Group RAF. On 29 January 1944, while bombing Berlin, Pat's Lancaster was shot down. Seven of the eight aboard, including Pat, were killed. Confusion began because eight, rather than just seven, were aboard. It turns out that the eighth was a second navigator. Confusion continued because the SS tossed all the bodies into one hole. Later the British had difficulties identifying the bodies when removing them to bury them properly. As an anomaly of war, details about this crash remain secret in Britain but are available here in Canada. Karl Kjarsgaard tells me fifty-six of our bombers,

---

23 Charlwood, *No Moon Tonight*, p. 9
24 Wikipedia, Don Charlwood

with about 390 aircrew, were shot down on Pat's Berlin combat sortie that night. Berlin was notoriously difficult to bomb because it was so far away, and so heavily defended.

Patrick Dennis: My friend, RCAF Colonel (Retd) and author is the nephew-in-law of Bomber Boy RCAF Flight Sergeant Peter Dutchak. Peter, the only maternal uncle of Pat's wife Wendy, was a mid-upper air gunner posted to 100 Squadron, No. 1 Group RAF, at Grimsby, only fourteen miles (22 km) east of Kirmington. Peter's pilot was killed on his 'second dickie' ride. Second dickie refers to an inexperienced pilot aboard for a single ride to observe how an experienced aircrew conducts a combat sortie before flying his own aircrew into battle. Peter and his crew were posted to 44 (Rhodesia) Squadron, No. 5 Group RAF where, incredibly, their new pilot was also killed on his 'second dickie' ride. On 24 February 1944 Peter and his crew were posted to 630 Squadron, No. 5 Group at East Kirkby, home today of 'Just Jane' (Lancaster NX611). On 18 March 1944, after successfully bombing Frankfurt, Peter and his six fellow aircrew were all killed in action near the Belgian coast, possibly by a coastal flak battery or by a radar-equipped German night fighter. Peter's pilot was RNZAF Bomber Boy Pilot Officer Kenneth Watson Orchiston. Peter was a musician. The RAF returned his violin to his family. Wendy now plays it.

In addition, Patrick has given me information for Bomber Boy Pilot Officer James Patrick Durkin, the uncle of Pat's next-door neighbour Cathy Kuhn in Kitchener, Ontario. He was a rear gunner aboard a Halifax in 424 Squadron, No. 6 Group RCAF. Pilot Officer Durkin's thirty-four combat sorties were from 13 March until 4 November 1944. Patrick compiled them for me from Durkin's logbook. I have included them in Chapter Twelve. Durkin's final sortie was bombing Bochum, a mining city near Essen in the Ruhr. He and his crew 'failed to return from this operation' and no trace was ever found of the aircraft or any of the crew. His death hit his parents hard – they died within a day of one another just before Christmas 1944.

Blain Fowler: My Camrose Alberta friend, and publisher of the Camrose Booster newspaper, is the nephew of 'Bomber Boy' Flying Officer Victor Thomas Fowler DFC. My Dad's younger brother, my Uncle Arthur MacKenzie, was Mayor of Camrose. Blain's Uncle Vic was born in Camrose in April 1920. The RCAF recruiter directed him into pilot training. Being only 5'2" and 122 pounds, Vic felt he was not strong enough to handle an aircraft, so he requested he be trained as a navigator/observer instead.

Overseas he, like my Dad, was seconded by the RCAF to the RAF. There he flew two tours of duty with 7 Squadron at RAF Oakington, near Cambridge. His first tour was aboard a Short Stirling, the first four-engine heavy bomber introduced into RAF service. He said its service ceiling was only 13,000 feet and that made him feel like a sitting duck.

On one sortie they were attacked by a night-fighter and landed in Tangmere, a village in West Sussex, with zero fuel and 300 holes shot into their aircraft. In

BOMBER COMMAND

August 1942, Vic's squadron was transferred into Bomber Command's Pathfinder Force. On 11 May 1943, the squadron was equipped with Lancasters which Vic said were excellent airplanes. He became a 'Master Pathfinder Navigator'. His final combat sortie was in December 1944, bringing his total to 60. He was told the survival rate of that many sorties was only 4%.

Blain married Maureen Smith, a steno at RAF Oakington Base Operations. In that position, Maureen knew where Vic would be flying on combat sorties before he did. After discharge from the RCAF in 1945, Vic became a Chartered Accountant who rose to serve as Alberta's Supervisor of Credit Unions and Co-operative Activities. He died in 2009.

Jim Haliburton: Three Haliburton brothers – Jim's father John ('Jack') Charles Haliburton and Jim's paternal uncles Bomber Boys Gilbert ('Gibb') Paul Haliburton and William ('Bill') Christopher Haliburton – all served in the Second World War as RCAF flying officer pilots. Jim's father was a flying instructor here in Canada. Jim's Uncle Bill flew with 408 (Goose) Squadron No. 6 Group RCAF. Jim's Uncle Gibb was killed in action on 31 March 1945 in 434 (Bluenose) Squadron also No. 6 Group RCAF. KB911's, his Lancaster, cockpit was hit by a rocket launched from a Me.262 jet. He was buried in 1946 in the CWGC Ohlsdorf Cemetery in Hamburg.

Brian Hann: My WVan friend is the brother of a Bomber Boy, and they are cousins of a second Bomber Boy. Brian's brother Flying Officer Raymond Hann was killed in April 1942, presumably in a crash in the English Channel. Their maternal cousin Gordon Wickson was killed a month later in May 1942. He was a Pathfinder. Both Bomber Boys were 22 years old when they were killed.

Ted Hawthorne: My friend and fellow lawyer is the son of Bomber Boy RCAF Flying Officer William Simpson Hawthorne in 433 Squadron (Porcupine), No. 6 Group RCAF. Ted's Dad flew thirty-seven combat sorties – his required thirty plus seven. He cherished his Ops Wing confirming completion of his tour. He told Ted that Ruhr Valley targets were the worst. Ruhr defences were so powerful it was like daylight at midnight, and the anti-aircraft grid system in the Ruhr was so good it meant you were almost always hit. Being hit meant death or becoming a PoW if your aircraft was disabled. Ted tells me his Dad was deeply upset by postwar defamation of Bomber Command, and especially CBC's *Death By Moonlight* on 19 January 1992. He and his aircrew took their work, and especially their targets, very seriously. They strived for accuracy. Their bombing was photographed for accuracy.

Elmer Harold ('Flip') Hunt: My friend and FitFellas senator is Bomber Boy Flip Hunt who disappeared just before I started writing this book. Flip resurfaced in a seniors' home in Kamloops, and then died on 1 November 2020. The Covid-19 pandemic prevented our getting together before his death. Flip was a rear gunner in a Halifax who flew thirty combat sorties in an RCAF Bomber Command squadron. Our FitFellas classmate Nigel Grant tells me Flip acquired his life-long nickname

'Flip' because, when his Halifax crash-landed, the gun turret flipped off with Flip in it. The Halifax then veered off the runway and burst into flames, killing everyone else in Flip's crew. Flip told me of his postwar exploration in England of a field where he thought his air base had been. A hostile farmer on a tractor challenged him with a gun, ordering him away. Flip explained his purpose. The farmer asked a few verifying questions, then put away his gun. He told Flip he was a small boy when Flip's squadron flew at his farm, that his Dad provided the aircrew with special treats of food from his farm, and that his family thought the world of the brave young Bomber Boys. The farmer then showed Flip where the base and runway had been. Afterwards, he took Flip back to his farmhouse for drinks and dinner in appreciation of Flip's wartime service.

Che Lafoy: His grandfather, and my Dad's maternal first cousin, was Bomber Boy Lloyd Stanley ('Red') Lafoy who flew thirty-one combat sorties as an upper gunner or rear gunner with RCAF Squadrons 426 (Thunderbird), 429 (Bison) and 425 (Alouette) in 6 Group RCAF primarily from RCAF Dishforth, Yorkshire. On one combat sortie, while they were being bombarded by flak, Red's rear turret jammed, so he asked fellow crewman Murray 'Tupp' Tupper to help him unjam it. Tupp did, then returned to his position to discover a large hole where his seat had been. Red's jammed turret saved Tupp's life. After completing his tour in 1944, Red attended officer training in the UK and became a gunnery instructor as a pilot officer on the Isle of Man while waiting for transfer to the Pacific. All ended when America bombed Hiroshima. Red attended my Dad's funeral in 1991.

Leah Lancaster: Sadly Leah, my friend, and the spouse of my cousin Trevor Lancaster of Lethbridge, died of cancer on 7 December 2021. She was the great niece of Bomber Boy Squadron Leader Robert George West. Her Great Uncle Bob piloted a Halifax in 76 Squadron RAF. On 23 June 1944 they bombed the marshalling yards at Laon to prevent Germans from sending reinforcements to Normandy. En route home, a Bf.110 night fighter attacked, disabling their inboard port engine. Bob kept flying on three engines, just as my Dad did on his final sortie. However, when they started to land, their 13-foot (4-m) diameter propeller broke off their disabled engine and spun into the cockpit, killing Leah's Great Uncle Bob and his wireless operator. Their pilotless, out-of-control Halifax nose-dived, killing everyone.

John MacLean: My friend and former Naval Officers Association of BC president is the cousin of Bomber Boys Thomas Rose and Donald Rose, both air observers/navigators RCAF sergeants. Tommy was killed when his 40 Squadron RAF Wellington from RAF Alconbury, Cambridgeshire was coned by searchlights and descended in flames on a sortie to Boulogne on 13 March 1941. His first and second pilots, Bomber Boys Douglas William Gough and Thomas Geoffrey Webb, were New Zealanders and his other aircrew English. All were only 19 years old – at that time they were the youngest RAF bomber aircrew certified for operations.

BOMBER COMMAND

They are buried together at Wimille Communal Cemetery in the Pas de Calais near where their aircraft crashed.

Bomber Boy Donald Rose was killed on 29 January 1944 when his Halifax LK640 in 434 (Bluenose) Squadron RCAF from RCAF Croft, Yorkshire was shot down by a German night-fighter pilot during a thousand-plane sortie to Berlin. He is buried in the Commonwealth Cemetery in Berlin. Tommy's and Donald's younger brother Bomber Boy Douglas Rose survived two tours of duty as a Lancaster pilot with 'the finest aircrew a man could hope to serve with'.

Keith Macrae: My friend and Elsham Wolds *Newsletter* editor is the son of RAF Bomber Boy flight engineer Malcolm Edward Thomas Macrae. Keith's dad flew his combat sorties with 103 Squadron RAF from Elsham Wolds from April to July 1944. My Dad flew his combat sorties nearby at Kirmington from April to August 1944, so they may have met. Returning on 29 July 1944 from bombing Stuttgart, that being Keith's dad's twenty-eighth combat sortie, his Lancaster was shot down about twenty-eight miles (45 km) south-east of Nancy at the village of Glonville in Lorraine. There the French Resistance hid him and his navigator for about ten weeks. Then the daughter of the woman in whose house they were hidden led Keith's dad and his navigator through a no man's land minefield to the approaching American army. They were saved. Of his dad's remaining five aircrew, two became PoWs and three were killed and are buried in Glonville. Their Scottish pilot was almost 21; their wireless operator and rear gunner were both only 18 years old.

Keith Maxwell: My friend and retired RCAF colonel is the son of Bomber Boy Flying Officer Allan Maxwell, a Lancaster pilot who served in No. 6 Group RCAF Bomber Command. Keith's superb talk on 'WWII Strategic Bomber Command' I attended on 10 April 2019 stressed the extremely high quality of the Plan's aircrew training – Keith told me on 12 April 2021 the examples he used for that impressive talk were his dad's experiences.

Dorothy Milne Miller: My friend and cousin-in-law in Saskatoon, age 91 in 2022, is a cousin of Bomber Boy David Reid of Duff, Saskatchewan. He was a bomb aimer who survived.

Margaret Moppett: My friend is the sister of Bomber Boy Flight Sergeant Dennis Eastcott, a wireless operator who flew in my Dad's 166 Squadron. He was killed on his twenty-first sortie on 23 February 1945 when his Lancaster AS-L2 was shot down over Pforzheim, near Stuttgart. His 1945 diary is attached as Appendix IV.

Chris Newey is the nephew of Bomber Boy Flight Sergeant Gerry Newey, a Royal New Zealand Air Force wireless operator/air gunner in Bomber Command. Gerry's aircrew consisted of three New Zealanders, two Canadians and an Englishman who 'crewed up' together, and afterwards a Scot who joined as flight engineer. They flew thirty-two combat sorties with 75 (New Zealand) Squadron, nineteen of which were aboard Lancaster HK601 JN-D-Dog C. While training in No. 12 OTU just after midnight on 12 July 1944, they crashed their Wellington, BJ622. They and their Canadian pilot instructor miraculously emerged unhurt from this belly landing, but their Wellington was destroyed in the fire that followed. Gerry died in 1977, aged 56.

Calvin, Randy and Guy Pocock: Calvin and I have been friends since we were fifteen in Calgary. Calvin's younger brother Randy is a fellow lawyer in Lethbridge, and their youngest brother Guy an architect in Calgary. These three brothers are sons of Bomber Boy RCAF Pilot Officer Eric Arthur Pocock, a wireless operator/air gunner. He died in 1984, aged 72. Like so many of the Bomber Boys, he volunteered because 'it was the right thing to do'. Calvin and I paid our respects at his grave in September 2020.

The Selman Family: My friend since Chief Crowfoot Elementary School in Calgary in the 1950s, Beverly Selman Smith of Champion AB, her brother Gordon Selman of Sherwood Park AB, and their sisters Marilyn Woolf of Utah and Sharan Gainor of Nicaragua, all helped me with this. They are the offspring of Bomber Boy John Francom ('Frank') Selman who was shot down at 21,000 feet on his thirteenth combat sortie, destination Dusseldorf. I am assuming he was aboard a Lancaster because I saw a framed photo of one on her wall when I visited their mom, Mary Wolfater Selman, shortly before her death on 2 July 2009. She told me her husband served in Bomber Command. The German who shot him down was flying a four-engine British Stirling, and so was able to get too close before they realized it was the enemy. In Frank's words, the 'Stirling behind us opened up with cannon and machine guns and just blew us to pieces'.

While parachuting down, Frank was shot three times – twice in the head and once in the leg. On landing, he sprained his ankle. He was bleeding badly, so he had to get medical help. He hobbled to a Belgian farmhouse. There the farmer's wife cleaned him up while the farmer sought Belgian police, one of whom spoke English. Frank told them his story, thinking they would help him. But then the door burst open, and in came three German soldiers with machine guns. Frank spent two years as a PoW, taken first to Stalag Luft III of the 1963 movie *The Great Escape*, and later north to Stalag Luft VI on the Baltic Coast about the same latitude as Fort McMurray, Alberta, where winters were bitterly cold. Towards the end of the war, they were force-marched freezing and starving out of their PoW camp in an attempt by their German guards to evade the Allies, but finally a tank appeared gloriously flying the Union Jack. The British Army liberated them.

Fred Wright: My friend since we were thirteen is the stepson of Bomber Boy John Lorne Wright, an RCAF mid-upper gunner in Bomber Command.

Martyn Wright: My first and best 166 Squadron friend Martyn is the son of Bomber Boy 166 Squadron Sergeant Jim Wright. Jim was a wireless operator who completed thirty-one combat sorties with 166 Squadron from October 1944, and then in France with his 166 Pilot Chas Martin (RNZAF) monitored the retreat of the invading forces. On one sortie, flying home over the Channel, they activated an auto flak gun from below. Normally it fired two bangs and the third one got you. However, after two bangs Chas dived, so the third missed them. But they then found themselves over London where they were shot at even though they fired identification flares. Somehow they survived. Jim served in combat in those last seven months of the Second World War solely because he altered his birth certificate to convince the RAF he was a year older than he actually was. That is a classic example of the dedication of Bomber Command aircrew, all volunteers.

Postwar, Jim attained the rank of squadron leader as CO of 2275 ATC Squadron. Since 1978, Jim led the 166 Squadron Association and, with his son Martyn, organized the annual Friday to Sunday reunions, until poor health prevented Jim in about 2008. Martyn has carried on with abbreviated reunions, and RAF Wing Commander Tony Lark has willingly continued with the 166 Memorial, including persuading me with my sons Guy Roland and Ruaridh MacKenzie to participate in 2018. Jim died on 1 December 2013.

In 1996 Jim published his magnus opus – *On Wings of War: A History of 166 Squadron*. It helps hugely in writing my book. Jim's book has been described as the most beautifully written book on Bomber Command. Tragically, the publishers' premises were burnt to the ground a couple of years after it was published, destroying everything needed to reprint Jim's wonderful book.

Coastal Command Family Anecdote: To conclude these family remembrances, this one veers off Bomber Command, but it's my family, and it's heartwarming. The husband of my Dad's sister, my Aunt Thelma Irvine, was Dr Warren Irvine. Uncle Warren was a wartime RCAF pilot in Coastal Command in Britain and the Mediterranean. The youngest of their five children, my cousin Sandra Irvine of Nelson BC, told me this touching anecdote about her dad. At one point Uncle Warren was assigned elsewhere, so another pilot flew his aircrew and crashed in bad weather. All but one were killed. Uncle Warren took photos of their graves. Postwar, he visited their families to convey his condolences in person, and to talk to them about his experiences with their deceased member of his aircrew. Uncle Warren later became a medical doctor in Dawson Creek BC, whose mayor told me my Uncle Warren delivered virtually every baby in Dawson Creek for years.

A Marvellous Discovery at Churchill College Cambridge

On 22 May 2019, the Director of Churchill Archives at Cambridge, Allen Packwood, accredited me for three years as a Churchill reader. That was astonishing because I thought he was going to accredit me for three days. Being accredited entitled me to review original documents in the Churchill Archives. And there's more. That same day Allen and I made an amazing discovery. It started with me finding a 16 May

1945 telegram from Harris to Churchill expressing gratitude. What on earth could Harris be grateful for after Churchill's failure to mention Bomber Command in his victory speech? To what mysterious document was Harris replying? It reminded me of the Letters of St Paul in the *New Testament* of the Bible. St Paul's letters were largely to sort out the endless internal problems of his new churches. I wonder what was in the letters to which St Paul was replying. Likewise, what was Harris replying to here? Knowing that this discovery could well go to the core of my Bomber Command quest, Allen warned me the originating document to which Harris was replying may no longer exist, or that even if it does, we might not be able to find it. But the search was on. And guess what? That very afternoon Allen appeared with his biggest smile. He was proudly holding the document. He had found it. It was a 15 May 1945 telegram from Churchill to Harris. Churchill's message, and the appreciation Harris expressed, are how I conclude this book. Read on.

Chapter Twenty-four

Conclusions

My Bomber Command quest was to discover what my Dad did in the Second World War. That led to my discovery of what Bomber Command accomplished, and how all this happened. I was astonished to learn that Bomber Command's contribution to defeating Germany was huge. I had had no idea what Bomber Command accomplished. I certainly did not know that Bomber Command was vital to victory. And until now I was singularly unclear how this all happened.

For starters, the air forces. I did not know how Bomber Command came to be four Commonwealth Air Forces working as one. Nor did I know how independent the Royal Canadian Air Force became, and how that worked to the great advantage of the Allies. I also did not know how closely Bomber Command and the Mighty Eighth worked as one, also to the great advantage of the Allies.

I found fascinating the opinions of giants such as Churchill, FDR, Eisenhower and Montgomery, as well as Royalty about Bomber Command. And it is wrong that, just like Bomber Command, two leaders were seriously abused postwar – Mackenzie King and Harris. Our failure of proper remembrance is unworthy of us. By way of contrast, postwar America has been supportive of the Mighty Eighth, indeed proud and appreciative, just as we should have been of Bomber Command. This divergence of attitude has led to the myth that the Mighty Eighth was more effective than Bomber Command, when in fact the reverse was true.

In this seamless joint strategic bombing offensive of Bomber Command and the Mighty Eighth, Bomber Command was the leader and did the heavier lifting for five reasons – the RAF and Dominion air forces had long been focused on strategic bombing to which America was the newcomer, Lancasters and Mosquitoes were the most effective aircraft, the Tallboys and Grand Slams were the most effective bombs, the Plan produced the world's best aircrew, and Harris with Churchill's support provided continuous outstanding leadership from his 22 February 1942 appointment by Churchill right through to Germany's 8 May 1945 surrender. Eisenhower was right – Harris accomplished miracles.

I am glad my Bomber Command quest led me to German sources because the Germans knew far better than we what Bomber Command accomplished. Germany's Research Institute for Military History has documented carefully how catastrophic Bomber Command was. In a word, Bomber Command destroyed Germany's ability to wage war. Thank goodness Hitler failed to heed Albert

CONCLUSIONS

Speer's warnings until it was too late. In addition, I was happy to learn that Bomber Command reduced Göring to a figure of ridicule and unleashed an internally destructive power struggle in the highest ranks of the Reich.

And finally, I'm glad I learnt that much, perhaps most, of what I thought I knew about Bomber Command and my Dad was wrong. My Bomber Command quest has created a massive paradigm shift for me. I hope it will for you too.

The Last Bomber Boy to Die

Here is a touching concluding anecdote. RCAF Flight Sergeant Kenneth Earl Clifford Slack of Toronto flew with 433 (Porcupine) Squadron in 6 Group RCAF Bomber Command. He was shot down, then liberated as a PoW on 22 April 1945. However, he lost his life on 9 May 1945, the day after Germany's surrender. He died trying to save a German guard who had fallen into the River Elbe near Schonebeck.[1] Slack being one of the last Bomber Boys to die in the Second World War, coupled with the reason for which he lost his life, reflects the heartwarming humanity of these idealistic young men, our Bomber Boys.

My Big Four Discoveries

- Bomber Command was vital to victory.
- Our failure of Remembrance is unworthy of us.
- I've undergone a full paradigm shift in how I perceive my Dad and his brothers-in-arms who endured the unendurable for us.
- Bomber Command was indeed Churchill's Greatest Triumph!

Colin Bell's Summation of Bomber Command Accomplishments

A magnificent summation of Bomber Command accomplishments was given to me on 22 July 2021 by Colin Bell, a Second World War Pathfinder pilot now over 100 years old. The occasion was a dinner at the RAF Club in London attended by eighty and watched via Zoom by 120, including me. Colin flew a Mosquito in fifty combat sorties over Germany, fifteen of which were over Berlin, the most difficult and dangerous target in the Third Reich. He credits his miraculous survival of these fifty sorties to his Canadian navigator Doug Redmond. I asked Colin: 'How do you feel about how poorly Bomber Command has been acknowledged and misrepresented postwar?' Colin's reply is unforgettable. He said:

---

1 *International Bomber Command Centre Newsletter* article referred to me on 9 May 2020 by Barbara Hunter of the New Zealand Bomber Command Association

Well, a bit angry really. But it gives me an opportunity to make the point that the whole objective of Bomber Command was to destroy the German capability of attacking us. When I say 'us', I mean our men, our women, and our children. We went out to destroy that capability and we only attacked those cities that were involved in war production, and I might add that includes Dresden. Dresden had 10,000 workers producing things like periscopes for submarines, bits for the Luftwaffe and in addition Dresden had marshalling yards through which, believe it or not, twenty thousand troops went each and every day. So Dresden was quite properly a target, and it was attacked [by us] and also attacked by our heroic Americans in daylight. Bomber Command has been misrepresented by a lot of rather ignorant people that know no better, and I might add who would never have come into existence if Bomber Command in this country hadn't won the war.

Colin's statement was rewarded with enthusiastic applause.

Bomber Command was Churchill's Greatest Triumph!

Last but not least, Bomber Command was indeed Churchill's greatest triumph, for without his support Bomber Command might not have flourished as it did and the Second World War would have been a very different story. Bomber Command was essential to our taking control of the air, Churchill was essential to Bomber Command's survival and Mackenzie King was essential to funding the British Commonwealth Air Training Plan which produced the world's finest aircrew. Roosevelt was right in declaring to the world that Canada was the Aerodrome of Democracy.

Sadly, Churchill's Bomber Command legacy is tarnished by his Dresden silence in February 1945, his ill-considered signal to General Ismay in March 1945, and his appalling omission of Bomber Command in his speech praising the armed forces at the end of the war. But he certainly captured Bomber Command's massive achievement with his 15 May 1945 telegram to Bomber Command. I can think of no finer way in which to conclude this book than with the Harris thanks, followed by that which Churchill said to generate thanks from Harris. Here they are:

MESSAGE FROM AIR CHIEF MARSHAL ARTHUR HARRIS
FOR BOMBER COMMAND TO PRIME MINISTER
16 May 1945

Bomber Command is deeply grateful to you for your message on behalf of His Majesty's Government. We do not forget your personal understanding of our needs and of the difficulties which beset us

CONCLUSIONS

in our darkest hours, some were dark indeed. It was your unfailing encouragement, your inspiring determination to hold to the course through everything, which brought us through to dawn, and to victory. To us, you were the foremost of the Pathfinders.

MESSAGE FROM PRIME MINISTER TO AIR CHIEF MARSHAL ARTHUR HARRIS FOR BOMBER COMMAND
15 May 1945

Now that Nazi Germany is defeated, I wish to express to you on behalf of His Majesty's Government the deep sense of gratitude which is felt by all the Nation for the glorious part which has been played by Bomber Command in forging the victory.

For over two years, Bomber Command alone carried the war to the heart of Germany, bringing hope to the peoples of occupied Europe, and to the enemy a foretaste of the mighty power which was arising against him. As the Command expended (sic), in partnership with the Air Forces of our American Ally, the weight of the attacks was increased, dealing destruction of an unparalleled scale to the German military, industrial and economic system. Your Command also gave powerful support to the Allied Armies in Europe and made a vital contribution to the war at sea. You destroyed or damaged many of the enemy's ships of war and much of his u-boat (sic) organization. By a prolonged series of mining operations you sank or damaged large quantities of his merchant shipping. All your operations were planned with great care and skill; they were executed in the face of desperate opposition and appalling hazards; they made a decisive contribution to Germany's final defeat.

The conduct of these operations demonstrated the fiery gallant spirit which animated your aircrews and the high sense of duty of all ranks under your command.

I believe that the massive achievements of Bomber Command will long be remembered as an example of duty nobly done.

WINSTON S. CHURCHILL

Appendix I

Royal Air Force Distinguished Flying Cross
Citation for Flight Lieutenant Roland W MacKenzie

This Canadian officer has now completed 30 4/3 faultless attacks on enemy targets, ranging from Germany to occupied territory. He has consistently shown himself to be a pilot of great skill and has displayed high qualities of leadership and courage. He has been determined to press home his attack regardless of the opposition and has always been successful. His tenacity of purpose was magnificently displayed on his last sortie on the 16th*August 1944 when, on proceeding to the target, an engine failed. He made no less than three runs over the target, despite heavy flak, to ensure that his bombs fell in the target area.

On the ground, as Deputy Flight Commander, he has shown willingness and enthusiasm which have been an inspiration to the whole squadron. For his determination and devotion to duty, he is strongly recommended for the award of the Distinguished Flying Cross.

Explanatory Notes 19 August 2018 of Roland W. MacKenzie's son Roddy:

The Distinguished Flying Cross was awarded to Dad effective 1 December 1944 as per *London Gazette* dated 12 December 1944 and AFRO 337/45 dated 23 February 1945.

30 4/3 sorties means Dad flew thirty-four sorties, but four were abandoned and so count as only 1/3 of one sortie each. The four abandoned sorties were:

2 June 1944 to Calais, France because of 10/10th cloud over target

---

* 16 August 1944 is an RAF typo. Dad's last sortie was on 11 August 1944. The target was Douai, France, just a few kilometres from Vimy Ridge.

288

ROYAL AIR FORCE DISTINGUISHED FLYING CROSS

17 June 1944 to Aulnoye, France because of 10/10th cloud over target

28 June 1944 to Aachen, Germany because the bomb doors wouldn't open

12 July 1944 to Revigny-sur-Ornain, France on Master Bomber instructions

Appendix II

Royal Bank of Canada *Quill & Ledger* Letter

The only writing of which I am aware by my Dad about his experiences in Bomber Command is his 1975 letter published in RBC's *Quill & Ledger* newsletter.

Dear Editor,

Recently my path crossed that of W.H. (Bill) Wood. It was my pleasure to work with Bill before the war. We both joined the Air Force; he was in aircrew on a Halifax Squadron; I was pilot on a Lancaster Squadron, flying aircraft 'L' for 'Love'. We didn't know it then, but our paths had crossed while we both were with Bomber Command. It happened on April 24, 1944.

My flight and Squadron were placed on alert about 1000 hours. Almost immediately my crew knew something special was up because our kite, 'Love' was receiving a full load of petrol, a full load of H.E. and incendiary bombs, plus 1,500 pounds of 'Window' – far in excess of the usual load. Window consisted of strips of foil two inches wide of various lengths and was dropped at regular intervals in the hopes it would jam enemy radar.

Some 30 miles away, Bill's Halifax was being loaded with 1,500 gallons of petrol, a different type of bomb load and their usual load of Window, about 100 pounds. It looked like a routine trip.

At 1900 hours we had our usual before flight meal of bacon, eggs, and fried potatoes – all very tasty but highly indigestible. The food was, I am sure, designed to keep us from getting hungry for hours. At 2000 hours we were in the briefing room and given our assignment. The main target was Munich where the famous 'Dam Buster' Squadron was to try a new target marking technique. They were using Mosquito aircraft for the first time and because of that aircraft's limited range (long range petrol tanks were not available), timing was most important. Our Squadron was assigned to a spoof and a diversionary target at Karlsruhe in the hopes that enemy fighters would be drawn away, thereby enabling the Munich raiders to have as trouble free a trip as possible.

ROYAL BANK OF CANADA *QUILL & LEDGER* LETTER

At 1900 hours the Halifax crews sat down to their before flight meal of bacon, eggs and fried potatoes, and at 2000 hours were given their assignment. They were to go to Karlsruhe where the target would be marked by Pathfinder Group at 0140 hours, immediately before our spoof. They were told that fires might already be burning when they arrived. They were also told the weather would be terrible.

We took off at 2100 hours and climbed immediately over base as high as we could before setting course. The Meteorological people were right – the weather was terrible and icing conditions bad, resulting in the loss of some of our instruments such as the all important 'air speed indicator'. We climbed above the dangerous icing level.

At 2215 hours, as we were leaving England, the Halifax Squadron began taking off. Icing conditions had worsened, with the result ice formed on their wings to such an extent many could not climb over 10,000 feet. They were to stagger along in solid cloud at that height for the entire trip. It was far from being a routine operation.

We cruised along at 22,000 feet, dropping 'Window' like mad, till we reached Dijon in France at midnight. We then doubled back on our tracks in an effort to confuse the enemy and at 2430 hours turned East toward Karlsruhe, again dropping 'Window'.

The Halifax Squadrons and the Dam Buster Lancasters were now only 15 minutes behind us and were flying under our 'window' cover. Ironically the Dam Buster Mosquitoes were a few miles east at 14,000 feet in CLEAR weather!

At 0130 we broke out of the cloud. Below was the Rhine River with Karlsruhe just ahead. We bombed at 0132 and then turned South with the idea of again leading defences astray. As we turned away, we saw the Pathfinders' markers go down right on schedule at 0140. At 0145 we turned for home, our supply of 'Window' almost gone. With a much lighter load we were now cruising above cloud at 25,000 feet.

The Halifaxes dropped their bomb loads almost right on schedule and then plunged back into the cloud and headed West. The Dam Busters carried on to Munich.

At 0205 hours we arrived at a point near Nancy where the main bomber stream was turning for home. Our Radar (fish pond) revealed many four engined aircraft far below us, hidden from the naked eye by their blanket of cloud. This was good because the ruse had worked. Enemy fighters were all over the sky looking for the bombers which were hidden below and hadn't yet realized a large force was now over Munich almost unmolested. The Dam Busters were proving their new technique was excellent!

BOMBER COMMAND

At 0400 hours we broke cloud near base and announced our position. Almost instantly the airdrome sprang into life with all lights on and a charming female voice replied, 'Prepare to land, Love'. She meant it, too, because she was my engineer's fiancée.

Twenty years later it was indeed interesting to compare notes with Bill and see just how important teamwork was to the overall success of such an operation.

Roland MacKenzie

Appendix III

Halifax 57 Rescue (Canada) to Rescue Halifaxes[1]
We Leave No Halifax Behind

In 1994 Ian Foster[2] of Scotland founded the charitable organization which Karl Kjarsgaard now leads. Under the inspiring heading above, it proclaims: We Leave No Halifax Behind.[3]

Halifax 57 Rescue (Canada) is an aircraft recovery and restoration group that operates worldwide and is international in its scope and mandate to save the Handley Page Halifax heavy bombers that flew with the RAF and RCAF in the Second World War.

From the early days of our group, when we set a world record for a heavy bomber underwater recovery with a lift of RAF Halifax NA337 from 240 metres depth in Lake Mjosa, Norway to the 'impossible' but successfully completed deep swamp recovery of RCAF Halifax LW682 in Belgium, with her missing crew still on board, Halifax 57 Rescue (Canada) has done its duty to bring the legend and important history of the Halifax bomber back to the people of Canada and the world.

Our mission is to bring home Halifaxes to Canada and the historic aviation world for these Halifaxes are the unknown and hidden symbol, thanks to the media and press, of the great effort and sacrifice of our RCAF and RAF bomber crews who gave all of us our freedom and peace that we enjoy today.

In the years to come, as we search out our holy grail of RCAF Halifax LW170 lying in the deep off Ireland as well as all the other Halifaxes we can find, we will not rest for we know the following to be a fact.

On every street, in every town of our nation, are families whose fathers, grandfathers, and uncles flew in bombers. The majority of those crew (in Canada over 60 per cent) flew their beloved Halifaxes, above all others, to victory in the Second World War.

---

1 Maggie Macintosh 'Recovering 'the greatest airplane in all 110 years of flight in Canada' costs $120K, CBC News, posted 2 July 2019, updated 8 July 2019

2 Karl Karlsgaard, Project Manager Halifax 57 Rescue Canada posted an Update on 'Support the Recovery of a RCAF Halifax Bomber', 4 November 2018 www.fundrazr.com/stories/dE0w36

3 Halifax 57 Rescue (Canada) http://www.57rescuecanada.com/tablet/index.html

BOMBER COMMAND

People all over the world long for a true symbol of the excellence and honour of their heroes in a just cause. There was, and still is, no better symbol to Canada and the world of a mighty sword of freedom wielded by young warriors who defeated tyranny and it is the Handley Page Halifax..

Under the equally inspiring heading of 'Study and Remember This', Halifax 57 Rescue (Canada) goes on to declare:

70 per cent of all RCAF Canadian airmen killed in action in bombers were flying in combat in their beloved Halifax.

28,000 of the 40,000 bomber combat flights done by the RCAF, in RAF Bomber Command, were flown on the Halifax.

70 per cent of the (1,592) RAF British airmen killed in action, while flying with the Canadian RCAF bomber squadrons, were flying the Halifax.

70 per cent of the (840) 'RCAF Americans' killed in action, who volunteered to fly for Canada and joined the RCAF, were flying the Halifax bomber.

The facts are obvious and the numbers so compelling that to any student of history, any person who appreciates their freedom of today, will see that this precious item was won for you over seventy years ago by young warriors whose average age was 21. And they flew the Halifax.

So if we were to select one, just one aircraft of Bomber Command, that symbolizes this great and honourable effort and sacrifice of our bomber crews, that ties together the nations of Canada, the USA, and the UK with a common bond of our lost young aircrews then surely it must be the Halifax, above all others, that we would seek out and preserve in memory of the bomber boys of our three nations.

We hope you will join us in our journey and support us in this worldwide quest to bring all things Halifax and her glorious heritage back to our people as the ultimate tribute for our bomber boys of Canada, the USA, and the UK.

Remember, WE LEAVE NO HALIFAX BEHIND

Appendix IV

Military Life Diarized by 166 Squadron
Airman Dennis Eastcott

This diary belongs to 166 squadron wireless operator Flight Sergeant Dennis Eastcott. I learned much from it. I hope you do, too. His sister Margaret and her husband Cedric Moppett of Waterlooville, Hants, have become my friends. Sadly Cedric died on 29 October 2021. The Moppetts kindly gave me a copy of his diary. It reveals numbing boredom, coupled with the stress of never knowing what will happen next, such as which sorties will be scrubbed after everyone is suited up. It also reveals that fighting the weather was a reality for Bomber Boys, the majority of whom became casualties.

For me, the story Dennis tells is powerful. Here it is in its entirety, omitting only the parts where he is on leave. I have even included all of his dots, the meaning of which I know not. Commencing on New Year's Day 1945, here is everything Dennis Eastcott tells us about life at RAF Kirmington.

* * * * *

January 1945

Monday 1st *Stand down all day.*

Tuesday 2nd *Not on battle order - drying room crew. Hope to get away on leave in afternoon, but had to wait until crews returned from op. (Nuremburg). Very fed up.*

Wednesday 3rd *Got up at 6.0 am. Walked .... to Barnetby station for 8.03 train.*

Thursday 4th to Tuesday 9th – *on leave.*

Author's note: While Dennis was on leave on 5 January a German flying bomb exploded in London only 200 yards (180 m) from him.

BOMBER COMMAND

Tuesday 9th *Heavy snow. Left home at 2.0 pm to return to camp.*

Wednesday 10th *D.I. in morning, and shifting in afternoon.*

Thursday 11th *D.I. in morning, snow shifting in afternoon. .... Fed up with walking to & from flights in wellingtons* [boots, not planes]

Friday 12th *Flew in afternoon on training. Weather terrible & we were recalled by W/T.*

Saturday 13th *On training in morning - scrubbed. On battle order - scrubbed also. Lecture on Radar in afternoon.*

Sunday 14th *Took off on ops on Merseburg. Starboard inner engine cut just after take off. Flew to North Sea to jettison bombs and returned to base - abortive.*

Monday 15th *No battle order .... Discovered bike at Committee of Adjustments.*

Tuesday 16th *Completed 13th op on Zeist-Troglitz. Lovely prang - bags of fires. Very long trip but no incidents. One flak hole.*

Wednesday 17th *Nothing doing all day.*

Thursday 18th *Not in battle order. Day off from lunchtime. Very wet day.*

Friday 19th *On training in afternoon. Terrible blizzard. Worst I've ever seen. Cycled to flights in it. Eventually took off on Y bombing at 5.30 till 6.15.*

Saturday 20th *Standing by all day for ops. Scrubbed at 4.40*

Sunday 21st *Standing by all day for ops. Scrubbed at teatime .... Went to bed early ready for daylight op.*

Monday 22nd *Up at 7.0 am for daylight op. Scrubbed at a/c and laid on again at night. Target changed at last minute to Duisberg/Hamborn Coking Plant. Got H2S scanner shot away.*

Tuesday 23rd *Terribly cold weather with bad visibility. Stood down from lunchtime.*

Wednesday 24th *Stand down again from lunch-time.*

Thursday 25th *Stand down again. Confined to camp till 4.30.*

Friday 26th *Stand down again.*

MILITARY LIFE DIARIZED BY 166 SQUADRON

Saturday 27th *Whole squadron on Y X-country in afternoon for air test. Fishponds exercises - I had best log.*

Sunday 28th *Snow clearing in afternoon. Should have been on again in evening but skived off.*

Monday 29th *On battle order - briefed & then postponed 2 hours - scrubbed when dressed up.*

Tuesday 30th *Very heavy snow during night. Terrific drifts. No mail, no papers. Transport snowed up on perimeter track.*

Wednesday 31st *Thaw started. Stood up, but ops scrubbed.*

February 1945

Thursday 1st *Did 15th op on Ludwigshaven. Heavy defences - saw 6 fighters. Jack Allman missing in it. Also J2, Spankie and W, Pollock.*

Friday 2nd *Did 16th op on Wiesbaden. Very easy, bombed through thick cloud. Little flak and saw no fighters.*

Saturday 3rd *Small battle order out; we were not on it.*

Sunday 4th *Nothing doing all day .... mended puncture.*

Monday 5th *On battle order but scrubbed after briefing.*

Tuesday 6th *Stand down all day.*

Wednesday 7th *Briefed for long op - scrubbed. Army support target put on. Cleve - very away trip. Bombed from 5,000ft.*

Thursday 8th *Briefed for long op again & scrubbed. Politz, near Stettin on instead. Near Russian front. Very long trip - returned via Sweden.*

Friday 9th *On battle order - scrubbed in early afternoon.*

Saturday 10th *Not on battle order.*

Sunday 11th *Stand by for ops all day. Scrubbed while in mess at 5 o'clock.*

Monday 12th *Very bad weather. No battle order out.*

BOMBER COMMAND

Tuesday 13th *Standing by all day for ops. Took off at 21.15 for raid on Dresden. Very long trip but uneventful. Landed at 7.0 am on following morning.*

Author's note: Interrupting here for a moment, Dennis Eastcott's diary reveals what many authors also say – at that time, Dresden was seen as a routine combat sortie. Author and 166 Squadron navigator Don Feesey also flew the Dresden sortie. He says 166 aircrew were told pre-flight that Dresden was of significant military importance, and its road and rail junctions were essential to German troop movements to block the advance of our Allies the Russians.[1]

However, Dresden was eventful for 166 Squadron:

> *An aircraft of 166 Squadron, flown by Pilot Officer Churchward, had just completed its bombing run over Dresden when it was hit by a burst of heavy flak which made several holes in the fuselage and also blew one of the incendiaries back into the aircraft. It ignited, but the wireless operator managed (despite a lack of oxygen) to extinguish the fire.*[2]

In addition:

> *One aircraft of 166 Squadron had anything but an easy trip to Dresden and back. Lancaster LM289 – Y flown by Squadron Leader Harold Whowell took off at 21.25 from its base at Kirmington, Lincolnshire. When they were 450 miles short of Dresden the starboard outer engine failed and the propeller had to be feathered. There was no hesitation and the crew decided to carry on: due to the excellent judgement of the flight engineer, Sergeant Lemming, they reached Dresden on time although flying 3,000 feet below the ordered height.*

For successfully carrying out this sortie flying on only three engines for eight of the 10.5-hour Kirmington-Dresden-Kirmington roundtrip, Whowell was awarded the DFC.[3]

Wednesday 14th *Left for home without any sleep.*

---

1 Feesey *The Fly By Nights* p 137
2 Alan Cooper *Target Dresden* p 203
3 Cooper, p. 170-1

MILITARY LIFE DIARIZED BY 166 SQUADRON

Dennis was on leave from this point. His diary ends on 17 February 1945. Four days later, on 21 February, Dennis flew his twentieth combat sortie. About this time, he was promoted to flight sergeant. He was killed on his twenty-first sortie on 23 February 1945 when his Lancaster AS-L2 was shot down over Pforzheim, near Stuttgart.

On this final combat sortie, twenty-three Lancasters from 166 Squadron were among the main force of 367 Lancasters which included fifty RCAF Lancasters. There were also thirteen Mosquitoes. A dozen Lancasters were shot down by German fighters or flak. These included the 166 Squadron Lancaster Dennis was aboard.

Pforzheim was a significant transportation target, and it had specialized light industry manufacturing precision instruments. Massive road, rail and bridge damage was inflicted. Most of the identifiable factories were destroyed.[4]

Flight Sergeant Dennis William Eastcott* was the wireless operator aboard 166 Squadron Lancaster AS-L2 ND506 when it was shot down. Its crew were:

Pilot:	Flying Officer Ernest Lewis Ellis
Flight engineer:	Sergeant R.C. Finlayson
Bomb-aimer:	Flight Sergeant Dennis Taylor
Navigator:	Flying Officer J.W. Rae
Wireless operator:	Flight Sergeant Dennis William Eastcott*
Mid-upper gunner:	Sergeant Arthur George Chapman
Rear gunner:	Sergeant Ralph Richards

Finlayson and Rae were the only survivors. The other five, including Dennis, are buried at Durnbach War Cemetery in the Bavarian Alps near Tegernsee Lake.[5]

That night Don Feesey was also on the Pforzheim sortie which he says is 'near Nuremburg.' Regarding the loss of Dennis Eastcott and his 166 Squadron crew that night, Don says: 'We lost an experienced crew who had flown alongside us on many an outing. They were on their twenty-first operation. Five crew members were killed and the other two were taken prisoner.'[6]

---

4 Bashow, p. 394

5 Wright, pp 140-1

6 Feesey, p. 147

Bibliography

Addison, Paul, *Churchill – The Unexpected Hero,* Oxford University Press, Oxford, 2005

Barris, Ted, *Dam Busters – Canadian Airmen and the Secret Raid Against Nazi Germany*, Patrick Crean Editions, HarperCollins Publishers Ltd, Toronto, 2018

Bashow, David L., *No Prouder Place – Canadians and the Bomber Command Experience 1939-1945*, Vanwell Publishing Limited, St Catharines ON, 2005

—*Soldiers Blue – How Bomber Command and Area Bombing Helped Win the Second World War*, Canadian Defence Academy Press, Kingston ON, 2011

Beevor, Anthony, *Ardennes 1944*, Penguin, London, 2016

Bekker, Cajus, *The Luftwaffe War Diaries – The German Air Force in World War Two*, Da Capo Press, New York 1994. First Published in German as *Angriffshohe 4000* by Gerhard Stalling Verlag, Hamburg, 1964

Bennett CB CBE DSO, Air Vice-Marshal D.C.T., *Pathfinder – A War Autobiography*, Sphere Books Limited, London, 1972 (First Published in Great Britain by Frederick Muller Ltd, 1958)

Bergstrom, Christer, *The Ardennes: Hitler's Winter Offensive 1944-1945*, Casemate Publishers, Havertown, Pennsylvania, 2014

Birrell, Dave, *FM159 The Lucky Lancaster*, Nanton Lancaster Society, 2002 (5th Edtn, 2015)

—*Johnny – John Fauquier DSO & 2 Bars DFC – Canada's Greatest Bomber Pilot*, Nanton Lancaster Society, 2018

Bishop, Patrick, *Air Force Blue – The RAF in World War Two*, William Collins/HarperCollins Publishers, London, 2017 (p/back 2018)

—*Bomber Boys – Fighting Back 1940-1945*, HarperPress, London, 2007

Black, Conrad, 'Canada must return to being a grown-up nation, now and post-COVID-19', *National Post*, 3 April 2020

Bomber Command – The Air Ministry Account of Bomber Command's Offensive Against the Axis September, 1939- July 1941, HMSO, London, 1941

Bousfield, Arthur and Garry Toffoli, *The Queen Mother and Her Century: Queen Elizabeth The Queen Mother On Her 100th Birthday*, Dundurn Press, Toronto, 2000

Broadfoot, Barry, *Ten Lost Years: 1929-1939: Memories of the Canadians Who Survived the Depression*, Doubleday Canada Ltd, Toronto, 1973

BIBLIOGRAPHY

Brookes, Wing Commander Andrew, 'An Interview with 'Bomber' Harris 8 September 1975,' *Royal Air Force Historical Society Journal*, No. 74

Buchanan, Patrick J., *Churchill, Hitler, and the Unnecessary War – How Britain Lost Its Empire and the West Lost the World*, Crown Publishers/ Random House Inc., 2008

Canada, Library and Archives Canada, *William Lyon Mackenzie King*

Charlwood, Don, *No Moon Tonight*, Goodall Publications Ltd London 1984(First published by Angus & Robertson Australia, 1956)

—*Journeys Into Night*, Burgewood Books, Warrandyte, Victoria, Australia (Third Edition, 2013. First published by Hudson Hawthorn, 1991)

Chorlton, Martyn, *The RAF Pathfinders: Bomber Command's Elite Squadrons*, Countryside Books, Newbury, Berkshire, 2012

—*The Thousand Bomber Raids*, Countryside Books, Newbury, Berkshire, 2015

Churchill, Sir Winston S., *The Hinge of Fate – Second World War, Volume IV*, Houghton Mifflin Harcourt Publishing Company, New York, NY, 1950

—*Closing the Ring – Second World War Volume V*, Houghton Mifflin Harcourt Publishing Company, New York, NY, 1951

—*Triumph and Tragedy – Second World War Volume VI*, Houghton Mifflin Harcourt Publishing Company New York, NY, 1953

Churchill War Rooms Guidebook Imperial War Museums

Claridge, Brian, 'Bomber Harris's VERY elegant bunker: 18th Century house which was home to RAF Marshal Harris could be yours for £3.75 million,' *The Mail on Sunday*, 24 June 2017

Cohen, David, *Churchill & Attlee – The Unlikely Allies Who Won the War*, Biteback Publishing, London, 2018

Cohen, Ronald (ed), *The Heroic Memory – The Memorial Addresses to the Rt Hon. Sir Winston Spencer Churchill Society Edmonton Alberta 1990-2014*, The Churchill Statue and Oxford Scholarship Foundation, 2016

Colville, Sir John Rupert ('Jock'), *The Fringes of Power – Downing Street Diaries 1939-1955*, Hodder and Stoughton Limited, London, 1985

Cook, Tim, *The Fight for History: 75 Years of Forgetting, Remembering, and Remaking Canada's Second World War*, Penguin, Canada, 2020

Cooper, Alan W., *Target – Dresden*, Independent Books, Bromley, UK, 1995

Costigliola, Frank, 'Pamela Churchill, Wartime London, and the Making of the Special Relationship,' *Diplomatic History*, Vol. 36, No. 4, September 2012, The Society for Historians of American Foreign Relations (SHAFR), Wiley Periodicals Inc., Oxford, 2012 www.jstor.org/stable/44376171?s

Cote, Mark, *That Lucky Old Son: Re-discovering My Father Through His World War II Bomber Command and PoW Experiences*, Friesen Press, Victoria BC, 2018

Cothliff, Kenneth B., *Under the Maple Leaf – The Remarkable Story of Four Canadian Volunteers Who Flew With Bomber Command During the Second World War*, Fighting High Ltd. www.fightinghigh.com, 2015

Coulter, Rebecca Priegert, 'War Brides', *The Canadian Encyclopedia*, published online 21 February 2006, updated by Tabitha Marshall, 9 August 2019

Courtenay, Paul, 'Churchill as Honorary Air Commodore,' *Finest Hour*, No. 185, Third Quarter 2019

Crow, David, *Jimmy Stewart and the WW2 Mission That Almost Broke Him,* Den of Geek 21 March 2021 www:denofgeek.com/movies/jimmy-stewart-ww2-mission-air-force/

Curnow, John M., *Shot Down – When his bomber exploded over Nazi-occupied France, only John survived – and found a new life,* Pacific Press Publishing Association, Oshawa, Ontario, 2006

Currie, Jack, *Lancaster Target – The Story of a Crew Who Flew From Wembley*, Crecy Publishing, Manchester (First Published by Goodall, 1981. Published as New Edition by Goodall, 1997. Reprinted 2012)

DeLuca, Diana M., *Extraordinary Things*, iUniverse Inc., Lincoln, Nebraska, 2007

Dennis, Patrick M., *Reluctant Warriors – Canada's Conscripts and the Great War*, UBC Press, Vancouver, 2017.

D'Este, Carlo, *Warlord – A Life of Winston Churchill at War 1874-1945*, HarperCollins Publishers, NYC NY, 2008

Dilks, David, *The Great Dominion – Winston Churchill in Canada 1900-1954*, Thomas Allen Publishers, Toronto, 2005

Dunmore, Spencer & William Carter, *Reap The Whirlwind – The Untold Story of 6 Group, Canada's Bomber Force of WW II*, McClelland & Stewart, Toronto, 1991

Ellin, Dan, 'A "Lack of Moral Fibre" in Royal Air Force Bomber Command and Popular Culture', *British Journal for Military History*, Vol. 6, No. 3, 2020

Evans, Tom Parry, *Squadron Leader Tommy Broom DFC – The Legendary Pathfinder Mosquito Navigator*, Pen & Sword Books, Barnsley, 2007 (reprinted 2011)

Ewing, Jack, 'Albert Speer Jr, Architect and Son of Hitler Confidant, Dies at 83,' *New York Times*, 27 September 2017

Falcon, Jonathan, *RAF Bomber Command 1939-45 Operations Manual*, Sparkford, Somerset, UK, 2018

Feesey, Donald W., *The Fly By Nights: RAF Bomber Command Sorties 1944-45*, Pen & Sword Books, Barnsley, 2007

Filey, Mike, 'The Way We Were – Historic Avro Lancaster will one day take to the SKIES again,' *Toronto Sun*, 30 May 2020

Fleming, Kevin, 'New Jobs for Calgary's Aviation Industry,' CTV News, 6 April 2022

Foot, Richard, 'D Day and the Battle of Normandy,' *The Canadian Encyclopedia*, published 7 February 2006.. Last Edited 3 May 2019 www.thecanadianencyclopedia.ca/en/article/normandy-invasion

Freeman, David, 'Prelude to Power: Churchill and the American Presidency before the Second World War' *Finest Hour* No. 192 Second Quarter 2021

BIBLIOGRAPHY

Fyfe, James, *'The Great Ingratitude' – Bomber Command in World War 2* G.C. Book Publishers Ltd Wigtown Scotland 1993

Garbett, Mike and Brian Goulding, *The Lancaster at War.* Foreword by Sir Arthur Harris Musson Book Company Toronto 1971 (2nd Impression 1973)

Geddes, John, 'Lest We Forget Again – For decades, Canada largely ignored World War II. What prompted our national change-of-heart?' *Maclean's, Canada's National Magazine*, June, 2020

German Research Institute for Military History, See Research Institute for Military History

Gibb, Robin, Jim Dooley, Gordon Rayner, Steve Darlow and Sean Feast (Editors) *Bomber Command Memorial – We Will Remember Them*, Fighting High Ltd, Stotfold, Hitchin, 2012

Gibson VC, Guy, *Enemy Coast Ahead*, Goodall Publications Ltd, 1986 (First Published by Michael Joseph Ltd, 1946)

Gilbert, Martin, *Finest Hour – Winston S. Churchill 1939-1941*, Stoddart-General Publishing Company, Don Mills ON, 1983

—*Never Despair* Stoddart Publishing Co. Limited, Toronto 1988

—*Road to Victory – Winston Churchill 1941-1945* Stoddart, Toronto 1986

Glueckstein, Fred *'An Extraordinary Advantage – Winston Churchill, Robert Watson-Watt and the Development of Radar'* International Churchill Society No. 195 First Quarter 2022

Goldie, Mark, (Picture Editor Barry Phipps), *Churchill College Cambridge – The Guide*, published by Churchill College, Cambridge, 2009

Grant, Lachlan 'The Australians of Bomber Command who helped defeat Nazism were brave, not shameful,' *The Sydney Morning Herald*, Australia, 2 June 2017

Grehan, John & Martin Mace (Compilers), *Bomber Harris – Sir Arthur Harris' Despatch on War Operations 1942*-1945, Pen & Sword Books Ltd, Barnsley, 2014

Hampton, James, *Selected for Aircrew – Bomber Command in the Second World War*, Surrey Air Research Publications, Walton on Thames, 1993

Hansen, Randall, *Fire and Fury – the Allied Bomber of Germany 1942-45*, Doubleday, Canada, 2008

Hardman, Robert, 'How a Handful of Heroes beat the officials who tried to sabotage the new memorial to Bomber Command,' *Daily Mail*, 26 June 2012

Harmon, Christopher, *'Are We Beasts?' Churchill and the Moral Question of World War II 'Area Bombing',* Naval War College, Newport, RI, 1991

Harris GCB OBE AFC, Marshal of the RAF Sir Arthur, *Bomber Offensive*, Collins, London, 1947 (Published by Greenhill Books/Lionel Leventhal Limited, 1998. Published by Frontline Books/Pen & Sword Books Ltd, Barnsley, 2015)

—'Straight From the Horse's Mouth,' Speech delivered by Sir Arthur Harris to Royal Air Force Bomber Command Reunion Dinner, London, 30 April 1977 www.lancaster-me699.co.uk>arthur.harris

Hastings, Max, *Bomber Command*, Penguin Group, 1979 and Zenith Press, Minneapolis MN, 2013

—*Winston's War – Churchill 1940-1945* (Published as *Finest Years: Churchill as Warlord 1940-45* by HarperPress, London, 2009) Borzoi Book/Alfred A. Knopf, NY, 2009

Hewer, Howard, *In for a Penny, In for a Pound – The Adventures and Misadventures of a Wireless Operator in Bomber Command*, Stoddart Publishing Co. Limited, Toronto, 2000

History TV Channel, *Prisoners of War*, A+E Networks AETN www.history.co.uk/history-of-ww2/prisoners-of-war

Holland, James, *Big Week – The Biggest Air Battle of World War II*, Atlantic Monthly Press, New York, 2018

Holledge, Richard, 'They Were the Means of Victory,' *Wall Street Journal*, 2 July 2012

Holmes, Richard, *In the Footsteps of Churchill – A Study in Character*, Basic Books, 2009 (First Published, 2005)

Hunt, Irmgard A., *On Hitler's Mountain – Overcoming the Legacy of a Nazi Childhood*, First Harper Perennial Edition, New York, 2006. (Hardback, William Morrow, an imprint of HarperCollins Publishers, 2005)

Hutchinson, Bruce, *The Incredible Canadian – A Candid Portrait of Mackenzie King, His Works, His Times and His Nation*, Oxford University Press, Oxford, 1952

Irvine, Thelma, *What Did You Do in the War?* Riftswood Publishing, Parksville, BC, 1995

Iveson, Tony DFC and Brian Milton, *Lancaster – The Biography*, Andre Deutsch, London, 2009

Jacobs, Peter, *Bomber Command Airfields of Yorkshire*, Pen & Sword Books, Barnsley, 2017

—*Night Duel Over Germany – Bomber Command's Battle Over the Reich During WWII*, Pen & Sword Books, Barnsley, 2017

James, Robert Rhodes (Editor), *Winston S. Churchill 1897-1963, His Complete Speeches 1897-1963, Volume VII 1943-1949*, Chelsea House Publishers in association with RR Bowker Company, New York and London, 1974

Jenkins, Roy, *Churchill – A Biography*, Macmillan, London, 2001

Johnson, Boris, *The Churchill Factor – How One Man Made History*, Riverhead Books/Penguin Group, New York, 2014

Johnson, Paul, *Churchill*, Viking/Penguin, NYC, NY, 2009. (Published in Penguin Books 2010)

Jones, Amanda Jane, *Bringing Up War Babies – The Wartime Child in Women's Writing and Psychoanalysis at Mid-Century*, Routledge, Abingdon, 2018

Kane, Robert B., Lt Col USAF, 'The Doolittle Raid – 75 Years Later,' *Air & Space Power Journal* www.airpower.au.af.mil

Katz, Catherine Grace, *The Daughters of Yalta – The Churchills, Roosevelts, and Harrimans: A Story of Love and War*, Houghton Mifflin Harcourt, New York, 2020

Lagrandeur, Philip, *We Flew We Fell We Lived – Stories from RCAF Prisoners of War and Evaders*, Vanwell Publishing Limited, St Catherine's, Ontario, 2006

BIBLIOGRAPHY

Lake, Jon, *Halifax Squadrons of World War 2*, Combat Aircraft Volume 15, Osprey Publishing Ltd, Botley Oxon (Fifth Impression 2009, First Published 1999)

Lancaster Squadrons 1944-45, Combat Aircraft Volume 35, Osprey Publishing Ltd Botley Oxon (Fifth Impression, 2005, First Published 2002)

Langworth, Richard M. (Editor), *Churchill's Wit: The Definitive Collection*, Ebury Press/Random House Group, London, 2009

'HM Queen Elizabeth The Queen Mother 1900-2002,' *Finest Hour* 114, Spring 2002

Larson, Erik, *The Splendid and the Vile – A Saga of Churchill, Family, and Defiance During the Blitz*, Crown, New York, 2020

Lee, Peter and Colin McHattie, 'Winston Churchill and the Bombing of German Cities, 1940-1945,' *Global War Studies,* Vol. 13, No. 1, 2016 http://doi.org/10.5893/19498489.130102.

Lincolnshire Aviation Heritage Centre Brochures and Guide Map 2018

Loewenheim, Francis, Harold Langley and Manfred Jonas (Editors), *Roosevelt and Churchill: Their Secret Wartime Correspondence*, Da Capo Press Inc., NY, 1975

Macintosh, Maggie, 'Recovering 'the greatest airplane in all 110 years of flight in Canada costs $120K.' CBC News, posted 2 July 2019, updated 8 July 2019

MacKenzie, Roland W. DFC, *Royal Canadian Air Force Pilot's Flying Log Book 16 March 1942 to 17 September 1944* Unpublished

— 'Karlsruhe Bombing 24 April 1944,' *Quill & Ledger*, Royal Bank of Canada, 1975

MacKenzie, Simon, *Bomber Boys on Screen – RAF Bomber Command in Film and Television Drama*, Bloomsbury Academic, London, 2019

Mackenzie King, William Lyon, *Canada at Britain's Side*, Macmillan Company of Canada Limited, Toronto, 1941

Manchester, William and Paul Reid, *The Last Lion – Winston Spencer Churchill Defender of the Realm, 1940-1965*, Little, Brown and Company, New York, 2012

Marks, Richard, *Avro Lancaster,* Air Vanguard 21, Osprey Publishing, Botley, Oxon, 2015

Marr, Andrew, *The Making of Modern Britain – From Queen Victoria to V.E. Day*, Macmillan, London, 2009

Martin, John, *Raid Over Berlin – A Miraculous True-Life Second World War Survival Story*, Parthian, Cardigan, Wales, 2018

Matzen, Robert, *Mission: Jimmy Stewart and the Fight for Europe*, GoodKnight Books, an Imprint of Paladin Communications, Pittsburgh, 2019

Maurer, John H., 'How Churchill Dodged the Flu Pandemic, and Others Were Not So Lucky,' The Churchill Project Hillside College Articles, 13 April 2020 www.winstonchurchill.hilldale.edu/maurer-flu-pandemic/

'Churchill, Air Power, and Arming for Armageddon.' *Finest Hour*, No. 185 Third Quarter, 2019

McCaffery, Dan, *Battlefields in the Air – Canadians in the Allied Bomber Command*, James Lorimer & Company, Toronto, 1995

McKinstry, Leo, 'They took a lot of flak: the lives of the Lancaster bombers – But their courage, and the dark missions they flew, eventually won the war,' *The Spectator*, 6 June 2020

McNeil, Bill, *Voice of a War Remembered – An Oral History of Canadians in World War I,I* Doubleday Canada Limited, Toronto, 1991

McQuaid, Peter, *Bomber Command Memorial*, Royal New Zealand Air Force www.airforce.mil.nz/about-us/archive/102/bomber-command

Metcalfe, Tom, 'Wreck of WWII battleship with Nazi symbol discovered off Norway,' *Live Science*, 11 September 2020 www.livescience.com

Middlebrook, Martin, *The Berlin Raids – The Bomber Battle, Winter 1943-1944*, Viking, London, 1988 (Reprinted Pen & Sword Books, Barnsley, 2010)

— and Chris Everitt, *The Bomber Command War Diaries – An Operational Reference Book 1939-1945*, Viking, London, 1985 (Reprinted Pen & Sword Books, Barnsley, 2014)

Militargeschichtliches Forschungsamt. See Research Institute for Military History

Moran, Lord (Charles Wilson), *Churchill Taken From the Diaries of Lord Moran – The Struggle for Survival 1940 – 1965*, The Riverside Press, Cambridge, 1966

Nahum, Andrew, 'The PM and the Boffins – Churchill and His Scientists,' *Finest Hour*, No. 195, First Quarter, 2022

Nichol, John and Tony Rennell, *Tail-End Charlies – The Last Battles of the Bomber War 1944-45*, Viking, New York, 2004

— *The Last Escape – The untold story of Allied prisoners of war in Germany 1944-45*, Penguin Books, London, 2003 (First Published, Viking, 2002)

Nicholas, Major Donna C. and Major Albert H. Whitley, 'The Role of Air Power in the Battle of the Bulge,' Air Command and Staff College, Air University, Maxwell Air Force Base Alabama April 1999

Nowarra, Heinz, *Heinkel He 111: A Documentary History*, Janes Publishing, London, 1980

North Shore News, Community Newspaper North & West Vancouver nsnews.com

Olson, Lynne, *Citizens of London*, Bond Street Books/Random House of Canada Limited, 2010

Otter, Patrick, *Lincolnshire Airfields in the Second World War*, Countryside Books, Newbury, 1996

Overy, Richard J., *The Air War 1939-1945*, Stein and Day Publishers, NY, 1981

— *Bomber Command 1939-45*, First Published in Great Britain by HarperCollinsPublishers 1997. (An Imprint of Bookmart Limited, Leicester; HarperCollins Publishers Ltd for Silverdale Books, 2000)

— 'World War Two: How the Allies Won the War,' Article in the BBC Website Archives, last updated 17 February 2011

Packwood, Allen, *How Churchill Waged War – The Most Challenging Decisions of the Second World War*, Frontline Books, Yorkshire & Philadelphia. 2018

— (Ed.) *Cosmos Out of Chaos*, Churchill College, Cambridge, 2009

BIBLIOGRAPHY

Parker, Winston Churchill, *Saddles and Service – Winston Parker's Story as Told to Elaine Taylor Thomas*, Calla Communications, Inc. La Grange Texas, printed & bound by Blitzprint Inc., Calgary, October 2011

Paterson, Michael, *Winston Churchill – The Photobiography*, David & Charles Books, Cincinnati, Ohio, 2006

Peden, Murray, *A Thousand Shall Fall, The True Story of a Canadian Bomber Pilot in World War Two*, First Published Canada's Wings Inc. 1979; reprinted 1981. Published Stoddart Publishing, Toronto, 1988; reprinted 2000

Phillips DFC MiD, Flight Lieutenant Humphrey, with Sean Feast, *A Thousand and One – A Flight Engineer Leader's War from the Thousand Bomber Raids to the Battle of Berlin*, Bomber Command Books/Mention the War Ltd, Leeds, 2017

Porter, Bob, *The Long Return – A True Story of a Young WWII Airman – One of Two Survivors of a Plane Which Was Blown Up Over Nazi-Occupied Holland* http://www.intergate.bc.ca/business/boport, Printed in Canada, copyright 1997 by Bob Porter 4th Edition June 1998 ISBN 0-9681953-O-X

Porter, Lisa, 'Guy Martin buys village pub in Kirmington,' *Lincolnshire Live*, 2 January 2017, updated 6 June 2017 www.lincolnshirelive.co.uk

Probert, Henry, *Bomber Harris, His Life and Times – The Biography of Marshal of the Royal Air Force Sir Arthur Harris, Wartime Chief of Bomber Command*, Stoddart Publishing Co. Limited, Toronto, 2001

Reardon, Terry, *Winston Churchill and MacKenzie King – So Similar, So Different*, Dundurn A.J. Patrick Book, Toronto, 2014

— 'History has been kind to Mackenzie King,' *Waterloo Regional Record*, 22 July 2013

Research Institute for Military History (*Militargeschichtliches Forschungsamt*) *Germany and the Second World War* (*Das Deutsche Reich und der Zweite Weltkrieg*) Vol. II *Germany's Initial Conquests in Europe* Freiburg im Breisgau, Germany, Translation Clarendon Press, Oxford, 1991

— Vol. V, *Organization & Mobilization of the German Sphere of Power* Part Two *Wartime administration, economy, and manpower resources 1942-1944/5* Potsdam, Germany, Translation Clarendon Press, Oxford, 2003

— Vol. VI, *Economy, and manpower resources* edited by the *Militargeschichtliches Forschungsamt* (Research Institute for Military History) Potsdam, Germany, Translated by Clarendon Press, Oxford, 2003

— Vol. VII, *The Strategic Air War in Europe* edited by the *Militargeschichtliches Forschungsamt* (Research Institute for Military History) Potsdam, Germany, Translated by Clarendon Press, Oxford, 2006

— Vol. IX, *German Wartime Society 1939-1945* Pt One *Politicization, Disintegration, and the Struggle for Survival* Edited by the *Militargeschichtliches Forschungsamt* (Research Institute for Military History) Potsdam, Germany, First published Deutsche Verlags-Anstalt, Munich 2004. Translated by Clarendon Press, Oxford, 2008

Reynolds, David, *In Command of History – Churchill Fighting and Writing the Second World War*, Allen Lane/Penguin Books, London, 2004

Riley, Gordon, *British Aircraft Museums Directory* (6th Edition), Aston Publications, distributed by Springfield Books Limited

Roberts, Andrew, *Churchill – Walking With Destiny*, Allen Lane/Penguin Books, London, 2018

— *Masters and Commanders – How Roosevelt, Churchill, Marshall and Alanbrooke Won the War in the West*, Penguin Group, London, 2008

Robson, Martin (Ed), Air Ministry *The Lancaster Bomber Pocket Manual 1941-1945*, Conway of Pavilion Books Group, London, 2012

Ruane, Kevin, 'The Professor and the Prime Minister – Frederick Lindemann and Winston Churchill,' *Finest Hour* No. 195, First Quarter 2022.

Ruston, Abby, 'Speed star Guy Martin 'breathes life back into' village where he grew up by buying the local pub,' *The Mirror*, 24 December 2016, www.mirror.co.uk

'Science and Technology 11 Series, Military and Defence Technology, Bombing in WWII,' narrated by Gwynne Dyer, ST0057 VH, 1983

Shirer, William L., *The Rise and Fall of the Third Reich – A History of Nazi Germany*, Simon & Shuster, New York, 1960 (23rd Printing)

Skaarup, Harold A., *Canadian Warplanes*, iUniverse Inc., New York, 2009

Smith, Steve, *A Short War – The History of 623 Squadron RAF*, Bomber Command Books/Mention the War Publications, 2015

Speer, Albert, *Infiltration – How Heinrich Himmler Schemed to Build an SS Industrial Empire*, MacMillan Publishing, New York, 1981

— *Inside the Third Reich – Memories*, Simon & Schuster, New York, 1970

— *Spandau – The Secret Diaries*, Macmillan Publishing, New York, 1976

Stacey, C.P., *A Very Double Life: The Private World of Mackenzie King*, Macmillan, 1976

Sterling, Christopher H., 'Marriage of Convenience: Churchill and 'Bomber' Harris,' *Finest Hour*, Winter 2012-13

Taylor, A.J.P., *Beaverbrook: A Biography*, Hamish Hamilton, London, 1972

Thompson, Neville, *The Third Man – Churchill, Roosevelt, Mackenzie King, and the Untold Friendships That Won WWII*, Sutherland House, Toronto, 2021

Tooze, Adam, *The Wages of Destruction – The Making and Breaking of the Nazi Economy*, Viking Penguin Group, London, 2006. (First American edition Viking Penguin, New York, 2007)

Vickerman, Lorraine Denise, *My Father's Keeper*, First Choice Books and Victoria Bindery, Victoria, 2016

Waite, P.B., *Lord of Point Grey – Larry MacKenzie of UBC*, The University of British Columbia Press, Vancouver, 1987

Webster, Sir Charles and Dr Nobel Frankland DFC, *The Strategic Air Offensive Against Germany 1939-1945* (four volumes) HMSO, London, 1961

Williamson, Murray, *The Luftwaffe – Strategy for Defeat*, Secaucus, New Jersey: Chartwell, 1986

Wilmot, Chester, *The Struggle for Europe*, London, Wordsworth, 1998

BIBLIOGRAPHY

Wilson, Gordon, *The Lancaster*, Amberley Publishing, Stroud, Gloucestershire, 2011

Woodworth, John and Halle Flygare, *In the Steps of Alexander Mackenzie*, John Woodworth, Kelowna, British Columbia, 1987

Wright, Jim, *On Wings of War – A History of 166 Squadron,* 166 Squadron Association Merseyside, 1996

Acknowledgements

It is astonishing how many people it has taken to write this book. I scarcely know where to begin in acknowledging and thanking them. When in doubt as where to start, I say to myself, start at the beginning. So I will.

Two Giants In My Life

Two men who caused me to write this book never knew it, because both died before I began. They are my Dad, Roland W. MacKenzie DFC; and my inspiration, Sir Winston Churchill.

Roland W. MacKenzie DFC. First and foremost, I have written this book to discover my father's work to help win the war. He died 24 August 1991, age 79.

Sir Winston Churchill whose inspirational leadership continues today for so many, and who was Bomber Command's greatest champion, inspired me to write this book. He died 24 January 1965, age 90.

My Four Awesome Mentors

David Freeman is worldwide Director of Publications of the International Churchill Society and Editor of both The Churchill Bulletin and the Society's impressive magazine 'Finest Hour' in which he published my paper 'Churchill's Greatest Triumph: Bomber Command' in Issue 185, Third Quarter 2019. The whole issue is devoted to Churchill's relationship with the Royal Air Force. David asked me to write the Bomber Command portion. And, in the spring of 2019, David decided Allen Packwood and I needed to know one another, so he brought us together. Every step of the way, including at the Churchill International Annual Conference David ran in Washington DC in 2019 and participated in with me in London in 2021, David has helped, guided and motivated me through all the ups and downs of writing this book. David was a nuclear reactor operator for six years with the United States Navy. He taught

ACKNOWLEDGEMENTS

at Saddleback College and teaches at California State University Fullerton and Coastline College.

Karl Kjarsgaard is Founder, CEO and Curator of Canada's Bomber Command Memorial & Museum in Nanton Alberta of which I am a Life Member. Countless times I've consulted with Karl. He always responds quickly and thoroughly, and is a treasure advising me of the fate of many Bomber Boys, delighting their families. He's an awesome authority of his beloved Halifaxes, and their greatest champion. The Halifax was of crucial importance to the RCAF. On Christmas Eve 2018, the Governor General of Canada awarded Karl the Sovereign's Medal for Volunteers for his dedication to preserving the history of Second World War aircraft and his recovering from the sea and rebuilding Halifax bombers. My time with Karl in Nanton and Vulcan has been solid gold both personally and for this book. Karl's instant availability by telephone regardless of where in the world he is has saved me several times from saying or writing something wrong, and he has enriched my book in so many ways. In addition, his enthusiasm fires me up.

Allen Packwood as Director of Archives at Churchill College Cambridge University warmly welcomed me, thanks to David Freeman's introduction, to Cambridge University in May 2019, made me an official Churchill reader, and accommodated me on campus for three separate, equally successful visits. In October 2019, Allen reviewed my full book's first draft of 60,000 words. Then, at Cambridge, Allen articulated his impressions in great detail with me and another of my treasured mentors, RAF Air Vice-Marshal Paul Robinson. Afterwards, I removed 15,000 words and added 35,000, thereby producing a fresh draft book of 80,000 words. At the 2019 Washington DC International Churchill Conference Allen, to my delighted astonishment, volunteered to review this new draft over Christmas of 2019 and January 2020. This led to David Freeman and Paul Robinson volunteering to do so too. That review by these three men launched this book. Allen and David also welcomed me into the 2021 London International Churchill Conference the program for which Allen organized as he will again in 2023 in Edinburgh. Allen is an OBE, a Fellow of Churchill College and the Royal Historical Society, and a Churchill Fellow at Westminster College in Fulton MO, a Member of the International Churchill Society International Committee and Operating Committee, and the author in 2018 of 'How Churchill Waged War'.

RAF Air Vice-Marshal Paul Robinson has contributed enormously, drawing on his deep knowledge from his long years of service with the RAF and his many presentations on Bomber Command. Paul even chauffeured my sons and me to places of Bomber Command importance in Lincolnshire in 2019 and 2021, the most important of which turned out to be RAF College Cranwell. In addition, Paul has given me wonderful wording to so perfectly clarify complex RAF information. Best of all, in February 2022, Paul edited my entire book, cover to cover, for a second time. In so doing, his helpful suggestions and important insights smashed the writer's block which paralyzed me that month, and blasted me back into action. Scarcely a week passes when we are not in contact on whatever interests us, be it Bomber Command or pretty much any other aspect of our lives. Paul is an OBE, a Fellow of the Royal Aeronautical Society, a Canon of Lincoln Cathedral and a Trustee of the International Bomber Command Centre in Lincoln.

My Hero

Peter Mansbridge from 1988 until his retirement in 2017 was Chief Correspondent for CBC News and Anchor of CBC's The National, CBC's pre-eminent nightly news. To me, Peter is the most trusted person in Canada, our Walter Cronkite, who was the most trusted man in America. Peter was a staunch defender of Bomber Command even in its darkest days. And so, in trepidation, I emailed him mentioning he is only twelve days older than I am, that our fathers were both in Lancasters in Bomber Command, and our fathers were both awarded DFCs. Peter's father, Wing Commander Stanley Mansbridge DFC, was a navigator who flew an astonishing 51 combat sorties with 49 Squadron Five Group Bomber Command including to bomb top secret Peenemunde.

And so, in trepidation, I asked Peter to review my book. His response overwhelmed me. On 13 October 2022, Peter emailed me saying:

Roddy, 'Bomber Command' is a tour de force. It is simply a masterpiece of reflection, anecdotes, and history. It puts the reader in the cockpit, in the navigator's and bomb aimer's sights, in the tail gunner's turret. It brings you inside Bomber Harris's inner thoughts and his internal battles over the value and import of the bombing campaign. There's so much here I didn't know, and I thought I knew a lot. I wish our dads were alive to read this. But future generations will and they bloody well should.

Sadly, my book's dust jacket had already been printed, so I was unable to put Peter's treasured response on the back cover of my book. Isn't it awesome?

My Special Friends

Dr. John Blatherwick OC is a published author who has the singular distinction of having earned his ranks separately in each of the Royal Canadian Air Force, the Royal Canadian Navy and Canada's Army. He came into my life in 1976 when I became City Solicitor and he Chief Medical Health Officer for the Royal City of New Westminster. The breadth of John's knowledge, his interest in me and my book, and his continuous contact and many suggestions all help me hugely.

ACKNOWLEDGEMENTS

Brooke Campell whose persuasive power first planted the seed for this book. He convinced me I had both the ability and the duty to research Bomber Command, find out what really happened, and write this book. Brooke was one of the finest men I ever knew, and one of the best friends I ever had. He died suddenly of a brain aneurism at home in West Vancouver on 02 September 2018. I miss him.

Jack Miles whose wartime experiences paralleled my Dad's. Jack brought alive for me what they both endured. Like Brooke, Jack's persuasive power also pushed me into writing this book, especially his 2019 impassioned speech at the RCAF 95th Anniversary Dinner urging me to write it. Jack was always delighted when I contacted him, which was several times a month, and he continually reminded me how important this book is, right up until just days before his death. Jack died peacefully at home in Surrey BC on 11 December 2021. He was 103 years old!

My Word Count Editing Friends

When the word count in my manuscript was too high in early 2022, two who volunteered to help me with the daunting task of editing out words are:

RCAF Colonel (ret) **Patrick Dennis** of Kitchener Ontario, a published author who was Canada's Deputy Representative to NATO in Brussels and our Defence Attache to Israel. Pat is a Canadian Military Historian and the Honorary Vice-President of the Western Front Association of Canada. In 1986, the Governor General of Canada invested him as an Officer in the Order of Military Merit.

His Honour Judge **William ('Bill') Rodgers** of Metro Vancouver, who was an Honorary Colonel of the 15th Field Artillery Regiment of the Royal Regiment of Canadian Artillery, President of the Provincial Court Judges Association of BC, a Judicial Council of BC and Commonwealth Judges Association member, and a Civilian Instructor with 103 Thunderbird Squadron, Royal Canadian Air Cadets.

Others By Category

Bomber Boy Families Canada: Jim Bartlett, Kamloops BC; Frank Borowicz KC, Vancouver; Roy Brand, WVan; Christopher Gaze, Vancouver; Jim Haliburton, WVan; Brian Hann, WVan; Ted Hawthorne, Coquitlam BC; Elmer ('Flip') Hunt, Kamloops deceased; Che Lafoy, Oshawa ON; Leah Lancaster, Lethbridge deceased; John MacLean, Burnaby BC; Betty Manning, New Westminster; Dorothy Miller, Saskatoon; The Eric Pocock Family -- Calvin & Guy of Calgary and Randy of Lethbridge; The Frank Selman Family – Beverley Smith of Champion AB & Gordon Selman of Sherwood Park AB, Sharan Gainor of Nicaragua & Marilyn Woolf of Utah; and Fred Wright, Kenora ON.

BOMBER COMMAND

Bomber Command Britain: Greg Algar, Dambusters Inn; Stuart Altoft 166 Squadron; Graham Brett, Elsham Wolds; Dan Ellis, Lincolnshire Bomber Command Archives; Dave Gilbert, Lincolnshire Bomber Command Memorial; Robin Lingard, Elsham Wolds Museum; Keith Macrae, Elsham Wolds Newsletter Editor; Cedric & Margaret Moppett, both deceased, 166 Squadron; Andrew Paton, Lincolnshire Aviation Heritage Centre East Kirkby; David Waldron, Elsham Wolds; and Martyn Wright of Liverpool and Sweden, son of Jim Wright, who was author of 'On Wings of War – A History of 166 Squadron'.

Bomber Command Down Under: Editor Geoff Raebel Australia; and Phil Furner, Barbie Hunter & Editor/CEO Peter Wheeler New Zealand.

Family, Friends & Colleagues Inside Canada: Dick Bennet, WVan; Dave Birrell, Nanton AB; Brother Luke Couillard, Westminster Abbey BC; Brother Maximus Spoeth, Westminster Abbey BC; John Chalmers, Edmonton; Ernie Davis, High River AB; Eric de Ridder, Calgary; Glen DuPre, Hope BC; Father Mark Dumont, Westminster Abbey BC; Blain Fowler, Camrose AB; Barbi Graham, WVan; Roy MacKenzie Graves, Calgary; Jaap Nico Hamburger, Montreal; Russ Hudson, Lancaster Restoration Sydney BC; Gord Johnsen, Commemorative Air Force, Camrose AB & Gilbert Arizona; Sunny Joseph, formerly Fairmont The Palliser, Calgary (now Fairmont Olympic, Seattle); Ken Lane, Monarchist League President, Vancouver Island; Phil Little, Saltair Ladysmith BC; David MacKenzie, Calgary; Doug & Peggi MacKenzie, Edmonton; Major-General Rob Roy MacKenzie, Ottawa; Don Marlatt, Vancouver; Mathieu Fairmont Queen Elizabeth, Montreal; Jan McAmmond, Sannichton BC; Jim McIlwaine, Sunshine Coast BC; Hon. David McLean, Vancouver; Allan Nielsen KC, Calgary; Jeff Noakes, Canadian War Museum, Ottawa; Mary Oswald, Canadian Aviation Hall of Fame 'Flyer' Editor, Wetaskiwin AB; Neil St. John, Toronto; Henk Snoeken, Former Dutch Consul-General Vancouver (now Berlin); Harry Somers, Fairmont Chateau Whistler; and Dean Winram, Vancouver.

Family, Friends & Colleagues Outside Canada: Jane Walker Bealby, Nottinghamshire UK; Alan Berridge, Chartwell UK; Lord Boateng Parliament UK; Doreen Charlwood Burge, Don Charlwood's Daughter, Warrandyte Australia; Mike Groves, Churchill Society of New Zealand; MacKenzie Clan Chief the Earl of Cromartie John Mackenzie, Castle Leod Scottish Highlands UK; Dwight Merriam, Connecticut; Beryl Nicholson, Chartwell UK; Miles Pooley RAF Club London UK; Justin Reash, International Churchill Society Washington DC; Tim Riley, National Churchill Museum, Fulton Missouri; Celia Sandys, Sir Winston Churchill's Granddaughter, London UK; Eric Stathers, Bellevue WA; and Fiona MacKenzie Try & Geoff Try, Windsor UK.

Librarians: Julie Backer, WVan Memorial Library; Annie Gleeson, Churchill College Librarian; and Howard 'Tim' Pierce, RAF College Cranwell Library.

ACKNOWLEDGEMENTS

Lincolnshire & North Lincs: Terry Marsden, Sally Martin and Lynne Williams.

Royal Air Force: Colin Bell, Sir Christopher Coville, Sir Michael Graydon, Tony Lark, Andy Marson, Richard Tillotson-Sills & Mark Wood.

Royal Canadian Air Force: Past Air Force Officers Association of BC (AFOA) President Wes Bowers, Surrey BC; Gordon Cowley, WVan; Past AFOA President Dick Dunn, Vancouver; Derrick Hotte, Ottawa; RCAF Deputy Commander Major-General Colin Keiver; Jack McGee, WVan; George Miller, Abbotsford BC; Ralph Langemann, Calgary; Past AFOA President Mike Matthews, Richmond BC; Keith Maxwell, Sunshine Coast BC; George Plawski, Vancouver; Allan Snowie, Bellingham WA; Hank Starek, Vancouver; Past AFOA President Jerry Vernon, Burnaby; and AFOA President Bud White, Vancouver.

And My Family

My sons **Guy Roland MacKenzie** and **Ruaridh MacKenzie** of London for representing Canada with me at their Grandfather Roland W. MacKenzie's 166 Squadron Kirmington Remembrance Service & Ceremony; joining me on North Lincolnshire & Lincolnshire expeditions; and being with me on my multiple visits to London, including at the RAF Museum, the RAF Memorial at Runnymede, and the Bomber Command and other London Memorials. Their ongoing participation, interest, support, encouragement and suggestions greatly enrich this book. In addition, all three of my sons know economics – each has a Masters in Economics – Guy Roland from the London School of Economics, Ruaridh from Oxford and Kai from Queens, the University which is mentioned several times in this book because of its important connections with FDR & Canadian Prime Minister William Lyon Mackenzie King. His knowledge of economics was vital.

My wife **Ka Hyun MacKenzie Shin** whose ceaseless support, her review and editing of my book in its entirety twice, her organization and printing of drafts for revision, her unique perspective, her wise counsel, her doing the monumental task of inserting page numbers into our enormous Index, her meeting with my Publishers in England, and her ongoing encouragement and assistance were essential. Without Ka Hyun helping me so much in so many ways, this book could not have happened.

And to others I have missed mentioning who also helped me create this book, I apologize and say THANKS!

I must emphasize though that any error or omission in this book is strictly mine. **And if you discover any, please let me know through emailing me at Roddy MacKenzie roddymmackenzie@gmail.com.**

Index

A10 German Rocket, 170, 249
ABC Airborne Cigar, RAF jammer, 164, 174, 176
AC2 Aircraftsman 2nd Class, 39, 141
AFOA (Air Force Officers Association) of British Columbia, ix, 95
AFU (Advanced Flying Unit), 140, 145
API (Air Position Indicator), 178
ATA (Air Transport Auxiliary), 67, 77, 109, 113, 123
ATS (Auxiliary Territorial Service), 119, 170
AWOL (Absent Without Leave), 127, 238
Aachen, Germany, Dad's 16th combat sortie, 27 May 1944, 145, 188, 230, 288
    1st German US Army Battle, 145
Abingdon, UK, RAF 1 Group HQ, 219, 303
Abraham Lincoln Battalion, Spain, 214
Admiral Graf Spee, 245
Admiral Hipper, German heavy cruiser, 245
Admiral Scheer, German heavy cruiser, 245
Advance Air Striking Force, RAF, 162
African Star Ship Safmarine, 75–7
Aiken, Max of New Brunswick, *see* Lord Beaverbrook, 41-42, 44-45
Air Force Officers Association of British Columbia, ix, 95

Air Museum of Canada Calgary 9
Air Training Plan, *see* British Commonwealth Air Training Plan
Air Transport Auxiliary, *see* ATA
Air War Crisis Areas in Germany, 186
Airborne Cigar jammer, 164, 174, 176
Airborne Grocer jammer, 164
Alanbrooke, Viscount Field Marshal, 83
Alberta Foothills, 2
Aldernest, Hitler's Eagle's Nest at Berghof, Berchtesgaden, 171–3, 253
Algar, Greg, proprietor, Dambusters Inn & Pub, Scampton, 37
Alkett Munitions Plant, Berlin, 208
Allied blockade of Fortress Europe, 218, 246
Altoft, Stuart, Bomber Boy stepson, 174
Altona, Borough of Hamburg, 206
American Fighter Aces Association, 93
American Legion, 93
American Patriots of WWII Through Service With the Canadian & British Armed Forces Gold Medal Act, US Congress 2019 Bill, 93
American War Memorials Overseas 93
An Airman's Letter, published anonymously, 18 June 1940, 119
Anderson, General Fred, USAAF, 233, 235
Antonov, General Aleksei, Soviet Red Army Chief of Staff, 155

316

INDEX

Anvil Flight Crew, US Navy, 234
Ardennes Offensive, 16 December 1944 – 25 January 1945, *see* Battle of the Bulge
Area Bombing Directive to Bomber Command, 14 Feb 1942, 162–3
Argentina, 92, 158
Armistice (WWI), 11 November 1918, 56
Arnhem, *Market-Garden,* 189
Arras, France, 2nd Battle of WWI, 275
Article XV squadrons, 86, 113–14, 226
Aspirin, Codename for Countermeasures, 224
Asquith, Prime Minister H.H., 44
Assheton, Nicholas, Treasurer to the Queen Mother and Harris' son-in-law, 87
Astaire, Fred, US dancer & actor, 58
Atlantic Wall, German defence, 144, 146, 183, 198, 249, 257
Attlee, Prime Minister Clement, 300
Augsburg, Bavaria, U-Boat diesel engine factory, 100, 211
Aulnoye, France, Dad's 2nd combat sortie, 10 Apr 1944, and 21st combat sortie, abandoned 17 Jun 1944, 10/10th Clouds, 117, 141, 148, 180, 288
Australia, 16, 53, 56–7, 70, 83, 88–92, 97, 105, 107, 113, 115, 121, 123, 126, 144, 161, 163, 210, 219, 229, 243, 268–70, 272–4, 276, 302
Australian Flying Corps, 22 Oct 1912 to 31 Mar 1921, 57
Australian War Memorial Sculpture Garden, Canberra, 272
Automatic Tail Turrets, *Village Inn*, 170
Auxiliary Territorial Service, *see* ATS
Avro, A.V. Roe & Company, British Aircraft Manufacturer Lancasters, 102
Avro Arrow Fighter Jet, RCAF, 18

Avro Canada, 102
Avro Lancaster bomber, 99–100

B-17 Flying Fortress Bomber, 105, 132, 234, 227, 248
B-24 Liberator Bomber, 125, 132, 170, 227
Baby Boomer generation, viii, 118, 264
Baker, Air Vice-Marshal & C-in-C, 12 Group, RAF, 75
Banana, Canaan, First President of Zimbabwe, 73
Banfield, John, 'Chaster Aircrew', 16
Banff National Park, Canada, 2, 94, 267
Banff, Scotland RAF Training, 130, 135
Bank of London and South America, 95
Banks, Mayor John, 273
Barmen, Ruhr Valley 229
Barnetby, RR Station for Kirmington and Elsham Wolds, 107, 116–17, 294
Barrin, W. 'Bill', Dad's Aircrew, 140
Bartlett, Christopher Smales 'Chris', 274–5
Bartlett, Jim, Author's Friend, 16, 274
Bartlett, Richard Edward 'Dick', 275
Bashow, David, Author, 240, 247, 299
Bataan Death March, 225
Battle, Fairey, Single-Engine British Light Bomber Aircraft, 162
Battle of the Atlantic, 3 September 1939 – 8 May 1945, 47, 218, 240, 244
Battle of Bataan, 7 Jan – 9 April 1942, 225
Battle of Berlin, 18 November 1943 – 31 March 1944, 231
Battle of Britain, 55, 74, 76, 101, 159, 161, 214–15, 221–22, 224, 227, 230, 258, 275
Battle of Britain Memorial Flight at RAF Coningsby, Lincolnshire, 101, 272

317

Battle of the Bulge, Ardennes, Belgium, 16 Dec 1944 – 25 Jan 1945, 192–3, 252–3, 305
Battle of Culloden, 16 April 1746, 59
Battle of Dieppe, Dad's 11th Combat Sortie, 10 May 1944, 144
Battle of Hamburg, 25 July - 3 August 1943, 231
Battle of Hong Kong, 8 – 25 December 1941, 158–9, 225
Battle of Midway, 4 June 1942, 225
Battle of Normandy, 6 June – 25 August 1944, Codename Operation *Overlord*, 14, 147, 254, 302
Battle of the Rhine, 25 August 1944 – 7 March 1945, 255
Battle of the Ruhr, 5 March – 31 July 1943, 116, 229–30
Battle of Singapore, 8 – 15 February 1942, 225
Battle of Stalingrad, 17 July 1942 – 2 February 1943, 191, 194, 200
Battle of Waterloo, 18 June 1815, 106, 257
Bay of Biscay, 242, 246
BCATP, *see* British Commonwealth Air Training Plan
Beaches Speech, Churchill, 7
Beam Approach, Enabled Bombers in Bad Weather, 135, 165
Beaverbrook, Lord, ix, 41-45
Beer Hall Putch, Munich, 212
Beevor, Anthony, 215, 299
Belgium, 15, 17, 92, 104–105, 252, 292
Bell, Colin, Pathfinder Pilot Age, 102, 105, 109, 284–5
Bella Coola, 22
Belleville-sur-Mer, France, 149
Bennett, AVM Don, C-in-C 8 Group Pathfinders, 16, 77, 163, 180
Bennett Jones, Calgary, Law Firm, 42
Bennett, Richard Bedford, Canadian Prime Minister, 41–2

Beppo, Josef 'Beppo' Schmidt 213, 215
Berchtesgaden, Germany 170–2, 253
Bergander, Gotz, 191
Berlin (now Kitchener), Ontario, 277
Berlin, Germany, 56, 62, 104, 109, 154, 160, 164, 184, 195–6, 201–208, 213–14, 221–2, 230–2, 234, 258, 261, 276–7, 279, 284, 304–306
Bethune, Dr. Norman, 48, 214
Bielefield Viaduct, 253
Big Valley, Alberta, 23
Billion Dollar Gift, 1942, Canada to UK, 47
Birrell, Dave, author & Bomber Command Museum of Canada, Nanton Alberta, 10, 64, 227, 299
Bishop, Air Marshal William Avery 'Billy', RCAF and WWI Ace, 93, 155–6
Black, Conrad, author, 47, 299
Blair Castle, Ancestral home of the Chiefs of Clan Murray, 13
Blatherwick, Dr. John, author, historian and author's mentor, 14–15, 100, 126
Blenheim, Bristol, 162
Bletchley Park, 113, 185
Blitzkrieg, fast powerful attacks using surprise & air superiority, 57, 260
Blom QC, Joost, Former Dean UBC Law, 38–9, 49
Blucher, German heavy cruiser, 245
Bochum, Ruhr Valley, 116, 230, 271, 278j
Boer War, 11 October 1899 – 31 May 1902, 77
Bombardment, The, Danish movie, 162
Bomber Boys on Screen by Simon P. MacKenzie, 159, 161, 304
Bomber Command Memorial & Museum of Canada at Nanton, Alberta, 10, 72, 84, 90, 97, 272–3
Bomber Command Memorial Spire, Canwick Hill, Lincoln, 39, 271

INDEX

Bomber Command Memorial Upkeep Club, 271
Bomber Harris, See Harris, Sir Arthur
Bomber Harris Trust, 32
Bomber Support, 163
Bomber Training Unit, *see* BTU
Bombing Ethics, WWII, 154
Bombing Reports:
    Butt Report on RAF Bombing Accuracy, 163, 165
    Singleton Report War Cabinet on bombing Germany, 259
    US Consul General in Geneva Report to US Secretary of State, 259
    British Intelligence Report No. 346, 259
    British Intelligence '*Report on Bombing's Effect on Housing and Division of Effort*', Autumn 1942, 259
    Chiefs of Staff Committee for the War Cabinet '*An Estimate of the Effects of the Anglo-American Offensive Against Germany*, 3 November 1942, 259
    United States Strategic Bombing Survey, 208 Volumes, 139, 237
Bombing Statistics, 72, 75, 91, 158, 197, 237–8
Bonaparte, Napoleon, Emperor of the French, 106, 257
Bonar Law, Andrew, 41–4
Bonar Law Memorial High School, Rexton, New Brunswick, 42
Book of the Month Club Selected Goebbels' Diaries, 203–209
Bordeaux, France, 151
Borg, Horst, Chief Historian, German Research Institute of Military History, 191
Bormann, Martin, Hitler's Private Secretary, 176, 226
Borowicz KC, Frank, 40, 275

Borowicz, Marilynn, Frank's wife, 275
Borsig Munitions Plant, Berlin, 208
Boulogne Channel Port, France, 252, 279
Bouman, Dutch General Ben, 37–8
Bouncing Bombs, 102, 169
Bourg Leopold, Military Depot, 249
Bowers, Wes, Former President AFOA, xviii, 314
Bowes-Lyon, Elizabeth, *see* Queen Elizabeth, The Queen Mother
Boy Scouts, 23
Boys in the Royal Naval Service, 85
Bracken, Brendan, Information Minister & Churchill confidant, 70
Brand, Frederick Roy, Bomber Boy, 275
Brand, Roy Jr., 276
Brandenburg, Germany, 212
Brandon, Manitoba, 29, 96–7, 128, 132–3, 273
Brest, Channel Port, France, 252
Brett, Graham, Author's Friend, 174
Bristol Blenheim, 162
Bristol Hercules Aircraft Engines, 103–104
British Army, 102, 254, 281
British Columbia Aviation Museum, 18, 100
British Commonwealth Air Training Plan, 8, 11, 29–31, 65, 85, 88–100, 113, 128, 273, 285
British Commonwealth Air Training Plan Flying Schools:
    No. 2 MD (Manning Depot) Brandon MB, 29, 96, 128, 132
    No. 2 ITS (Initial Training School) Regina SK, 133
    No. 2 FIS (Flying Instructors School) Vulcan Alberta, 94, 128, 130, 134
    No. 4 SFTS (Service Flying Training School) Saskatoon SK, 30–1, 96, 128, 130–1, 134

319

No. 15 SFTS Claresholm AB, 11, 94–5, 128, 130, 134–5
No. 16 EFTS (Elementary Flying Training School), Edmonton AB, 130, 133
No. 33 SFTS Carberry MB, 133
No 37 SFTS Calgary, 95
British Commonwealth of Nations, 88–90
British Imperial War Museums 89, 300
Brittain, Donald, *Canada at War,* 160
Broadfoot, Barry, Canadian Author of 'Ten Lost Years', 25, 300
Brooke, Field Marshal Alan, Later Viscount Alanbrooke, 83
Broom, Tommy DFC, 'Legendary Pathfinder Mosquito Navigator', 301
Brother Luke, Benedictine Monk, Westminster Abbey Mission BC, 46
Brother Maximus, Benedictine Monk, Westminster Abbey Mission BC, 268
Brownings, 169
Bruce, Rochelle, 276
BTU (Bomber Training Unit), 114
Buckingham Palace, London, 87, 152
Bufton, Sydney, RAF Air Vice-Marshal and a Director of Bomber Operations, 75
Bull Housser & Tupper, Law Firm, Vancouver, 29
Bullitt, William, US Ambassador, 68
Burge, Doreen, Charlwood of Australia, 144, 161, 276
Butt, David, British War Cabinet Secretariat, 162
Butt Report on RAF Bombing Accuracy, 162–3, 165

CBC *The Valour and the Horror,* 32–3, 63, 159–60, 267
Cairo, Egypt, 58
Calais, France, Dad's 17th combat sortie, 2 June 1944, abandoned

10/10th Clouds, 145–6, 181, 248, 251, 278
Calgary Herald Newspaper, 3, 7
Calgary International Airport, 3, 95
Calgary International Airshow, Lynn Garrison 1963-1966, 9
Calgary Public Library, xvi, 6–7
Calgary Public School Board, 147
Cambridge American Military Cemetery, 78
Cambridge University, viii, ix, 40, 175–6
Campbell, Hugh, RCAF Air Marshal & Chief of Air Staff, 8
Campobello Island, New Brunswick Vacation Home of F.D.R., 50
Camrose, Alberta, 277
Canada at Britain's Side, book by Mackenzie King, 304
Canada at War, 1962 documentary, 159
Canada Inflation Counter, 89
Canada Munitions & Supply Department, 49
Canada's Stalingrad, Ortona, 156
Canadian Air Force, 17 May 1920 – 1April 1924, 57
Canadian Army:
    Royal Rifles of Canada Quebec, 158, 225
    Seaforth Highlanders of Canada, ix, 37, 156
    Winnipeg Grenadiers, 158, 225
Canadian Army Medical Corps (Royal Canadian Army Medical Corps), 121, 126, 225
Canadian Encyclopedia, 22, 24, 38, 45, 49, 91–2, 147, 301–302
Canadian Foreign Enlistment Act, 214
Canadian Pacific Railway, 46-47
Canadian Parliament, Ottawa, 38, 46, 49
Canadian Revolt at Cranwell, 228–9
Canadian Rocky Mountains, 2, 267
Canadian Senate, Ottawa, 33, 50

INDEX

Canadian War Museum, Ottawa, 9, 33, 127
Canadian Warplane Heritage Museum at Port Hope ON Hamilton Airport, 101–102, 112
Canadian Women's Army Corps, 29
Canwick Hill, Lincoln, 39, 271
Cap Gris Nez, France, 147, 252
Cape Town, South Africa, 76
Carinhall, Göring's Hunting Lodge, 212
Carpet, RAF Jammer 164
Casablanca Conference, 67, 257
Casablanca Directive, 4 February 1943, 163, 183
Castles of the North, 139, 264, 266
Castle Leod, Scotland, 11–12, 314
Catherine, Duchess of Cambridge, now Princess of Wales, 85, 87, 95, 113, 185
Ceylon, now Sri Lanka, 92
Chadwick Centre, 100
Chadwick, Roy, Creator of the Lancaster, 99–100
Chamberlain, Prime Minister Neville, 57
Channel Ports, 252
Chapman, Arthur George 'Eastcott', 298
Chartwell, Churchill's home, Kent, 71
Chaster, Barry, RCAF Bomber Boy and New Westminster City Planner, 14–16
Chateau Bernapre, France, Dad's 23rd Combat Sortie, 27 June 1944, VI Rockets, 149
Chatham, New Brunswick, 42
Chequers, Country Home of British prime ministers, 55, 65, 69–71
Cherbourg, France, Dad's 18th Combat Sortie, 5 June 1944, and Kriegsmarine HQ, 146
Cherkley Court, Country Home of Lord Beaverbrook, 43

Chiang Kai-shek, Nationalist leader of China in WWII and postwar Taiwan, 12
Chicago Black Hawks, Hockey Team, 275
Chief Crowfoot Elementary School, Calgary, the author's Alma Mater, viii, 5, 131, 280
Children War Diaries Symphony, 40
Children's Evacuation Scheme, Germany's KLV, 184
Chinese Army, WWII,
  30th Division, 12
  89th Division, 12
Chopper, Marrowbone & Cleaver Pub, Kirmington, 34
Chorlton, Martyn, 64, 163, 300
Christ The King, Seminary, Mission, 268
Chuikov, General Vasily, Soviet 8th Guards Army Commander, 202
Churchill and the Movie Mogul, 125
Churchill, Clementine, Winston's wife, 59
Churchill College, Cambridge University, ix, 40, 175, 241, 282, 302, 306
Churchill, Pamela, 58, 300
Churchill, Randolph, Winston's son, 58
Churchill, Sarah, Winston's daughter, 58
Churchill, Winston, Prime Minister, vii, 6, 41, 43, 53, 56, 59–61, 98, 110, 160–2, 218, 221–23, 268, 286, 300–304, 306–307
Churchward, Pilot Officer, 166 Squadron, 297
Circular-Error Probability (CEP), 167
Civil War, USA, 12 April 1861, 124
Clan MacKenzie, ix, 61, 136
Clarendon Press, an imprint of Oxford University Press, 176, 225, 306–307
Claresholm, AB, 11, 94–5, 128, 130, 134–5

Clayton Knight Committee, Recruiting American Noncombat RCAF Pilots, 93
Cochran, Jacqueline, US pioneer aviator and wartime WASP, 67
Cochrane, Alberta, 94
Cochrane, Sir Ralph, RAF Air Vice-Marshal & C-in-C 5 Group, 16, 75, 180
Cold War, 1947-1991, viii, 33
Cologne, Germany, Dad's 4th combat sortie, 20 April 1944, 141–2
Cologne Ford Works, Germany, 259
Combined Bomber Offensive from the United Kingdom, 112, 182
Comet Escape Line, Belgium, WWII, 17
'Commies', Slang for Communists, 12
Commonwealth War Graves (CWGC), 277
Condor Legion, German Military Aiding Franco in Spanish Civil War, 214
Confederate Air Force, *see* Commemorative Air Force
Congress, United States House of Representatives and Senate, 53, 93
Conscription Crisis, Canada, 1944, 49
Continuously-Computed Impact Point (CCIP), 167
Cook-Radmore, Derry, Chair of the Translators Guild, 176
Copenhagen, Denmark, 162, 246
Copp, Terry, 161
Corona, RAF Spoofer, 164
Cossey, Ted & Norah, Devonshire, 13
Coville, RAF Air Marshal Sir Christopher and Lady Coville, 35, 37, 129
Cranwell Aviation Heritage Museum, 174
Cranwell Mutiny, 228–9
Crewing-up Process at the OUT, 114
Crimes Against Humanity, 195
Crisbecq Gun Batteries, D-Day, 146
Crossbow Committee, 179, 181, 234

Crown Lumber, Later Crown Zellerbach, 23
Crown Prince Wilhelm of Germany, 212
Crown Prince Wilhelm's Regiment (112th Infantry), 211
Crüwell, General Ludwig, German General and PoW, 179
Cryers Hill, 69
Curnow, John, 101–102, 301
Curzon, Frederick, 7th Earl Howe 271
Czechoslovakia, now Czechia and Slovakia, 92

D-Day, Normandy Invasion, 6 June 1944, 4, 83, 145–8, 151, 192, 209, 247–8, 250–1, 254, 279, 302
Dahlem, Suburb of Berlin, 260
Daily Express, 44, 77
Dalhousie University, Halifax 164
Dambusters, 617 Squadron 5 Group, 16, 118, 275
Dambusters, 1955 Movie, 6
Danson, Barney, Former Canadian Minister of Defence, 160
Das Deutsche Reich und der Zweite Weltkrieg, [Germany and the Second World War] published by the Deutsche Verlags-Anstalt, 176, 306
Dashwood, Ontario, birthplace of the author's maternal Grandfather, 5
Davis, Ernie, the author's friend, 276
de Havilland Mosquito, *see* Mosquito
de Ridder, Anne and Ben, the author's friends & survivors of Japanese WWII Indonesian prison camp, 158
de Ridder, Eric, the author's friend, 38, 158
DECCA Navigational Aid, 225
Defence of the Reich Campaign, German Luftwaffe Response to Allied Bombing, 69, 218, 237, 239
Denmark, 246, 262, 269
Dennis, RCAF Colonel Patrick, author & Historian, 24, 153, 277

INDEX

Dennis, Wendy, Patrick's wife and Bomber Boy niece, 277
Desjardins, Brian, Executive Director Hangar Flight Museum, Calgary, 8, 95
Devon, 13
Diefenbaker, John, Canadian Prime Minister & honorary bomber, 46
Diefenbaker, William, father of John and teacher of Mackenzie King, 46
Dieppe, Battle of, 12 August 1942; Dad's 11th Combat Sortie, 10 May 1944, 144
Dietrich, Sepp, German General and former chauffeur for Hitler, 192, 253
Disraeli, Prime Minister Benjamin, 238
Distinguished Flying Cross (DFC), vi, 5, 151, 175, 287
Distinguished Service Order (DSO), 5, 86
Ditchley Park, Churchill's wartime country retreat, 71
Dixon, USAF General Robert, 90
Dobbs, Lord Michael, author and politician, 6–7
Dobson, Sir Roy, Managing Director of Avro. Postwar founder, Avro, Canada, 99, 102
Dobson, Royal Bank of Canada General Manager, WWII, 29
Doenitz, Karl, German Admiral & Dollar-a-Year Men, Canada, 49
Dollar-a-Year Men, Canada, 49
Doolittle, USAAF General Jimmy, 68, 233–5, 304
Dorchester Hotel, London, 58
Dornier Do 17, Light Bomber, 215
Dortmund, Germany, Dad's 15th combat sortie 22 May 1944, 145
Dortmund Tunnels, 184
Dortmund-Ems Canal, 244
Douai, France, Dad's 34th and final combat sortie, 11 Aug 1944, 151, 277

Douglas, RAF Air Marshal Sholto, 77, 87
Dow Brothers, Calgary High School band leaders, 42
Dowding, Air Chief Marshal and C-in-C of Fighter Command Hugh, 44, 76
Dresden, Germany, 71, 82, 154–7, 160–1, 190, 193, 203, 210, 226, 244, 253–4, 285, 297, 300
Dresden Commission of Historians for the Ascertainment of the Number of Victims of the Air Raids on the City of Dresden on 13/14 Feb 1945, 154
du Pont, Ethel, F.D.R. Jr's wife, 59
Duchess of Cambridge, Now Princess of Wales, Catherine 85, 87, 95, 113, 185
Duchess of Gloucester, Princess Alice Sister-in-Law of King George VI 70, 86
Duchess of Sutherland, Anne Hay-Mackenzie, Countess of Cromartie, 59
Duisburg, Germany, Dad's 14th combat sortie, 21 May 1944, 145, 203
Duke of Atholl, Chief of Clan Murray, 13
Duke of Cambridge, *see* Prince William
Duke of Edinburgh, *see* Prince Philip
Duke of Kent, King George VI's brother and RAF Air Commodore, 70, 86
Duke of Marlborough Charles 'Sunny', 59
Duke of Sussex, *see* Prince Harry
Duke of Windsor, *see* King Edward VIII
Durkin, James Patrick, Bomber Boy, 142
Durnbach War Cemetery, Bavarian Alps by Tegernsee Lake, 'Eastcott', 298
Dusseldorf, Germany, Dad's 5th combat sortie, 2 Apr 1944, 142, 236

Dutch Resistance, WWII, 17
Dutchak, Peter, Bomber Boy, 277

E-Boats, 147–8
Earl of Cromartie, John Mackenzie, current Chief of Clan MacKenzie, 11
Earl Howe, Minister of State in the House of Lords for Defence, 271
Earls of Seaforth, historic chiefs of Clan MacKenzie, ix
East Kirkby, Lancaster, *Just Jane*, 36–7, 101, 277
Eastchurch, Isle of Sheppey, 55
Eastcott Aircrew 166 Squadron, 116, 128, 280, 294, 297–8
Eastern Front, Soviet Union, 155–6, 215, 238–9, 261
Ebeling, Dr. Ministerialdirigent of the Reich Transport Ministry, 250
Edith, Lady Londonderry, 59
Edmonton, Alberta, 3, 7, 9, 26, 31, 96, 130, 133, 139, 265, 300
Edmonton Eskimos football team, 275
Edmonton #16 Flying Training School, 31, 96, 133
Edzell Scotland, RAF Training, 130, 135
Eilean Donan Castle, Scotland, 12–13, 136
Eisenhower, Dwight 'Ike', US General, Supreme Commander and US President, ix, 54, 63, 66, 78, 80, 82, 153, 181, 223, 233, 236, 239, 250, 269, 283
El Alamein, Egypt, 223, 225
Elbe River, 284
Elberfeld, Ruhr Valley, 230
Ellef Rignes Island, Canadian Arctic, 10
Ellesmere Island, Canadian Arctic, 10
Ellin, Dan, IBCC Digital Archivist, 121–2
Ellis, Ernest Lewis, *see* Eastcott
Elvington Yorkshire (Halifax), 104
Emden, German light cruiser, 245
Emerson, Ralph Waldo, 22–3
Emphysema, 20, 267

Empire Air Training Plan, *see* British Commonwealth Air Training Plan
Epenstein, Hermann Ritter von, Jewish lover of Goering's mother, 211
Ernest Hall Aviation Museum, USA, 93
Esens, near Wilhelmshaven, 227
Essen, Ruhr, Goebbels inspects bomb damage, 10 April 1943, 183

Fairey Battle, 162
Fairmont Chateau Frontenac, Quebec, 51
Fairmont Hotel MacDonald, Edmonton, 139
Fairmont Palliser, Calgary, 264
Fairmont Queen Elizabeth Hotel, Montreal, 40, 266
Fairview, Alberta, 25–7
Fauquier Johnny, *Canada's Greatest Bomber Pilot*, 5, 21, 54, 64, 86, 148, 163, 180, 218, 229, 299
Falla, P.S. (Paul Stephen), translation editor, 176
Falsterbo, 104
Fake news, 155
Fantasy of Flight, Kermit Weeks Orlando, Florida, 9
Fast-Attack Torpedo Boats, *see* Torpedo Boats
Father of Manitoba, *see* Louis Riel
Fatherland, *see* Germany
Feesey, Don author & 166 Squadron Navigator 116, 123–4, 297–8
Few, Royal Air Force Aircrew, 54
Fiji, 92
Finest Hour, International Churchill Society Magazine, 40, 44, 50, 55, 59–61, 222–3, 301–302, 304–305, 307
Finland, 55, 92, 220
Finlay, Gregory & Co, Montreal Fur Traders, 22
Finlayson, RC, 298
  see also Eastcott

INDEX

Flak Happy, (USAAF PTSD), 125
Fleur, France, Dad's 22nd combat sortie, 24 Jun 1944, 149
Flying Bombs, 179, 215, 239, 251, 294
Flying Fortress, 105, 132, 227, 234, 248
Fontenay Le Marmion, Normandy Dad's 33rd combat sortie, 07 Aug 1944, 151
Force Substitution Churchill/Trenchard Concept for Offense Use of RAF, 56
Foret-Du-Croc at Freulleville France, Dad's 26th combat sortie, 149
Fort Chipewyan, Alberta, 22
Fort MacLeod, Alberta, 7
Fort McMurray, Alberta, 281
Fort Ord, Monterey Bay, CA, 12
Fortress Europe, 57, 209, 218
Foster, Ian founder of Halifax, 57, 104, 292
Fowler, Blain, Bomber Boy Vic's Nephew, 277
France, 17, 57–8, 63, 84–5, 92, 100, 103, 117–18, 121, 143–51, 162, 168, 171, 180–2, 250, 254, 269, 275, 281, 287–8, 290, 301
Franco, Francisco, Spanish dictator, 214
Frank, Anne, Teenage diarist, 158
Frankfurt, Germany, 208, 230, 277
Freeman, David, Churchill International, my mentor, 40, 50, 108, 129, 302
Freiberg, Germany, Jimmy Stewart, 170
Freya, Luftwaffe radar, 164
Frick, Wilhelm, Reich Minister of the Interior, 206
Friedenstal Historical Society, AB, 26
Friedrichshafen Germany, Dad's 7th combat sortie, 143, 152–3, 230, 236
Fuhrerbunker, Berlin, 227
Fürth, Germany, 125
Fyfe, James, author of *The Greatest Ingratitude*, 169, 193, 253, 268–9, 302

GCB – Order of the Bath, British Knighthood, 87
GPI (Ground Position Indicator), 168
GPS (Global Positioning System), 168
Gabaldon, Diana, author of *Outlander* series and a Guardian of Castle Leod, 11
Gainor, Sharan, Bomber Boy daughter, 108, 280
Galland, Adolph, 192, 213–16, 236
Gander, Newfoundland, airport, 159
Garner, Donald, 166 Squadron CO from 30 Apr 1944 for the duration of Dad's Tour, 137, 143, 146
Garrison, Lynn, RCAF 403 Squadron, 7, 9
Gauleiter, 201
Gelsenkirchen, Ruhr Valley, 230
General der Jagdflieger (Luftwaffe General of Fighters), 192, 216, 236
Geneva, Switzerland, 259
George Washington Battalion, Spain, 214
Gerhardinger, German artist, 204
German 6th Panzer Army in Belgium, 253
German air armaments, 177–8, 182
German Army Social Sciences Studies Centre, 174
German blockade, 246
German industrial capacity, 260–1
German Steel Syndicate, 192
German WWII atrocities, 158, 195
Germany and the Second World War [*Das Deutsche Reich und der Zweite Weltkrieg*] published by the Deutsche Verlags-Anstalt, 176, 307
Germany's merchant marine fleet, 242, 246
Gestapo, 17, 69, 105, 162, 186–7, 191, 207, 213
Gibbons, Pilot Officer Dudley, 166
Gibson, Guy, RAF Dambusters leader, 16, 23, 34, 37, 111–12, 135, 219, 302

325

Gilbert, Dave Lancaster Memorial Spire, Lincoln, 37, 77–8, 272
Givors France, 151
Glassborow, Valerie, WWII Bletchley Park codebreaker, Grandmother of Catherine, Duchess of Cambridge, 185
Gleason, Annie, Churchill College Head Librarian at Cambridge University, 175
Glueckstein, Fred, author, 222, 302
Godfrey, Vice-Admiral John Henry, Head of RN Naval Intelligence, 70
Goebbels, Joseph, German Minister of Propaganda and Total War, vi, x, 105, 154–5, 160, 176, 183, 189, 201–10, 212, 226, 230–1, 235, 261
Goebbels, Magda, wife of Joseph, 202
Goering, Reich Marshal Hermann, 61, 104, 176, 181–2, 185, 192, 198, 204, 206, 210–15, 218, 221–3, 225–6, 230, 241, 256, 284
Gospel of St. Matthew, 97
Gotenhafen, Baltic Sea port, 246
Gotha, Germany, 125
Gough, Douglas, Bomber Boy, 279
Grade, Michael Channel Four TV, 160
Graham, Bill, Minister of National Defence Canada, 272
Graham, David, RCAF Brigadier General, 272
Graham, Isabelle, New Westminster, 15
Graham, Jim, Isabelle's son, 15
Granatstein, Jack Canadian, historian, 32
Grand Slam bombs, 37, 72, 102, 167, 169, 234, 244, 253, 283
Grant, Lachlan, *Sydney Morning Herald,* 302
Grant, Nigel, WVan FitFella, 278
Grant, Rebecca, author *Air Force Magazine,* 64, 67
Graz, Germany, 184
Great Depression, 1930s, Canada, viii, 25, 28, 42, 45, 300

Great Escape, 1963 Movie, 275, 281
Great Kingshill, Bucks., 70
Great Cross-Channel Adventure, Churchill's D-Day Description, 247
Greatest Briton, see Churchill
Greatest Generation, WWII, viii
Greatest Person of the 20th Century, 53
Greece, 92, 126
Green Hill, Pictou County, Nova Scotia, 21–3, 48
Green, L., Dad's aircrew, 140
Green Park, London, 87, 269–71
Grindel, Albert, Comet Escape Line, 17
Grindel, Jean, Comet Escape Line, 17
Gneisenau, 245
Greatest Ingratitude by James Fyfe, 169, 193, 253, 268
Guardians of Castle Leod, 11
Gyro, *see* SABS

H2S Ground Mapping Radar, 164–5, 167–8, 236, 295
Hagen, Germany, 187
Haigerloch, Germany's Black Forest, 260
Haliburton Gilbert, Bomber Boy, 277
Haliburton Jim, West Vancouver, 277
Haliburton, John, Flying Instructor, 277
Haliburton William, Bomber Boy, 277
Halifax,
    57 Rescue (Canada), vi, 103–104, 292–3
    RAF Halifax (NA337), Recovered From Lake Mjosa, Norway, is on display in Trenton Ontario, 292
    405 Squadron Pathfinders Halifax (HR871), rescued in Sweden Baltic Sea, 104
    426 Squadron RCAF Halifax (LW682), 271
Halle, Kay, author of Churchill books, 58
Hamborn, Ruhr Valley, 230, 295

INDEX

Hamburger, Jaap Nico, composer & conductor, 40

Hampton, James, Author of *Selected for Aircrew*, 71, 83, 156, 247, 261, 268–9, 302

Handley Page Halifax, 72, 104, 275, 292–3

Handley Page V/1500, WWI bomber, 56

Hangar Flight Museum, Calgary, 95

Hanks, Thomas 'Tom', US actor and WWII veterans champion, viii

Hann, Brian, Bomber Boy's brother, 277

Hann, Raymond, Bomber Boy, 277

Hanover, Germany, 231, 253

Harriman, Averell, WWII US diplomat, 45, 58–9, 68, 76, 304

Harris, Jackie, Sir Arthur's daughter, 69, 76–7, 87

Harris, Jill, Sir Arthur's wife, 68–70, 77

Harris, Sir Arthur, 41, 48, 55, 62–3, 68, 71, 73–6, 79–80, 88, 99, 102, 114, 160, 247, 270, 302–303, 306

Harris, Walter, 'Chaster Aircrew', 16

Harrison, Glen, author's paternal uncle-in-law, 24

Harvard University, 49

Hawthorne, Edwin 'Ted', Honorary Colonel and Bomber Boy's son, 278

Hay-Mackenzie, Anne, Countess of Cromartie and Duchess of Sutherland, 59

HCU (Heavy Conversion Unit), 92, 136, 166

Headache, codename navigation, 224

Head Smashed In Buffalo Jump, 11

Hector, ship bringing Scots to Canada, 22

Heenan, Joseph, Comet Escape Line, 17

Heer (German Army), 186

Heimatflak, 181

Heinemann, Gustav, President of West Germany, 87

Heinkel He 111 and He 177 planes, 214–15

Heligoland, German Archipelago, 144, 234

Heligoland Bight Mining, Dad's 12th combat sortie, 12 May 1944, 100, 144

Hellyer, Paul, Canada's controversial Minister of Defence, 9

Helm, Major Erwin, 187

High Flight, Poem, John Magee, 93, 137

High Wycombe, RAF, Bomber Command HQ, Walters Ash Village, 34, 68, 70, 86

Himmler, Heinrich, SS Reichsfuhrer and Chief of German Police, 176, 180, 194–5, 206–207, 210, 213, 226, 307

Hindenburg, Paul von, German President, 213

History of the Second World War Series, 78, 243

Hitler, Adolf, 6–7, 45, 57–8, 61, 69, 71, 82, 84, 120, 145–7, 150, 153, 160, 170–2, 176–7, 181–4, 186, 191–202, 206, 209–16, 218, 221–2, 224–5, 230, 234, 238–9, 241, 243, 248, 252–3, 256–8, 260, 283, 299–301, 303

Hixon, Staffordshire RAF Training, 130, 135–6

HMCS *Mackenzie*, Canadian destroyer, ix

HMCS *Ontario*, light cruiser, 10

HMS *Arc Royal*, aircraft carrier, 275

HMS *Prince of Wales*, 45

Holmes, Richard, UK professor, 47, 303

Holocaust, 154, 158, 193

Hong Kong, 158–9, 225

Hongerwinter, Dutch Hunger, 1944-45, 38, 189

Horrocks, Sir Brian, British general and corps commander in Normandy, 83

327

Houdremont, Edouard, professor and Essen Krupps Works Controller, 192
House of Cards, Lord Dobbs, 6
Howe C.D., Canada's Wartime Minister of 'Everything', 49
Howe, Earl, 271
Hudson, Russ, Victoria Lancaster, 18, 100
Huggins, Godfrey, Prime Minister of Southern Rhodesia (Zimbabwe), 70, 72
Huls, Ruhr Valley, 230
Humberside International Airport, Kirmington, North Lincolnshire, 35
Hunt, Elmer Harold 'Flip', Author's Friend, FitFella & Bomber Boy, 278
Hunt, Irmgard, 170–2, 303
Hunter, Barbie, New Zealand Bomber Command Association, 119
Hunter, Ken, husband of Barbie, 119
Hutson, Arthur, husband of Elizabeth MacKenzie, the author's cousin, 12
Hutson, Daniel Frank Arthur 'Danny', son of Arthur and Elizabeth Hutson, 12
Hutson, Anna Elizabeth, daughter of Danny & the author's cousin, 12
Hyde Park, New York, Home of FDR, 51–2
Hyde Park Corner, London, 271
Hyde Park Declaration, 20 Apr 1941, 52
Hydrogenation plants, 198–9

IBCC (International Bomber Command Centre), Lincoln, 37, 100, 109, 121, 272
ILA (German Interministerial Committee on Bomb Damage), 183, 196, 200, 220, 232
Imperial War Museums, 89, 300
Independent Bomber Force RAF, 54–6, 175
Inside the Third Reich, Albert Speer, 195
Inspectorate for Civil Air War in Germany, 183

Interministerial Committee on Bomb Damage in Germany, *see* ILA
International Bomber Command Centre Lincoln, *see* IBCC
Iron Lung for polio, 9, 265
Irvine, Dr. Warren, the author's paternal uncle-in-law, 24, 106, 281
Irvine, Sandra, the author's paternal cousin, 282
Irvine, Thelma Elizabeth MacKenzie, the author's paternal aunt, 129, 147, 267, 281, 303
Isle of Sheppey, 55
Isle of Skye, 136
Ismay, Hastings Lionel, vii, 57, 79, 285

Jagerstab (Fighter Staff) to increase fighter plane production with SS slave labour, 182
Japan, 67, 93, 131, 157–9, 166–7, 220, 225, 233, 268
Japanese archipelago, 233
Japanese WWII atrocities, 158
Jasper National Park Alberta, 267
Jazz (*Schrage Musik*), Luftwaffe upward firing cannon for night fighters, 236
Jenkins, Roy, author & British politician, 156, 303
Jewish Physics, Hitler's name for nuclear physics, 198
Joan of Arc, France, 141
Johnsen, Gord, the author's friend, 132
Johnson, Boris, UK Prime Minister and author, 41, 54–5, 59, 303
Johnson, Paul, author, 155–6, 238–9, 303
Jones, R., Dad's aircrew, 140, 148
Jones, Reginald, RAF Assistant Director of Intelligence (Science), 216, 223–5
Jostle, RAF jammer, 164
Junkers Ju 88, 161
Just Jane Lancaster, 36, 101, 165, 304

INDEX

Justice Ministry Germany, 186–7
Jutland, Island in Denmark, 236

Kaiser Wilhelm Institute for Physics, 260
Kaiser Wilhelm II, German emperor, 150, 202
Kammhuber, Josef General of the night-fighters, 213, 215–16
Kananaskis, Alberta Rocky Mountains, 2
Karlsruhe, Germany, Dad's 6th combat sortie 24 April 1944, 142–3
Karlsruhe German light cruiser, 245, 289–90, 304
Kassel, Germany, V1 manufacturing site, 178, 183, 231
Kato, Toshiyuki Japan's Parliamentary Vice-Minister for Foreign Affairs, 159
Kay, Archibald Thomas 'Archie', 110
Keiver, Major-General Colin, Deputy Commander RCAF, x
Kellogg-Briand Pact, 1926, 218
Kelly, De-Anne, Australian Minister of Veteran Affairs, 272
Kennedy, John F., US President, 53
Kennedy, Joseph, JFK's brother, 234
Kerr, President Clark, University of California Berkeley, 12
Kesselring, Albert, German Field Marshal of the Luftwaffe, 192
Kiel, Germany, Dad's 29th combat sortie, 23 July 1944, and Last Raid, WWII, 150
Killiecrankie Pass, Scotland, 13
Kindersley, Saskatchewan, 23
King Edward VIII, 53
King George V, 5, 43, 57
King George VI, 44–5, 60, 70, 85–7, 89, 152, 221, 233, 256
King Willem-Alexander, Netherlands, 38
King, PM, *see* Mackenzie King
King's Royal Regiment of New York, 22

Kirmington and Croxton Parish Council, 35
Kirmington village, 35, 37
Kitchener, Ontario, 277
Kjarsgaard, Karl, Curator & Director Bomber Command Memorial and Museum of Canada in Nanton AB, 94, 103–104, 271–2, 274, 276, 292
KLV – Germany's children's evacuation scheme 184
Knapp, Bud, *Canada at War,* 1962, 160
Knight, Clayton, of Canada's WWII Clayton Knight Committee, 93
Knights of the Garter, 87
Knipfer, Kurt, German bombproof construction, 184
Knox United Church, the author's family church Calgary 27, 264, 266
Koller, Karl, German Chief of General Staff and Luftwaffe operations, 192
Koln, German light cruiser, 245
Konigsberg, German light cruiser, 245
Korean War, 94
Krefeld, Ruhr Valley, 230
Kriegsmarine, 141, 146, 241–2, 245–6
Krupp, German weapons producer in both world wars, 235
Kuhn, Cathy Bomber Boy niece, 277

Lack of Moral Fibre (LMF), 21, 120–1, 123, 301
La Pallice, 24 July 1941, 103
Lachine, (Montreal) Quebec, 139
Lafoy, Floyd ('Red') Bomber Boy, 278
Lafoy, Gary ('Che') Bomber Boy's grandson, 278
Lagrandeur, Philip Author *We Flew, We Fell, We Lived,* 16–17, 304
Lancaster Bomber Aircraft viii, 2–3, 5–11, 13–20, 32, 34, 36–8, 43, 72, 77, 83, 92, 95, 99–104, 106, 108, 111–12, 115–18, 122, 124, 127, 129, 136–7, 140–51, 159, 164–5, 167, 169, 192, 225, 231,

234, 236, 239, 244, 248–9, 253–4, 265–6, 270–3, 275–7, 279-80, 283, 289–90, 297–99, 301–05
Roy Chadwick, creator of the Lancaster, 99–100
166 Squadron Lancasters AS-J2 & AS-V collided. AS-J2 crashed, no survivors, 151
166 Squadron Lancaster AS-E crashed. All seven aircrew are buried in one box at Belleville-sur-Mer, 149
166 Squadron Dad's Lancaster AS-L for Love (ND757), 116, 140, 146
166 Squadron Eastcott Lancaster AS-L2 (ND506), 280, 298
166 Squadron Gibbons' Lancaster AS-F, for Freddie, 117–18, 141
166 Squadron Gibbons' Lancaster AS-W, 118
Battle of Britain Flight Lancaster (PA474), 101
Calgary Lancaster (FM136), 3
Calgary Airshow Lancaster (KB976), 9
Canadian Lancaster (KB732) flying most sorties, 101
East Kirkby Lancaster (NX611), 36, 277
Haliburton Lancaster (KB911), 277
Hamilton Lancaster (FM213), 18
Nanton Lancaster (FM159), 10, 101, 299
Red Deer Lancaster (KB885), 9
Ruhr Express Lancaster (KB700), 101
Toronto to British Columbia Lancaster (FM104), 18
Lancaster, Dorothy, the author's maternal aunt, 10–11
Lancaster Experience, East Kirkby, 101
Lancaster, Ken, the author's maternal uncle-in-law, 11

Langemann, Ralph, RCAF 403 Squadron, 9
Lansbury, Angela, beloved British and American actress, 43
Lansbury, George, British Labour Leader of the Opposition, 43
Laon, France, 279
Larkin, Peter, Royal Westminster Tank Regiment and NW City Clerk, 14
Lark, RAF Wing Commander Tony, the author's friend, 35–7, 101, 108, 118, 281
Laurier, Sir Wilfrid, Canadian Prime Minister, 50
Law of Unintended Consequences, 213
Le Havre, France, Dad's 19th combat sortie attacking E-Boats, 14 June 1944, and 30th Combat Sortie, 2 August 1944, attacking Flying Bomb site, 147, 150
Leipzig, German light cruiser, 246
Lefkowitz, 'Lefty' B. Dad's aircrew, 136, 140
Leipzig, Germany's Supreme Court, 209
Lemming, Sergeant and Flight Engineer, 166, 297
Lend-Lease, 51–2, 90
Lethbridge, Alberta, 4, 10–11, 18–20, 25, 278, 280
Letters of St. Paul, New Testament, 282
Lichtenstein, Luftwaffe radar, 164
Lincoln, Abraham, US President, 214
Lincoln, capital city of Lincolnshire 37, 110, 271
Lincolnshire Aviation Heritage Centre, East Kirkby, 36, 101, 165, 304
Lindemann, Frederick, physicist and Churchill's scientific advisor, 162–3, 223–4, 259
Lindholme, Yorkshire, RAF, 130, 136
Lineker, Ivan, 16
Link Trainers – flight simulators, 133, 135

INDEX

Lintott, Graham, Air Vice-Marshal & Chief of Royal New Zealand Air Force, 27
Lloyd George, British Prime Minister David, 43, 56
Loch Duich, MacKenzie Clan lands Scotland, 12, 136
Lochbroom, MacKenzie Clan lands Scotland, 22
Lochner, Louis, confirmed Goebbels' diaries, 203
Loerzer, Bruno, Goering's friend, 212
London Declaration 26 April 1949 reconstituting Commonwealth, 88–9
London Gazette, 74, 175, 287
Lord Cherwell, *see* Lindemann, Frederick
Lord President of the Council, UK, 219
Lougheed, James, Canadian senator, 42
Lougheed, Peter, Premier of Alberta, 42
Lübeck, Germany, 181
Lucero, 164
Ludlow-Hewitt, Sir Edgar Rainey, RAF Air Chief Marshal, Bomber Command C-in-C, 1937 to 1940, 65
Ludwigshafen, Germany, 238
Luftwaffe, vi, 5, 16, 56, 58, 64, 105, 112, 119, 144, 150, 163–4, 169, 178, 181–2, 186, 192, 195–6, 198, 204, 206, 210–11, 213–16, 218–30, 235–8, 241–2, 250–1, 258–9, 285, 299, 308
Lutzow, German heavy cruiser, 245

McArthur, John Duncan, ('JD') Peace River Country railroader, 26
McCall, Fred, WWI Flying Ace, 3
McEwan, Clifford 'Black Mike', RCAF Air Vice-Marshal C-in-C 6 Group, 72
McGregor, Blair, Seaforth Highlanders of Canada CO, 37

McIntosh, Hugh, the author's boyhood friend, 265
McKay, Donald, RCAF F/O Oyen AB, 132
McKenna, Brian & Terrance, CBC/NFB 'The Valour & The Horror', 32–3
McKenzie Portage Road, ON, 96
McKenzie, William, teacher aboard ship *Hector*, 22
Macintosh, Maggie, CBC News, 104, 292, 304
Mackenzie, Alexander, Canadian Prime Minister, 13, 46–7
Mackenzie, Alexander, explorer, 21–2
MacKenzie, Arthur, the author's uncle, 277
MacKenzie, Bruce M., the author's uncle, 9, 23–4, 27, 105, 147
MacKenzie, Chester, the author's great uncle, 23
MacKenzie Clan Chief, 11
MacKenzie, Elizabeth, the author's cousin and Arthur Hutson's wife, 12
MacKenzie, Guy Roland, the author's son ix, 13, 22, 33, 35–7, 50, 55, 92, 101, 119, 174–5, 281
Mackenzie, Ian, Canada's First Minister of Veterans' Affairs, 49
Mackenzie, Isabel, Grace, mother of Mackenzie King, 46
MacKenzie, John R., ('Jack') the author's uncle, 23, 140, 147
MacKenzie, Joyce Lenore Miller, the author's mother, 3, 50, 264
MacKenzie, Kai, the author's son, 51
Mackenzie King, William Lyon, Canadian Prime Minister, ix, x, 41–2, 45–54, 58, 60–1, 72, 88–91, 98, 114, 134, 202, 226, 228, 283, 285, 300, 303–304, 306–308
Mackenzie King Scholarships, 49
MacKenzie, Larry, (Dr. Norman A.M) WWI hero and UBC President, 48, 308

MacKenzie, Leslie, the author's great uncle, ix, 11–12, 23
MacKenzie, Mary Anne, the author's daughter, 8, 13, 50
MacKenzie, Mary Catherine Gunn, the author's paternal grandmother, 22
MacKenzie, Dr. Norman A.M. 'Larry', 48, 308
Mackenzie-Papineau Battalion, Spain, 214
Mackenzie-Papineau Rebellion, 1837, 46
Mackenzie River, District of Mackenzie, Northwest Territories, 22
MacKenzie, Roderick the author's grandfather, x, 4, 21
MacKenzie, Roderick MacKay the author's grandfather, 22, 121
MacKenzie, Roderick Winter, see MacKenzie, Ruaridh
MacKenzie, Roland W., DFC the author's father, vi–x, 2–7, 9, 11–14, 17–35, 38–40, 56, 66, 89, 93–6, 107–108, 114–18, 121–2, 124–5, 127–53, 156, 165, 168, 175, 178, 180, 226, 229, 236, 239, 243, 249, 251, 264–7, 273, 279, 283–4, 287, 289
RCAF Record of Service, 2, 20–2, 27, 129, 175, 264, 287, 291, 304
see also RAF Kirmington, 166
MacKenzie, Ruaridh, the author's son, ix, 22, 35–7, 55, 77, 92, 101, 119, 158, 174–5, 281
MacKenzie, Sheila Manning, the author's paternal aunt, 8
MacKenzie Shin, Ka Hyun, the author's wife, 11, 22, 26, 34–5, 38, 40, 50, 95–6, 211
MacKenzie, Simon P., author, 159, 304
MacKenzie, Susan, author's sister, 3–4
MacKenzie, Verna Tate the author's stepmother, 25
Mackenzie, William Lyon, First Mayor Toronto and Mackenzie King's grandfather, 46

McLean, David, HCol Seaforths, 314
MacLean, John, Cousin of Bomber Boys Thomas, Douglas & Donald Rose, 279
Maclean's, Canada's National News Magazine, 33, 57, 61, 302
MacLeod, Mary Anne, see Mary Anne Trump, 22
Macmillan, Harold, British Prime Minister, 75, 78
Macrae, author's friend, Bomber Boy Malcolm's son and Elsham Wolds Newsletter Editor, 279
Macrae, Malcolm, (Edwin Thomas) Bomber Boy and Keith's dad, 279
Magee, RCAF Pilot Officer John Gillespie Jr, *High Flight*, 93, 138
Magic Weapons To Enable Germany to Win, WWII, 177, 197–8
Mailly, Panzer Military Camp Dad's 9th combat sortie, 3/4 May 1944, 143
Maisky, Ivan, Soviet Ambassador to UK, WWII, 68
Malton ON Victory Aircraft factory, 18
Manchester Bomber Aircraft, Failure Predecessor of the Lancaster, 99-100
Manchester News, 276
Mandela, Nelson, South Africa President, 264
Mandrell, RAF jammer, 164
Manning, Elizabeth 'Betty', Doug Manning's wife, 14
Manning, Doug, New Westminster City Administrator & author's mentor, 14
Mao Zedong, founder of the People's Republic of China, 12
Mansion House, London, 60
Mantenon ammunition dump near Rouen France Dad's 8th combat sortie, 143
Mark XIV Gyro, see SABS

INDEX

Market-Garden, 189
Marrowbone & Cleaver Pub, Kirmington, *see* Chopper
Marsden, Terry, Kirmington, 35
Marshall, George C., US General of the Army, Marshall Plan 66–8, 155
Marson, Squadron Leader Andy, RCAF, Aviation Heritage Lincolnshire, 165, 168
Martin, Guy, owner of the Chopper Kirmington, 34, 306–307
Martin, John, 166 Squadron Lancaster wireless operator and author, 239
Martin, Sally, manager of the Chopper Kirmington and sister of Guy, 34
Marwood, Gordon, 'Chaster Aircrew', 16
Mason, Frank, US Military Attaché in Berlin who identified the Goebbels Diaries, 202
Massey, Vincent, Canadian High Commissioner to UK, 1935-46, 70, 228–9
Master Bomber, 144, 148–9, 151, 165, 179–80
Matthews, Mike, Air Force Officers Association of BC President and the author's friend, 96, 128–9
Matzen, Robert, author, 125, 170, 305
Maxwell, Allan, Bomber Boy, 279
Maxwell, Colonel Keith, RCAF, the author's friend & Bomber Boy's son, 279
Mayer, Professor Hans Ferdinand, author of *Oslo Report,* 1-2 November 1939, 179
Medicine Hat, Alberta, 4, 23
Memory Project Veteran Stories, 120
Mercer, Rick, CBC, 112
Merkel, Angela, German chancellor, 155
Merritt, Lt. Col Cecil VC Dieppe distinguished postwar lawyer, 29
Messerschmitt Me262 jet fighter, 200, 216, 258, 277

Meurer, Manfred, Luftwaffe ace, 16, 230
Middle Land Canal, 244
Middleton, Peter, DFC, paternal grandfather of Catherine, wife of Prince William, 95, 105, 185
Mighty Eighth USAAF, vii, x, 67–8, 125–6, 155, 161, 166–7, 170, 203, 218, 227, 231–4, 245, 253, 283
  Second Bomb Division, 170
  Second Combat Wing, 170
  389th Bombardment Group, 238
  445th Bombardment Group, 125
  Tibenham, US Airbase, 125
Milch, Erhard, German Field Marshal, 182, 192, 196, 204, 220, 230
Miles, Jack, WWII RAF pilot & the author's friend, 95–6, 128–9, 133
Miles, John, Jack's Grandson, 96
Miller, Dorothy Milne, the author's cousin-in-law, Saskatoon, 280
Miller, Eleanor, the author's maternal grandmother, 5
Miller, John W., the author's maternal grandfather, 5
Miller, Gordon, the author's maternal uncle, 5
Miller, Pearl Hanson, the author's maternal aunt-in-law, 5
Miller, Wanda, the author's maternal aunt-in-law, 5
Mimoyecques, German WWII V-3 long-range guns site, 239
Mining, by Bomber Command, 106, 144, 152, 240–2, 277, 286
Mitze, Ilse, beheaded looter, 187
Moger, Bill, 'Chaster Aircrew'
Mohne Dam, bombed by Dambusters, 17 May 1943, 16
Monroe Doctrine, 2 December 1823, 51
Monroe, James, US President, 51
Monterey Bay, California, 12
Montgomery, Bernard, (Monty) British Field Marshal, ix, 62, 70, 77, 82–3, 223, 225, 254–5, 283

Moppetts, Cedric & Wife Margaret, Bomber Boy's sister, 280, 294
Morgenthau, Henry, US Secretary of the Treasury & FDR's Hyde Park neighbour, 52
Morley Flats/Plateau, west of Calgary, 2
Morrison, Herbert, UK home secretary, 70
Moscow, Russia, Soviet Union, 45
Moskito Panik, German nickname for Mosquito damaging impact on German morale, 105
Mosquito, de Havilland, 11, 16, 95, 99, 104–105, 142, 162–3, 166, 179, 205, 208, 225, 268, 283–4, 289–90, 298, 301
Mosley, Oswald, British fascist, 73
Mount Pleasant, Calgary, 265
Mt. Pleasant Cemetery, Toronto, burial place of Mackenzie King, 49
Munich, 102, 203–204, 212–13, 230, 289–90, 307
Munich Art Exposition, 204
Munich Beer Hall Putsch, 212
Murphy, Charles 'Spud', Dad's aircrew, 136, 140
Murrow, Edward, CBS, London, WWII, 58
MusiCares Person of the Year, 265
Muskeg, Cree for Low-Lying Marsh, 26

NAAFI (Navy, Army & Air Force Institutes), 109
Namibia, formerly South West Africa, 211
NANOOK, Operation RCAF Ice Reconnaissance Patrols, 10
Nanton, Alberta, 10–11, 19, 72, 84, 90, 97, 272–3
Nanton Lancaster Society, 11, 299
National Air Force Museum of Canada at Trenton Ontario, 104, 271

National Association of County Veteran Service Offices, USA, 93
National Foundation for Infantile Paralysis, Warm Springs Georgia, 50
NATO (North Atlantic Treaty Organization), 51, 94, 275
Naval Officers Association of British Columbia, 122, 240, 279
Naval Protocol With the Luftwaffe, Between Raeder & Goring, January 1939, 241
Navigation Aid H2S, 164–5, 167–8, 236, 295
Navy, Army & Air Force Institutes 109, 241
Netherlands, 15, 17, 37–8, 92, 156, 244
Neuville, See Oisemont, France, 149
New Westminster, BC, 14, 156
New York City, 21–2, 41, 47–8, 50–1, 162
New Zealand, 53, 57, 84–5, 87–90, 92, 97, 107, 119, 126–7, 210, 219, 221, 268–70, 273–4, 280, 284, 305
New Zealand Bomber Command Association, 92, 97, 127, 268–9, 273–4
Newey, Chris, and Bomber Boy Gerry, 280
Newtonmore, Clan MacPherson, 13
NFB (National Film Board), *The Valour and the Horror*, 33, 159
NICKEL Ops., Bomber Command leaflet drops 136, 140
Nielsen, Erik, deputy PM, Canada, 164–6
Nielsen, Leslie actor & Erik's brother, 164
Night Fighters, German Heavy Fighters and Light Bombers Modified to Fight at Night or in Poor Visibility, 19, 105, 112, 143–4, 163–4, 166, 188, 213, 215–16, 227, 232, 235–6, 248, 277, 279

334

INDEX

Nissen Huts, Bomber Command NCO accommodation, 118–19
No Moon Tonight, Don Charlwood, 107, 161, 229, 276, 300
No Price to High, Canadian TV, 160
No Prouder Place author David Bashow, 155, 178, 240, 247, 259, 299
Noakes, Jeff, senior WWII historian Canadian War Museum, Ottawa, 9, 127
NORAD, North American Air Defence Command until 1981, now North American Aerospace Defense Command, 51
Normandy, Battle, *see* Battle of Normandy
Normandy, D-Day Invasion, *see* D-Day
North Sea, 144, 190, 234, 236, 242, 246, 295
North West Company, Canadian Fur Traders, Montreal, 22
Norton Rose Law Firm Vancouver, 29
Norway, 84, 92, 104–105, 179, 216, 245, 292, 305
Nose Hill Park, 2–3
Nuremberg Trials, 190, 193–5, 211
Nürnberg, German light cruiser, 246
NZ Bomber Command Association Newsletter, 92, 97, 128

Oberhausen, Ruhr Valley, 148, 230
Obersalzberg, Berchtesgaden, 171
OCU (Operational Conversion Unit), 166
Official History of the Royal Air Force Strategic Air Offensive in WWII, 78
Ogdensburg Agreement, 17 Aug 1940, 51
Ohlsdorf Cemetery, Hamburg, 277
Oisemont/Neuville, France, Dad's 24th Combat Sortie, 30 June 1944, Daylight Bombing Flying Bomb Sites, 149

Old Bistro, Fairview AB, 26
Oldman, Gary, actor playing Churchill in *Darkest Hour*, 6–7
Olivier, Laurence, British Actor, 160
Ontario Court of Appeal, 33
Operation Aphrodite, US bombing, 234
Operation Anvil, US bombing, 234
Operation Crossbow, Anglo-American Campaign against German long-range weapons, 179, 181, 234
Operation Hydra, the bombing of Peenemunde 17/18 Aug 1943, began *Operation Crossbow*, 179
Operation Manna, feeding the Dutch, 38, 164
Operation Market-Garden, 189
Operation Overlord, 14, 147, 254, 302
Operation Paperclip, 180
Orchiston, Kenneth Watson, Bomber Boy RNZAF, 277
Organization Todt, civil & engineering organization, 186, 196
Orleans, France, Dad's 13th combat sortie, 19 May 1944, snd 25th sortie, 4 July 1944, bombing railway yards, 149
Ortona, Italy, 'Canada's Stalingrad' battle 20-28 Dec 1944, 156
Osers, Ewald, translation editor, 176
Oslo Report, authored by Prof. Hans Ferdinand Mayer, 1-2 Nov 1939, 179
Ossington Notts., 130, 138
Ottawa, Canada's capital city, 9, 28, 33, 38, 46, 49, 89–91, 97, 101, 103, 127, 131, 214, 272–3
OTU (Operational Training Unit), 114, 136, 138, 280
Ottawa Civic Hospital, 38
Outlander books & drama Series author, Diana Gabaldon, 11
Overy, Richard, author & British Bomber Command authority, 155, 191, 218, 256, 260, 306

335

Oxford University Press, 49, 176
Oyster Bay, New York Home of Theodore Roosevelt family, 50

Packwood, Allen, author's mentor and Churchill College Archives director at Cambridge University vii, 6, 40–1, 129, 240, 282, 306
Paley, William, CBS London, WWII, 58
Panton, Andrew, Lincolnshire Aviation Heritage Centre at East Kirkby, 37
Panton, Christopher, Whitton Bomber Boy killed in action, 37
Panton, Fred, Andrew's uncle, 37
Panton, Harold, Andrew's uncle, 37
Paris, 23, 117, 134, 140–1, 197, 238
Parkdale Junior High School, Calgary, the author's alma mater, viii
Parker, Charlie, My Red Deer Lancaster owner, 10
Parliament, UK, 42, 54, 57, 219
Parliament, Canada, 27, 38–9, 46, 49, 214
Pas de Calais, phony Patton D-Day ploy Dad bombed to delude Hitler, 145–6, 181, 248, 251, 279
Pass of Killiecrankie, Scotland, 13
Pathfinders, Bomber Command, 16, 76, 77, 86, 104–105, 109, 111–12, 114–15, 122, 155, 163, 165, 167–8, 180, 192, 200, 225, 229, 236, 242, 277, 284, 286, 290, 299–301
Patton, General George, Commander US 3rd Army, 146, 156
Pauillac (Bordeaux), France, Dad's 32nd combat sortie, 5 Aug 1944, 151
Peace River, town in Alberta, 26
Peace River Country, 25–8
Pearl Harbor, Hawaii, 58, 67, 93, 131, 134, 225
Pearson, Lester 'Mike', Canadian Prime Minister, 91, 126

Peden, Murray, RCAF pilot & author, 62, 90, 114–15, 157, 233, 306
Peenemunde, top secret German Army rocket development centre, 160, 178–81, 197, 207, 269
Pelly-Fry, James, RAF Group Captain, 71
Perfectos, RAF radio device to detect night fighters, 163, 169
Pentagon, 32, 35–6
Person of the Year, MusiCares, 265
Petain, Phillipe French Marshal, 224
Petrolinas, Kasimir, executed by German firing squad, 187
Petwood Hotel, Woodhall Spa, Lincolnshire, 116, 118–19
Pforzheim, Germany near Stuttgart, Eastcott's last combat sortie, 280, 298
Pictou County, Nova Scotia, 21–3, 48
Pierce, Howard ('Tim'), Assistant Librarian RAF College Cranwell, x, 174
Pinetree, Mighty 8th HQ at Wycombe Abbey, 68
Pitlochry, Scotland, 13
Place Ville Marie, Montreal, 40, 266
Placentia Bay, Newfoundland, 45
Pocock, Calvin, Bomber Boy's son and the author's friend, 94, 280
Pocock, Randy, Calvin's brother, 280
Pocock, Guy, Calvin's brother, 280
POINTBLANK, directive to both bomber forces, 19 June 1943, 112, 182
Poland, 92, 158, 213
Polio, Poliomyelitis, caused by the polio virus, 3–4, 9, 50, 264–6
Politz, near Stettin, Eastcott combat sortie, 296
Polo – RAF College Cranwell RAF & Army Reserve team, 175
Popeye, American cartoon character, 106

INDEX

Portal, Sir Charles 'Peter', RAF Chief of Air Staff, 65, 71, 103, 156, 182, 233
Porter, Bob, author, 306, 17
Post-War Problems Committee of the National Conference of Canadian Universities, 48, 308
Potsdamer Platz, Berlin's busiest, 207
Powley, Frank, 166 Squadron commander, 117, 143
Prang, a crash, 137, 144, 149–50, 295
Premier Inn, Canwick, Lincoln, 39, 271
Prince Albert, *see* King George VI
Prince Charles, Prince of Wales, now King Charles III, 89, 101, 264, 270
Prince Edward Island, Canada, 22
Prince Philip, Duke of Edinburgh, 4, 270
Prince William, Duke of Cambridge, now Prince of Wales, 85, 87, 95, 101, 270
Princess Alice, head of WAAF and wife of Duke of Gloucestershire, Governor General of Australia, 70
Princess Alice, wife of Earl of Athlone, Governor General of Canada, 86
Princess Beatrix of The Netherlands, 38
Princess Margriet of The Netherlands, 38
Prinz Eugen German heavy cruiser, 246
Privy Council Office Canada, 43
Profumo Affair, 79
Pugh, Ken, 'Chaster Aircrew', 16

Queen Beatrix of The Netherlands, 38
Queen Elizabeth II, 4–5, 8, 14, 22, 77–8, 85–7, 89, 109, 270
Queen Elizabeth II Highway, Alberta, 9
Queen Elizabeth High School, Calgary, 6, 42, 131, 147
Queen Elizabeth, The Queen Mother, and King George VI Consort, 46, 62–3, 70–1, 75, 78, 85–7, 160, 270, 299, 304

Queen, John, Mayor of Winnipeg, 46
Queen Mary, King George V, Consort, 38, 86
Queen Victoria, 13–14, 86, 134, 304
Queen's Park, Ontario Legislature in Toronto, 214
Queen's University, Kingston Ontario, 51
Queen's View, Pitlochry, Scotland, 22

RAF Club, London, 129, 271, 284
RCAF, *see* Royal Canadian Air Force
RCAF Memorial Brandon Manitoba, 96
RNZAF, Royal New Zealand Air Force, 57, 84–5, 113, 277, 281
Rae, J.W., Eastcott Aircrew, 297
Raeder, Erich, Grand Admiral, 241
Randolph Field of USAAC, 90
Ratagan Youth Hostel, Loch Duich, 12
Rathenau, Walther, Organizer of Germany's WWI economy, 196
Reagan, Ronald US President 13, 126
Reardon, Terry Author 41, 47–50, 53–4, 60–1, 88, 91, 98, 306
Red Arrows, RAF Aerobatics, 37
Red Baron, Manfred von Richthofen, 230
Red Deer, Alberta, 9–10
Redmond, Doug Colin Bell's Navigator, 284
Regina, Saskatchewan, 4, 133
Reich Chancellery, Germany, 202
Reichsgau, *see* Gauleiter
Reich Inspectorate for Civil Air War, 183, 210
Reich Ministry of Transport, 250, 257
Reich Plenipotentiary for Total War, *see* Joseph Goebbels
Reichstag, German Parliament, 212–13
Reid, David, Bomber Boy Duff SK, 280
Reminisce with Freidenstal, 26
Remscheid, Ruhr Valley, 230–1
Renaud, Paul French Prime Minister, 224

Rennes St. Jacques, France, Dad's 10th combat sortie, 7 May 1944, 144
Research Institute for Military History Germany, vi, x, 5, 69, 105, 109, 120, 154–5, 164, 174–9, 181–9, 191, 199–200, 209–10, 220, 225, 229–32, 235–8, 241, 250–1, 253, 257–8, 260–1, 273, 302, 305–307
Revigny-Sur-Ormain, France, Dad's 27th combat sortie 12 July 1944, bombing RR yards aborted due to heavy cloud, 149
Rhineland, 188
Rhodesia (southern is Zimbabwe, northern is parts of Zambia), 70, 72–3, 76, 92, 100, 277
  1st Rhodesian Regiment, WWI, 73
Richards, Denis, Introduction to Harris' *Bomber Offensive* 1990, 71
Richards, Ralph Eastcott, aircrew, 298
Riddell, Sir George, 59
Riley, Angela, Cranwell Aviation Heritage Museum, Lincolnshire, 174
Rinickendorf munition plants, Berlin, 208
Ritchie, Gordon, DFM, 120
River of Disappointment, *see* Mackenzie River
River Elbe, 284
Roberts, Andrew, historian, 157, 160, 307
Robinson, E., pilot-mechanic who taxied Red Deer Lancaster, 10
Robinson, Paul, RAF Air Vice-Marshal and the author's mentor, x, 16, 34–5, 37, 40–41, 92, 96, 107, 109, 111–13, 115, 119–20, 122, 127–9, 138, 140, 158, 162–6, 174–5, 220, 242
Robinson, Sarah Assistant Deputy Lord Lieutenant of Lincolnshire, 35
Rocanville, Saskatchewan, birthplace of the author's mother, 4–5
Rockefeller, John, D. Jr., 49

Rockney, Knut Chaster, aircrew, 17
Rogers Hill, Pictou County, Nova Scotia, 48
Rohrer, CEO Canadian Warplane Heritage Museum, Port Hope, ON, 112
Rommel, Erwin, German Field Marshal, 191, 198
Roosevelt Campobello International Park, New Brunswick & Maine, 50
Roosevelt Eleanor, First Lady, 50, 52
Roosevelt, Franklin Delano US President, ix, 6, 38, 41, 45–6, 48–54, 58, 67, 82, 91–2, 155–6, 202, 209, 233, 237, 257, 269, 283
Roosevelt, Franklin Jr., FDR's son, 59
Rose, Bomber Boys Donald, Douglas and Thomas, 279
Rosewarne, Vivian Alan William Noall, RAF 36(B) Sqd., *An Airman's Letter*, 120
Ross, Don, Director The Hangar Flight Museum, Calgary Airport, 8
Rouen, France, Dad's 3rd combat sortie, 18 Apr 1944, 141
Royal Air Force,
  Advance Air Striking Force, 162
  83 Squadron, 180
  97 Squadron, 122
  100 Group (Bomber Support) Electronic Warfare and Countermeasures, 105, 112, 114, 163–4, 166, 192, 236
  101 Squadron, 164–5, 169, 170
  156 Squadron, 180
  166 Squadron, the author's father, vi, viii, 34–7, 56, 115–18, 123–4, 129, 135, 137, 140–53, 156, 167, 171, 236, 239, 254, 280–1, 294–5, 297–8, 308
  617 Squadron, Dambusters, 78, 167, 245, 275
  No. 1 Lancaster Finishing School, 137

INDEX

RAF Abingdon, 1 Group HQ, 219
RAF Banff, 135
RAF Bawtry, 34
RAF Coningsby, Battle of Britain Memorial Flight Lancaster, 101
RAF College, Cranwell, 174, 229, 276, 279
RAF Elsham Wolds, 34–5, 37, 101, 107, 112, 116, 123, 144
RAF High Wycombe, Bomber Command HQ, 34, 68, 70, 86
RAF Hixon, OTU Operational Training Unit, 130, 135–6
RAF Kirmington, the author's father, 34–7, 107, 112–13, 115–19, 129–30, 137, 140–1, 143–4, 148–51, 165, 175, 254, 276–7, 279, 294, 297, 306
RAF Lindholme, 1656 HCU (Heavy Conversion Unit) South Yorkshire, 130, 136
RAF Metherington, 165
RAF North Killingholme, 117
RAF Scampton, 35, 37, 55, 78, 119
RAF Wyton, HQ 8 Group Pathfinders, 86
RAF Woodhall Spa, 116, 118–19
Royal Air Force Internet Forum Chat Room, 267
Royal Aircraft Establishment Farnborough, 110, 223
Royal Australian Air Force, 57, 83, 92, 121, 161–2, 262, 272, 274, 276
Royal Australian Air Force Bomber Command Memorial, Canberra, 272
Royal Bank of Canada, 24–9, 40, 132, 134, 266, 289

Royal Bank Magazine Christmas 1942, 29–30
Royal Commonwealth Society of Mainland British Columbia, 118
Royal Canadian Air Cadets, 265
Royal Canadian Air Force, viii, ix, 3, 8–11, 15–18, 21, 24–6, 28–31, 36, 38, 47, 55, 57, 61, 72, 76, 84, 86, 90–8, 101, 103–104, 106, 113–14, 120–1, 126–8, 131–5, 138–9, 141–2, 144–50, 153 155, 160, 162, 164, 175, 179, 203, 223, 226–9, 232–3, 237, 242, 244, 246, 264–5, 271–2, 274–82, 284, 292–3, 298, 304
6 Group (RCAF) Bomber Command, 72, 76, 86, 92, 101, 103, 106, 114, 120–1, 134, 146, 160, 179, 226–8, 242, 246, 271–5, 277–9, 284, 301
405 (Vancouver) Squadron, RCAF's first bomber squadron, 86, 101, 104, 226, 229, 244
408 (Goose) Squadron, 272, 277
418 Intruder Squadron, 275
419 (Moose) Squadron, 101, 242
425 (Alouette) Squadron 278
426 (Thunderbird) Squadron, 271, 278
428 (Ghost) Squadron, 242
429 (Bison) Squadron 120, 278
434 (Bluenose) Squadron, 274, 277, 279
441 Fighter Squadron, 147
RCAF Comox Vancouver Island, 10
RCAF Dishforth, Yorkshire, 278
RCAF Linton-on-Ouse, a 62 'Beaver' RCAF operational base, 86
RCAF Middleton, St. George Airfield, Yorkshire, 72
RCAF Vulcan, Alberta, Flight Training School, 94, 128, 130, 134

339

Royal Canadian Air Force Cadets, 265
Royal Canadian Air Force Women's Division, 86
Royal Canadian Army Medical Corps, 121, 126, 225
Royal Canadian Navy, 10, 29–30, 47, 147, 240, 275
Royal City, *see* New Westminster BC
Royal Commonwealth Society of Mainland British Columbia, 118
Royal Flying Tour South America, 1962, 95
Royal Military College, Sandhurst
Royal Navy, 56, 92, 221, 240, 244–5, 268
Royal Navy Fleet Air Arm, 92, 245, 275
Royal New Zealand Air Force 57, 84, 87, 92, 273, 280
Royal New Zealand Air Force Bomber Command Memorial, Auckland, 272–3, 305
Royal Rifles of Canada, Quebec, 158, 225
Royal tour, Canada, 1959, 4–5
Royal tour Canada, 2011, 95
Royal Westminster Tank Regiment, the 'Westies' of New Westminster, 14
Ruhr Valley, Germany, 116, 230, 271, 278
Russian Army, *see* Soviet Red Army
Russian front, 220, 296
Rutte, Mark, Dutch Prime Minister, 38–9
Ryan, Congressman Tim Ohio, 93

SABS (Stabilized Automatic Bomb Sight), 165, 167–8
Safmarine, South African Marine Corporation, Sir Arthur Harris, 76–7
Sai Wan War Cemetery, Hong Kong, 158
Sair, David, Bomber Boy, 276
Salinas, California, 12
Sandys, Duncan, father of Celia, Operation Crossbow, 179
San Francisco, 93
Saorstat Eireann, Ireland, 88
Saskatoon, Saskatchewan, 7, 29–31, 96, 128, 130–1, 134, 280
Saskatoon Service Flying Training School, RCAF, 31, 96, 128, 131
Saskatoon *Star-Phoenix* newspaper, 30
Savio, Mario, Berkeley University Student Movement leader, 12
Scandinavia, 212, 242
Scharnhorst, German battlecruiser, 103, 245
Schicklgruber, Maria Anna, Hitler's grandmother, 211
Schlesien, German pre-Dreadnought battleship, 245
Schleswig-Holstein, German pre-Dreadnought battleship, 245
Schlossberg Tunnel, Graz, Austria, 184
Schmid, Josef ('Beppo') Luftwaffe intelligence commander, 213, 215
Schonebeck, Germany, 284
Schrage Musik (Jazz), Luftwaffe upward firing cannon for night fighters, 236
Schultz, US Secretary of State for Ronald Reagan, 13
Scotland, 11, 13, 21–2, 42, 104, 110, 130, 135, 292
Scouts Canada, 27th Vancouver Scouting Group, 13
SD (Security Service of the Reichsfuhrer-SS), 231
Seaforth Highlanders of Canada in Vancouver, ix, 37, 156
Searby, John, Master Bomber for 17/18 August 1943, Peenemunde raid, 180
Selected for Aircrew author James Hampton, 71, 83, 132, 268, 302

INDEX

Selman, James Francon ('Frank'), Bomber Boy, then PoW, 108, 280
Selman, Gordon, Bomber Boy Frank's son, 108, 280
Selman, Mary Wolfater, Bomber Boy Frank's wife, 108, 280
Senate of Canada, 33
Sergeant, John, IBCC host, 276
Serrate, RAF homer radio device to detect night fighters, 163
Shadow in My Eye, 2021 Danish Movie, 162
SHAEF (Supreme Headquarters Allied Expeditionary Force), 153, 239
Short Stirling, *see* Stirling bomber
Sicily, Italy, 54
Siemens factories, 222
Siemenstadt, Germany, 222
Simpson, Bill, President, New Zealand Bomber Command Association, 273
Sinclair, Archibald, UK Secretary of State for Air, 70
Singleton, Mr. Justice John, '*Report to the War Cabinet on the Bombing of Germany*', 29 May 1942, 259
Skoda works, near Pilsen, Germany, 204
Slack, Kenneth Earl Clifford, RCAF, Flt Sergeant, died 09 May 1945; trying to save German guard, 284
Smith, Beverley Selman, Bomber Boy Frank Selman's daughter, 108, 280
Smith, Ernest ('Smokey') VC, Seaforth Highlander, New Westminster, 156
Smith, Gordon, RCAF, navigator, 275
Smith, Mel, Edmonton eskimo, 275
Smith, Terry, Chicago, Black Hawk, 275
Smithhurst, Cliff, Dad's aircrew, 140
Smuts, Jan, South African Prime Minister & general, 70, 77–8
Snoeken, Dutch consul-general, Henk, 38
South Africa, 70, 76–8, 85, 88–9
South African Air Training Schools, 89
South African Marine Corporation, *see* Safmarine

South West Africa, now Namibia, 211
South-West African Campaign, WWI, 73
Southern Rhodesia (Zimbabwe), 72, 92
Soviet Red Army 154–6, 242, 246, 254
Soviet Union, USSR, 45, 47, 58, 76, 158
Spandau Prison, Berlin, 195
Spandau: The Secret Diaries by Speer, 195, 307
Spanish Civil War, 1936-39, 214
Speer, Albert Reich Minister of Armaments & War Production, vi, x, 56, 153, 176–8, 182, 189–91, 193–200, 202, 210, 216, 225–6, 230–1, 243–4, 256–7, 260, 284
Speer, Albert Jr. Speer's son and Berchtesgaden schoolboy, 170–1, 195, 301
Speer myth, 195–6
Spokane, Washington State, 93
Springfields, Harris' wartime home, 68–9
SS (Schutzstaffel), Nazi German paramilitary surveillance, security & terror, 172, 180, 182, 253, 276, 307
St. Andrew's Heights, Calgary, viii, 265
St. Malo, France, 252
St. Martin-de-Varreville gun batteries, 146
St. Medard-en-Jalles explosive works, 249
St. Paul's United Church, Fairview, Alberta, 27
Stabbed in the Back Nazi German Post-WWI myth, 56
Stabilized Automatic Bomb Sight, 165, 167–8
Stacey C.P. (Charles Perry), Canadian military historian, 45, 307
Stafford Cripps, Sir Richard, Lord Privy Seal & House of Commons leader, 70

341

Stalag Luft III POW Camp of *The Great Escape* movie fame, 275, 281
Stalag Luft VI POW Camp Baltic coast, 281
Stalin, Josef Soviet Union dictator, 42, 52, 57, 82, 110, 155–7, 161, 254
Stark, Harold, US Admiral Commander, US Naval Forces, Europe, WWII, 70
Stathers, Eric, the author's friend, 46
Sterkrade, Germany, Dad's 20th combat sortie, 16 Jun 1944, synthetic oil, 148
Stettin, Germany, February 1945; near Russian front, 230, 296
Stettler, Alberta, MacKenzie family hometown, 1927-67, 23–8, 132, 139
Stettler Museum, 23
Stewart, Jimmy, US actor & Air Force, 124–6, 170, 238
Stirling bomber, 72, 92, 248, 280
Stock Market Crash, 1929, 25
Stornoway, Outer Hebrides, Scotland, 21–2
Strachey, John, British Under-Secretary of State for Air, 73
Strategic Bombing Offensive, UK, US & Commonwealth Bombing Germany, 55, 63, 66, 68–9, 79, 120, 124, 126, 157, 160, 166, 181, 183, 190–2, 200, 209–10, 218–20, 222, 226–7, 234–5, 237–9, 257, 261, 279, 283
Stuttgart, Germany, Allies lost 300 aircraft, 230, 279–80, 298
Superior District Courts in Germany, 186
Supreme Headquarters Allied Expeditionary Force, 153, 239
Sutton, Bertine, RAF Air Marshal & Air Member for Personnel, 55, 228
Sydney Morning Herald newspaper, Sydney Australia, 259, 274, 302
Synthetic oil facilities bombed, 148, 152, 251

Tabun nerve gas, 260
Tactical Air Command USAF, 35, 90, 157, 304
Tallboy bombs, 72, 102, 148, 165, 167, 169, 234, 244–5, 253, 276, 283
Taras, David, Canadian lawyer, 32
Taylor, Dennis, *see* Eastcott
Taylor, Edward Plunkett, Canadian business tycoon, 49
Tedder, Sir Arthur, RAF Chief of Air Staff & SHAEF Deputy Commander, 75, 77–8, 87, 153, 239, 249
Tegernsee Lake, Bavarian Alps, 298
Tempelhof Airfield, Berlin, 222
Texas, USA, 90
Thatcher, Margaret British Prime Minister, 270
THE (Times Higher Education), 48
Thiel, Walter, German V-2 rocket, von Braun's engine designer, 180
Thunderbolt, US fighter aircraft, 166, 238
Thuringia, 12,000 A4 Missiles relocated from Peenemunde, 181
Tibenham, Jimmy Stewart airbase, 125
Tiergarten, Berlin's diplomatic quarter, 208
Tiger Force, very long-range Lancaster bomber force to attack Japan, 10
Tiger Moth, training aircraft, 11, 133
Tillotson-Sills, Richard, Battle of Britain Flight Lancaster, RAF Coningsby, 101
Time Magazine, 44
Tizard, Sir Henry, radar patron, 222
Tobruk, Libya, 225
Todt, Dr. Fritz, Nazi Minister of Armaments & Munitions, 186, 196
Tomlinson, Peter, godfather of Harris' daughter Jackie, 76
Tooze, Adam, author, 181, 230, 308
Toronto, 11, 18, 24, 33, 46, 49, 91, 101, 126, 214

INDEX

Torpedo boats, 147
Trans-Canada Highway, 2, 4, 96
TRE (Telecommunications Research Establishment (100 Group)), 164
Treaty of Versailles 1919, 213, 218
Trenchard, Hugh, *Father of the RAF*, ix, 54–7, 70, 77–8, 80, 85, 160, 219
Trossy, France, Dad's 31st combat sortie, 03 Aug 1944, bombing flying bomb storage site, 150
Truman, Harry, US President, 76, 158
Trump, Donald, US President, 209
Trump, Fred, Donald's father, 22
Trump, Mary Anne, Donald's mother, 22
Try, Fiona MacKenzie & Geoff, Windsor, UK, 36
Tudor aircraft, 100
Tupper, Murray ('Tupp'), RCAF, 278
Turner, John Canadian Prime Minister, 41, 45

USS *Cory*, American destroyer sunk by Crisbecq gun battery on D-Day, 146
USS *Hornet*, aircraft carrier, 233
USSR, *see* Soviet Union
Udet, Ernst, Luftwaffe Colonel-General & Chief of Procurement & Supply, 230
Unconditional Surrender, 157, 218, 257
United Church of Canada, 26–7, 264, 266
University of British Columbia (UBC), the author's alma mater, 38, 48, 266–7, 308
The United States Army Center of Military History, 253
United States Army Air Corps (USAAC), 56, 67, 90
United States Army Air Force (USAAF), *see* Mighty Eighth
United States Agency for International Development (USAID), 172

University of British Columbia, 38, 48, 266-67, 308
University of Calgary, the author's alma mater, viii, 12, 28, 131, 266
Upkeep Club, 169, 271
Urquhart, Bob, *Operation Manna*, 164
US Consul General in Geneva's report to US Secretary of State, 22 Jun 1942, 259

Van Raalt, Flt Lt, RAAF, LMF, 122
Vancouver, ix, 13, 19, 24, 29–30, 38, 47–9, 91, 96, 121, 129, 156, 266–7, 276
Vassall Affair, 79
Vassall, John, 79
Veldenstein, castle of Goering's boyhood, 211
Vickers Wellington, *see* Wellington bomber
Victoria, British Columbia, 214, 276
Victoria Cross, 5, 29, 156
Victoria Day Weekend, Canada, 134
Victoria International Airport, 18
Victory aircraft at Malton, Ontario, 18
Victory Bonds WWII, Canada, 47, 90
Victory Honours List, Britain, 73
Victory ships, 74
Village Inn, automatic tail turrets, 170
Villeneuve-Saint-Georges, Dad's 1st combat sortie 9/10 Apr 1944, 140–1
Villers Bocage, Bomber Command destroyed 2nd and 9th Panzer Divisions, 251
Vimy Ridge, Canadian military victory & WWI memorial, 64, 151, 275, 287
Violins of Hope Concert, Place des Arts, Montreal, 2 Nov 2019, 40
Viscount Bennett, *see* Bennett RB
Viscount Bennett High School, Calgary, 42
Volkssturm, national militia Hitler created through Nazi Party, not army, 181

von Braun, Wernher, German & American rocket scientist, 180–1
Von Hindenburg, Paul, German President who made Hitler Chancellor, 213
von Richthofen, Manfred, 'Red Baron', 230
von Rosen, Carin, Göring's Wife, 212
von Rundstedt, Gerd, German Field Marshall and Commander-in-Chief in the West and a commander in the Battle of the Bulge, Ardennes Offensive, 193, 250, 253
von Toma, Wilhelm Ritter, German general and PoW, 179
von Zeppelin, Ferdinand, 143
Vulcan, Alberta, 94, 128, 130, 134
Vulcan, aircraft, 100
Vulcan's Forge, Industrial Region of Rhineland and Westphalia, 229

Walker, Rebecca, of Victoria BC Bomber Boy Pat Rothera's great niece, 276
Wallis, Barnes, 102, 106, 169, 234, 253, 271
Walters Ash Village, RAF HQ High Wycombe, 68, 70
War Crimes, 195
Warm Springs, Georgia, FDR Polio, 50
Wartime Information Board Canada, Chaired by Larry MacKenzie, 48
Wartime Prices & Trade Board, Canada, 49
Waterloo, Battle, 18 Jun 1815, 106, 257
Waterton Glacier International Peace Park, Montana & Alberta, 11
Watson, Roy & Jean, the author's maternal great uncle & aunt, 4
Watson-Watt, Robert, radar expert, 222, 302
Webb, Saskatchewan, 23
Webb, Thomas, Bomber Boy, 279
Webster, Sir Charles, author, 78–9, 308

Weeks, Kermit, legendary aviator & aircraft collector, 9
Wehrmacht, 181, 207, 215, 232, 259
Weimar Republic, 1918 to 1933, Germany, 150, 206, 213
Weise, Hubert, Luftwaffe general, 206
Wellington bomber, 11, 72, 99, 106, 113, 115-16, 136, 138, 169, 214, 242, 244, 279–80
Westdeutscher Beobachter, magazine of Nazi Party Cologne/Aachen area, 253
Westerbork, Nazi death camps transit camp in The Netherlands, 158
Western Front, 151, 243, 252, 261
Westies, Royal Westminster Tank Regiment, 14
Westminster Abbey Benedictine Monastery, Mission, BC, 46
Westphalia, German industrial area, 188
Westville, Nova Scotia, birthplace of the author's father, 22-23
Wever, Walther, German general, the Luftwaffe's first Chief of Staff, 219
Wheeler, QSM, Peter, editor *NZ Bomber Command Association News,* 97, 117
White, John, Wing Commander, flight commander of 156 Squadron, 180
White House, Washington DC, 48, 52–3, 67
Whitehorse, Yukon capital, 164
Whowell, Harold 'Eastcott', 207, Wilhelmshaven, Germany, 227
Wickson, Gordon, Bomber Boy, 278
Wilhelmplatz, Berlin, 207
Williamson, Murray, American historian & author, 258–9, 308
Willy, Lt. Wilford John, US Navy, 234
Wilson, Harold, UK Prime Minister, 79
Wimille Communal Cemetery, 279
Wimpy, J. Wellington of Popeye, 106
Wimpy, nickname of Wellington bomber, 106, 242

344

INDEX

Winant, John, US Ambassador to UK, 58, 68
Winnipeg General Strike, 1919, 46
Winnipeg Grenadiers, 158, 225
Winnipeg, Manitoba, 2, 45–6, 115, 139, 158
Winston Churchill's War, 2021 TV mini-series documentary, 161
Winston's War by Lord Dobbs, 6–7
Winter, Guy, RCAF Radar, the author's 1st father-in-law, 223
Wizernes, France, Dad's 28th combat sortie 20 July 1944, bombing six flying bomb launching sites, 150, 251
Wolsley Barracks, No. 1 District Depot London, Ontario, 30
Women Airforce Service Pilots (WASP), USA, 67
Women's Auxiliary Air Force (WAAF), 70, 109, 113, 143, 179
Women's Auxiliary Ferrying Squadron (WAFS), USA, 67
Wood, RAF Flt. Lt. Mark, RAF at Scampton, 02 Sep 2018, 37, 55
Wooden Wonder, see Mosquito Bomber
Woodhall Spa, Lincolnshire, 116, 118–19
Woolf, Marilyn, Bomber Boy's daughter, 108, 280
World Bank, 172
Wright, Fred, Bomber Boy's stepson, 96, 281
Wright, Jim, author & RAF 166 Squadron, 34, 56, 115–18, 140–3, 146, 148, 150, 152, 281, 298, 308
Wright, Martyn, the author's friend and son of Jim Wright, 34, 36, 281
Wuppertal, Ruhr Valley, 230
Wurzburg, Luftwaffe radar, 164
Wycombe Abbey, became Pinetree, 68

Yalta Conference, Roosevelt, Churchill & Stalin 04-11 February 1945, 52, 155–6, 254, 269, 304
Yorkton, Saskatchewan, 4

Zeppelin von, Ferdinand, German general and an airship inventor 143
Zhou Enlai, Premier of the People's Republic of China, 12
Zimmerman, Hauptmann, Chief Air Raid Warden at the Port of Bremen, 221, 244
Zurich, Switzerland, Jimmy Stewart, 170